WOMEN, MEDIA AND SPORT

WOMEN, MEDIA AND SPORT

Challenging Gender Values

edited by
PAMELA J. CREEDON

 SAGE Publications
International Educational and Professional Publisher
Thousand Oaks   London   New Delhi

For information address:

SAGE Publications, Inc.
2455 Teller Road
Thousand Oaks, California 91320

SAGE Publications Ltd.
1 Olivers Yard, 55 City Road
London EC1Y 1SP

SAGE Publications India Pvt Ltd
B-42 Panchsheel Enclave
PO Box 4109
New Dehli 110 017

Printed in the United States of America

Library of Congress Cataloging-in-Publication Data

Main entry under title:

Women, media and sport : challenging gender values / edited by Pamela
    J. Creedon.
        p. cm.
    Includes bibliographical references and index.
    ISBN 0-8039-5233-3. —   ISBN 0-8039-5234-1 (pbk.)
    1. Sex discrimination in sports. 2. Mass media and sports.
GV706.32.W66   1994
796'.0194—dc20   93-41211

00   10 9 8 7 6 5 4 3

Sage Production Editor: Astrid Virding

Contents

Preface

"When will you make an end?" This question kept ringing in my ears over and over as I worked on this book. In my mind's eye the scene from the movie *The Agony and the Ecstasy*, in which the Pope Julius II (Rex Harrison) shouts this question at Michelangelo (Charlton Heston) while he paints, kept replaying. Don't misunderstand. I'm not comparing this book to the ceiling of the Sistine Chapel. It's simply that I just couldn't seem to "make an end" with this book. The most time-consuming part for me was piecing together a contribution herstory of women sportswriters and sportscasters for the book.

And the work still isn't finished. Last week a very helpful reference librarian at the Cleveland Public Library asked if I'd heard of *Lady in the Locker Room* by Susan Fornoff. I knew that the Oakland A's Dave Kingman sent her a live rat when she worked for the *Sacramento Bee*, but I hadn't heard of her book. I finished it today. This week I received a postcard from Paul Bauer, the owner of a sports specialty bookstore in Kent, Ohio, who kept open long after closing one Friday evening as I poured through his collection of *Best Sports Stories*. He wrote: Did I know that Tallulah Bankhead supposedly auditioned to call the New York Giants' baseball games but was refused the job? Nope, but I'm checking it out.

Many other people helped me in the project. Maurine Beasley, Susan Henry and Marion Marzolf gave me names and citations to investigate. Keith Richwine generously shared his work on Sadie K. Miller. Janet Schneider shared her research on Mary Bostwick. Dale Myer helped me try to find material in the Hoover Presidential Library Archives. Judy Cramer and Linda Williams gave me names of women sportscasters and African-American sports journalists.

Research assistants George Estrada and Jackie Krawetz tracked down leads, reviewed microfilm and checked references. Gail Chryslee provided cover and interior page art, and Ingrid Hubbard provided art for Figure 5.1 and Table 13.1. Sue Lafky found someone to do library work for me at the University of Iowa. Members of the Association for Women in the Sports Media looked over my lists of "firsts."

Support from a number of sources helped to make this book possible. Many contacts and ideas for the book came from the 1991 and 1992 Women in Sports Conferences at Ohio State. Jean Girves was instrumental in securing grants from the Committee for Institutional Cooperation of the Big Ten Conference that made the conferences possible. The Miller Research Fund of the School of Journalism at Ohio State also provided grants that allowed me to visit archives and to hire some students, including Gail Chryslee, Patty Skidmore and Lo'litta Snow, who did research for the exhibit that was created for the conferences. Walter Bunge provided additional support from the Ohio State School of Journalism as did Susan Hartmann and Mary Margaret Fonow of the Center for Women's Studies.

I owe a special thanks to Pamela J. Shoemaker, Chair of the School of Journalism at Ohio State, who supported my professional leave proposal that allowed me to finish this book. She also put me in touch with several sources who contributed valuable information.

Why a Book on Sports?

A number of people have asked why I decided to do a book on sports. Nostalgia is a big reason. I grew up about 40 minutes east of Cleveland, listening to Jimmy Dudley announce the Indians, games on WERE radio. I remember May 7, 1957, almost as vividly as most baby boomers remember November 22, 1963, when President Kennedy was assassinated. I was glued to the radio, when a line drive off the bat of Yankees shortstop Gil McDougald hit Herb Score in the left eye. Aided by sportscasters with a flare for the dramatic, the radio coverage took on the aura of a major American tragedy. Score recovered, but never pitched as well again. By 1964, he was announcing baseball for WJW-TV. I also loved the Indians because they gave any kid in a Cleveland area elementary school seven pairs of free tickets for earning "straight A's." Fourteen free tickets! It was an incredible promotional idea. It motivated me to do well in school, and we usually ended up buying several more tickets so that the entire family could go to the game. I always kept the line score during games with my glove on my lap ready to nab foul balls. The ritual also included waiting outside of the clubhouse door at Municipal Stadium after games to get autographs. I recognized most of the players, and they were usually willing to sign my scorecard. My favorites—Vic Power and Rocky Colavito—aren't destined for Cooperstown, but they'll always have a special place in my memory.

Feminism is another reason for the book. In the early 1970s, I used to walk through a men's locker room nearly every afternoon at 5 p.m. with Jane Clark, Chandi Rudolph, Peggy Smith, Jann Sykora and Carol Wearstler. Why? Because the college that I worked for had built a new gymnasium with two racquetball courts that were accessible only through the men's locker room. Inspired by our muse, Helen Reddy, we opened the locker room door and roared, "Women coming through." We had no idea of how to play racquetball at the time and often all six of us were on the small court at one time, but it didn't matter. Eventually, the college knocked a hole in an outside wall and dug a stairwell for us. A little later, I "sponsored" the first women's softball team at that same college when the Athletic Department said it couldn't afford it. I arranged to purchase uniforms and pay for travel and meals from my Public Information Office budget. I justified spending the PIO budget in this way because I saw the team members as public relations representatives of the school. If they looked sharp, the college would make a good impression. The owner of the store where we purchased the uniforms, called "Grandma" by the players, coached the team.

The 1990 National Women's Studies Association conference in Akron, Ohio, provided the impetus for the book. I walked up and down the crowded rows of tables filled with books from feminist publishers, searching in vain for one on women and sport. Although I have since found several volumes devoted to women and sport, none attempts to do what this book sets out to do. We link women, sports and the mass media with feminist perspectives from history, psychology, women's studies, sociology, kinesiology and mass communication.

Special Thanks

It's always a pleasure to work with the editorial and production staff at Sage Publications. Sophy Craze and Astrid Virding were particularly helpful with this project.

My family, friends and animals tried to help me keep one foot in their reality for the past 15 months. Thanks to Kelly, Benji, Holli and Sadie for letting me be—most of the time. I never thought it would end either! Thanks to Louise, Barb, Jim and Tina for their support, acceptance and understanding as I found my voice this year. And thanks to my late father, James, whose kindness and generosity still affects us all.

Pamela J. Creedon

PART I

Overview and Definitions

c. 1890

Women, Media and Sport

Creating and Reflecting Gender Values

Pamela J. Creedon

> Suppose a spaceship flew into our atmosphere and beamed up every
> ball on the planet? Every last football, baseball, tennis ball, basketball,
> volleyball, golfball, shot put, softball, squash ball, soccer ball, pool
> ball, bowling ball, even croquet and polo balls, all of them. What
> would happen? Would the male population go slowly berserk?
> Would blood flow in the streets? Would you boys just curl up and die?
> Or would it expedite the evolution of a higher species of mammal?
>
> Tom Robbins, *Skinny Legs and All* (1990, p. 383)

Much of my research focus in the last several years has involved
an analysis of the gendered nature of sport. I say "sport"
instead of "sports" because I define *sport* as a cultural institution
and *sports* as activities or games that are only one component of the
institution of sport. I define *sex* as a culturally constructed biological
characteristic and *gender* as an ongoing cultural process that constructs differences between women and men (cf. Rakow, 1992).

Two recurrent themes emerged from my analysis of the work of
numerous sport historians and sociologists. Sport is an expression
of the sociocultural system in which it occurs; and sports mirror the

---

AUTHOR'S NOTE: I want to thank Lana F. Rakow, Pamela J. Shoemaker and Lee B.
Becker for comments on a draft of this chapter.

rituals and values of the societies in which they are developed (Boyle, 1963; Guttmann, 1978, 1986, 1988, 1991; Luschen, 1981). Sport influences our language, clothing styles and concepts of heroes and heroines. Its athletes and teams become our symbolic warriors defending the honor of our schools, towns or nation. Its games and contests become symbolic representations of personal and societal struggles for such things as property, fairness, honor and economic gain.

To function effectively in our culture, we must be adept with its metaphors. During intense business negotiations when a colleague suggests throwing a "Hail Mary" pass, knowledge of football as well as Catholicism is needed to decipher the metaphor. The other day a government spokesperson announced that delicate negotiations with a foreign government were "in the bottom of the ninth." She was trying to tell us that the negotiations were almost over. Instead she told us we were losing. Perhaps, if she'd had the opportunity to play Little League baseball, she would have known that a team only bats in the bottom of the ninth if it's behind![1]

During the Cold War of the 1950s, the victories of the U.S. Olympic team became symbols for Americans of the triumph of democracy over communism. In 1980 President Carter used sport as a symbol of political disapproval by refusing to allow American athletes to participate in the Olympics after the Soviets invaded Afghanistan. The 1984 Olympics in Los Angeles earned the nickname of the "Hamburger Olympics" because of the ubiquitous use of sponsorship symbols. Organizers of the Special Olympics and the Gay Olympics use sport to challenge stereotypes and prejudice.[2]

The nicknames and mascots of athletic teams also give clues to understanding cultural values imbedded in sport. Most American collegiate and professional sports teams use symbols of aggression, ferocity or colonialism such as Savages, Bulldogs, Pirates and Redskins (Fuller & Manning, 1987). The nicknames for women's teams are likely to be diminutive such as Tigerettes or Wildkittens or contradictory such as Lady Rams, Lady Bulldogs or Lady Centaurs (Eitzen & Zinn, 1989).

Although many of these scholars did not approach sport from a feminist perspective, their writings underscored my belief that sport is a microcosm of gender values in American culture. With apologies to Shakespeare, "All the world's a playing field, and all of the men and women are merely players." One purpose of this book is to expand the insights of earlier scholars to show how the playing field—gymnasium, arena, court, stadium or anywhere else that sports are played—serves as a metaphor for gender values in American culture. At the most fundamental level, gender even influences which games or activities are defined as "real" (read "macho") sports. Synchronized swimming and fishing, for example, have peripheral status in the U.S. sports world because they involve values such as grace and patience, not often associated "real," that is with male professional, sports.

Gender values are at the core of the media system as well. Just look at the one annual television event—started ever so humbly in 1967—that continues to capture a large share of our collective attention. Of course, it's the Super Bowl. The epitome of media sport spectacles, it's an incredible source of information about gender values. Communication scholar Michael Real (1975) describes the Super Bowl as the American mythic spectacle, "a collective reenactment of symbolic archetypes that express the shared emotions and ideals" (p. 96) of our culture. Novelist Tom Robbins (1990) describes it as "the pure spirit of America. It sums up this country, it's what we're all about" (p. 381).

What does this synthetic super media spectacle tell us about the differences between males and females in our culture? At a minimum, because professional football remains a male-only preserve, we learn that being male in our culture confers a degree of privilege. By denying women access to the game as players, we are taught that women are less qualified, powerful or physical than men. By limiting women to largely stereotypical support roles (e.g., cheerleader, spectator, perhaps hostess for a Super Bowl party), we also learn that women should be subservient.

At a more critical level, we learn alarming lessons about violence. We are reminded that violence and aggression in pursuit of property gain are socially sanctioned. Moreover, with "its atmosphere of heightened aggressiveness, drinking, gambling and the onslaught of sexually charged advertising—[the Super Bowl] sets up a scenario that further reinforces a cultural mindset of antagonism against women" (Lurie, 1991, p. 132). In 1993 concerns about the increase in domestic violence associated with the Super Bowl had reached such a significant level that a television public service campaign was launched during the week preceding the game to raise public awareness.

A second purpose of this book is to look at the role of the media in constructing gender values through their sports coverage. Contemporary mass media, like the plays, epic poems, fairy tales, fables, parables and myths before them, preserve, transmit and create important cultural information. News functions as a window that frames our view of the world (Tuchman, 1978). And five principal journalistic norms and conventions frame what is presented as news:

- Objectivity (reporters are taught to deny their experience of the world)
- News values (emphasis on conflict, controversy, crime and outcome)
- Sourcing (use of "official" or institutional sources)
- Work routines (i.e., beats that privilege certain types of news)
- Structural constraints (i.e., deadlines or space limitations)

The result is that news brings us the event, not its context or multiple meanings. And it also brings us a value system. Feminist research has shown that each of the five journalistic norms listed above privilege a patriarchal world view (Strutt & Hissey, 1992; Theberge & Cronk, 1986; Tuchman, 1978). For example, what is the sex and color of those most likely to be used as "official" news sources? What values support the amount of space and time devoted routinely to male professional sports? Why are few—if any—reporters assigned to the women's sports beat? Why do studies show that professional football is the beat (e.g., job assignment) most coveted by male and female reporters alike? Why do male sportscasters earn much higher salaries than female sportscasters for the same work? What values suggest that women athletes should be called by their first names in television commentary more than men? What values justify devoting less than 5% of a newspaper sports page to women's sports?

Finding answers to these questions involves uncovering the gendered value system of American culture that underlies and supports both sport and traditional sports media.

The "F" Word in Sport

The "F" word in sport is not a four-letter word; it has eight. Feminism, according to sportswriter Susan Fornoff (1993) is the "F" word in sport. Why? Simple: The four-letter word means business as usual; the eight-letter word threatens to change things.

The threat is relatively recent, however. Feminist scholarship virtually ignored sport until the late 1970s (Messner & Sabo, 1990). Many early feminist scholars viewed sport as an inherently inappropriate site for their energy because of its institutional sexism. Janice Kaplan (1979) explains the crux of the issue:

> The women's movement has rallied around vaginal politics: abortion, contraception, gynecological arrogance. But sports has been a stepchild to feminism, since the issue of who gets to play kickball with whom never seems to be quite worthy of political upheaval. But it is important, because at stake is how women view themselves in general. (p. x)

Two authors in this book—Susan Birrell and Susan Greendorfer—produced some of the first scholarship that brought sport from the margin to the mainstream of feminist critical analysis.[3] Today feminist critiques of sport can be found in nearly every issue of significant journals in the field, such as the *Sociology of Sport Journal*.

When reading these critiques, it's important to remember that there are many feminisms or feminist approaches to understanding. Several communication scholars have described specific feminist theoretical positions in detail (e.g., Cirksena & Cuklanz, 1992; Steeves, 1987), and several sport sociology scholars have applied them to sport (e.g., Boutilier & SanGiovanni, 1983; Messner & Sabo, 1990). Here, however, I will simply describe the two overarching categories of feminism. Both challenge the values of the existing sport system but differ in terms of the desired outcome. The first is *reform*. Based on theoretical concepts such as equal opportunity, reform feminists often use legal strategies, such as Title IX to the Higher Education Amendments Act of 1972, to achieve equity within the existing system. The second is *transform*, which seeks to change the fundamental values on which the system is based. Since both desire change, both can lead to empowerment for women in sport (Duncan & Brummett, 1993).

In this book, valuing difference and developing a nonhierarchical theory means not privileging one feminism over another, thus, reform and transform perspectives are provided in various chapters. Authors in this book agree that the media play a role in the way women are oppressed, marginalized or disenfranchised by the current sport system, but they disagree on the nature of the oppression and how to eliminate it. For example, authors approach the journalistic norm of "balance" differently. In a recent study, Suzanne Strutt and Lynne Hissey (1992) described feminist critiques of the journalistic norm as either *bad balance* or *balance as usual* perspectives. To authors using a reformist perspective, the problem is one of *bad balance* and achieving *good balance* in media coverage means more coverage, better coverage, or equal coverage of women's sports. To those using a transformist perspective, the norm itself is problematic because increased or equal coverage does not guarantee change in any of the values that construct what is considered a newsworthy sport event. From this point of view, balanced coverage means *balance as usual* and would only render the "media more ideologically effective as patriarchal institutions" (Strutt & Hissey, 1992, p. 62).

Because the mass media industry is one of the dominant structures of our economic, social and political system, the remainder of this chapter will discuss the role of the media in the construction of gender. The next several pages of this chapter will discuss three major areas of media research: effects, content and production. It will also examine what research has been done in each area concerning sport. Feminists—reformists and transformists—need to understand these research traditions to effectively seek change in the current media system and in its representations of women in sport.

For the purposes of this book, *mass communication* is "communication from one person or a group of persons through a transmitting device (a channel) to a large audience or market" (Biagi, 1992, p. 546). The mass media are the channels used to transmit the communication such as newspapers, magazines, radio, television, movies, books and recordings.

Theoretical Issues in Mass Communication Research

Do the mass media create, reflect or possibly refract cultural attitudes about female athletes? About women's sports? What role do the media play in stereotyping female athletes? Is there a relationship between sports violence, media content and audience behavior?

If we expect to find answers to these questions, we are going to be disappointed. After nearly seven decades of research, there is still little agreement on how powerful the media is, how the power works, and why it works. Three models, however, have emerged over the years from the theoretical ferment in mass communication attempting to describe media effects, and a fourth is described in this chapter.[4] Although the exact lines between the categories have generated controversy, they are useful in tracing the general development of effects research. By tracing the historical development of media effects research, we will also see how this body of literature has developed from a patriarchal perspective and how it continues to ignore feminist theory.

1. All-Powerful Effects

Effects research in the U.S. took shape in the 1930s, when people feared that they could be manipulated by evil forces in control of the mass media because of propaganda's significant role in World War I. Communication scholar James Carey (1978) suggests that powerful effects of communication were feared in the 1930s because the Depression and political currents surrounding the war created a fertile seed for the production of certain kinds of effects.

One proponent of the all-powerful media model, Harold Lasswell, developed the "magic bullet" or "hypodermic needle" theory of mass communication effects. Essentially it stated that the media, like a serum injected into the bloodstream, directly shape public opinion and mold behavior. Researchers using this linear, hypodermic/bullet model viewed the audience as passive. "The model held that 'rightly-formed' messages were nearly irresistible by the common person" (Anderson & Meyer, 1988, p. 167). Research of this period focused primarily on the channel or medium delivering the message.

2. Limited Effects

The pendulum swung as evidence accumulated that other factors affected the mass communication process. Beginning with a 1940 study, researchers—notably Paul Lazarsfeld—declared that intervening effects in the process could no longer be ignored. Studies showed that people actively processed information and that many factors influenced mass communication effects including personal contact, social environment and motives for attending to a particular medium. The active audience concept essentially "killed" the hypodermic/bullet model and replaced it with a limited effects model. Bernard Berelson (1948) summed up the paradigm shift: "some kinds of *communication* on some kinds of *issues*, brought to the attention of some kinds of *people*, under some kinds of *conditions*, have some kinds of *effects*" (italics in original) (p. 172). Joseph Klapper (1960) helped to further switch the focus "toward a view of the media as influences, working amid other influences, in a total situation" (p. 5). In large part because of Berelson's and Klapper's pronouncements, the audience became central to the paradigm as an active processor of messages. And the mass communication effects model shifted from one of media "potency" to one of media "impotency."[5]

3. Powerful but Contingent

The antiwar, antiestablishment climate of the late 1960s spawned research to examine the relationships between the fundamental nature of the media and its relationship to the social structure. A powerful, but contingent, media effects model gained popularity in the 1970s, and researchers described media effects on several levels. Whereas the primary measure of media effect in the all-powerful and limited effects models had been behavior change, this model— rooted in research by Carl Hovland from World War II—described a hierarchy of media effects such as awareness, understanding, attitude change and behavior. Further refinements—for example, research by Maxwell McCombs and Donald Shaw (1972)—suggested that the media may not be able to tell the public what to think, but they could tell them what to think about. These agenda-setting theories argued for powerful media effects in terms of awareness, which were contingent on a number of audience characteristics. Another example of powerful but contingent media effects came from studies done in what became known as the knowledge-gap hypothesis (Tichenor, Donohue & Olien, 1970). These studies linked economic status and education to the rate at which particular kinds of information is diffused through a community. These researchers theorized that the growth of certain kinds of knowledge is greater and faster among higher status groups. Another in this strain of effects research, the uses and gratifications approach, focused on "what people do with the media" rather than "what the media do to them" (McLeod, Kosicki & Pan, 1991, p. 201).

A brief look at follow-up studies on these theories illustrates the difficulty in making generalizations about media effects.

Agenda Setting. Denis McQuail (1988) argues that current evidence for agenda-setting effects "is inconclusive and assessments . . . tend to leave agenda-setting with the status of a plausible, but unproven idea" (p. 276). Drawing from the more than 200 articles and a dozen books that have refined understanding of agenda-setting, Gerald Kosicki (1993) describes the nature of agenda-setting effects as "subtle, highly contingent" (p. 100).

Knowledge Gap. Follow-up studies in the knowledge-gap hypothesis suggest that the media can close gaps in small communities on issues of general concern (Donohue, Tichenor & Olien, 1975), that it is important to know the utility of the information to the group being studied (Novak, 1977) and that different media work in different ways (Robinson, 1972).

Uses and Gratifications. Relationships between strong motivations for media use and learning have been found, as has evidence that strong motivations interfere with agenda-setting effects (McLeod & Becker, 1974). However, intervening effects from the gendered context of media and audience characteristics have also been postulated (Creedon, 1988). The relationship of gendered context to motivations for viewing sports will be explored a little later in this chapter.

4. Powerful, Contingent and Contextual Effects

Perhaps because 70 years of empirical effects research largely failed to produce a macro-level general theory that adequately explained media effects, cultural and critical feminist theory gained a modicum of respect in the late 1980s and early 1990s in mass communication scholarship. In light of this, a new rupture in thinking about media effects is gaining momentum. This proposed fourth model builds on the accumulated knowledge from the earlier models and integrates critical insights about context. Most important, it uses the conjunction *and* rather than *but* when describing media effects. It acknowledges that the media are powerful, *and* that the power is contingent *and* contextual; that is, it accounts for the fact that different individuals view the world differently based on the way that they have experienced it.

Cultural theories, for example, have been used to explain media effects in interactive settings including economic, social and political contexts. Critical feminist theories have extended cultural studies to include the intersection of gender within other contexts such as class, race, ethnicity and sexual preference. Both traditions suggest that to understand media effects one must understand the cultural contexts in which the messages are received. For example, cultural studies scholar Sut Jhally (1989) argues that a capitalistic context affects the production, content and reception of media messages about sport. Critical feminist scholars Nancy Theberge and Alan Cronk (1986) suggest that the gendered nature of journalistic norms and production processes affects the wider coverage enjoyed by men's sports.

As the next section of this chapter will argue, the powerful, contingent and contextual effects model holds some promise to solve the enigma. In addition, since a large portion of the work that led to the development of the existing effects models was done—and continues to be done—in political communication, studies in sport communication could broaden the field of effects research. The next section of this chapter reviews current research into the effects of sports coverage and then looks at a case study of a research program to see how context can be integrated in media effects studies examining sport.

Developing a Powerful, Contingent and Contextual Effects Model Through Sport

Existing work in media effects involving sport communication falls into three broad categories: motivations for viewing, locus of exposure and effects of exposure. A series of studies investigating motivations for sports viewing found that fanship ("to thrill in victory"), a desire to "let loose," and learning motivate sports viewing and that differences exist in motivations between men and women (Gantz, 1981; Wenner, 1989; Wenner & Gantz, 1988). The locus of exposure—that is, whether one views with friends, at a sports bar or alone—has been shown to affect perceptions (Gantz, 1981; Sapolsky & Zillmann, 1978; Wenner, 1989). Sociological research has suggested that the aggressive actions of players often serve as catalysts for the violent behavior of those who are spectating; the related effect of violent television sports programming and/or commentary on viewers is another strain of mass communication audience research (Celozzi, Kazelskis & Gutsch, 1981; Comisky, Bryant & Zillmann, 1977).

Virtually nothing had been done to explore audience preferences for televised sports involving women until 1985 when Lee Becker, my colleague at Ohio State, and I began a research effort. A review of the literature found at least three theoretical constructs that could help account for stated audience preferences to view male sports on television: people do not like the unknown; female sports are perceived as inferior; and some sports are viewed as inappropriate for women (Becker & Creedon, 1989). How we went about applying these explanations to sports involving women illustrates some of the complexities of media effects research and how the powerful but contingent effects model differs from the proposed powerful, contingent and contextual effects model.

The program involved survey as well as experimental research (Becker, 1991; Becker & Creedon, 1988, 1989, 1990; Creedon, 1988; Creedon & Becker, 1986a, 1986b). Over a six-year period, we surveyed more than 1,200 residents of the Columbus, Ohio, metropolitan area and 354 Ohio State University students regarding their sports viewing preferences. The survey work showed that audiences perceive women's sports as inferior and less exciting.

We also conducted controlled exposure experiments with more than 460 college students. The experiments were designed to see if viewing videotaped segments of various sporting events involving women could alter these perceptions. In all experiments, subjects completed pre- and post-viewing questionnaires. In the first experiment, students, either in groups or individually, viewed either male or female volleyball; in the second experiment they viewed male or female basketball. In later experiments subjects viewed either women's figure skating or women's soccer. The first exposure experiment did not alter interest in or views about the inferiority of women's sports (Becker & Creedon, 1988), whereas the second showed that those high in modeling motivation (e.g., those who were interested in learning specific skills by viewing competent athletes performing) were willing to learn from athletes regardless of sex and that those high in spectating motivation preferred to watch men's sports (Becker & Creedon, 1989). The third experiment provided evidence that forced exposure to female athletics that are not viewed by society as sex appropriate (i.e., women's soccer) stimulates negative responses (Becker, 1991).

Generally, these results fit nicely into the powerful but contingent effects model, under the rubric of uses and gratifications research. In sum, exposure did not change individual preferences for viewing more women's sports or alter the fact that some sports are viewed as inappropriate for women or change perceptions that some women's sports are inferior to men's sports. The experiments, however, did provide empirical evidence that audience motivations affect sport viewing preferences.

Although one could argue that we weren't seeking to understand these findings at a mega-theoretical level, the fact is that after six years of work, we have only succeeded in reconfirming what other researchers had already reported (i.e., women's sports are perceived as inferior to men's) and in confirming that modeling and spectating motivations exist in television sports viewing preferences. We still don't understand why preferences exist for men's sports or why exposure did not alter them. Or do we?

In the beginning of the work, I naively believed that we could conduct a stimulus-response experiment, test for possible intervening variables, and arrive at an understanding of audience behavior.

Yes, the experiments have provided empirical proof that some intervening variables affect some perceptions and some behaviors for some people some of the time. But is that the best we can do?

In our studies, we attempted to measure media effects through gross quantitative categories (i.e., male responses or female responses), which ignored or minimized within group variability (Hare-Mustin & Marecek, 1988). To study the effects of sports viewing, a great deal more time must be spent conceptualizing gender and ways to measure varying gendered responses. Equally important, when we asked our respondents to compare men's and women's athletics, we prompted them to use an implicit frame of reference, that is, male sports as the norm. Other research has shown that because of the gendered context of this norm, women playing as well as men are perceived as aberrant and women playing differently than men as inferior. Measures of competitiveness and quality of play assume a male norm, so why not use alternative measures such as fun and enjoyment on the part of the athletes? Would such measures alter the viewer's perception? If these values were to become part of the institutional norm for professional sport, might this affect preferences for mediated sports in general?

There are several contributions that critical feminist and cultural theory can make at this juncture. First, assumptions about gender— sexuality, beauty, femininity and so forth—produce powerful, contingent and contextual effects. Naomi Wolf (1991), for example, provides ample anecdotal, as well as some qualitative and quantitative, proof of the powerful effect of the media in perpetuating what she calls the beauty myth. The relative power of this effect, however, is contingent on a number of factors, including economic, political and social variables that construct responses to the myth. For example, according to Wolf, beauty is defined as white, Western, blonde and youthful. If we add context to the analysis, then we must ask a series of related questions. What long-term effect have the mediated representations of this myth had on women? Are all women affected the same? All African-American women the same? All African-American women in various social classes the same? All bisexual African-American women in various social classes the same? These are not questions that can be answered by plugging factoids about salary levels, education, race and sexual preference into an equation to determine statistically significant differences. If some highly educated African-American women with prestigious, white-collar jobs, for example, are not the least bit interested in assimilating white values, presumably, then, the beauty myth would not affect them in the same way it might affect other women and other African-American women. However, the beauty myth is part of the cultural context for all women—and men. Even those who consciously reject the beauty myth must contend with it because it permeates media messages.

To move this research program—and a good deal of media effects research—significantly forward more time must be spent conceptualizing ways to measure a range of responses by acknowledging their gendered contexts. Adding gendered contexts to the formula might help us link some of the contingent effects into meaningful chains of understanding.

Media Content and Production

Researchers studying media content and production have also built a large body of literature. Content analyses of newspapers, magazines, radio and television have provided numerous data on what people buy, read and view. Chapter 2 details many of the descriptive studies that have been done concerning sports content in the media.

More recently scholars have focused considerable effort trying to understand how differences in content are produced (i.e., Shoemaker & Reese, 1991). "[C]ontent differences are a function of a network of influences, ranging from communication workers' personal attitudes and role conceptions, routines of media work, media organizational structure and culture, the relationship between media and other social institutions and cultural and ideological forces" (Shoemaker & Reese, 1990, p. 650). Nancy Theberge applied several of these concepts in her research on work routines in sports departments (1986) and in her study of how media accounts of violence at a hockey game framed the incident as a problem with certain individuals rather than as a problem with the institution of sport (1989).

Gatekeeping theory is an area of media content and production research that has considerable interest to our investigation of sport. Gatekeeping, according to Pamela J. Shoemaker (1991), is "the process by which billions of messages that are available in the world get cut down and transformed into the hundreds of messages that reach a given person on a given day" (p. 1). The process involves selecting, producing, transmitting and shaping information. Nearly everyone involved in the news production process functions as a gatekeeper. In newspapers, for example, the primary news source (i.e., coach or athlete) selects, produces, transmits and shapes the information provided to the sports reporter who repeats the process and then passes the information along to an editor or several editors who repeat the process again. But it doesn't end there. Advertisers, publishers, public relations practitioners and other opinion leaders can influence message selection, shaping, production and transmission. Geographical distribution and production processes also affect content. Sports news in *USA Today*, for example, will differ from that appearing in a local paper both in terms of general content and detail.

A related body of research has emerged on the role of information subsidies such as news releases, interviews, background briefings and so forth in the news construction process (Gandy, 1982; Turk, 1985, 1986). Sources of quick and inexpensive information for reporters, information subsidies clearly influence media content. In one study, judgments about the salience of certain facts and priorities set by public relations sources influenced news content about government agencies in about 50% of the stories examined (Turk, 1986). No comparable empirical study of information subsidy influence on newspaper sports page content has been reported in the literature. However, as the former supervisor of a collegiate sports information function, I would estimate the overall percentage of subsidy influence on the daily sports page—throughout all levels of sports coverage and from all public relations sources—to be significantly higher than 50%. A study of newspaper editors' perceptions of public relations practitioners lends some support to my contention: sport editors viewed PR folks more favorably than did either business or news editors (Pincus, Rimmer, Rayfield & Cropp, 1991). Presumably, the sports editors viewed PR practitioners in sport favorably because they provided useful, quick and inexpensive content subsidies. Another factor affecting this positive attitude, explored in more detail in Chapters 4 and 7, involves the traditional "cheerleader" role that sports reporters play with the sports they cover. A series of interviews with contemporary women sportswriters in Chapter 6 provides additional insight on these relationships.

Media Research, Feminist Theory and Sport

Clearly, neither the all-powerful, the impotent, nor the powerful but contingent model has provided a satisfactory explanation of the power of the media. Even without any empirically proven mega-theory, however, general agreement remains that the media, like family, education, church and occupation, are a powerful socializing institution in America that presents a relatively homogenous picture of the world.

The lesson of common sense and everyday observation, as well as of research, should tell us that mass media constitute a public institution that may rarely initiate change independently but that does provide the channels, the means and an arena for the playing-out of societywide processes in which many actors and interests are involved, often in competition (McQuail, 1988, p. 291).

How do we then produce a body of literature that will answer the questions about the power of mass communication? First, the boundary line between traditional media effects, content and production research on the one hand and critical feminist and cultural studies research on the other must be erased to allow more creative and less dualistic (e.g., male versus female) conceptions of how individuals produce meaning to be included. Some feminist scholars, for example, have suggested that women make meaning differently than men (i.e., Gilligan, 1982; Rakow, 1992). Others have made arguments for oppositional, subverted or resisted readings of media content—including football games—by women (i.e., Brown, 1990; Duncan & Brummett, 1993).[6] In my view, integrating these arguments for gendered context with the scientific method will not result in the absolute relativism that many empiricists fear; instead it will provide for a more sophisticated recognition of diverging patterns and dis-symmetries (symmetries in opposite directions).

Although most attempts to date to incorporate feminist perspectives into larger media effects traditions have failed, sport communication research is a relatively young and unmined field that could provide the much needed avenue to integrate context with the scientific method and challenge "disciplined, homogenized and commodified" gender values (Jansen, 1993, p. 141). Because there has been no *universal* agreement about a *single* answer, an opportunity is at hand. Increased interest in the potential of cultural and critical theory to assist in understanding communication effects provides feminist scholars a chance to help reframe, expand and diversify the perspectives used in the investigations. Sue Curry Jansen's (1993) argument for "communication as situated knowledge" (p. 137) and Kathryn Cirksena's (1987) discussion of the "inescapable contextuality of knowledge" (p. 21) provide us with some useful theoretical starting points.

Several other factors that have contributed to paradigm paralysis in mass communication must also be addressed. Researchers, eager to produce publications, have jumped onto theoretical bandwagons, entered conceptual labyrinths and designed experiments to generate statistically significant results that do little to advance understanding. Yiannakis (1979, cited in Boutilier & SanGiovanni, 1983) described the problem in the context of sport sociology, then an emerging subdiscipline of sociology, over a decade ago:

> [G]reater emphasis should be placed on creating a climate of intellectual discourse on matters theoretical, conceptual, and normative, and emphasize less the current obsession with "piecemeal" quantitative research. Until the domain has been adequately excavated theoretically, statistically significant results are often theoretically meaningless in and of themselves. (p. 1)

Because mass communication is a hybrid discipline, borrowing from "parent" disciplines such as psychology, political science, economics and communication, conceptual research in the field calls for a broad understanding of many theoretical traditions. Particularly since the onset of effects research, mass communication scholarship has suffered from severe conceptual myopia.

At this juncture in media research, it may be less important to seek *The Answer* than to find *The Questions*. Asking better questions will permit us to move closer to understanding the power of the mass media and the gendered underpinnings of its value system.

Women, Media and Sport

In the table of contents of their recent book *Megatrends for Women*, Patricia Aburdene and John Naisbitt put "the sporting life" in second position right after politics (1992, p. xi). They suggest that women have become a critical mass in sports, which they define as an "unstoppable, accepted phenomenon" (p. xvii). They cite sports researchers who predict that women will beat men's times in the marathon by 1998. "The 1992 Olympics was the metaphor: U.S. women brought home all **5 gold medals** [bold in original]—in total 9 of 11 medals won by Americans" (p. xx).

Because much of the recorded history of sport in the United States is rooted in American sports journalism, by examining media coverage in combination with traditional and nontraditional historical sources, feminist sport historians and sociologists have been able to piece together a fairly comprehensive record of women's sport history. No one, however, has taken a close look at the relationship of women, media and sport in the manner of this book. We examine the values of the media system, the values used to construct media representations of women and the values of the women who work in the media system. We also critique the values of the sport system, the economic structure that supports it and the media system that is part of that economic structure. Finally, we take a look at a new sport model based on very different values and how it could change sports coverage as we know it.

The first part of the book looks at the mediated context of gender values in sport. A critique of media coverage of women's sport is the focus of Chapter 2 by Mary Jo Kane and Susan Greendorfer. They also look at the role of the media in presenting stereotyped images of women in sport. In Chapter 3, Linda Williams offers an in-depth look at coverage of women's sports from the 1920s to the 1940s in what was then called the Negro Press and reviews research on how women of color are covered in the mainstream press.

Taken together, Chapters 4 and 5 are a first—an attempt to provide a complete historical account of women in American sports journalism. As a feminist, I realize that such a contribution history is flawed because it uses a penile yardstick. Unfortunately, except for a few notable feminist efforts in magazine journalism, the standard for sports news in our culture has been and remains men's sports. Retrieving the herstory of women journalists who "measured up" is presented in this context. The material in these chapters is meant to be seen as a first step in recovering the history of women sportswriters and sportscasters. It is also a starting point for future scholarship that will add context and meaning to their contributions and perhaps contribute to a further examination of the role of women in the sports media in creating, preserving, transmitting and, perhaps, resisting gendered norms.

Although many male sportswriters and sportscasters have written about the development of sport from the perspective of a journalist and many others have written about their own experiences in sport, until 1993 only *one* nonfiction book documented the experience of a female sports journalist in the American media market. Published in Canada, it dealt with *Toronto Star* reporter Alison Gordon's (1985) experiences while covering the Blue Jays.[7] Interviews with women in print and broadcast sports journalism in Chapter 6 by Judith Cramer make an important contribution toward helping us understand the context of women's experiences in sport reporting. They also provide significant insights about their roles as gatekeepers.

The concluding chapter in this part examines the relationship between economics, sports and the media. It also explores the current state of promoting and marketing women's collegiate and professional sports. It includes data from two surveys of college sports information managers responsible for publicizing women's sports and describes how information subsidies affect the media agenda in sports coverage.

Cultural contexts for gender values are presented in Part II. In Chapter 8, Susan Birrell and Cheryl Cole show how the media struggled to (re)construct tennis player Renée Richards after her sex change operation. Karlene Ferrante provides an essay in Chapter 9 on the construction of gender values in the All-American pastime, baseball. In Chapter 10, the global context of women as TV spectators is examined by Anne Cooper-Chen.

The three chapters in the final part of the book work together to develop a new model for women's sports. Women in this model are empowered to challenge the cultural ideals represented by exclusionary sports such as football.[8] Chapter 11 traces the cultural mythology that surrounds the strong woman archetype and how it has affected her representation in contemporary American culture. Molly Merryman looks at how the archetype is represented in modern film in Chapter 12. In the final chapter, Pamela Highlen provides the structure for the new model, called the Co-Essence Model of Sport, and examines how it is used by Stanford University's Basketball Coach Tara VanDerveer.[9]

Women's increasing participation in American sport will certainly act as a catalyst for numerous challenges to traditional gender values. Whether it will help "expedite the evolution to a higher species of mammal" remains to be seen (Robbins, 1990, p. 383). The remainder of this book examines the way in which the media are communicating—and have communicated— about women in sport and sports journalism.

Notes

1. I assumed that the spokesperson missed out on Little League acculturation because girls have been allowed to play in it only since 1974 (Aburdene & Naisbitt, 1992). In fact, in 1975 a girl was ejected from a game for not wearing "the required protective cup on her groin" (Aburdene & Naisbitt, p. 45). A recent report of the percentage of white-collar women involved in athletics shows that 51% played youth sports, 38% high school sports, 29% intramural sports, 9% college sports, and 12% participate in post-college amateur sport (Lawton, 1993, p. 13).

2. In 1987 the Supreme Court upheld a lawsuit by the United States Olympic Committee to block leaders of the gay community from using the word *Olympics* on the grounds that it was a trademark violation (Sage, 1990, p. 211). The fact that the case was brought to trial underscores the symbolic power of sport. Approximately 1,300 athletes participated in 14 events at Gay Games I in San Francisco in 1982; 15,000 participants in 31 events from 50 states and 40 countries are expected for Gay Games IV in New York in 1994 (*Fact Sheet*, n.d.).

3. Messner and Sabo (1990, p. 2) provide a useful list of references to pioneers in feminist analysis of sport.

4. Historical revisionists in the field are disputing several traditional accounts of the development of media effects research (see McLeod, Kosicki & Pan, 1991). These include: (1) attributing of the origins of concern about media effects to the 1940s when roots can be traced to the late 1800s, (2) representing the findings of complex effects research by Lazarsfeld and Hovland as a simplistic stimulus-response model, and (3) misunderstanding the construction and acceptance of the limited effects model. Of particular note is recent revisionary work by Chaffee and Hochheimer (1985), which suggests that some of the early reports of research that led to the all-powerful effects model did not reflect the research design or actual findings but may have been used instead to establish credibility for later work—partly sponsored by commercial interests—in what became widely known as the limited effects model.

5. The limited effects model has been criticized extensively because of the murky relationship between the sponsors of the research that led to its development and the interpretation of the findings (see, e.g., Gitlin, 1978). The criticism suggests that the use of the limited effects model privileged commercial interests because it supported policy decisions of non-interference and non-intervention in media development and content. Interestingly, commercial, government and marketing research continues in large part to support the limited effects model. For example, research done by the three major television networks does not show much effect for television content, especially on children, whereas academic research shows much the opposite.

6. This is not an essentialist argument. Gender is a social construction and as such women's experience of the world differs from that of men's. Similarly, all women do not experience the world the same, nor do all men.

7. Now there is a second book, Susan Fornoff's (1993) *Lady in the Locker Room*. Both Gordon (1985) and Fornoff (1993) include discussions of gender differences in sports reporting experiences such as issues of locker room access and credibility. The books by male sportswriters tend to be either social commentary or reflections of shared glory. Sportswriter Kay Gilman (1974) also wrote a book about the New York Jets during their 1973 season, but it does not focus on her experiences as a female sportswriter; rather it provides a description of the season. To date there are no books based solely on the experience of women sportswriters covering women's sports. Of course, there are few sportswriters, if any, who have made a career of covering women's sports (see Chapters 4 and 5).

8. Women are currently playing high school football after Beth Balsley waged a legal battle in 1985 for the right to try out for the Annandale, New Jersey, football team (Carlson, 1992). Since 1985, most states have amended their policies to permit girls on boys teams, but school boards and coaches still play a role. For an interesting fictional account of an eighth-grade basketball team dealing for the first time with girls at the tryouts, see Levy (1979).

9. Two areas of related interest are not covered in this book: physiology and nutrition. See Greta Cohen (1993) for a discussion of these issues.

References

NOTE: Readers may note that we have violated American Psychological Association style in chapter reference lists by including the first names of book and article

authors where available. This was done to provide an additional context for the
reader to evaluate the arguments made throughout the book.

Aburdene, Patricia & Naisbitt, John. (1992). *Megatrends for women*. New York: Villard
Books.

Anderson, James A. & Meyer, Timothy P. (1988). *Mediated communication: A social
action perspective*. Newbury Park, CA: Sage.

Becker, Lee B. (1991, May). *Audience values and sports preferences*. Paper presented at
the International Communication Association, Chicago.

Becker, Lee B. & Creedon, Pamela J. (1988, August). *Altering stereotypes about female
sports: The effects of exposure to television coverage of female athletes*. Paper
presented at the International Association for Mass Communication Research, Barcelona, Spain.

Becker, Lee B. & Creedon, Pamela J. (1989, November). *Coming to grips with sports
viewing on television: Conceptual and methodological work on motivations for watching sports*. Paper presented to the Midwest Association for Public Opinion
Research, Chicago.

Becker, Lee B. & Creedon, Pamela J. (1990, August). *Motivations for watching sports:
Modeling and spectating as goals*. Paper presented at the International Association for Mass Communications Research, Bled, Yugoslavia.

Berelson, Bernard. (1948). Communications and public opinion. In Wilbur Schramm
(Ed.), *Communications in a modern society* (pp.162-185). Urbana, IL: University of Illinois Press.

Biagi, Shirley. (1992). *Media/impact: An introduction to mass media*. Belmont, CA:
Wadsworth.

Boutilier, Mary A. & SanGiovanni, Lucinda. (1983). *The sporting woman*. Champaign,
IL: Human Kinetics.

Boyle, Robert H. (1963). *Sport: Mirror of American life*. Boston: Little, Brown.

Brown, Mary Ellen. (1990). *Television and women's culture*. Newbury Park, CA: Sage.

Carey, James. (1978). The ambiguity of policy research. *Journal of Communication,
28*(3), 114-119.

Carlson, Alison. (1992, March). Where the boys are: Why women choose to join guys
on the playing field. *Women's Sports and Fitness*, p. 72.

Celozzi, Mathew J., Kazelskis, Richard & Gutsch, Kenneth U. (1981). The relationship
between viewing televised violence in ice hockey and subsequent levels of
personal aggression. *Journal of Sport Behavior, 4*, 157-162.

Chaffee, Steven H. & Hochheimer, John L. (1985). The beginnings of political communication research in the United States: Origins of the 'limited effects
model.' In M. Gurevitch & Mark R. Levy (Eds.), *Mass communication review
yearbook, 5* (pp. 75-104). Beverly Hills, CA: Sage.

Cirksena, Kathryn. (1987). Politics and difference: Radical feminist epistemological
premises for communication studies. *Journal of Communication Inquiry, 11*(1),
19-28.

Cirksena, Kathryn & Cuklanz, Lisa. (1992). Male is to female as —— is to ——:
A guided tour of five feminist frameworks for communication studies. In
Lana Rakow (Ed.), *Women making meaning: New feminist directions in commu-
nication* (pp. 18-44). New York: Routledge.

Cohen, Greta L. (1993). *Women in sport: Issues and controversies*. Newbury Park, CA: Sage.

Comisky, Paul, Bryant, Jennings & Zillmann, Dolf. (1977). Drama in sports commentary. *Journal of Communication, 27,* 150-153.

Creedon, Pamela J. (1988, November). *Analyzing the audience of mediated sport: The hidden variables.* Paper presented at the Midwest Association of Public Opinion Research, Chicago.

Creedon, Pamela J. & Becker, Lee B. (1986a, August). *Audience expectations and sport: The role of the female athlete.* Paper presented to the International Association of Mass Communication Research, New Delhi, India.

Creedon, Pamela J. & Becker, Lee B. (1986b, November). *Television sports viewing and leisure behavior.* Paper presented to the Midwest Association for Public Opinion Research, Chicago.

Donohue, George A., Tichenor, Phillip & Olien, Clarice N. (1975). Mass media and the knowledge gap. *Communication Research, 2,* 3-23.

Duncan, Margaret Carlisle & Brummett, Barry. (1993). Liberal and radical sources of female empowerment in sport media. *Sociology of Sport Journal, 10,* 57-72.

Eitzen, S. Stanley & Zinn, Maxine Baca. (1989). The de-athleticization of women: The naming and gender marking of collegiate sport teams. *Sociology of Sport Journal, 6,* 362-370.

Fact Sheet: Unity '94. (n.d.). Available from Unity '94, 19 W. 21st Street, Suite 1202, New York, NY.

Fornoff, Susan. (1993). *Lady in the locker room.* Champaign, IL: Sagamore.

Fuller, John R. & Manning, Elisabeth Anne. (1987). Violence and sexism in college mascots and symbols: A typology. *Free Inquiry in Creative Sociology, 15,* 61-64.

Gandy, Oscar H., Jr. (1982). *Beyond agenda setting: Information subsidies and public policy.* Norwood, NJ: Ablex.

Gantz, Walter. (1981). An exploration of viewing motives and behaviors associated with television sports. *Journal of Broadcasting, 25,* 263-275.

Gilligan, Carol. (1982). *In a different voice: Psychological theory and women's development.* Cambridge, MA: Harvard University Press.

Gilman, Kay. (1974). *Inside the pressure cooker.* New York: Berkeley Medallion.

Gitlin, Todd. (1978). Media sociology: The dominant paradigm. In G. Cleveland Wilhoit & Harold deBock (Eds.), *Mass communication review yearbook, 2* (pp. 73-121). Beverly Hills, CA: Sage.

Gordon, Alison. (1985). Foul ball: Five years in the American League. New York: Dodd, Mead.

Guttmann, Allen. (1978). *From ritual to record: The nature of modern sports.* New York: Columbia University Press.

Guttmann, Allen. (1986). *Sports spectators.* New York: Columbia University Press.

Guttmann, Allen. (1988). *A whole new ball game: An interpretation of American sports.* Chapel Hill, NC: University of North Carolina Press.

Guttmann, Allen. (1991). *Women's sports: A history.* New York: Columbia University Press.

Hare-Mustin, Rachel T. & Marecek, Jeanne. (1988). The meaning of difference: Gender theory, postmodernism, and psychology. *American Psychologist, 43*(6), 455-464.

Jansen, Sue Curry. (1993). "The future is not what it used to be": Gender, history and communication studies. *Communication Theory, 2*(3), 136-149.

Jhally, Sut. (1989). Cultural studies and the sports/media complex. In Lawrence A. Wenner (Ed), *Media, sports, & society* (pp. 70-93). Newbury Park, CA: Sage.

Kaplan, Janice. (1979). *Women and sports.* New York: Viking.

Klapper, Joseph. (1960). *The effects of mass communication.* New York: The Free Press.

Kosicki, Gerald M. (1993). Problems and opportunities in agenda-setting research. *Journal of Communication, 43*(2), 100-127.

Lawton, Lynnore S. (1993, March/April). Working women work out. *The Women's Sports Experience.* East Meadow, NY: Women's Sports Foundation.

Levy, Elizabeth. (1979). *The tryouts.* New York: Four Winds Press.

Lurie, Rachel. (1991, Jan. 29). The Super Bowl and wife beating: Unnecessary roughness. *Village Voice,* p. 132.

Luschen, Gunther. (1981). The interdependence of sport and culture. In Marie Hart & Susan Birrell (Eds), *Sport in the sociocultural process* (3rd ed., pp. 92-108). Dubuque, IA: William Brown.

McCombs, Maxwell E. & Shaw, Donald L. (1972). The agenda-setting function of the press. *Public Opinion Quarterly, 36,* 176-187.

McLeod, Jack M. & Becker, Lee B. (1974) Testing the validity of gratification measures through political effects analysis. In Jay G. Blumler and Elihu Katz (Eds), *The uses of mass communication: Current perspectives on gratifications research* (pp. 137-164). Beverly Hills, CA: Sage.

McLeod, Jack M., Kosicki, Gerald M. & Pan, Zhongdang. (1991). On understanding and misunderstanding media effects. In James Curran & Michael Gurevitch (Eds.), *Mass media & society* (pp. 235-266). London: Edward Arnold.

McQuail, Denis. (1988). *Mass communication theory: An introduction* (2nd ed.). Newbury Park, CA: Sage.

Messner, Michael A. & Sabo, Donald F. (1990). *Sport, men, and the gender order: Critical feminist perspectives.* Champaign, IL: Human Kinetics.

Novak, K. (1977). From information gaps to communication potential. In M. Berg et al. (Eds), *Current theories in Scandinavian mass communication.* Grenå, Denmark: GMT.

Pincus, David J., Rimmer, Tony, Rayfield, Robert E. & Cropp, Fritz. (1991, August). *Newspaper editors' perceptions of public relations: How business, news and sports editors differ.* Paper presented at the Association for Education in Journalism and Mass Communication conference, Boston, MA.

Rakow, Lana F. (1992). *Women making meaning: New feminist directions in communication.* New York: Routledge.

Real, Michael. (1975). Superbowl: Mythic spectacle. *Journal of Communication, 25*(1), 31-43.

Robbins, Tom. (1990). *Skinny legs and all.* New York: Bantam.

Robinson, John P. (1972). Mass communication and information diffusion. In F. Gerald Kline & Phillip J. Tichenor (Eds.), *Current perspectives in mass communication research* (pp. 71-93). Beverly Hills, CA: Sage.

Sage, George H. (1990, September). Sport and the social sciences. *Annals of the American Academy of Political and Social Science, 445,* 1-14.

Sapolsky, Barry S. & Zillmann, Dolf. (1978). Enjoyment of televised sport contests under different conditions of viewing. *Perceptual and Motor Skills, 46,* 29-30.

Shoemaker, Pamela, J. (1991). *Gatekeeping.* Newbury Park, CA: Sage.

Shoemaker, Pamela J. & Reese, Stephen D. (1990). Exposure to what? Integrating media content and effects studies. *Journalism Quarterly, 67*(4), 649-652.

Shoemaker, Pamela J. & Reese, Stephen D. (1991). *Mediating the message: Theories of influences on mass media content.* New York: Longman.

Steeves, Leslie H. (1987). Feminist theories and media studies. *Critical Studies in Mass Communication, 4,* 95-135.

Strutt, Suzanne & Hissey, Lynne. (1992). Feminisms and balance. *Canadian Journal of Communication, 17,* 61-74.

Theberge, Nancy. (1986). Sport and women's empowerment. *Women's Studies International Forum, 10*(4), 387-393.

Theberge, Nancy. (1989). A feminist analysis of responses to sports violence: Media coverage of the 1987 World Junior Hockey Championship, *Sociology of Sport Journal, 6,* 247-256.

Theberge, Nancy & Cronk, Alan. (1986). Work routines in newspaper sports departments and the coverage of women's sports. *Sociology of Sport Journal, 3,* 195-203.

Tichenor, Phillip J., Donohue, George A. & Olien, Clarice N. (1970). Mass media and the differential growth in knowledge. *Public Opinion Quarterly, 34,* 158-170.

Tuchman, Gaye. (1978). *Making news: A study in the construction of reality.* New York: The Free Press.

Turk, Judy VanSlyke. (1985). Information subsidies and influence. *Public Relations Review, 11*(3), 10-25.

Turk, Judy VanSlyke. (1986, December). Information subsidies and media content: A study of public relations influence on the news. *Journalism Monographs, 100.*

Wenner, Lawrence A. (Ed). (1989). *Media, sports & society.* Newbury Park, CA: Sage.

Wenner, Lawrence A. & Gantz, Walter. (1988, May). *Watching sports on television.* Paper presented to the International Communication Association, New Orleans.

Wolf, Naomi. (1991). *The beauty myth.* New York: William Morrow.

Yiannakis, Andrew. (1979, July). From the editor. *Newsletter: The North American Society for the Sociology of Sport, 1,* 1-5.

2

The Media's Role in Accommodating and Resisting Stereotyped Images of Women in Sport

Mary Jo Kane
Susan L. Greendorfer

On the surface, media coverage of the two most recent Olympic Games, 1988 and 1992, departed from past practices, as women athletes appeared finally to have achieved visibility in the national media. Few can forget images of Florence Griffith Joyner (FloJo) at the 1988 Olympics running down the track in her multicolored, high-fashion "outfit." Media coverage of female athletes at the 1992 games focused on gymnasts—little pixies whose bodies were shown in graceful, aesthetic motion. Thus, after decades of denial and invisibility in our culture, the female athlete had finally arrived. Or had she? In this chapter we argue that although the presence of women athletes in the media appears to represent fundamental social change—that sportswomen have gained widespread social acceptance—in reality, these "feminized" images represent a modernized attempt to reinforce traditional stereotypical images of femininity and female sexuality. More important, we also argue that these feminized and sexualized portrayals are simply new variations on very old themes: media images as a product or tool of patriarchal oppression of women—and their bodies—through an institutionalized socially constructed system of gender roles and values.

When we speak of "gender roles and values," we are focusing on the social definitions of female and male that have traditionally represented two mutually exclusive, dichotomous polar opposites. Whereas *male* and *female* are biological terms that represent physical differences in size, structure and reproductive capacity, *feminine* and *masculine* correspond to social, historical and cultural meanings that have been associated with these biological differences (Betterton, 1987; Birrell & Cole, 1990; Smith-Rosenberg & Rosenberg, 1987; Vertinsky, 1987). We suggest, however, that the relationship between sexual difference and gender difference is more than a mere association—sexual (physical) difference *becomes* gender (social) difference. Thus, the biological signifiers of being female (e.g., physical attributes, size, structure and reproductive capacity) require individuals to look, dress and act differently, in terms of gender roles and gender values, than those individuals who carry the biological signifiers of being male.

Although few would argue that, for the most part, women and men conform to these gender role expectations, our analysis extends beyond gender difference and how that difference is linked to sexual or physical difference. We are suggesting that gender *difference* is translated into gender *hierarchy*, because in existing social arrangements females are defined not only as "other than" but as "less than" their male counterparts. In Western culture, normative expectations hold that males are "active, aggressive, and spontaneous whereas [females are] weak, passive and responsive" (Nead, as cited in Duncan, 1990, p. 25). The critical point underlying these normative expectations is that being active, aggressive and spontaneous is considered superior to being weak, passive and responsive.

Overview of Chapter

How do the issues raised in the preceding discussion relate to sport and the mass media? In this chapter we outline how sport in general, and media portrayals of female athletes in particular, are vehicles through which sexual difference, gender difference and gender hierarchy are reified. We further argue that one important consequence of this reification is the maintenance of the status quo, a power structure in which males and male athletes are perceived and portrayed as different from (sexual and gender difference) and better than (gender hierarchy) females and female athletes. Returning to our earlier example of media portrayals of female athleticism during the 1988 Olympics, what are the dominant images and themes that remain in our minds? Do we remember Florence Griffith Joyner, an outstanding athlete who won three Olympic gold medals in track and field? Or do we remember "FloJo," a fashion model/designer who performed in "long tresses, lavish makeup, and racy one-legged running suits that emphasize sexual difference" (Duncan, 1990, p. 28)? This latter portrayal clearly depicts Florence Griffith Joyner as "FloJo," a woman who is portrayed (and therefore socially constructed) as different from and other than her athletic male counterparts—primarily because the dominant media themes emphasized her femininity and sexuality, not her athleticism.

A similar example occurred in professional sports when Chris Evert announced her retirement in the late 1980s. This event was seen as so significant that Evert appeared on the cover of *Sports Illustrated*, something that rarely happens to sportswomen. However, rather than focusing on her brilliant tennis career, *Sports Illustrated* chose to frame her retirement with the caption, "I'm going to be a full time wife" (August 28, 1989). Finally, in a very recent example of this type of stereotypical portrayal, *Sports Illustrated* again chose to focus on sportswomen's physical, sexual appearance. In the world of figure skating there is a debate about allowing former Olympic figure skaters who turned professional to return to amateur status in order to compete in the 1994 Olympics. One athlete affected by this debate, 1988 gold medal winner Katarina Witt, was portrayed not as a serious, committed athlete with a discipline and desire for athletic excellence but as a sexy female who recently appeared in a German magazine in a "peekaboo" photo "posing in a veritable buffet of semi-naughty attire" (Swift, 1993, p. 23).

In all of these examples, female athleticism is constructed by the media as a "bastardized, perhaps even counterfeit version of the 'real' (men's) sport" (Kane & Snyder, 1989, p. 92). More significant, we would argue that by portraying female athletes as feminized and sexualized others, the media trivialize and therefore undermine their athletic achievements. This type of media portrayal results in constructions of female athleticism as less important than male athleticism.

Sport, Physicality and Gender as Power

A number of authors have argued that perhaps more than any other social institution sport perpetuates male superiority and female inferiority (Birrell & Cole, 1990; Donnelly, 1987; Duncan, 1990; Duncan & Hasbrook, 1988; Duquin, 1982; Greendorfer, 1990; Kane & Parks, 1992). Essentially this argument is based on the notion that sport represents a potent medium through which biological or physical differences interface with social and cultural interpretations of gender role expectations. For example, Hargreaves (1986) has argued that physical size or muscularity is an essential symbol of male power in Western culture. Because sport is ultimately about physical activity, sport offers an arena for reproducing concrete, everyday examples of male physicality, muscularity and superiority. In lay person's terms, males run faster, jump higher and throw farther than females (Willis, 1982). In short, the physicality of the male body represents power and dominance, whereas the physicality of the female body represents subservience, frailty and weakness (Greendorfer, 1990; Kane & Disch, 1993; Messner, 1988). However, as previously indicated, the reproduction of male superiority in sport is not limited to biology. As Kane and Snyder (1989) summarize from the arguments posited by Clarke and Clarke (1982), Theberge (1985) and Willis (1982), sport provides symbolic and tangible proof that physical superiority of males is equated with social superiority:

> Sport reproduces the ideology of male supremacy because it acts as a constant and glorified reminder that males are biologically, and thus inherently superior to females. Ultimately, this physical, biological, "natural" supremacy of males in sport becomes translated into the "natural" supremacy of males in the larger social order. (p. 77)

Given the argument that definitions of masculinity and femininity are closely bound to the ways in which the human body is perceived and represented (Betterton, 1987; Bryson, 1990; Featherstone, 1983), and that notions of power reside in the human body and in sport, it is not difficult to understand how sexual (physical) difference, gender difference and gender hierarchy are taken to extreme cultural forms in athletics and physical activity (Kane & Disch, 1993; Messner, 1988).

Sport, Gender and Social Change

In light of the previous discussion about the relationships among sport, gender and power it is not surprising that traditional definitions of "female" have been antithetical to traditional definitions of "athlete." Historically, these social definitions and gender role expectations have served to exclude women from sport for generations. However, within the last two decades there have been significant changes regarding women's roles in general and women's involvement in sport in particular. Title IX, which became a watershed in women's sport, was a reflection of this social change.[1] Since the passage of this federal legislation in the early 1970s a number of significant changes have occurred with respect to women's sports. For example, close to 2 million young women participate in interscholastic sports on a nationwide basis compared with 300,000 before the passage of Title IX (Becker, 1988; National Federation of State High School Associations, 1991). Currently, 158,000 women—approximately one third of all intercollegiate athletes—participate in college sports, compared to 31,000 or 15% who participated in college sports in 1971 (National College Athletic Association [NCAA], 1992). In addition, women's intercollegiate sports budgets have increased to over $116 million, compared to $4 million in 1974 (Sullivan, 1985); and at the present time, more than 500 institutions of higher education offer athletic scholarships to women, compared to a mere 60 in 1974 (Nyquist, 1979; Sullivan, 1985).

If one accepts the preceding arguments about sport as an essential institution of male dominance and control, then women's entry into this arena on such a national scale represents, by definition, a fundamental challenge to male power and privilege. Even though those in power may be uncomfortable with this challenge, because of federal legislation (e.g., Title IX) they can no longer exclude or limit women's participation in sport without fearing legal repercussions. However, it is unlikely that the dominant power structure would willingly embrace a social change that may fundamentally alter its base of control. Therefore, a central question to ask is what strategies of resistance can be employed by those in authority to accommodate this social change without fundamentally altering the balance of power.

It has been argued that one central mechanism for accommodating and resisting women's entry into sport has been through the messages socially constructed in the mass media (Clarke & Clarke, 1982; Kane & Disch, 1993; Kane & Parks, 1992; MacNeill, 1988; Messner, 1988). Returning once again to our example of media coverage given to women during the 1988 Olympic Games, Florence Griffith Joyner appeared on the covers of *Sports Illustrated* and *Time*, two nationally prominent magazines. As Duncan (1990) states, "[It was] no coincidence that Joyner's rapier-like intricately painted fingernails [were] often visibly represented in [these] photographs. . . . Griffith Joyner's nails are an external adornment that shouts femininity—and otherness" (p. 28). The important point about this portrayal is to note how accommodation and resistance have occurred simultaneously. Joyner's presence on the covers acknowledges that social change has taken place; yet the specific type of portrayal indicates a resistance to *fundamental* social change because she is primarily linked to her "appropriate" role as female, not athlete. Our point is highlighted in the coverage (or lack thereof) given to another outstanding female Olympian, Jackie Joyner Kersee. Joyner Kersee won gold medals in the heptathlon (all around athlete) in both the 1988 and 1992 Olympics; yet she has never received the type of media exposure that her more stereotypically feminine counterpart has. The comparison between Florence Griffith Joyner and Jackie Joyner Kersee illustrates how the mass media contribute to the maintenance of male dominance in sport.[2]

Perhaps this is why Messner (1988) has argued that the media's construction of female and male athleticism continues to represent major obstacles for any significant challenge to the existing power relationships between women and men in sport. In the remaining sections of this chapter, we will demonstrate how and why Messner has reached this conclusion by briefly outlining the research findings on the amount and type of coverage given to the post-Title IX female athlete.

Amount of Coverage: Underrepresentation and Symbolic Annihilation

One consistent finding well documented in the literature is the quite noticeable underreporting (and thus underrepresentation) of female athletes and their sporting events throughout all mass media (Kane, 1989). This severe underrepresentation often creates the impression that females are nonexistent in the sporting world, a portrayal that is particularly ironic given the significant increases in their active sport participation since Title IX. More important, this lack of coverage can easily result in the "symbolic annihilation" (Gerbner, 1978) of the female athlete. We should not underestimate the significance of this symbolic annihilation. As Tuchman (1978) points out, individuals, and the roles with which they are associated, are incorporated in the media as "symbolic representations of American society" (p. 8), because they reflect dominant American values and norms. In short, the media reflect who and what has value and prestige in this culture. By their symbolic annihilation of the female athlete, the media tell us that sportswomen have little, if any, value in this society, particularly in relationship to male athletes.

Evidence demonstrating the symbolic annihilation of women's sports comes from a variety of research studies that include print as well as broadcast journalism. For example, Boutilier and San-Giovanni (1983) analyzed covers of *Sports Illustrated* published from 1954 to 1978. They found that sportswomen represented less than 5% of all coverage given to athletes during this time period. In addition, several studies have found qualitative and quantitative differences in depictions of females and males in sport. Female athletes tended to be either absent or underrepresented in such magazines as *Runners World, Sport, Sports Illustrated, Tennis* (Bryant, 1980), *Young Athlete* (Rintala & Birrell, 1984) and *Sports Illustrated for Kids* (Duncan

& Sayaovong, 1989). In both print and visual media females were more likely to be depicted in individual rather than team sports (Kane, 1989), and along with significantly less airtime, fewer representations of team or individual "masculine" sports (such as shot putting) are offered photographically or through visual images (Duncan & Hasbrook, 1988; Kane, 1989).

Several of the most recent studies have replicated findings from earlier research. For example, an analysis of feature articles in *Sports Illustrated* between 1954 and 1987 indicated that male athletes (and their athletic accomplishments) received 91% of the total coverage given to athletes during this time period (Lumpkin & Williams, 1991). And, in the most recent studies of television and newspaper sports coverage, Duncan, Messner and Williams (1990, 1991) found no change in the pattern of underreporting and underrepresentation of women's sports. Ninety-two percent of television air time was given to men's sports, compared to only 5% allotted to women, and stories focusing exclusively on men's sports outnumbered exclusive coverage given to women's sports by a ratio of 23 to 1 (Duncan et al., 1990, 1991). In a similar finding, although television sports news did include women's sporting events on a regular basis, rarely was the focus on individual women as athletes. Relative to newspaper coverage, there were 28.8 times as many column inches devoted to men-only sports stories as there were to women-only sports stories (Duncan et al., 1990, 1991).

One study that illustrates the symbolic annihilation of women in sport is Rintala and Birrell's (1984) analysis of *Young Athlete* magazine. Examining the availability of sportswomen as athletic role models for female adolescents, the authors discovered that *Young Athlete* magazine created the impression that the world of sport is dominated by males. For example, less than one third of all photographs that appeared in this magazine between 1975 and 1982 included female athletes. The authors also discovered that the percentage of photographs depicting females decreased even further if the photograph was prominent (e.g., centerfold, cover).

In one of the few studies specifically addressing the absence of sportswomen of color, Lumpkin and Williams (1991) discovered that with respect to feature articles appearing in *Sports Illustrated* between 1954 and 1987, black females received less coverage than black males and white females. In an extraordinary manifestation of symbolic annihilation the authors also found that of the 3,723 articles examined over two decades, black female athletes were featured in only 16 articles.[3]

The overwhelming evidence from this literature clearly indicates that women continue to be severely underrepresented in the highly prestigious world of sport. This underrepresentation by the mass media does more than simply create an impression that women are absent from the sporting arena. Rather, it creates a *false* impression of women's athleticism by denying the reality of the modern female athlete. According to the National Sporting Goods Association (1993), over 7 million women participate in softball; more than 7.5 million women are involved in basketball; another 7.4 million participate in tennis; and 5.6 million participate in golf. Approximately 26 million bicycle, 44.6 million engage in exercise walking and close to 23 million participate in aerobic exercise (National Sporting Goods Association, 1993). We can only speculate as to whose interests are best served by the denial of this social reality.

Type of Coverage: The Female Athlete as Caricaturized Femininity

A second major finding from the literature suggests that even when sportswomen are depicted in the media, they are consistently trivialized and marginalized[4] through the type of coverage they receive. Specific findings from this research literature suggest that visual production techniques, language, terminology and commentary applied to women's sport are selectively imposed by the media to provide a highly stereotypical feminized view—one that tends to sexualize, commodify, trivialize and devalue (through marginalization) women's sporting accomplishments (Duncan & Hasbrook, 1988; Hilliard, 1984; Kane, 1989; Kane & Parks, 1992; Kinkema, 1989; MacNeill, 1988; Rintala & Birrell, 1984). For example, in 1979 *Sports Illustrated* published its Silver Anniversary issue, which was a collection of photographs highlighting significant sporting personalities, moments and events during the first 25 years of the magazine's existence. In an analysis of this coverage Boutilier and SanGiovanni

(1983) reported that approximately 60% of all photographs depicting females portrayed them in passive, nonathletic roles. In contrast, only 44% of the photographs depicting males portrayed them in a similar fashion. In a study that also examined trivialization through feminization, Hilliard (1984) found that media coverage given to professional female tennis players focused on their physical attractiveness rather than on their athletic accomplishments. He further noted that commentary alluding to female athletes' youthful or adolescent status also trivialized their athletic accomplishments by suggesting that "these players should not be taken seriously until they grow up" (p. 253). More significant, Hilliard found that specific references to (their participation as) "a teenage slumber party" and characterizations such as "not one but two Dumpling Queens" or as "all these pixies" (p. 254) had no analogues in commentary or themes that referred to the leading male players. In her discussion of Hilliard's findings, Kane (1989) pointed out an even more distressing pattern of coverage:

> Even when an article did emphasize how successful and talented these women were, another theme emerged: that they were plagued by such character flaws as emotional dependency, anxiety and depression, sexual identity conflicts and role conflicts. The overriding message in these articles was quite clear: female athletes should be recognized and remembered for their stereotypical gender role, not their athletic role. (p. 61)

Unfortunately, the most recent research demonstrates no change in this type of coverage. For example, the Duncan et al. (1990) study found that television treated women differently, both as spectators and as participants. Women spectators were treated as comical targets of newscasters' jokes and/or sexual objects, while at the same time, the technical framing (e.g., production techniques) of women's sporting events trivialized the seriousness of their athletic performance. A comparison of the coverage given to women's and men's basketball illustrates the unevenness in production techniques. Men's basketball contests were framed as dramatic spectacles of historic import, while women's basketball contests were given the feel of neighborhood pickup games.

In summary, the overwhelming theme that emerges from this stereotypical portrayal is that despite the new reality of the post-Title IX female athlete as an active, physical woman, historical stigmas of female athleticism are retained through selective and therefore inaccurate media coverage.

Ambivalence as a Means of Accommodation and Resistance

Ambivalence is the term initially used by Duncan and Hasbrook (1988) to explain how (or the way in which) media portrayals of women athletes contain mixed or contradictory messages. Their findings indicated that verbal and visual depictions of sportswomen often combined positive and flattering portrayals with subtly negative suggestions that trivialized or undermined their sports performance. One example of ambivalence was revealed in the verbal narratives used by television commentators when they were describing female basketball players. These athletes were described as powerful, skillful and courageous, while at the same time they were also characterized as vulnerable, cute, dependent and anxious (e.g., Duncan & Hasbrook, 1988; Kane & Parks, 1992). In a related fashion, ambivalence toward the female athlete was also demonstrated when it became apparent that sportswomen were given coverage not because of their physical ability but because they were glamorous and conveyed sex appeal. For example, during an interview with a female athlete who was competing in the New York City Marathon, the announcer asked the athlete if she thought the television audience expected to see her competing in a bathing suit.

The preceding example involving the marathon runner is an overt and obvious manifestation of ambivalence toward the female athlete. However, as Duncan and Hasbrook (1988) point out, there are more subtle and insidious forms of ambivalence that frequently occur in media portrayals. Consistent with the contradictory messages that result from ambivalent portrayal is what Duncan and Hasbrook (1988) have described as "narrative and visual incongruity." This can occur when the visual portrayal focuses on female performance yet the narrative description accompanying this visual image focuses on male performance. Returning to the New York City Marathon, at one point during the coverage the camera focused on Greta Waitz as she crossed the finish line in victory. At the exact moment that her visual image appeared on the television screen, the verbal narrative, and thus the commentator's attention and emphasis, focused on who had finished third in the men's race. Interestingly, ambivalence in media portrayal was found only in coverage given to female athletes. As Duncan and Hasbrook (1988) noted, "Not once could this narrative/visual incongruity be identified within the coverage of the men's marathon" (p. 16).

According to Duncan and Hasbrook (1988), a consequence of ambivalent media portrayal is that it denies sportswomen the power and prestige that should be their due. Although we do not disagree with this conclusion, we are suggesting that ambivalence serves an equally important function—that of allowing those in power to acknowledge (and therefore to accommodate) the social changes that have taken place within the last two decades while simultaneously offering resistance through the maintenance of the status quo. As was just mentioned, females, not males, are subjected to conflicting and contradictory messages about their physical abilities and accomplishments as serious sportswomen.

Conclusions and Implications

At one point in our history there was serious debate about whether young girls and women should participate in sports. In recent decades, however, so many women have penetrated this once exclusive male preserve, and continue to do so with increasing frequency, that the debate regarding women's participation is no longer relevant. As we have tried to explain throughout this chapter, what is relevant is that strategies employed by those in power have denied women their full potential within the realm of sport. In this sense, as Greendorfer (1990) has noted, the fundamental relationship between women, gender and sport has remained virtually unchanged. The social realities surrounding the post-Title IX female athlete is that the "revolution" in women's athletics represents a continuation of the status quo rather than a true transformation of hegemonic masculinity. The question is why?

It is our contention that increased interest and participation rates represent only superficial social change because deep-seated *ideological* change has not occurred. The mass media have been used as one means of resisting ideological change, as media practices, production, content and messages continue to perpetuate notions of sexual difference, gender difference and gender hierarchy (Greendorfer, 1990). The media have transformed the meanings of women's physicality—women becoming active agents with and of their own bodies, and women using their bodies in skilled, physical activity—to commodification, sexuality and femininity. As such, the dominant belief system of patriarchy has successfully incorporated women's challenge to male superiority by transforming it in a way that it (the challenge) becomes compatible with stereotypical ideological themes related to sportswomen and their bodies. As a consequence, we find the media not only focusing attention on but also dictating and legitimating the ways in which women's physicality will be acknowledged.

The key point is that this acknowledgment will only occur when women's physicality is associated with traditional, stereotypical beliefs regarding the female body and its "proper" use—in graceful and aesthetically pleasing ways (Greendorfer, 1990; MacNeill, 1988). For these reasons, it should not be surprising that women receive greater social acceptance and media coverage when they participate in such "feminine" sports as gymnastics and figure skating (Kane, 1988; Lumpkin & Williams, 1991). This is clearly not the case with women who use their bodies as instruments of physical power or force, characteristics that are required in such "masculine" sports as basketball and rugby.

Admittedly, we have analyzed the media's role in resisting social change in sport with a rather critical eye. We have indicated how the media have consistently and systematically portrayed modern sportswomen with messages and themes that limit their potential in sport. This is not to suggest, however, that the media cannot or should not alter their coverage. Media messages are not immutable or fixed; ideological meanings are subject to challenge and transformation (Greendorfer, 1990). In fact, Betterton (1987) argues that particularly in times of social change, it is erroneous to view stereotypes as rigid, fixed and resistant to change. Clearly, media practices are not neutral. To date, media portrayals of women in sport have reinforced gender stereotypical ideology, and by so doing have set limits to interpretations and meanings of women's engagement in physical activity, as well as limiting how their athleticism is to be demonstrated.

This same media bias systematically obscures and diffuses the intersections between race, class and gender. Although not specifically addressing media coverage, Birrell's (1990) analysis of race, class and gender could easily apply to an analysis of media portrayals when she points out that: (1) constructions of "black athlete" typically equate with "black male athlete," and (2) analyses of class become analyses of race/class where two separate variables are far too often perceived as one and the same.

The media are active agents in the construction of meanings that come to be identified with specific images and themes. By the same token, they also have the ability, power and means to produce counterstereotypical images. We should take seriously the notion that ideological bias, once recognized and acknowledged, is subject to modification. The modern sportswoman is anything but the cardboard, unidimensional individual constructed by the media. She represents a multiplicity of ethnic and racial backgrounds. She is actively participating in a variety of sports in numerous athletic settings. In this sense, sport represents a potential site for empowering and liberating women in much the same way it has enabled minorities to challenge the ideology of subservience attached to them. At the very best, the mass media can play an active role in this ongoing liberation that is empowering countless young girls and women in sport. We challenge the media to reflect the reality of women as athlete and not as caricature.

Notes

1. Title IX, an extension of civil rights legislation, was part of the Education Amendments Act of 1972 that stated: "No person in the United States shall, on the basis of sex, be excluded from participation in, be denied the benefits of, or be subjected to discrimination under any education program or activity receiving federal financial assistance." Interestingly, only 4% of the text of Title IX dealt with athletics; yet the majority of comments and cases have focused on sport.

2. It is not the purpose of this chapter to debate whether this type of portrayal is conscious or nonconscious on the part of the media. We are, however, arguing that regardless of the intentions of the media, the end result is the same —that female athletes are consistently and systematically associated with oppressive and restrictive stereotypes of femininity and sexuality.

3. The symbolic annihilation of female athletes of color also exists in virtually all scientific investigations/analyses of media coverage given to sportswomen. As this chapter demonstrates, a body of knowledge examining female athleticism in general, and how women are constructed by the media in particular, has accumulated over the past decade. Much of this literature is grounded in feminist analysis. Unfortunately, how race, as well as other salient variables, such as social class and sexual orientation, may mediate the sport experience for females has been virtually ignored by social scientists. Media coverage given to the black female athlete is a much needed topic that is addressed in Chapter 3 of this book.

4. Marginalization occurs when individuals or groups occupy less desirable or noncentral roles or positions. Typically such roles or positions are less prestigious and less powerful.

References

Becker, Debbie. (1988, September 16). Courts kick the teeth out of Title IX. *USA Today*, pp. 1C-2C.

Betterton, Rosemary. (Ed.). (1987). *Looking on: Images of femininity in the visual arts and media*. London: Pandora Press.

Birrell, Susan. (1990). Women of color, critical autobiography and sport. In Michael A. Messner & Donald F. Sabo (Eds.), *Sport, men and the gender order* (pp. 185-199). Champaign, IL: Human Kinetics.

Birrell, Susan & Cole, Cheryl L. (1990). Double fault: Renee Richards and the construction and naturalization of difference. *Sociology of Sport Journal, 7*, 1-21.

Boutilier, Mary A. & SanGiovanni, Lucinda. (1983). *The sporting woman*. Champaign, IL: Human Kinetics.

Bryant, James. (1980). A two-year selective investigation of the female athlete in sport as reported in the paper media. *Arena Review, 4*, 32-44.

Bryson, Lois. (1990). Challenge to male hegemony in sport. In Michael A. Messner & Donald F. Sabo (Eds.), *Sport, men and the gender order* (pp. 173-184). Champaign, IL: Human Kinetics.

Clarke, Alan & Clarke, John. (1982). Highlights and action replays ideology, sport, and the media. In Jennifer Hargreaves (Ed.), *Sport, culture and ideology* (pp. 62-87). London: Routledge & Kegan Paul.

Donnelly, Peter. (1987). Sport as a site for "popular" resistance. In Richard Gruneau (Ed.)., *Popular cultures and political practice* (p. 69-81). Toronto: Garamond Press.

Duncan, Margaret Carlisle. (1990). Sports photographs and sexual difference: Images of women and men in the 1984 and 1988 Olympic Games. *Sociology of Sport Journal, 7*, 22-43.

Duncan, Margaret Carlisle & Hasbrook, Cynthia A. (1988). Denial of power in televised women's sports. *Sociology of Sport Journal, 5*, 1-21.

Duncan, Margaret Carlisle, Messner, Michael & Williams, Linda. (1990). *Gender stereo-typing in televised sports*. Los Angeles: Amateur Athletic Foundation of Los Angeles.

Duncan, Margaret Carlisle, Messner, Michael & Williams, Linda. (1991). *Coverage of women's sports in four daily newspapers*. Los Angeles: Amateur Athletic Foundation of Los Angeles.

Duncan, Margaret Carlisle & Sayaovong, Amoun. (1989, November). *Visual images and gender in* Sports Illustrated for Kids. Paper presented at 9th Annual Conference of North American Society for Sociology of Sport, Washington, DC.

Duquin, Mary. (1982). Feminism and patriarchy in physical education. In Aidan O. Dunleavy, Andrew W. Miracle & C. Roger Rees (Eds.), *Studies in the sociology of sport* (pp 167-179). Fort Worth, TX: Texas Christian University Press.

Featherstone, Michael. (1983). The body in consumer culture. *Theory, Culture and Society, 1*(3), 18-33.

Gerbner, George. (1978). The dynamics of cultural resistance. In Gaye Tuchman, Arlene Kaplan Daniels & James Benet (Eds.), *Hearth and home: Images of women in the mass media* (pp. 46-50). New York: Oxford University Press.

Greendorfer, Susan L. (1990, August). *Media reinforcement of stereotypic ideology of women in sport*. Paper presented at the Institute for International Sport Seminar, "The Media and International Sport: Ethical Issues," University of Rhode Island, Kingston, RI.

Hargreaves, Jennifer A. (1986). Where's the virtue? Where's the grace? A discussion of the social production of gender through sport. *Theory, Culture and Society, 3*, 109-121.

Hilliard, Dan C. (1984). Media images of male and female professional athletes: An interpretive analysis of magazine articles. *Sociology of Sport Journal, 1*, 251-262.

Kane, Mary Jo. (1988). Media coverage of the female athlete before, during, and after Title IX: *Sports Illustrated* revisited. *Journal of Sport Management, 2*, 87-99.

Kane, Mary Jo. (1989, March). The post Title IX female athlete in the media: Things are changing but how much? *Journal of Physical Education, Recreation and Dance, 60*,(3), 58-62.

Kane, Mary Jo & Disch, Lisa J. (1993). Sexual violence and the reproduction of male power in the locker room: A critical analysis of the Lisa Olson "incident." *Sociology of Sport Journal, 10*(4), 331-352.

Kane, Mary Jo & Parks, Janet B. (1992). The social construction of gender difference and hierarchy in sport journalism—Few new twists on very old themes. *Women in Sport and Physical Activity Journal, 1*(1), 49-83.

Kane, Mary Jo & Snyder, Eldon E. (1989). Sport typing: The social "containment" of women in sport. *Arena Review, 13*(2), 77-96.

Kinkema, Kathleen M. (1989, November). *Towards a model for studying the mediated sports audience*. Paper presented at the 9th Annual Conference of the North American Society for Sociology of Sport, Washington, DC.

Lumpkin, Angela & Williams, Linda D. (1991). An analysis of *Sports Illustrated* feature articles, 1954-1987. *Sociology of Sport Journal, 8*, 1-15.

MacNeill, Margaret. (1988). Active women, media representations and ideology. In Jean Harvey & Hart Cantelon (Eds.), *Not just a game* (pp. 195-212). Altona, Manitoba: University of Ottawa Press.

Messner, Michael. (1988). Sports and male domination: The female athlete as contested ideological terrain. *Sport Sociology Journal, 5*(3), 197-211.

National College Athletic Association (NCAA). (1992). *Gender Equity Study*. Overland Park, KS: Author.

National Federation of State High School Associations. (1991). *National High School Sport Participation Survey*. Kansas City, MO: Author.

National Sporting Goods Association. (1993). *NSGA Sports participation study: 1988-1992*. Mount Prospect, IL: Author.

Nyquist, Ewald B. (1979). Win, women, and money: Collegiate athletics today and tomorrow. *Educational Record, 60*(4), 374-393.

Rintala, Jan & Birrell, Susan. (1984). Fair treatment for the active female: A content analysis of *Young Athlete* magazine. *Sociology of Sport Journal, 1*, 231-250.

Smith-Rosenberg, Carroll & Rosenberg, Charles. (1987). The female animal: Medical and biological views of women and their role in nineteenth-century America. In J. A. Mangan & Roberta J. Park (Eds.), *From "fair sex" to feminism: Sport and the socialization of women in the industrial and post-industrial eras* (pp. 1-37). London: Frank Cass.

Sports Illustrated. (1989, August 28). New York: Time Inc.

Sullivan, Robert. (1985, March 4). A law that needs more muscle. *Sports Illustrated*, p. 9.

Swift, E. M. (1993, March 22). Teen ice queen. *Sports Illustrated*, pp. 22-23.

Theberge, Nancy. (1985). Toward a feminist alternative to sport as a male preserve. *Quest, 10*, 193-202.

Tuchman, Gaye. (1978). The symbolic annihilation of women by the mass media. In Gaye Tuchman, Arlene Kaplan Daniels & James Benet (Eds.), *Hearth and home: Images of women in the mass media* (pp. 3-38). New York: Oxford University Press.

Vertinsky, Patricia. (1987). Body shapes: The role of the medical establishment in informing female exercise and physical education in nineteenth-century North America. In J. A. Mangan & Roberta J. Park (Eds.), *From "fair sex" to feminism: Sport and the socialization of women in the industrial and post-indus-trial eras* (pp. 256-281). London: Frank Cass.

Willis, Paul. (1982). Women in sport and ideology. In Jennifer Hargreaves (Ed.), *Sport, culture and ideology* (pp. 117-135). London: Routledge & Kegan Paul.

3

Sportswomen in Black and White

Sports History From
an Afro-American Perspective

Linda D. Williams

Prior to the mid-1980s, sport historians focused primarily on the experience of the white male. It has only been within the past 20 years or so that sports historians have expanded their research to include women. However, this work suffers from several shortcomings. First, when sport historians began to examine the legacy of women's athletes, they often did so through the lens of the white male, which produced scholarship that reflected these values and "fit" the experience of sportswomen into existing norms and roles.

Second, historians often began retrieving women's story in sports without concern for context or standpoint. This resulted in a story that consisted largely of upper/middle-class white experiences in sport. Several scholars have pointed out that this experience cannot be extrapolated to other social classes or racial groups (Boutilier & SanGiovanni, 1983; Howell, 1982; Lerner, 1977, 1979; Struna, 1984). Boutilier and SanGiovanni wrote:

AUTHOR'S NOTE: I wish to thank Pamela J. Creedon for her comments and suggestions on this chapter and to express my appreciation to The Ohio State University Women's Studies Program for providing funds for my initial research at the dissertation stage.

> Women who are members of an oppressed racial or ethnic group,
> who are poor, women who are powerless rural women, and older
> women, fat women do not necessarily adhere to or value the dominant
> image of the acceptable woman in our society. (p. 118)

To remind the reader of the need for contextualizing historical knowledge, this chapter uses the terms *Negro*, *black* and *Afro-American* in their appropriate historical contexts.

Third, sport historians have not used social science techniques, which would allow them to interpret and to analyze events within the context of society and to provide a "more comprehensive picture of the meaning of sport" (Adelman, 1983, p. 98). Adelman urged sports historians "to apply quantification techniques to the study of social, religious and ethnic backgrounds of sport participants and owners, club members and officials" (p. 98).

The remainder of this chapter addresses these three concerns, provides a brief overview of women's sport history from an Afro-American perspective and examines the portrayal of black female athletes in the Negro press of the 1920s to the 1940s.

Black Women in Sport History

From its beginnings, sport history patterned itself after "mainstream" history and, thus, developed through similar evolutionary stages of history. Gerda Lerner (1979) classified women's historiography into two levels: compensatory history and contributory history. Historians initially wrote compensatory history in which they identified "notable" women and their achievements. Consequently, these works pertained primarily to the accomplishments of the middle/upper-class female and they were based on white and male standards. Because it does not include working class or ethnic females, compensatory history does not accurately describe nor represent the history of women in society as a whole. Contributory history, the next level, includes women's contributions, and it also describes their status in society.

In a synthesis of women's sports history, Nancy Struna (1984) found that "few women other than educated presumably middle class women are considered, and the potential breadth of what sport was and what it offered and meant at any given point in time is ignored" (p. 128). The literature she studied consisted mainly of descriptive, chronological accounts, for the most part documenting the participation of white, middle/upper-class females such as Gertrude Ederle and Helen Wills in sex-appropriate sports such as swimming and tennis or the participation of sports heroines such as Mildred "Babe" Didrickson. At best, these accounts explored the milieu in which women's involvement in sports took place, but they failed to examine their context and meaning.

In recent years, scholars have given greater attention to the contribution of black women in America (Williams, 1988a). They have suggested that the experience of the black female in American society, and particularly in sports, has differed from that of her white counterparts. Although she has been visible in her own community for decades (Henderson, 1939), the black woman has been essentially invisible in white culture.

There are several explanations for this paradox of visibility. First and foremost, society's standard of femininity, which applied to white, educated, middle-class women and restricted their participation in sports, did not apply to working women, black women or other minority groups. One sociologist contended that black women were not perceived as women, since "a racist culture did not define them as 'real women,' therefore "black women formed the vanguard of those individuals who broke new sports ground for women in general" (Murphy, 1984, p. 199). Hart (1979) also asserted that the black sportswoman had more freedom in sporting activities and received more recognition for her sporting accomplishments than her white counterpart. She contended the black female athlete "can be strong and achieve in sport and still not deny her womanness" (p. 25).

The inattention to and disregard of the black female athlete by white culture has resulted in a distorted picture, which suggests that the black sportswoman's experience in sport paralleled that of her white sisters. This distortion is compounded by the fact that existing literature on the black female in sports is both limited and contradictory. Mostly descriptive, it documents the participation and accomplishments of individual black women, particularly in one sport, track and field. Wilma Rudolph in track and Althea Gibson from tennis are probably the two most eminent black female sport heroines. Sporting activities of black women before Gibson and Rudolph remain obscure.

Excluding autobiographies or biographies, only three books have been written that focus exclusively on the black sportswoman: Sloan-Greene, Oglesby, Alexander and Franke (1981), Bentley (1983) and Davis (1992). Of these, two provide a limited overview of her achievements in the past two decades, and Davis (1992) documents track and field competitors in the Olympic Games through 1988. The first, *Black Women in Sport* (1981), is a collection of monographs that focus on athletes and administrators in the late 1970s and early 1980s. It illustrates the athletic accomplishments of Rudolph and Gibson, as well as those of Anita DeFrantz and Nell Jackson. Contributors examined obstacles that prevented or limited participation by black women in sports. The collection is limited, however, by its lack of historical perspective.

A 23-minute film accompanies the second book, *Going for the Gold: The Story of Black Women in Sports* (1983). This work contains biographical sketches of elite black female athletes in various sports including: Wilma Rudolph, Wyomia Tyus, Jeanette Bolden, Carol Lewis and the Howard sisters in track; Cheryl Miller, Pam and Paula McGee and LaTaunya Pollard in basketball; Leslie Allen and Zina Garrison in tennis; and "lone black stars" in volleyball, gymnastics and equestrianism. Bentley featured national champions, Olympians or potential Olympians, who lived or trained primarily on the West Coast. Several prominent national champions and Olympians, as well as American and world record holders from the Midwest and the East, were omitted.

Also of note is Henderson's seminal work in 1939, the first comprehensive book on Negro athletes, which devoted a single chapter exclusively to women. "Negro Girls in Sport" sketched a brief history of prominent female athletes and teams in the Negro community. It includes mention of the success of the Tuskegee Institute in producing outstanding female athletes in track and field and of the overwhelming success and travels of the *Philadelphia Tribune* Girls, an amateur basketball team, who played by boys' rules. Henderson's book also provided some social context for the participation of blacks in athletics; however, he described the participation of black female athletes in terms of white cultural values (for a full discussion of Henderson and other early historical works on the black sportswoman, see Williams, 1988a).

The Contributions of Black Women to America, edited by Marianna W. Davis (1981), also contained a history of black sportswomen. She identified multiple roles and contributions of the black female in society and her achievements in sports. Her edited volume examined five different areas: an overview of the sports scene, tennis, track, team sports and individual sports.[1]

In recent years, sport historians have begun to examine women outside of the mainstream. Emery and Toohey-Costa (1988) found "the roles of Mexican, black and native American women differed, noticeably from their white counterpart, yet a common theme of stubborn persistence by which barriers of all kinds were thrown back can be identified in all of their personal histories" (p. 41).

A three-volume history titled *A Hard Road to Glory* written by an Afro-American traced the development of African-American athletes from the 17th century through the 1980s (Ashe, 1988a, 1988b, 1988c). Similar to other books written on black athletes, "blacks are men." Information on early black sportswomen was scanty and derived from Henderson's work and Thaxton's (1970) dissertation. Unlike Henderson, Ashe minimized the participation of black women in sports alleging that "most black women spent very little time engaged in competitive organized sport" (1988b, p. 75). He attributed black women's low participation in sports to work outside of their own homes and to the lack of leisure time and reported that less than 5% of black college women participated heavily in athletics. Although these numbers may be representative of black women in the South, the North, which had an industrial economy, offered more employment and recreational opportunities for blacks and women (Chicago Commission on Race Relations, 1968; Drake & Cayton, 1945).[2] In contrast to the picture painted by early sports history scholarship, "the black sportswoman's experience in many respects resembled that of the males in the black community. Excluded from competition with whites, she participated in leagues for blacks (Foreman, 1975; Lumpkin, 1982).[3] Some black female basketball teams played by "men's" rules, and there was a more favorable climate for competitive sport among women in the black community (Williams, 1988a). Moreover, as this chapter will show, the Negro press was supportive of the achievements of black sportswomen.

Race in the Sport Media

Coverage of the black athlete by the U.S. press has long been problematic. Initially, the problem was a total exclusion of sports news about black athletes and teams in the mainstream, white press. Occasional news coverage prior to 1960 featured the black male "superstar," who successfully overwhelmed his competition as the "only" one, who participated in a traditionally white institution or team or who represented his country at the Olympics or in boxing. For example, only 6% of *Sports Illustrated*'s 96 male athlete covers from 1954 to 1959 featured a black athlete.[4]

The appearance of black athletes on the cover of *SI* after the 1960s revealed an increase in coverage, which was aided by the continued success of black Olympic boxers and achievements of black athletes in professional basketball. The recruitment of black athletes by professional teams and colleges, which were previously all-white, also occasioned a surge in the coverage of Afro-Americans (Williams & Lumpkin, 1990). The presence of black athletes on *SI* covers largely coincided with a period that focused on racial injustices. In fact, the first of a five-part *SI* series by Jack Olsen (1968) titled "The Black Athlete—The Shameful Story" was featured on the cover. It investigated "the roots and validity of the black athlete's unrest" (Olsen, p. 12).

However, the increase in coverage was not without problems. The concern over a lack of coverage soon shifted to a concern with biased coverage. For example, a comparison of press coverage of football and basketball at the University of Maryland, a predominantly white institution, and Howard University, a historically black institution, found that Maryland received greater coverage and better placement of stories than Howard (Braddock, 1978). More important, black athletes at the University of Maryland received more than twice the amount of unfavorable coverage when compared to their white teammates.

Gender and Race in the Sport Media

In the white press, the female is often portrayed as an extension of her spouse or as a sex symbol. Stories usually emphasize her social and physical attributes from a male perspective. The initial publicity given to women by newspapers was primarily limited to the "society pages." Although women have gained acceptance in other sections of the newspaper over the years, the sports page has been slow to acknowledge women's participation in sport or to accept women as sportswriters (Bryant, 1980; Miller, 1975).

As Mary Jo Kane and Susan Greendorfer point out in Chapter 2, when women have been included, the length and the frequency of the articles and/or photographs have been minimal. In an analysis of photographs printed throughout daily newspapers, for example, Susan Miller (1975) found that only 5%-6% of the photographs of women ran in the sports section, whereas almost three fourths of all the photographs of men appeared in this section. Other studies show that stories generally focus on gender roles rather than the athletic event or the participant's performance, and photographs often contain sexist symbolism (Bryant, 1980; Miller, 1975).

Designers tell us that no feature is so important to a magazine as its cover (Nelson, 1978). Magazine editors realize that the editorial decision of what to put on the magazine's cover will create "the all-important first-impression" (Click & Baird, 1983, p. 204). Johnson and Christ (1988) suggest that as historical benchmarks magazine covers show relationships of cultural power and influence. For magazines such as *SI*, which depend heavily on over-the-counter sales, the cover is a very important selling tool. It allows the magazine to catch the potential reader's attention by featuring recognizable individuals and sports.

Williams and Lumpkin (1990) studied the presence or absence of women and blacks on the cover of *SI* from 1954 to 1989.[5] Sportswomen appeared on about 6% (114) of the 1,835 *SI* covers examined. The black sportswoman appeared on only five of the 114 covers during the 35 years studied. In 1957, Althea Gibson was the first black woman on the cover. A span of three decades marked the gap between Gibson and the appearance of the second black female, Jackie Joyner-Kersee, in 1987. Further, of the five *SI* covers featuring black female athletes, four appeared between 1987 and 1989. These photographs highlighted Joyner-Kersee's world record in the heptathlon, Florence Griffith-Joyner's world records at the Olympic Trials and their success in the 1988 Olympics.

Aside from covers, several scholars have examined the treatment of gender and race in content of stories in the sports media. Condor and Anderson (1984) reported that *SI* published more and longer feature articles on white athletes than on black athletes; they also concluded that "the stereotypes of black athletes seem to be upheld over the 21-year time period" (p. 40). Lumpkin and Williams (1991), who conducted the only thorough examination of feature articles by race and gender in every issue of *SI* from 1954 through 1987, reaffirmed that sport in *SI* is primarily a white and male domain. Less than 10% (320) of the 3,273 feature articles examined reported on sportswomen. Blacks were mentioned in less than 25% of these articles.

Although the elite black male athlete receives a significant amount of coverage today in the white, mainstream press, concerns remain regarding negative images, stereotyping and the dearth of coverage of the black female sportswoman. Gerda Lerner (1979) describes the absence of media coverage as "built-in distortion":

> How we see and interpret what we know about women has been shaped for us through a value system defined by men. (p. 160)

For the black sportswoman, the built-in distortion flows from the fact that our understanding of attitudes toward women of color in sports has emerged largely from the examination of the national press. Very few scholars have examined how constituent subgroups in society, such as the Afro-American community, have perceived the participation of women in sports.[6] The remainder of this chapter attempts to provide some of that perspective.

The Negro Press

According to Myrdal (1972), the development of the Negro Press closely paralleled two interrelated trends: the increasing protest against racial discrimination and the growing number of educated Negroes in society. The Negro Press shaped and influenced opinions of blacks and actions of the black leadership. The first Negro newspaper, *Freedom's Journal*, was started by John B. Russwurm and Samuel E. Cornish in 1827. Henry L. Suggs (1983) asserted that the primary objective of *Freedom's Journal* "is still symbolic of the press: 'We wish to plead our case. Too long others have spoken for us' " (p. 3). As Henderson's (1939) work suggested, the black sportswoman has been visible for many years in the black community and in its press. In fact, her athletic endeavors were well covered in the Negro Press, which has been an important institution in black American culture since the early 1800s.

The Negro Press evolved because the white, mainstream press did not, or could not, fulfill the needs of blacks. When the national press contained stories about blacks, these accounts depicted blacks in crimes of violence, especially against whites. The white, mainstream press neglected to publicize news on black achievements and accomplishments. As Americans, Negroes yearned to have their successes and triumphs published. Frederick Detweiler (1968) wrote that throughout the Negro Press

> flows an undercurrent of feeling that race considers itself a part of America and yet has no voice in the American newspaper. Members of this group want to learn about each other, they want the stories of their success, conflicts, and issues told, and they want to express themselves in public. (p. 79)

Research has shown that the mainstream, white press plays a major role in establishing and perpetuating stereotypes (e.g., Edwards, 1973; Tuchman, Daniels & Benet, 1978; Wiggins, 1983a, 1983b). Although the white press printed news stories reinforcing negative stereotypes and attitudes about Negroes in a segregated and racist society, the Negro Press sought to eliminate racial discrimination and inequality in America. The advocacy role played by the Negro

Press created many myths and stereotypes about Negro publications. Generally, whites perceived the coverage as limited to blacks, as anti-American and as read only by blacks. Instead, the Negro Press covered the same issues and events as the white press but from a black perspective. Within the pages of the Negro press, racism and discrimination served as rallying points to unify blacks—males and females.

Sportswomen in the Negro Press

The black community provided a favorable environment for sportswomen, and the Negro Press supported and published their achievements and accomplishments as athletes on its sport pages (Williams, 1988a). My in-depth study of the coverage of sportswomen in two Negro newspapers, the *Pittsburgh Courier* and the *Chicago Defender*, illustrates the support within the black community for sportswomen. The study is important because it uses a source other than that of the white, mainstream press to study women in sports. Second, it uses both quantitative and qualitative methods to analyze the content of articles in order to identify bias for or against women. Finally, it is comprehensive and examines every issue of the national edition of each paper. For the *Courier*, this represents a 25-year span from 1924 to 1948. For the *Defender*, the study covers 17 years from 1932 through 1948.

Although the time frame examined in the Chicago paper represented eight fewer years, its coverage of sportswomen exceeded the number of sports stories found in the *Courier* by more than 300. The *Defender*'s coverage of women's sports never equaled that given to men, yet 70% of the 884 papers studied contained news about sportswomen (see Figure 3.1). Further, more than one-half of the issues without news of women's sports occurred between October through December, which may be due to the absence of women's sporting activities in the fall as well as to the increasing popularity of football. In contrast, the *Courier*'s coverage of women's sports between 1932 and 1948 totaled 771 stories, not even half the number of stories (1,741) published in the *Defender* from 1932 to 1948. The number of issues without news of sportswomen in the *Courier* constituted more than one-half of the issues published.

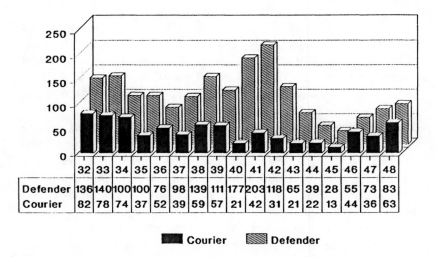

	32	33	34	35	36	37	38	39	40	41	42	43	44	45	46	47	48
Defender	136	140	100	100	76	98	139	111	177	203	118	65	39	28	55	73	83
Courier	82	78	74	37	52	39	59	57	21	42	31	21	22	13	44	36	63

■ Courier ▨ Defender

Figure 3.1. Coverage of Women's Sports by Year for *Courier* and *Defender*

NOTE: This figure shows the actual number of stories about women's sports run in the *Chicago Defender* and the *Pittsburgh Courier* from 1932 to 1948. The number of stories peaked in 1941 at 203 for the *Defender* and then tapered off rather dramatically. The number of stories in the *Courier* was highest in the 1930s but increased again in the late 1940s.

In the *Defender*, the content of stories about sportswomen was similar to coverage given to men. Nearly 85% of the news about female athletes appeared on the first or second page of the sport section. Photographs constituted 23% of these 1,741 accounts. Occasionally, a column designated specifically for Women's Athletics or Women's Sports was run. Most of the stories with bylines were written by men, although several women wrote sports articles for the paper or had their own columns. One columnist, Zelda Hines, who was identified as the women's bowling editor, routinely covered both men's and women's bowling results (Williams, 1988a, 1988b).

Some women occasionally wrote stories about other male sporting events such as boxing, horse racing and football. Often these reports emphasized the social aspects of the event rather than the contest. For example, Nettie George Speedy's narrative of the 1924 Carpenter-Gibson fight for the *Courier* identified notable people and celebrities in attendance (Williams, 1989c). Stories about horse racing often contained a "who's-who" list of those in attendance.

Coverage of women's sports in the *Defender* peaked in 1941, a non-Olympic year. Three of the six years with the greatest number of stories about female athletes occurred after the 1936 Olympic Games and prior to World War II. Overall, women's basketball, tennis and track were the most heavily covered sports, accounting for slightly less than two-thirds of the stories in the *Defender*. These three sports also comprised almost three-fourths of the *Courier*'s coverage between 1932 and 1948 (see Figure 3.2). Although basketball received the greatest number of stories, the location of tennis articles on page 1 or above the fold of the newspaper and the identification of the writer indicated that women's tennis was perceived to have greater prestige than basketball or track and field by the sport editors at both the Chicago and Pittsburgh papers.

Many of the Chicago paper's stories featured local female athletes in golf, badminton, bowling, softball and other recreational sports. Track and field, which was third on the list of sports covered, received its greatest coverage during the periods surrounding the Olympics. Occasionally, sports coverage of golf, bowling, basketball and tennis exceeded that of track, traditionally perceived as the most prevalent sport among black sportswomen. The *Defender* clearly provided its readers with news about a wide range of women's sporting activities. Four sports (golf, tennis, bowling and track) accounted for 19 of the 23 items on the front page (Williams, 1988a).

In both papers, the greatest number of track articles and photographs appeared in 1948, when nine Negro women made the United States Olympic Track Team. It is important to remember that track provided a unique opportunity for black athletes, especially females, since this sport did not openly ban competition against whites. In 1932, Tydie Pickett and Louise Stokes became the first black women to earn berths on the U.S. Olympic Team; they repeated as Olympians in 1936.[7]

The coverage of the black female athlete in the *Chicago Defender* and the *Pittsburgh Courier* reveals a far more active sporting culture for women in competitive sport in the black community than for the white female athlete in the white community during the 1920s, 1930s and 1940s. These accounts also demonstrate that black women engaged in many of the same sporting activities that white women did, including the "country club" sports such as tennis and golf.

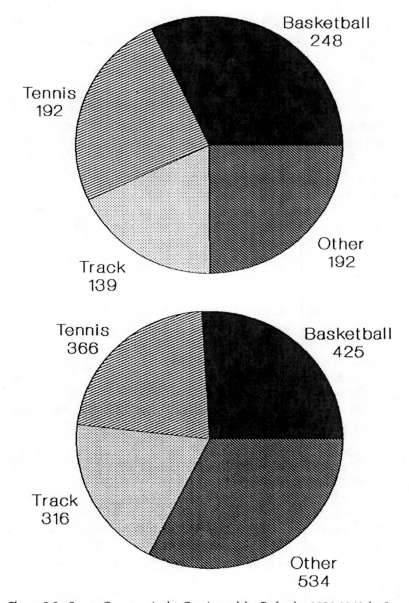

Figure 3.2. Sports Coverage in the *Courier* and the *Defender,* 1932-1948, by Sport

NOTE: A comparison of women's sports that received coverage by the two papers shows that basketball topped the list with tennis coming in second and track third for both papers.

Tennis was an extremely popular sport, as the number of events sponsored at the local, regional, state and national levels attest. The National Tennis Association Championship, for example, was the "social and athletic event" for Negroes (Francis, 1928).

Black women also competed for a national crown in golf. Female golfers from Chicago, Washington, DC and Indianapolis emerged as pioneers and leaders in the sport (Williams, 1989a, 1991b). Women from Chicago and Indianapolis participated in the United Golf Association (UGA) First Women's Championship.[8] By 1937, at least two all-black women's golf clubs existed in the United States (Williams, 1989a).[9] In addition to being athletes, some women held leadership and administrative positions as coaches, owners and trainers in sports.

Negro newspapers also sponsored leagues or teams in basketball, softball and bowling. As early as 1925, the *Pittsburgh Courier* announced that it would sponsor a girls' league "urged by lovers of the sport in an amateur way, with the hope of really bringing the game home to the girls and young women in a sense to emphasize its worth" ("Girls' Floor," 1925, p. 13). The *Defender* also sponsored a girls' basketball team out of New York City, known as Bessye Bearden's *Defender* Cracker-Jackers.

The famed *Philadelphia Tribune* Girls, which represented the Negro paper of the same name, were the best Negro women's five. Formed in 1931, these women dominated the sport between the 1930s and early 1940s prior to the death of their promoter, Otto Briggs, in 1943. Hailed as the Negro World Champions, the *Tribune* Girls captured "eleven-straight national championships" (Saunders, 1943, p. 16). These women played under boys' rules and competed against other Negro amateur teams and some white female teams, including the Lampeters of New York. Ora Washington, a distinguished tennis star and champion, served as the captain of the team.

The Chicago paper also started an annual playground softball championship in 1932 ("Chicago Defender's," 1932). In 1947, the *Defender* initiated the first bowling championship exclusively for women ("Defender's National," 1947). A promotional story for the *Defender*'s 2nd Annual Women's Diamond Sweepstake revealed Daisy Glenn, who captured a first place trophy, a diamond and $100 in cash for her victory in 1947 ("2nd Defender," 1948, p. 11).

In further research, I have found that women were among the top vote-getters in a 1943 *Courier* newspaper survey to determine "The Greatest Colored Athlete" in history (Williams, 1989b) and in an amateur sports contest conducted by the *Defender* (Williams, 1991a).[10] Tennis players received the greatest number of votes for women in both polls.[11]

The Chicago paper's poll in 1927 to identify the city's outstanding amateur athlete illustrated the popularity and acceptance of sportswomen within the city and in the black community. Readers had to clip a ballot located in the sport pages and submit it to the newspaper. The athlete named was awarded 10 points for each coupon submitted. At one moment when the points for the women were exceeding those for the men, one reporter wrote: "The women athletes seem to be more popular than the male folks, or else they have more friends" ("Mrs. Seames," 1927, p. 4). Although male sports fans responded to his cry by sending in votes for male athletes, women still captured the top four spots in the amateur athlete contest.[12]

These two polls conducted by the Negro Press illuminate an aspect of women's sport history that has received little attention. First, sports experts and readers in the Negro community acknowledged and recognized women's participation in sports. These acknowledgments also demonstrate that attempts to identify the greatest athlete or the best amateur athlete obscure the participation of other women athletes and sporting opportunities available to women. As Lerner (1979) noted, the "measure of men" is the standard for the evaluation of women. Therefore, women who regularly participated in an activity and who failed to obtain celebrity status or to capture numerous titles are eliminated instantly. Regional differences, the popularity of a sport and other factors also influenced the nomination and selection of these top vote-getters.

Another factor that deserves further study is the selection of a relatively unknown amateur athlete (Mrs. C. O. Seames) in the *Defender* contest over other nationally prominent black female athletes of the time. It suggests that some factor other than athleticism or participation in the community played a key role in the process. According to Rhodes (1989), "discussions of gender, race, and class rooted in critical theory have sought a framework for discussing women of color. . . . But little original research has been published to put this developing analysis into practice" (p. 113), especially for Afro-American sportswomen. Therefore, it is essential that black newspapers, diaries, oral histories and other primary sources be used to document and to uncover the complexities of the participation of Afro-American women in sports.

When sport historians reconstruct the history of black women athletes, it is important that they put them in context, as I have attempted to do in my studies, and avoid homogenizing their experiences into those of "victims" of a male-dominated arena or of racism. Frequently, feminism has been perceived "as a threat to the stability of the Black community, and black women were and still are often faced with demands from white feminists and Black men to choose which form of oppression is most important" (Rhodes, 1989, p. 114). Neither the black male nor the black female could have survived in America without the support of each other.

Further, the data collected from these two Negro newspapers indicate that other patterns exist across cities, sporting events and time. These patterns influenced the participation and acceptance of black female athletes differently than those that presumably affected the white female athlete. Racial analyses focusing on power and class prior to integration are somewhat meaningless, since racism and discrimination served to unite blacks. Sport historians need to identify the actual activities and experiences of black female athletes in their contemporary contexts without imposing modern-day theories on the past.

Although prohibitions against interracial competition hindered the visibility of the black female athlete in the white community, it is clear from this analysis that it did not hinder her participation in sport in the black community. On occasion, black females competed with or against whites in recreational activities such as basketball or at interracial high schools or colleges in the North.

The comparison of these two papers confirmed the existence of many of the problems associated with the "built-in distortion" in history as described by Lerner (1979). Similarities and differences between the papers illustrate that factors other than sexism and racism also influenced sports coverage. These include factors such as the geographical location, the time frame and the editor's or publisher's news judgment.

The issue now for sport historians and sportswriters is to be vigilant for cultural differences when interpreting the meaning of events and activities in the lives of female athletes. As chapters throughout this book explain, because the institution of sport not only supports white male dominance over women but reinforces an "intermale dominance hierarchy" (Nelson, 1991), the survival strategies and forms of resistance used by women and people of color are often trivialized or ignored when interpreted from a white male context. A concerted effort to expand historical and critical autobiographical studies of the sporting activities of female athletes of color could go a long way toward developing new interpretations of what it means—and has meant—to be an athlete and female in American culture.

Notes

1. Unfortunately, with the exception of time lines for each sport, Davis's study produced little new information. Slightly more than 47% (72 of 153) of the citations found in Davis's work are to four earlier sources, including Henderson. In essence, Davis simply aggregated these earlier works and continued to apply the white middle-class standard of femininity to the black female athlete.

2. See Chapter 5 in Chicago Commission on Race Relations (1968) for more information about interaction with whites at schools and in recreation in Chicago. In addition, also see Bart Landry's work (1987) for a discussion on class in black America. Although most Southern cities failed to provide social institutions for Negroes outside of the church—such as YMCA, public playground, welfare organizations, public library, gymnasium, orderly dance halls, public parks or theaters—Negroes in the North had "other places than the church for their leisure time" (Chicago Commission on Race Relations, 1968, p. 143). In Chicago, for example, the Wabash Avenue YMCA, the Southside Community Service, the Wendell Phillips Settlement, the Butler Community Center and the Woodlawn Community Association provided community activities and recreation for Negro boys and girls. Two organizations, the Phyllis Wheatley Home and the Indiana Avenue YWCA targeted women and girls, specifically. Similar community organizations in other northern cities provided recreational opportunities and activities for women and girls (Williams, 1991a).

3. According to Angela Lumpkin (1982), both blacks and women encountered similarities in their quest for athletic acceptance and equality. In response to both written and societal restrictions, these minority groups formed their own leagues for participation. A time line prepared by Williams (1988a) identified several sports including tennis, golf, track and basketball.

4. The study focused on gender and race of American athletes depicted on *SI*'s cover from 1954 to 1989. Covers containing one or more athletes of the same race and gender in 10 selected sports were analyzed for the time period. Photographs of whites with blacks or with members of other ethnic groups were excluded, as were those featuring both males and females. The sports analyzed were: baseball, basketball, boxing, football, golf, gymnastics, ice skating, swimming, tennis and track.

5. Preliminary results of the study from 1954 to 1987 were presented at the National American Society for Sport History Conference in Clemson, South Carolina. Data for 1954 to 1989 are part of an unpublished paper (Williams & Lumpkin, 1989).

6. Recent works that feature oral history and other primary sources to document Afro-American women in America have included some information about women in sport and recreation (see, e.g., Hill, 1991; Jones, 1990). Presentations at the 1993 National Convention of the American Alliance for Health, Physical Education, Recreation and Dance revealed that more sports historians are using ethnic newspapers (Emery, 1993) and oral histories (Costa, 1993) to study women outside of the mainstream.

7. National recognition of the success of black women in track actually began in 1936 when Tuskegee Institute finished second during their first competition at the National Amateur Athletic Union Track and Field Championships. When the Tuskegee women's team returned a year later to win the title, it marked the first time in American history that any black team—male or female—had won a national championship. For an overview of black Olympic sportswomen in track and field, see Davis (1992).

8. Marie Thompson, a Chicago golfer, edged Lucy Williams of Indianapolis to capture the first title. However, Mrs. Williams won the women's title in 1932, 1936 and 1937 and was runner-up during four of the five years in which she failed to win the title, between 1931 and 1937. Incidentally, her teammate, Mrs. Ella Able of Indianapolis, won the title in 1934 and 1935.

9. The Chicago Women's Golf Club was established almost six months after the formation of the Wake Robin Golf Club in Washington, DC. In 1940, the Chicago Women's Golf Club became the first women's club to host United Golf Association's National Championships. Incidentally, two separate national golf championships for Negroes were held in Chicago at the Palos Hill within one week of each other in 1941 (Williams, 1987). The National Amateur Golf Association sponsored a championship solely for amateurs.

10. Ora Washington, an outstanding tennis and basketball athlete, received 65 points in the *Courier*'s poll, which gave her fifth-place honors among the top 11 athletes named. Washington won eight of 10 National American Tennis Association ladies' singles' titles between 1929 and 1937. She also captured numerous doubles' titles. Unlike Althea Gibson or Jackie Robinson who broke the color line in baseball, Washington did not have her "moment in time." Althea Gibson had Alice Marble (a white woman), who advocated that the tennis championship should be decided on the playing field with the best athletes. The top white American tennis player refused to play Washington even in exhibition games (Williams, 1991c; 1992). By the mid-1940s, both "Alice Marble and Mary Hardwicke, two of the world's foremost women players" were scheduled in exhibition games at the ATA nationals ("150 Clubs," 1944, p. 12). Hardwicke of Britain and her spouse Charles Hare also played several interracial exhibition matches at the national in 1946 ("Lula Ballard," 1946).

11. The fact that black female athletes in tennis were the top vote-getters as opposed to members of the Tuskegee Institute Women's Track Team, which had won

the National Amateur Athletic Union title in interracial competition from 1937 through 1941, is an interesting finding. The reason may be linked to the abundance of outstanding male track stars. Other scholars may argue that the presence of a "country-club" sport supports division based on social class or "appropriate" sports for women. Nevertheless, the black tennis community worked, collectively, to develop and to produce a tennis champion to "break the color line." Althea Gibson's success represents only one of the many athletes, male and female, supported and trained by these black leaders.

12. The top vote-getters and their sports were: first, Irma Mohr, basketball, tennis and golf; second, Mrs. C. O. Seames, tennis; third, Corrine Robinson, track; and fourth, Virginia Willis, basketball. Hansel Jones, a high school athlete, finished fifth.

References

Adelman, Melvin L. (1983). Academicians and American athletics: A decade of progress. *Journal of Sport History, 10*, 80-136.

Ashe, Arthur, Jr. (1988a). *A history of the African-American athlete, 1916-1918* (vol. 1 of 3). New York: Warner Books.

Ashe, Arthur, Jr. (1988b). *A history of the African-American athlete, 1919-1945* (vol. 2 of 3). New York: Warner Books.

Ashe, Arthur, Jr. (1988c). *A history of the African-American athlete, since 1946* (vol. 3 of 3). New York: Warner Books.

Bentley, Kenneth. (1983). *Going for the gold . . . The story of black women in sports.* Los Angeles: Carnation Company.

Boutilier, Mary A. & Lucinda SanGiovanni. (1983). *The sporting woman.* Champaign, IL: Human Kinetics.

Braddock, II, Jomills H. (1978). The sport pages: In black and white. *Arena Review, 2*, 17-25.

Bryant, James. (1980). A two-year selective investigation of the female in sports as reported in the paper media. *Arena Review, 4*, 32-44.

Chicago Commission on Race Relations. (1968). *The Negro in Chicago: A study of race relations and a race riot.* Chicago: University of Chicago Press.

Chicago Defender's softball meet starts Sept. 5. (1932, September 3). *Chicago Defender* (National Ed.), p. 8.

Click, J. W., & Baird, Russell N. (1983). *Magazine editing and production.* Dubuque, IA: William C. Brown.

Condor, Robert & Anderson, Dean F. (1984). Longitudinal analysis of coverage accorded black and white athletes in feature articles of *Sports Illustrated* (1960-1980). *Journal of Sport Behavior, 7* (1), 39-43.

Costa, Margaret. (1993, March). *Nisei sports participation in southern California in the early decades of the 20th century.* Paper presented at the meeting of the American Alliance for Health, Physical Education, Recreation and Dance National Convention, Washington, DC.

Davis, Marianna W. (Ed.). (1981). *The contributions of black women to America* (vol. 1). Columbia, SC: Kenday Press.

Davis, Michael D. (1992). Black American women in Olympic track and field: A complete illustrated reference. Jefferson, NC: McFarland.

Defender's national women's diamond sweepstakes. (1947, April 12). *Chicago Defender* (National Ed.), p. 21.

Detweiler, Frederick. (1968). *The Negro press in the U.S.* College Park, MD: McGrath Publishing.

Drake, St. Clair & Cayton, Horace. (1945). *Black metropolis: A study of Negro life in a northern city.* New York: Harcourt, Brace and Company.

Edwards, Harry. (1973). *Sociology of sport.* Homewood, IL: Dorsey Press.

Emery, Lynne. (1993, March). *Ethnic women in sports in southern California, 1920-1950.* Paper presented at the meeting of the American Alliance for Health, Physical Education, Recreation and Dance National Convention, Washington, DC.

Emery, Lynne & Toohey-Costa, D. Margaret. (1988, May 20-23). The western sporting woman: An overview. [Abstract] *Proceedings of 16th NASSH (North American Society for Sport History) Conference*, Tempe, AZ, pp. 41-42.

Foreman, Thomas E. (1975/1957). *Discrimination against the Negro in American athletics.* San Francisco: R and E Research Associates.

Francis, Arthur. (1928, August 15). On the courts. *New York Amsterdam News*, p. 10.

Girls' floor league to be organized. (1925, September 19). *Pittsburgh Courier* (National Ed.), p. 13.

Hart, M. Marie. (1979). On being female in sport. In Stephanie Twin (Ed.), *Out of the bleachers: Writings on women and sports* (pp. 24-35). Old Westbury, NY: Feminist Press.

Henderson, Edwin B. (1939). *The Negro in sports.* Washington, DC: Associated Publishers.

Hill, Ruth E. (Ed.). (1991). *The guide to the transcripts of the black women oral history project* (vol. 1). Westport, CT: Meckler.

Howell, Reet. (Ed). (1982). *Her story in sports: A historical anthology of women in sport.* Old Westbury, NY: Leisure Press.

Johnson, Sammye & Christ, William. (1988). Women through Time: Who gets covered? *Journalism Quarterly*, 65(4), pp. 889-897.

Jones, Adrienne L. (1990). *Jane Edna Hunter: A case study of black leadership.* Brooklyn, NY: Carlson.

Landry, Bart. (1987). *The new black middle class.* Berkeley, CA: University of California Press.

Lerner, Gerda. (1977). *The female experience: An American documentary.* Indianapolis, IA: Bobbs-Merrill.

Lerner, Gerda. (1979). *The majority finds its past: Placing women in history.* New York: Oxford University Press.

Lula Ballard, McDaniel defeat English couple. (1946, August 31). *Pittsburgh Courier* (National Ed.), p. 17.

Lumpkin, Angela. (1982). Blacks and females striving for athletic acceptance. *The North Carolina Journal*, 28, 30-38.

Lumpkin, Angela & Williams, Linda D. (1991). An analysis of *Sports Illustrated* feature articles, 1954-1987. *Sociology of Sport Journal*, 8(1), 16-32.

Miller, Susan H. (1975). The content of news photos: Women's and men's roles. *Journalism Quarterly*, 52, 70-75.

Mrs. Seames still leads in contest; Others made gains. (1927, June 18). *Chicago Defender* (City Ed.), p. 11.

Murphy, Patricia J. (1984). Sport and gender. In Leonard, Wilbert M. (1984). *A sociological perspective of sport* (2nd ed., pp. 187-210). Minneapolis, MN: Burgess.

Myrdal, Gunnar. (1972). *An American dilemma: The Negro problem and modern democracy* (vol II, rev. ed.). New York: Pantheon.

Nelson, Mariah Burton. (1991). The rules of the game. *Women's Review of Books, 8*(4), p. 17.

Nelson, Roy Paul (1978). *Publication design* (2nd ed.). Dubuque, IA: William C. Brown.

Olsen, Jack. (1968, July 1). The black athlete: The shameful story. *Sports Illustrated*, pp. 12-27.

150 clubs invited to national net tourney. (1944, August 5). *Pittsburgh Courier* (National Ed.), p. 12.

Rhodes, Jane. (1989). Strategies on studying women of color in mass communication: Overview and theoretical framework. In Pamela J. Creedon (Ed.), *Women in mass communication: Challenging gender values* (pp. 112-116). Newbury Park, CA: Sage.

Saunders, Jack. (1943, November 6). Otto Briggs, diamond great, dies in Philadelphia. *Pittsburgh Courier* (National Ed.), p. 16.

2nd *Defender* diamond bowling sweepstake March 13 and March 14. (1948, February 14). *Chicago Defender* (National Ed.), p. 11.

Sloan-Green, Tina, Oglesby, Carole, Alexander, Alpha & Franke, Nikki. (1981). *Black women in sport*. Reston, VA: American Alliance for Health, Physical Education, Recreation and Dance.

Struna, Nancy L. (1984). Beyond mapping experience: The need for understanding in the history of American sporting women. *Journal of Sport History, 11*, 120-133.

Suggs, Henry L. (1983). *The black press in the South*. Westport, CT: Greenwood Press.

Thaxton, Nolan A. (1970). *A documentary analysis of competitive track and field for women at Tuskegee Institute and Tennessee State University*. Unpublished doctoral dissertation, Springfield College, Springfield, MA.

Tuchman, Gaye, Daniels, Arlene Kaplan & Benet, James (Eds). (1978). *Hearth and home: Images of women in the mass media*. New York: Oxford University Press.

Wiggins, David K. (1983a). The 1936 Olympic Games in Berlin: The response of America's black press. *Research Quarterly for Exercise and Sport, 54*, 278-292.

Wiggins, David K. (1983b). Wendell Smith, the *Pittsburgh Courier-Journal* and the campaign to include blacks in organized baseball, 1933-1945. *Journal of Sport History, 10*, 5-29.

Williams, Linda D. (1987, May). *The coverage of women in sports in the Negro press: The* Pittsburgh Courier, *1924-1948 and the* Chicago Defender, *1937-1941*. Paper presented at North American Society for Sport History Conference, Columbus, OH.

Williams, Linda D. (1988a). *An analysis of American sportswomen in two Negro newspapers: The* Pittsburgh Courier, *1924-1948 and the* Chicago Defender, *1932-1948*. Eugene, OR: Microforms Publications, College of Human Development and Performance, University of Oregon.

Williams, Linda D. (1988b, March). *An analysis of American sportswomen in the* Chicago Defender, *1932-1948*. Paper presented at the meeting of the Southern District, Alliance of Health, Physical Education, Recreation and Dance Conference, Little Rock, AK.

Williams, Linda D. (1989a, March). *Striving for par: Wake Robin golf club and black women in golf*. Paper presented at North American Society for the Sociology of Sport, Washington, DC.

Williams, Linda D. (1989b, April). *Bridging the gap: The Negro press and the invisible athlete, female and black*. Paper presented at Women's Studies Colloquium, Chapel Hill, NC.

Williams, Linda D. (1989c). *Viewing American sportswomen for a quarter of a century (1924-1948) through the writings of the* Pittsburgh Courier, *Negro weekly*. Unpublished paper.

Williams, Linda D. (1991a). *Before Wilma and Althea: Afro-American women in sports*. Unpublished manuscript.

Williams, Linda D. (1991b, May). *"Not only do we cook greens, we play on them, too": Chicago black female golfers, 1930 through 1937*. Paper presented at North American Society for Sport History Conference, Chicago, IL.

Williams, Linda D. (1991c, April). *A history of the black female athlete*. Paper presented at the meeting of Women in Sport Conference, Columbus, OH.

Williams, Linda D. (1992, April). *Race, ethnicity and gender*. Paper presented at the meeting of Women in Sport Conference, Columbus, OH.

Williams, Linda D. & Lumpkin, Angela. (1989, May). *An examination of the sport, gender, race, and sporting role of individuals appearing on the covers of* Sports Illustrated, *1954-1987*. Paper presented at North American Society for Sport History Conference, Clemson, SC.

Williams, Linda D. & Lumpkin, Angela. (1990). *An examination of the sport, gender, race, and sporting role of individuals appearing on the covers of* Sports Illustrated, *1954-1989*. Unpublished paper.

4

Women in Toyland

A Look at Women in American Newspaper Sports Journalism

Pamela J. Creedon

> I hear they're [Oberlin College] even letting w-o-m-e-n in their sports
> program now. That's your Women's Liberation, boy—a bunch of
> goddamn lesbians. . . . You can bet your ass that if you have women
> around—and I've talked to psychiatrists about this—you aren't going
> to be worth a damn. No sir! Man has to dominate. There's just no
> other way.
>
> Woody Hayes, 1973 (cited in Vare, 1974, p. 38)

I teach at The Ohio State University where on Saturdays in the fall
a sea of football fans clad in scarlet and gray transform the entire
campus into a five-ring circus. The Buckeye football ritual is the
legacy of legendary Coach Woody Hayes, who left the university in
temporary disgrace when he was fired in 1978 for slugging a Clemson University player during the Gator Bowl.

It wasn't the first time that Hayes had hit anyone. He had assaulted
players, referees and reporters over the years, and he had a particular

AUTHOR'S NOTE: I wish to thank Maurine Beasley, Mary Garber, Susan Henry,
Marion Marzolf, Tom Schwartz and Mary Ann Yodelis Smith for their comments on
this chapter.

disdain for the news media. In 1973, for example, he shoved a camera into the face of *Los Angeles Times* photographer Art Rogers, who suffered from double vision and swollen eyes for several weeks after the incident (Vare, 1974). The irony of Hayes's demise is that the final blow was captured by photographers and television cameras on a national broadcast.

Although Hayes may seem like an anachronism from a bygone era, his specter remains at Ohio State and can be found throughout men's sports. Today, it is particularly visible in attitudes about women in sports journalism, especially when it comes to granting women sportswriters access to the locker room.

Yet women have been covering sports—women's and men's—since sports reporting became a regular feature of newspapers. However, the involvement of women in sports journalism has not been documented well for several possible reasons. First, research on women in journalism history generally is relatively recent with most work completed in the last 20 years (Beasley & Silver, 1977; Henry, 1990; Marzolf, 1977; Mills, 1988). Most of this scholarship has focused on uncovering women who made contributions in more traditional areas of journalism such as political reporting, publishing and editing. Second, the field of sports reporting generally has not received much attention by mass communication scholars, probably because of the stigma that has long been attached to sports reporting. The sports department of newspapers or broadcast stations is often derided as the Toy Department or Toyland by other reporters. Sports news has traditionally been viewed as "soft" news or entertainment, which means it is of less consequence. This stigma may have influenced mass communication scholarship as well in the sense that research on sports journalism was not valued as highly or taken as seriously by the academy.

However, Toyland is changing and sports scholarship is becoming increasingly credible. If Coach Hayes were alive today, he could expect his misogynist remarks to be reported on the network news and the front pages. He would read about females playing football in high school. He would find female photographers and reporters asking to enter his locker room.

To add some perspective on how much sports journalism has changed over the years, this chapter will examine the role of American women in newspaper sports journalism and the gender values that have affected their roles from the 1800s to the present. The role of women in sports broadcasting, magazine and photojournalism is discussed in Chapter 5.

Women Journalists and the Development of the Newspaper Sports Page

Most accounts of the rise of the newspaper sports page agree that its popularity paralleled the growth of sports due to increased leisure time caused by industrialization (Garrison, 1985; Stevens, 1987).[1] Also, by the 1830s, increased literacy had increased newspaper circulation, which attracted advertising revenue, which in turn helped to lower the price of the paper and create the mass-marketed "penny press." Publisher James Gordon Bennett was one of the first to recognize the relationship of sports news to increasing circulation; consequently, his *New York Herald* was one of the first papers to include routine coverage of sporting events such as horse racing, cricket and prize fighting (Mott, 1962). Bennett also created news beats —specific areas of responsibility, and assigned reporters to cover sports news (Emery, 1954). In 1883, as the popularity of the mass-circulated, cheap papers grew, Joseph Pulitzer is credited with being the first to organize a separate sports department at his *New York World* (McChesney, 1989). Sports routinely covered at this point were horse and yacht racing, prize fighting and baseball.[2]

As the concept of beat reporting began to catch on and as sports news was gaining in popularity, Midy (Maria) Morgan walked into the editor's office at *The New York Times* looking for a job (see Table 4.1). As Nan Robertson (1992) describes it:

> On a September day in 1869, John Bigelow, the *Times* editor in chief, heard a gallumphing noise and looked up from his desk to see a hugh apparition bearing down upon him. The apparition was six feet two inches tall, garbed in rough Irish tweeds, and shod in thick-soled brogues. A whiff of the stables perfumed the air. A deep, melodious voice with an Irish lilt said, "I am Maria Morgan. I want a job." (p. 44)

Bigelow told Morgan that the only job available was that of livestock reporter, and she said, "I can fill it" (Ross, 1936, p. 145). She certainly could fill it; she grew up around horses in Ireland and hunted almost as soon as she could read. Before coming to the United States in 1869, her knowledge of horses had impressed King Victor Emmanuel of Italy so much that he had commissioned her to buy horses in Ireland for his stable (Ross, 1936, p. 146). Moreover, she had started her journalistic career covering the horse races at Saratoga, as a special correspondent for the *New York World* in July 1869 (Ross, 1936, p. 146). Morgan got the job at the *Times*, and for the next 23 years she covered livestock market news, horse racing and dog, cat and horse shows. According to Heath and Gelfand (1951), in the mid-1800s "the only member of a newspaper staff who in any way resembled the modern sports editor was the *turf man*" [sic; italics in original] (p. 14). As a "turf man," Morgan became so well known and widely respected that livestock breeders and General Ulysses S. Grant sought her opinion on horses.

According to accounts by Ross (1936) and Robertson (1992), Morgan's athletic ability was legendary. Although she walked with a limp because a horse had crushed one of her feet, she had transported six horses from Ireland, transferring them from steamer to train 32 times, as well as crossing one mountainous area on foot, to fulfill her commission from the King of Italy. Her work as a livestock market reporter meant that she had to walk miles over marshes and through livestock yards to meet with breeders and inspect the animals. Her death in 1892, according to Ross, was the indirect result of falling on ice while inspecting animals in the Jersey City stockyards.

In the West, women covered sports events for papers in California and Nevada from at least the late 1890s. Nellie Verrill Mighels Davis, editor and owner of the *Carson City Daily Appeal*, covered the Corbett-Fitzsimmons championship fight in Carson City in 1897 (Bennion, 1991). Annie Laurie (pen name of Winifred Black), a reporter for William Randolph Hearst's *San Francisco Examiner*, reportedly was the first female reporter in the city to cover a prize fight, and at the *San Francisco Bulletin* Pauline Jacobson covered fights and baseball stories and Inez Haynes Irwin covered wrestling in the early 1900s (Bennion, 1976/1977).

Stunt Girls as Participatory Sports Journalists

The development of the wireless, telephone and portable type-writer had a significant impact on news of the time, but the bicycle truly revolutionized news gathering. The bicycle, which had become an established part of American life before Queen Victoria died, allowed journalists, women and men alike, to pedal across town and gather news. The *Journal-American*, a Hearst newspaper, even sponsored the first transcontinental bicycle relay from San Francisco to New York, and magazines touted the invention as liberating for American women both in terms of dress and health (Boyle, 1963).

By 1895, the widespread recognition of sports as a stimulant to circulation led William Randolph Hearst to establish the first newspaper sports section in the *New York Journal* (McChesney, 1989). Competition between Hearst and Pulitzer for circulation and advertising revenue in the 1890s also opened the door for a special breed of women reporters. Following in the athletic footsteps of Midy Morgan, these female reporters, known as *stunt girls*, performed and wrote about athletic activities, even if their stories didn't always appear on the newspaper sports pages. Mary Bostwick, a reporter for the *Indianapolis Star*, defined the personality of a stunt girl: "[Y]ou had to have a brain approximating that of the praying mantis, and the firm conviction that you were both indestructible and immortal" (Bostwick, 1950, p. 12).

Nellie Bly, the pseudonym of 5-foot 3-inch Elizabeth Cochrane, is the best known of this genre of daredevil female reporter.[3] Working for Pulitzer at the *World* where she occasionally covered prize fighting (Garrison, 1985), her most famous stunt was a race around the globe in 72 days, six hours and 11 minutes, using every form of transportation and muscle in her body to outdo Jules Verne's fictional hero Phileas Fogg who circled the globe in 80 days (Ross, 1965, p. 196). Bly started out on November 14, 1889, on board a ship from New York and returned triumphant on January 25, 1890, aboard a special train from San Francisco after traveling 24,899 miles (Ross, 1936). However, no chartered trains or ships were available for the other parts of the journey. After reaching London, she had to make her own transportation arrangements from river boats to jinrikishas, and from camels to burros. The stunt was her own idea and, according to Ross

(1965), when Pulitzer told her it was really an assignment for a man, she told him that she would race anyone he would send—which convinced Pulitzer to send her.

> In three days, Nellie had assembled an odd wardrobe—an ulster with shoulder cape made at Ghormley's, a ghillie cap, a plaid cloth dress, and a camel's hair costume that she thought—mistakenly—would serve for the heat. She tucked in three veils, a jacket, a dressing gown, some flannel underwear, and comfortable shoes. A crocodile gripsack held her clothes, and her toothbrush was tucked in the knapsack that she slung over her shoulder. Her most valuable possessions were her twenty-four hour watch, five hundred dollars in American money, and two hundred pounds in sterling. (Ross, 1965, p. 196)

While she struggled to circle the globe, the *World* kept its readers in suspense. A chart tracing her progress was printed in the paper every day, and Bly sent back stories filled with plenty of first-person drama about bandits, filth, heat, insects, monsoons and beggars.[4]

Another notable stunt girl was Mary Bostwick at the *Indianapolis Star* from 1914 to 1958. Bostwick, who started her career as a reporter in Denver in 1903, spent about 25 years as the only woman in the city room at the *Star*.[5] During her career she covered a variety of topics including football, boxing, baseball, hunting and basketball, but her specialty was aviation and race car reporting (Schneider, 1992). One of her most clever stunts required that she disguise herself as a man.

> At this time, in the disguise of the famous khaki pants, and the goggles and the cap, it was necessary to keep an eagle eye out for Speedway officials and I'd have to crawl into a rain barrel, or behind a bush, or try and look like a spare tire every time one of them hove into view. It was nerve racking but I figured it would be worth it. I'd be the first woman to drive on the Speedway with a race car driver in a racing car. (Bostwick, 1922, p. 1)

Her disguise worked; the 36-year-old Bostwick, who had tried for years to get into the press pagoda, became the first female reporter to ride around the Indianapolis 500 Mile Speedway oval.[6] In May 1922, she completed seven windy, bumpy laps (17.5 miles) at speeds of up to 110 miles an hour in the open cockpit of driver Howdy Wilcox's Peugeot (Schneider, 1992). According to her front-page story following the ride, it "cured" her of race car fever, but she continued to take risks riding dirigibles, autogiros (a prototype of the helicopter) and hot air balloons, as well as piloting a glider.

Bly, Bostwick and numerous other stunt "girls" were the real pioneers of what has come to be known as *participatory sports journalism*. They were in their day what George Plimpton has become to contemporary sports journalism.[7] Plimpton, a journalist, "played" professional baseball, football and so forth as stunts and then wrote books such as *Out of My League* (1961) and *Paper Lion* (1966) to recount the experiences. He said the notion behind his books was "to play out the fantasies, the daydreams that so many people have—seeing themselves on the center court at Wimbledon, or sinking long putts in the U.S. Open or ripping through the Green Bay secondary" (1966, p. 2). The stunt girls fulfilled similar fantasies for newspaper readers from the 1890s through the 1920s with their athletic and daredevil antics.

Moreover, although their exploits were not covered on the sports pages of their day, the stunts were important to the history of women in sports journalism because they were stories by women reporters about women accomplishing tasks involving physical strength and some athletic ability. As such, they also provided the reading public with an alternative vision to the feminine mystique of passivity and frailty.

Other women reporters were involved in more traditionally defined sports journalism. Mrs. Sallie Van Pelt covered baseball for the *Dubuque* (IA) *Times* at the turn of the century (Rayne, 1884, p. 45). Mrs. Sadie Kneller Miller, who used the byline SKM to disguise her gender, covered the Baltimore Orioles as a reporter for the *Baltimore Telegram*.

At the time of her death, SKM had earned a national reputation as a journalist and photographer, primarily for *Leslie's Weekly*. She was arrested in Germany as a spy, flew in a zeppelin and panned for gold in the Yukon (Thomas, 1977). The 1885 graduate of Western Maryland College, however, may also have been the first woman to cover major league baseball. SKM began covering the Orioles in 1894 at age 26 and started her photography career to enhance her baseball stories (Richwine, 1983). And her readers didn't learn that she was a woman until 1897 when her sex was "discovered" while she was on a national tour with the team.

Aside from the "stunt girls," it is difficult to find definitive records of women in early sports journalism history, although several were routinely turning in newspaper sports copy from the turn of the century through the 1920s. In 1908, Eloise Young was sporting editor and reporter of the *Chronicle-News* of Trinidad, Colorado (G. Berlage, personal communication, January 25, 1993). Ross (1936) refers to Harriet Underhill, who worked at the *New York Herald Tribune,* as the pioneer woman sportswriter in New York. Others wrote feature stories about a wide range of sports events including the World Series, Kentucky Derby, Rose Bowl, Olympic Games and major tennis matches and prize fights. One such feature writer was Jane Dixon of the *New York Telegram,* who was one of the first newspaper women to cover "big" prize fights such as the Dempsey-Willard fight in 1919 (Ross, 1936). Another was Adela Rogers St. Johns, who wrote feature stories on sports for the Hearst newspapers beginning in 1925 (Chance, 1984).

In 1916, Nan O'Reilly, who used the pen name Jean Sanderson, started a golf column for the *New York Evening Post.* Like SKM, the pen name was used in the hope that readers would assume that the columns were written by a man. Her boss cooperated in keeping her identity a secret by sending her all her checks so that she didn't need to be seen at the office (Ross, 1936). In 1929, when she became golf editor of the *New York Evening Journal,* she described herself as the "only female in captivity who has conducted a daily golf column" ("Nan O'Reilly," 1937). She was also a frequent contributor both as a writer and a photographer for *The Professional Golfer* magazine.

Sob Sisters and the Golden Age of Sports Writing

Sports news continued to increase newspaper circulation, which attracted more advertising, and so sports gradually took up more space in the papers. The golden age of sports writing was also a boom period for women in journalism. It was the age of "sob sister" journalism. "Sob sister" reporters, according to Ross (1936), watched "for the tear-filled eye, the widow's veil, the quivering lip, the lump in

TABLE 4.1   Milestones for Women in American Newspaper Sports Journalism

1869	*Midy Morgan* joins the *New York Times* and covers racing.
1884	*Sadie Kneller Miller* covers the Orioles for the *Baltimore Telegram.*
1889	*Nellie Bly* joins the *New York World.*
1906	*Pauline Jacobson* covers sports for the *San Francisco Bulletin.*
1908	*Eloise Young* is sporting editor of the *Chronicle News* of Trinidad, Colorado.
1916	*Nan O'Reilly* starts a golf column in the *New York Evening Post.*
1920	*Mary Bostwick* of the *Indianapolis Star* rides in a race car around the Indianapolis Speedway.
1922	*Dorothy Bough* is a sportswriter for the *Philadelphia Inquirer.*
1924	*Lorena Hickok* covers Big Ten football for the *Minneapolis Morning Tribune.* *Margaret Goss* starts a regular "Women in Sports" column for *New York Herald Tribune.* *Nettie George Speedy* covers sports news for the *Chicago Defender.*[*]
1929	*Nan O'Reilly* is golf editor of *New York Evening Journal.* *Cecile Ladu* is sports editor of the *Albany (NY) Times Union.*
1932	*Maribel Vinson* (Owen) covers sports for the *New York Times.*
1942	*Lois Fegan* of the *Harrisburg (PA) Telegraph* covers professional ice hockey.
1943	*Jeane Hofmann* of the *New York Journal-American* covers baseball training camps. *Zelda Hines* is women's bowling editor for the *Chicago Defender.*[*]
1944	*Mary Garber* is sports editor at *Winston-Salem Sentinel.*
1973	*Karol Stringer* of the Associated Press enters the pits at the Indianapolis 500. *Betty Cuniberti, San Bernardino Sun-Telegram,* covers an NFL team from the training camp to the Super Bowl.
1976	*Betty Cuniberti* is a sportswriter for the *San Francisco Chronicle.* *Lawrie Mifflin* is a sportswriter at the *New York Daily News.* *Lesley Visser* covers the National Football League beat for the *Boston Globe.*[*]
1977	*Carolyn White* is a sportswriter for the *Akron Beacon-Journal.*[*]
1978	*LeAnne Schreiber* is sports editor at the *New York Times.*
1979	*Alison Gordon* covers American League baseball for *The Toronto Star.*
1982	*Claire Smith* joins the staff at the *Hartford (CT) Courant.*[*]
1985	*Christine Brennan* covers the Washington Redskins for the *Washington Post.*
1988	*Karen Hunter-Hodge* is the only black woman sportswriter on a major New York daily (*Daily News*).[*]

NOTE: This is intended to be a list of significant "firsts" for women in sports reporting. I welcome challenges to this list because the more one learns about history, the more one learns that it is never safe to say "first." In addition, almost every newspaper in the country can add its own "first" woman sports reporter to this list.
[*]Significant firsts for African-American women sports reporters.

the throat, the trembling hand" (p. 65). Yet, while the emotional and flowery prose of the sob sisters filled the front pages, a similar emotional writing style also filled a lot of column inches on newspaper sports pages during the 1920s and 1930s.

Sob sisters offered their readers emotional pathos, and sportswriters of the era offered emotion too. According to Grantland Rice, "sport's first tidal wave of popularity never struck full force until we came into the Golden Age of Competition after the First World War" (Rice, 1948). His argument is based on the fact that the period from 1919 into the 1930s produced the greatest collection of stars (e.g., Babe Ruth, Jack Dempsey, Knute Rockne, Helen Wills and Glenna Collett) that sport had ever known. Rice, however, neglects to mention the role of sportswriters like himself in creating these heroes through their purple prose and "Gee Whiz" style of sports journalism. Stories about baseball, boxing and college football helped fill the newspaper sports section of the 1920s with excitement and color. McChesney (1989) explains:

> It would have been difficult not to be a sports fan if one read a newspaper and had the slightest inclination in that direction. Sportswriters were major figures: at best, styles ranged from the colorful verse of Grantland Rice to the literary stylishness of Paul Gallico, Damon Runyon, and Westbrook Pegler. At worst, there was a pervasive cliché-ridden mediocrity. (p. 57)

Women had been officially granted the right to vote in 1920 and were beginning to organize their own sports associations such as the Women's Division of the National Amateur Athletic Federation (Sparhawk, Leslie, Turbow & Rose, 1989). Following the lead of women's colleges, women's sports became a part of the collegiate and recreational scene, and coverage of women's sports began to appear on the sports pages.

At least five women wrote regularly about women's sports during the 1920s. Margaret Goss's "Women in Sports" column appeared in the *New York Herald Tribune* starting in 1924 (Ross, 1936). In 1925, Dorothy Lindsay was named Women-in-Sports editor of the *Boston Herald* (Twyman, 1983). Ann Haber's "The Woman in Sports" column appeared in the *New York Evening World* several times in 1928. Janet Valborg Owen followed Haber at the *World* and wrote a sports column that appeared an average of four or five days a week, generally on page 3, the last full page of the paper's sports section. In 1929, Cecile Ladu was named women's sports editor of the *Albany* (NY)*Times Union* ("Woman Writes," 1929).

Owen's column covered women's sports news from coast to coast and from college to the industrial league. A graduate of Barnard,

Owen covered women's field hockey, basketball, fencing, gymnastics and bowling and news of meetings and conferences of women's athletic organizations. She often gave game scores, as well as individual names and point totals. In her column on March 1, 1930, for example, she covered an Industrial Athletic League tournament game played the previous evening between the "girls" of *The New York Times* and those from Metropolitan Life Insurance Company.

> The first half was played according to men's amateur rules; the second, professional. Both teams scored a field and a foul shot in the first quarter, each putting up such a stiff defense against alternating onslaughts that large scoring became impossible at either end. (p. 10)

The *Times* team prevailed 12-10, handing the Metropolitan quintet its first defeat of the season.

Owen's column also kept readers abreast of discussions regarding the direction of women's intercollegiate sport. In her column on February 15, 1930, she outlined the platform to be discussed at the sixth national conference of the Athletic Conference of American College Women, a organization formed in 1912.

> Among the four [policies of] most outstanding importance are the giant development of intramural sports; the many changes in point systems and in schemes of awards; the division of women's athletic associations in colleges and other large organizations into groups of smaller clubs; and the popularization of play days, each of which have added new problems to the organization of women's athletic associations. (p. 12)

Around the country during the 1920s, women were also covering men's sports in greater numbers.[8] In Philadelphia, Dorothy Bough became the first woman sportswriter at the *Inquirer* in 1922; Betty Hardesty started her sportswriting career in 1924 with the *Public Ledger* [9]; Helen O. Mankin started work at the *Evening Bulletin* in 1925; Dora Lurie joined the *Inquirer* in 1927 (Hardesty, 1944). In fact, about 15 women reported sports in Philadelphia during the 1920s, and they organized a Women's Sportswriters Association in 1929.

In Minneapolis about this time, Lorena Hickok earned her stripes as a sportswriter. Hickok, whose journalism career has been widely chronicled, may have been the first woman reporter to cover Big Ten football.[10] According to Ross (1936), Hickok wrote football stories for four years for the *Minneapolis Morning Tribune* and toured with the University of Minnesota team. According to Faber (1980), Hickok's first football assignment was a feature story on the 1924 season opener against Illinois. Her lead: "We have met the enemy and he is ours" (Faber, p. 66). Her story, which didn't mention the final score until the sixth paragraph, was accompanied by a play-by-play account. During the 1924 season, she traveled with the team on its special train and stayed in the same hotel as the team, often staying up late to play poker with the all-male press entourage.

But as the 1920s drew to a close, the American newspaper was changing. The number of newspapers declined while circulation increased (McChesney, 1989). Advertising became an increasingly vital source of newspaper revenue. To reduce costs, newspapers relied more heavily on wire services and press agents for information. The summary lead replaced chronological-style writing. Ultimately, the Great Depression forced many women out of the labor force so that men could have what few jobs were available.

A combination of these factors affected the number of women entering sports reporting. In all of the sources consulted for this chapter, only three new bylines by women were mentioned on the sports pages during the 1930s. The first was Frances Turner, a graduate of Goucher College. She began her sportswriting career at the *Baltimore Morning Sun* and the *Baltimore Sunday Sun* as a woman's sports reporter on January 13, 1930 (Luckett, 1942). She accompanied the U.S. women's lacrosse team on its four-week tour of Great Britain in 1935 and also wrote sports for magazines (Ross, 1936).

A precursor of the trend to hire ex-athletes for television sports announcing, Maribel Vinson, an Olympic skating champion, was hired by *The New York Times* as a sports reporter in the 1930s. According to Ross (1936), she "writes about baseball, basketball or anything that comes along, but she avoids any comment on skating, lest she run into a snag on her amateur standing" (p. 471). Later, she made headlines in 1956 as the coach of America's first Olympic gold medalist in figure skating (Tenley Albright), but in 1961 she and 18 members of the U.S. figure-skating team, including two of her daughters, were killed in a plane crash at the Brussels airport on the way to the world figure skating championships in Prague (Hollander, 1976).

In 1937, 16-year-old Jeane Hofmann started a lengthy sportswriting career with the *Hollywood Citizen*.[11] She went on to cover a wide variety of sports for the *Philadelphia Evening Bulletin,* King Features Syndicate and the *New York Journal-American.* In 1949, she became executive editor of the *Police Gazette* and may have been the first female reporter to cover major league baseball training camps in 1942, as well as the first female member of the Football Writers of America (Hofmann, 1944). Her story "The Chinese Spirit" for the *Los Angeles Times* was the only story by a female sports reporter to be included in the 1959 edition of *Best Sports Stories* (Marsh & Ehre, 1959).

Entries in Iona Robertson Logie's book, *Careers for Women in Journalism* (1938), indicate that at least three women were active as sports reporters in the 1930s. Although she does not use names in her volume, she writes of a woman on the Pacific Coast who worked in a secretarial position in a "prominent football league" by day, but marketed her magazine sports stories on her own time (p. 219). Another female sportswriter for an eastern metropolitan daily (presumably Maribel Vinson) is described as "a champion ice skater and college graduate" (p. 220). Her third example is that of woman who wrote a daily column on women's sports in the winter, spring and fall beginning in 1933 at a salary of $50 a week (p. 221).

Research by Linda Williams (1988) shows that Afro-American women were active as sportswriters in Chicago and Pittsburgh between the 1920s and 1940s. In the 1920s, Nettie George Speedy's byline appears in *Chicago Defender* sports stories, and Rose Atwood and Bernice Dutrieuille signed sports stories in the *Pittsburgh Courier* in the 1920s. Later, Rosemarie Barrie's byline appears with women's tennis stories in the *Courier* in the 1930s and Zelda Hines's coverage of bowling earns her the title of Women's Bowling Editor for the *Defender* in the 1940s. Williams also found that women's sports—bowling, baseball and tennis—were routinely covered by the Negro press during these decades.

War and the Press Box

Because of the shortage of male reporters during the war, women had unprecedented opportunities in sports reporting in the 1940s. Mary Garber of the *Winston-Salem Sentinel* and *Journal* (now *Winston-Salem Journal*) is probably the best-known of this generation. Often referred to as the "Dean of Women Sportswriters," Garber became sports editor at the *Sentinel* in 1944 when all available men had entered the armed services during World War II. As she explains:

> While the men were away fighting the war, a high school boy used to come by and put out the sports page before he went to school. Then he went into the navy [sic] and there wasn't anybody to take his place. The staff was all women at that time. I'm not sure why, but I was picked to handle the sports page. I just got fascinated by it and loved it. (Collins, 1980, p. 132)

When the men returned, Garber was moved to the high school sports beat and eventually on to collegiate sports. In the fall of 1946, she was back on the sports beat full-time where she remained until 1986. She was one of the first female sports reporters to challenge the rule prohibiting women in the press box:

> I went down to Duke to cover a football game with press credentials [in 1946] but the sports information director wouldn't let me sit in the press box because he said women were not allowed. And while I was talking with him, there was a little boy about ten years old hopping up and down . . . the steps. I said . . . "Is he covering for the Lilliputian Gazette?" And he didn't think that was very funny. He put me in what they called the wives' box. (Gentry, August 28, 1991, p. 44)

She went back and told her managing editor about her treatment, and he promptly wrote a letter to the athletic directors of the four universities in North Carolina that the paper routinely covered. He told them that they were turning away the paper, not simply a woman reporter. The letter worked, according to Garber, because the athletic directors didn't want to get involved in a dispute with one of the largest papers in the state. Garber, who grew up in a racially segregated era in the South, was the first white—and first woman—

sportswriter on her paper to spend time reporting on black high school and college players (Gentry, 1991, p. 10). Although Garber retired from full-time reporting in 1986, she continues to cover tennis, small college sports, coaches' conferences and special assignments for the *Sentinel.*

The feud over press box entry for women was not confined to North Carolina in the 1940s (see Table 4.2 for locker room incidents as well). In 1943, Doris Blackmer of the Associated Press was assigned to cover a game at Denver University stadium. She showed up with press credentials, but was quickly ejected "upon demand" of the *Denver Post* sports editor Jack Carberry, who said:

> The press box is exclusively for male sports writers. It's a tradition of the newspaper game—and the war is no excuse to change it. Sports writers have the privilege of using their own kind of language in their own domain—and it's no language for a girl to hear, even if she purports to be a sportswriter. Let the girl cover the game—I don't care how the Associated Press covers the game—but she can cover it from some place other than the press box. ("Feud Flares," 1944, p. 43)

After being seated for nearly 20 minutes, Marie Williams, also an Associated Press reporter in the Denver bureau, was ejected from the press box at the national Amateur Athletic Union tournament on March 24, 1944. Carberry, also president of the Denver Sports Writers Association at the time, spotted Williams in the press box area and had her ushered to another seat. Expressing sentiments that echo Woody Hayes's opening quote, he explained his reasons:

> When I'm covering a game, I don't want to hear a lot of feminine chit-chat about fashions, new cooking recipes and boy friends. And that's what the press box would be filled with, if girls were admitted. I know, I've been in some press boxes where women have been admitted. If we admitted women reporters, we'd been [sic] in for plenty of trouble so much trouble that it would interfere with our work. ("Feud Flares," 1944, p. 43)

Jean Buck, an Atlanta staff member of the International News Service, was among the first women to enter the press box at Georgia Tech in 1947 ("Lady Football," 1947, p. 24). Reaction from sports editors to the unprecedented open press box policy instituted by the university was mixed with comments ranging from sexist (let them in if they are blonde and pretty) to all-out war. Raymond Johnson of the *Nashville Tennessean,* president of the Football Writers Association, declared: "I expect to continue the campaign to rid the nation's press boxes of women" ("Lady Football," p. 24).

Lois Fegan, the only woman in the country from 1942 until 1952 to cover professional ice hockey, also had a press box "experience." While covering a mid-1940s playoff match between the Hershey Bears and the Cleveland Barons in Cleveland for the *Harrisburg* (PA) *Telegram,* she was blocked from entering the glassed-in press box by a security guard (Fegan, 1990). She took a seat on a step of the center aisle and opened her typewriter. However, she quickly realized that she was too far away from her Western Union operator to be able to send play-by-play action back to the paper. As she explains:

> In those pre-computer days, copy was transmitted by teletype. The reporters, using half-size sheets of paper, would write two or three paragraphs at a time, rip the sheet out of the machine and pass it over to the keypuncher whose line was connected to the newspaper's in-office wire system. (p. 48)

According to Fegan, when several of the male reporters realized her dilemma, they convened a meeting of those in the press box and voted to make an exception in her case. She was seated just as "The Star Spangled Banner" began.

Mary Flannery, another in the long line of Philadelphia's women sportswriters, joined the sports staff of the *Inquirer* in 1944, when she was promoted from copy "girl" as the male reporters went off to war.[12] A university official tried to bar her from the press box when she was assigned to cover the Philadelphia high school city title game on Penn State's field. As she recounts it: "The press-box manager told me, 'No women allowed in Penn's press box.' I told him that since the Interleague Commission had rented the field from Penn, it wasn't Penn's press box that day. And I kept on going" (Flannery, 1992, p. 29). Adeline Sumi, who worked for the *San Francisco Call-Bulletin* in the mid-1940s, also made the move from the copy desk to sports desk (Nelson, 1981). When she did, however, the paper shortened her first name to "Del" to disguise her sex from male readers.

Stagnant Fifties to the Title IX Seventies

Some of the women sportswriters continued to be active through the 1950s and early 1960s, but many apparently lost their jobs after World War II and elected not to re-enter the work force. History sources from this period are essentially devoid of references to women sportswriters, except for four unique individuals.

In 1961, at age 65, Beth Hightower began a full-time job at the *Sacramento Union* as a sportswriter (Scott, 1973, p. 24). Actually, her first sports story was written in 1942 for the *Sporting News*. The subject: Why women aren't allowed in the press box at Pacific Coast League baseball games. Before joining the *Union* as a staff reporter, she had covered golf on a part-time basis for 30 years and was reputed to be the best-known golf writer in the West.

MaryAnn Yodelis Smith, then Sister Mary Angelora of the Sisters of St. Francis of the Holy Family, covered the Briar Cliff College Charger basketball team—in her nun's habit—as a freelance sports-writer for the *Des Moines Register* and *Sioux City Journal* from 1962 to 1964 (Yodelis Smith, personal communication, December 15, 1992). Sister Mary Angelora was the publicity director at the formerly all-women's college when the decision was made to become co-educational. Briar Cliff's academic dean thought that the quickest way to attract male students would be to add basketball and to publicize it as much as possible. So Sister Mary Angelora visited the sports editors at the *Journal* and *Register* to see if they would run her stories of Briar Cliff's first season. They said they would, and did, although without bylines; she later left the convent and joined the ranks of college journalism faculty.

Joan Ryan launched her sportswriting career unexpectedly in 1964 when the sports editor of the *Cleveland Plain Dealer* called her and asked her to write for the paper (Moran, 1976). Her first pub-lished work was a twice-a-week football column called "Back Seat Brown." Her husband Frank just happened to be the quarterback of the Browns at the time, and by 1976 she was covering sports for the *Washington Post*.

Barbara Long started her sportswriting career in 1965 at the *Village Voice*. She wrote the *Voice's* first sports piece—"The Lady Saw the Punch"—following the heavyweight title fight between Sonny Liston and Cassius Clay (aka Muhammed Ali). Long watched the fight on closed circuit television and saw the knockout punch thrown by Clay that male sportswriters claimed they didn't see (Long, 1975).

In the early 1970s, sports news was changing. Two trends undoubtedly influenced this change to some extent. First, sports sociology was gaining status in the academy through its analyses of relationships between sports and race, class and gender. Second, feminism and feminist scholarship had also gained credibility and visibility, although sport was regarded with some disdain by a number of influential feminist scholars until the 1980s (Sabo & Jansen, 1992; Theberge, 1981).[13] These trends combined to place social issues such as violence and drug abuse on the news agenda. Without any prompting, the sports establishment put itself on the news agenda with stories of widespread steroid, cocaine and alcohol abuse.

As the examples throughout this chapter have shown, by the 1970s much of the pioneering groundwork for women interested in careers as newspaper sports journalists had been done. A lot of battles had been fought. In 1976, the joint Associated Press/United Press International stylebook committee recommended the elimination of the courtesy titles, "Miss" and "Mrs." in sports stories—but not elsewhere in the paper ("Media Women Object," 1976). Moreover, because of federal equal opportunity employment mandates issued in the early 1970s, doors were "magically" opening for women in sports reporting.

The career of LeAnne Schreiber provides a good example. After teaching English at Harvard, Schreiber joined *Time* as a staff writer in 1974 and covered the Olympics for the magazine in 1976 ("The New York," 1978). Then she spent about a year as editor of *womenSports* magazine, leaving it to join *The New York Times* as one of three assistant sports editors. In 1978, the *Times* settled a sex discrimination lawsuit out of court by agreeing to fill 25% of its management positions with women (Robertson, 1992). Not surprisingly, when the job of sports editor became available in November 1978, Schreiber got the job supervising 55 reporters and becoming the first woman sports editor in the history of the *Times*. She agreed to keep the job for two years and did, moving on to become deputy editor of the *Book Review* in 1980. After four years in that job, she left the daily journalism business to pursue a book writing career. Her first book *Midstream*, published in 1990, is the story of her mother's death from cancer and Schreiber's experience of it (Smith, 1990).

Betty Cuniberti was graduated from the University of Southern California in 1973 and starting working for the *San Bernardino Sun-Telegram*, moved to the *San Francisco Chronicle* in 1976 as its first woman sports reporter and then went to the *Washington Post* in 1977 (Marsh & Ehre, 1977, 1979). Lynn Rossellini joined the *Washington Star* as its first female sportswriter in 1974 and gained recognition for her series on homosexuality in sports. Melissa Ludtke, a 1973 graduate of Wellesley College, had never written about sports before she was hired at *Sports Illustrated* in 1974 ("Woman Sportswriter," 1978). Jane Gross and Stephanie Salter also joined the *SI* staff as researchers/sports reporters immediately after they were graduated from college in the early 1970s (Angell, 1979, 1982). Robin Herman, a member of the first class of female Princeton graduates in 1973, joined the *New York Times* that same year and in 1974 was assigned to cover the New York Islanders in the National Hockey League (Angell, 1979, 1982). Lawrie Mifflin, a 1973 graduate of Yale, became the first woman reporter in the sports department at the *New York Daily News* in 1976 and was later named deputy sports editor of the *New York Times* (Angell, 1979, 1982). Nancy Scannell switched from covering government, politics and courts to covering sports at the *Washington Post* in 1973 (Moran, 1976). Lesley Visser was hired by the *Boston Globe* in 1974 to cover high school football and by 1976 she was "the first female beat writer for an NFL team" (Jenkins, 1991, p. 85). Tracy Dodds started for the *Milwaukee Journal* as a sports writer in 1974 immediately after being graduated from Indiana University (Angell, 1979, 1982).

In 1975, Cyndi Meagher got the chance to write a three-day-a-week sports column at the *Detroit News* (Moran, 1976) and Judi Patton's column "Ms-Ports" appeared every Thursday in the Harrisburg (PA) *Patriot-News* (Gibboney, 1975). Also in 1975, Jenny Kellner started at *Newsday* as a sports assistant, moving to *The Record* (Hackensack, NJ) as a horse racing writer and handicapper, then to United

Press International in 1977 as a racing writer (Marsh & Ehre, 1978). At the *Boston Herald*, Marie Brenner was one of the first women baseball columnists in the major leagues in 1979 (Brenner, 1993; Lannin, 1987), and in the same year Alison Gordon of *The Toronto Star* became the first woman journalist to cover the American League baseball beat (Gordon, 1984). Linda Kay, who covered the Super Bowl for the *San Diego Tribune* in 1978, joined the sports staff of the *Chicago Tribune* in 1979 and was writing a five-day-a-week sports column for the paper in 1985 (Kay, 1985). Christine Brennan landed a sportswriting job at the *Miami Herald* right out of journalism school in 1980 (Ricchiardi & Young, 1991). As she explains:

> It would be naive to believe that I got a job simply because I was a fabulous writer. I'm aware that had I been a white male coming out of Northwestern University with the same degrees—everything else being equal—I wouldn't have landed one of the plum assignments at the *Miami Herald* at age 23. (Ricchiardi & Young, 1991, p. 162)

Some doors, however, weren't about to open easily for women sportswriters.

The advantage of immediacy in broadcast media coverage had drastically changed newspaper sports by the 1970s. Stories were no longer adequate with only box scores and game highlights. The baseball clubhouse or the football locker room became the newspaper sportswriter's beat. To be competitive, newspaper sports stories relied on post-game locker room interviews with players and coaches for "conflicting game stories, rumors, whispers of team feuds, hidden injuries, managerial pomposities, salary discontents, or incipient trades" (Angell, 1982, p. 132). However, locker room doors were often closed to women sportswriters.

Occasionally a few doors were opened, *if* a coach were willing to agree to it, but often that permission was granted on the spot and could be rescinded at a moment's notice. That's how it was for the first women to enter a National Hockey League locker room. They were permitted in by team coaches after the 1975 NHL All-Star game in Montreal (Angell, 1982). Robin Herman recalled the occasion:

> It was treated like a joke. Marcelle St. Cyr, who'd been broadcasting [Montreal] Canadiens games for station CKLM, in Montreal, and I

were the first women in. I had no plans to make it happen or anything.
I couldn't believe it. All-star games are sort of boring, and Marcelle
and I were the story that night, not the players. There were a lot of
jokes and pranks. (Angell, 1982, p. 141)

In 1977, *Washington Post* sportswriter Betty Cuniberti entered the
Minnesota Vikings locker room with the blessing of Coach Bud Grant.
She explained that "the locker room problem gets misconstrued as
a bunch of flaky broads wanting to get inside" (Shah, 1978). Diane
K. Shah, who worked as a sports reporter covering the baseball pennant race for the *National Observer* in 1972, found that the management
of the team made a big difference in how a woman sportswriter was
treated.

Earl Weaver, of the Orioles, is very accommodating and easy, and
so are his players. So is Chuck Tanner of the Pirates. The Red Sox
always make you feel sort of uncomfortable, but I think they're an
uncomfortable kind of team, even among themselves. The Yankees—
well, I rode on a team bus with them in Kansas City a couple of
times . . . aren't exactly a mature team, to put it mildly. (Angell, 1982,
pp. 143-144)

According to Tracy Dodds, locker room access has "nothing to
do with morality or privacy"; it's an issue of territoriality (Watson-
Rouslin, 1987, p. 22). For many women sportswriters in the 1970s,
entering the territory or locker room was a job security issue, involving crucial post-game interviews for their stories.

The issue of access came to a boiling point in the baseball clubhouse during the 1977 World Series, when Melissa Ludtke of *Sports
Illustrated* was denied access to the New York Yankees locker room,
and baseball commissioner Bowie Kuhn refused to overrule Yankee
management. Ludtke, 26 at the time, had worked for *SI* for more
than three years, covering baseball for two seasons.[14]

To gain access, Ludtke and *SI*'s parent company, Time, Inc., filed
a federal sex discrimination suit against the baseball commissioner's
office, the New York Yankees and the president of the American
League and against the mayor and other officials of New York City (as
owners of the stadium) ("Woman Sportswriter," 1978). The suit was
based on the argument that she could not perform her job without

access to the players for post-game interviews and that the exclusion was based on her sex, which violated her rights of equal protection and due process under the 14th Amendment to the U.S. Constitution. Time, Inc., argued that if one reporter was not given the same opportunity as another to acquire certain information, that reporter is being denied equal access. The suit also stated the fact that about half of the reporters at *SI* at the time were women and that the magazine "wants to assign its reporters to cover the 1978 baseball season on the basis of their talent and expertise and without regard to sex" ("Woman Sportswriter," 1978, p. 11).

By lot, the case was assigned to New York Federal District Court Judge Constance Baker Motley, the only female judge in the southern district of New York at the time ("Woman Sportswriter," 1978). She ruled that all reporters, regardless of sex, should have equal access to the athletes, including the locker room if necessary (Boutilier & SanGiovanni, 1983). Baseball Commissioner Bowie Kuhn asked for a stay for the order, which the judge denied. He then appealed the ruling arguing that baseball was a family game and that to let women in the locker room would "undermine the basic dignity of the game" (Angell, 1982, p. 129). That appeal was denied as well.

Roger Angell, a sports journalist who covered baseball at the time, described the scene on September 26, 1978, the first night that women were allowed in the Yankee clubhouse[15]:

> On the night that Judge Motley's order took effect, the Yankee clubhouse was suddenly crowded with strangers, male and female, who had come to report on the new socio-journalistic phenomenon. Most of the women . . . were local television reporters, and they smilingly asked the players what they thought about the presence of women in the locker room, while the cameras caught it all. (Angell, 1982, p. 133)

Judge Motley's ruling was interpreted as specific to the Yankees and not binding on other baseball clubs or other professional sports; in practice, it only opened the door to one locker room. Further, although the Yankees' clubhouse was opened to women sportswriters for the last week of the 1978 season, through the playoffs and the World Series—it was only open *when* the Yankees played in New York.

During the playoffs and World Series, when the games were played out of town, no women reporters were allowed in either locker room.

B. J. Phillips, associate editor of *Time* and its chief writer on sports at the time, was assigned to cover the 1978 World Series. After the first game in Los Angeles, even though she was not attempting to enter a locker room, she was harassed by two public relations men, representing Kuhn, who attempted to take her press credentials. She refused to comply, and they forced her out of a public interview area and onto the field. Television reporters saw her close to tears; she and her story made national news. As she explained it:

> I've picked up a severed leg outside a blown-out pub in Northern Ireland, I've interviewed women terrorists, I've heard the President of the United States lie at a press conference. But the first time in twelve years I've been forced to tears in public was there in Dodger Stadium. To think it was the World Series that did it—it's ludicrous. . . . I've been treated worse in sports than anywhere else. I've never felt that resentment anywhere else. (Angell, 1982, p. 139)

Ludtke paid a price for her victory too. According to Angell, the ruling brought out the worst in his sports journalism colleagues. He often heard Ludtke defamed by other reporters, her motives for bringing the suit and professional abilities questioned, and her appearance and private life vilified (1982, p. 135). Ludtke said that she felt *Time* had used her suit as a convenient way to symbolize its commitment to women since the company had recently settled a discrimination suit filed against it by female employees (1982, p. 146). Kuhn finally dropped his appeals in February 1979 and on March 9, 1979, he sent a memo to the major league baseball teams directing them to find ways to give equal access to all reporters (Boutilier & SanGiovanni, 1983).

Acceptance in the 1980s and 1990s

Access and acceptance are not synonymous. Women sportswriters eventually gained official access to most professional sports locker rooms by the mid-1980s, but it triggered an increase of incidents of locker room harassment and violence against women reporters (see

Table 4.2). Some teams chose to set up separate interview areas, which caused a backlash of resentment against female reporters by male reporters who were banned from the locker room.

However, the recorded incidences of harassment are by no means a good measure of how many have actually occurred during the 15 years since the Ludtke ruling. Many female reporters are not willing to complain, fearing that they may be reassigned to a less prestigious beat or thought of as crybabies who need special treatment or that "*they* [italics in original] might become the story rather than the team or game" (Watson-Rouslin, 1987, p. 24).

Undoubtedly, the most publicized incident involving a female newspaper sportswriter occurred in a football locker room in 1990. At the time of the incident, 26-year-old Lisa Olson had been a reporter for four years and had covered the New England Patriots for the *Boston Herald* for three months. On September 17, 1990, Olson was interviewing a Patriots player in the locker room when several naked players exposed their genitals and made lewd remarks; one stood next to Olson and one invited her to "take a bite" out of his penis (Kane & Disch, 1993).

Olson complained to the Patriots' media relations manager; her editor complained to the team's general manager ("Women: Not Welcome," 1991). Initially, she and her management at the *Herald* sought a private solution, similar to the manner in which Mary Garber and her editor solved her press box access issue in the 1940s. However, the *Boston Globe*, a rival paper, chose to run the story about Olson's treatment.

Olson quickly became a media event. She appeared on radio and television news and talk shows. She was booed by the crowd at a subsequent Patriots' game (Whitaker, 1990), even though the flurry of stories and editorials that followed the incident generally defended Olson as a professional journalist and attacked "Kiam [owner of the Patriots] and the Cavemen" (Jackson, 1990).[16] However, according to an analysis by Mary Jo Kane and Lisa Disch (1993), the underlying message of media reports was that Olson was either a classic rape victim (i.e., she asked for it by being there) or a classic hypersensitive female (i.e., she can't take a joke).

According to Olson, her editor decided to try her case in the court of public opinion.

My editor told me we were at war. I didn't think I could say no. But it was bad advice to do television interviews then. I was so blinded by anger that I came across as a very angry young woman. And that's because I was an angry young woman. (Henkel, 1993, p. 2)

National Football League Commissioner Paul Taglibue appointed former Watergate prosecutor Philip Heymann to investigate the charges. He issued a 60-page report on November 28, 1990, after taking a 1,760-page deposition from Olson. The report found no fault with Olson. Taglibue fined the players involved in amounts ranging from $5,000 to $12,500 (two or three days' pay) and fined the Patriots' owner, Victor Kiam, $50,000.[17]

Olson had become a symbol of a much deeper tension between gender values, hauntingly reminiscent of the sentiments expressed in the opening quote of this chapter by Woody Hayes. And there are several other angles to the story. First, the Patriots finished the 1990 football season with a 1-15 record. Sports psychologists suspect that being a loser in the "winning is the only thing" model that dominates in male professional sport can lead to aggression and hostility, which may be displaced in violent behaviors directed at others in the athlete's life such as wives, girlfriends, and, in the case of the Patriots, female sportswriters (Calhoun, 1987; Le Unes & Nation, 1989).

Also in spring 1990, *Washington Post* sports and staff writer Jane Leavy had toured the country promoting her book *Squeeze Play*, a fictional account of a female baseball reporter who works for a Washington tabloid. Her media blitz included appearances on *Larry King*, the *Today Show* and ESPN, interviews with CBS radio and NPR's *All Things Considered* and live radio sports talk shows with KMPC in Los Angeles and at WFAN in New York (Leavy, 1990). The book attracted so such attention from sports fans that even President Bush sent her a handwritten note promising to read it (Leavy, p. 62). Most of the interviews focused on two things: her experiences as a woman sportswriter in the locker room and the opening paragraph of her book.

You see a lot of penises in my line of work: short ones, stubby ones, hard ones, soft ones. Circumcised and uncircumcised; laid-back and athletic. Professionally speaking, they have a lot in common, which is to say they are all attached to guys, most of whom are naked while

TABLE 4.2   A Chronology of Locker Room Access and Incidents

1975   Jane Gross, a *Newsday* reporter, and Jennifer Quale, a *Times-Picayune* feature writer, are instrumental in opening NBA locker rooms for women reporters.

1977   Melissa Ludtke of *Sports Illustrated*, denied access to the New York Yankee locker room, sues major league baseball.
Betty Cuniberti, *Washington Post* sportswriter, is granted access to the Minnesota Vikings locker room by Coach Bud Grant.

1978   A federal district court judge rules that all reporters, regardless of sex, should have equal access to the locker room.

1979   Doris Goodwin becomes the first woman reporter to enter a baseball clubhouse with the official permission of the Boston Red Sox.
The Tampa Bay Buccaneers construct the "Himmelberg Wall," a partition between the entry area of the locker room and the rest of the room, in "honor" of Michele Himmelberg of the *Fort Myers News-Press*.

1980   Lesley Visser of the *Boston Globe* is physically ejected from the locker room after the Cotton Bowl.
Sally Jenkins, *San Francisco Examiner*, is harassed in the locker room by Fred Stanley of the Oakland A's.

1982   National Hockey League establishes equal access rule for reporters.

1983   Sara Frel/gh of the *Philadelphia Inquirer* is assigned the Penn State football beat and, rather than let her in the locker room, Joe Paterno sets up a separate interview room for all reporters.

1984   Associated Press Sports Editors approve guidelines concerning equal access to locker rooms for male and female reporters.
Lesley Visser of the *Boston Globe* and Christine Brennan of the *Washington Post* are denied access to the Giants locker room and are told to wait outside for interviews. A public relations representative provides them with a player (Casey Merrill) who had only played a down or two during the entire game to interview.
Jane Gross, of the *New York Times*, is verbally harassed by members of the Cleveland Indians during post-game interviews in the clubhouse.
Jackie McMullan, a *Boston Globe* sportswriter, is thrown across a hallway and into a wall when she attempts to enter a college basketball team's locker room.

1985   Major league baseball Commissioner Peter Ueberroth orders equal locker room access for female reporters. The National Football League adopts equal access rule for male and female journalists. USFL Commissioner Chet Simmons says that the league has a strict rule that provides for equal access.
Jill Lieber, *Sports Illustrated*, Nanci Donnellan, CBS radio, and Joan Ryan, *The Orlando Sentinel*, are told to leave the locker room of the Arizona Wranglers after the USFL Championship game in Tampa by an administrative assistant of George Allen.
Joan Ryan, *The Orlando Sentinel*, is surrounded by players in the locker room of the USFL Birmingham Stallions while one of them strokes her leg with a disposable plastic razor.

1986   Shelly Smith, *San Francisco Examiner*, is physically grabbed in the locker room and marched into the 49ers' shower room by Bubba Paris.
Lisa Nehus Saxon of the *Los Angeles Daily News* reports that Los Angeles Dodger baseball players harass her by fondling themselves in front of her and sticking dildos in her face as she tried to conduct interviews.

TABLE 4.2 Continued

Annalisa Kraft, a photographer for the *Cincinnati Enquirer*, who was attempting to take pictures, was "goosed" with a bat by Pete Rose as she bent over and then was greeted with obscenities.

1988 Karen Rosen, a sports reporter for the *Atlanta Journal-Constitution*, is denied an opportunity to interview two Vanderbilt players after a game—outside of the locker room. The American Society of Newspaper Editors writes a protest letter to Vanderbilt's president. The Southeastern Athletic Conference institutes the Karen Rosen Rule: all reporters must wait outside of the locker room for interviews.

1989 Melody Simmons of the *Baltimore Evening Sun* is harassed in the Baltimore Orioles' locker room by players chanting, "Wool, wool."

1990 Lisa Olson of the Boston Herald is harassed in the locker room by several members of the New England Patriots including Zeke Mowatt, Michael Timson and Robert Perryman.

Denise Tom, *USA Today* sports reporter, is barred from the Cincinnati Bengals' locker room by Coach Sam Wyche. He is fined $30,000.

A. J. Brown, of the *Daily Tar Heel*, the student newspaper at the University of North Carolina-Chapel Hill, is told to leave the locker room as she attempts to interview a player.

Jennifer Frey, sportswriter intern with the *Detroit Free Press*, is verbally harassed by Tiger Pitcher Jack Morris when she attempts to interview him.

1991 Beth Harris of the Associated Press is evicted from the Indiana University locker room by basketball coach Bobby Knight.

1992 Karen Crouse of the Orange County *Register*, Lisa Nehus Saxon of the *Riverside Press-Enterprise* and Karen Pearlman of the *El Cajon Daily Californian* are barred from the locker room at a San Diego State and Southern California football game.

Ailene Voisin of the *Atlanta Journal Constitution* is verbally abused by Charlotte Hornet rookie Larry Johnson. He shouted obscenities at her when she reminded him that female reporters have equal access to the locker room.

After a game with the New England Patriots, Miami Dolphins' player Mark Clayton screams obscenities about Lisa Olson to a locker room full of reporters.

NOTE: This chronology does not presume to cover all locker room incidents that women sportswriters have encountered. The incident, for example, in which Susan Fornoff of the *Sacramento Bee* received a live rat in the press box is not discussed in the chapter since it did not occur in the locker room. Many have tolerated the harassment in silence. The specific incidents recorded in this list were those that received media attention.

I am not, thus forming the odd dynamic of our relationship. They are athletes who believe in the inalienable right to scratch their balls anytime they want. I am a sportswriter. My job is to tell you the score. (Leavy, 1990, p. 3)

While women sportswriters were arguing that they were in the locker room to gather information vital for their jobs, Leavy's exposure on national television and radio programs, including sports talk shows, suggested that it was impossible for them not to look at male genitalia and make comparisons. Although it is not possible to prove a direct cause-and-effect relationship between Leavy's book and the Lisa Olson incident, the timing certainly suggests a relationship. Leavy was on the publicity circuit suggesting that women sportswriters were critiquing more than male athletic ability; Olson became a symbol of female challenge to male power, particularly in professional sports where athletic performance and sexual performance seem to go hand in hand.[18] Angell (1982) predicted the outcome of gender equity in the locker room a decade earlier with the Ludtke ruling, when he wrote:

> The new presence of capable, complicated women in the inner places of sports means that relations between the sexes cannot be relegated just to marriage, or just to hotel rooms, either. When women are not easy to sum up or dismiss, traditional male responses to them suddenly begin to look pathetic. (p. 158)

What Angell forgot to acknowledge is that even when traditional male responses look pathetic, power relationships don't shift. Six weeks after the incident, Lisa Olson was no longer covering football; she was assigned to cover hockey and basketball. Next she took an international assignment for the *Herald* in Australia, and then joined the *Sydney Daily Telegraph-Mirror* as a feature writer. Despite Olson's disappearance from sports journalism, the *Globe*, for reasons that are not clear, published a four-page report in June 1992 based on its examination of the material gathered by the NFL investigation— nearly two years after the original report was issued. The *Globe* report suggested that Olson was a "looker."[19] Olson, who chose not to directly respond to the "new" report, explained her "no comment" rationale:

> When the *Globe* beat me up in its piece, I decided I didn't want to get into another newspaper war with them. . . . But there were some real basic lies that were printed. I did not feel that I had any way to set the record straight. I also knew that as long as I kept fighting it, it would never go away. (Henkel, 1993, p. 3)

Her specter made locker room news again on December 27, 1992, when Miami Dolphin player Mark Clayton screamed from inside the Patriot's visitors' locker room, "Close the door, and keep Lisa Olson outside. Make sure to leave that dick-watching bitch outside" (Henkel, 1993, p. 2). Olson wasn't even on the North American continent at the time! Yet the new "incident" was reported by three Florida papers and the rival newspaper in Sydney.[20]

Today, as women sportswriters continue to battle the specter of Woody Hayes for acceptance within the locker room of professional men's sports, the issue of access is rearing its ugly head again. This time the focus is on college campuses, where, in the arbitrary hierarchy of sports news values, NCAA Division I and Division IA men's collegiate sport ranks just a cut below men's professional sport. In some media markets such as Columbus, Ohio, a town without a professional baseball, NFL or NBA franchise, news about Ohio State football and basketball fills the sports pages. Access to players and coaches in these programs is vital for a sportswriter. However, the Associated Press Sports Editors' association reports that an increasing number of universities are making female reporters into villains. For example, Notre Dame's locker room is open to reporters, except women. If women demand equal access, the locker room is closed to all reporters (Vacek, 1993). In fact, the two publicly recorded instances of female reporters being denied access to locker rooms in the early 1990s occurred on university campuses. In 1991, Beth Harris of the AP was ejected from the Indiana University locker room by basketball coach Bobby Knight. In 1992, three female reporters from California newspapers were barred from the locker room at San Diego State University.[21]

Yet, as Melissa Ludtke (1990) suggests: "Women in the locker rooms should not be the issue in 1990. Rather, the finger ought to be pointed at the infantile and repugnant behavior of some ballplayers and their inability to adjust to changing times, when gender equality should be assumed" (p. 97).

Even if gender equality is assumed, it's clear that black female reporters in locker rooms haven't achieved equity. The number of Afro-American women covering a sports beat remains minuscule, and they have had their share of hassles. *San Jose Mercury News*'s

Annette John-Hall was forced to wedge her foot in the door of the Golden State Warriors locker room to prevent a guard from locking her out (Turner, 1991). Police disregarded *USA Today* reporter Carolyn White's credentials and arrested her when she attempted to cover the 1988 Super Bowl parade (Turner, 1991)!

Outside of the locker room, the acceptance of Afro-American and other women of color in newspaper sports reporting by the "mainstream" press has been slow. Only a dozen or so black female reporters currently cover professional sports. Finding two black female sportswriters on the same staff is rare, but in 1991 *USA Today* employed both White and Valerie L. Dorsey. White started her sportswriting career in 1977 with the *Akron Beacon-Journal* (Turner, 1991). Another pioneer is Claire Smith, now with *The New York Times*, who started her sportswriting career in 1982 with the *Hartford* (CT) *Courant* (Turner, 1991). Other Afro-American female sports reporters in the 1990s include: Karen Hunter-Hodge, *Daily News* —the only black female employed at a major New York daily in the late 1980s (Layne, 1989); Donna Carter, *Denver Post*; Kelly Carter, *Dallas Morning News*; Merlisa Lawrence, *Pittsburgh Press* (Turner, 1991). In the black press, women are rare as sports reporters. Rhonda Smith, sports editor of the *Los Angeles Sentinel*, is perhaps the most prominent ("Should Women," 1990).

The Status of Women in Newspaper Sportswriting

The newspaper sports pages continue to have a major role in supplying the basic information that fans can't get by watching or listening to the games as they occur. *USA Today* provides routine coverage of men's and women's marquee sports for a national audience. Weekly papers are playing an increasingly important role covering women's high school and community sports. Today, according to Sabo and Jansen (1992), "the sports section of the daily paper is the most widely-read section of major metropolitan newspapers, and more ink is devoted to sports than any other topic, including national and international news" (p. 170). Moreover, 64% of women are regular sport page readers, compared with 85% of men (Simmons, 1991).

Awards and Recognition

Women newspaper sportswriters are being noticed outside the locker room. Although awards and recognition are not a perfect way to measure achievement, they do provide some evidence that women sportswriters have broken through more doors than those with naked, sweaty athletes behind them.

A volume of *Best Sports Stories* has been printed annually since 1944. Irving T. Marsh and Edward Ehre initiated, compiled and edited the volume through 1982. They started by soliciting entries from "sports editors, sports writers, columnists, photographers, copy boys [sic], publishers and men on the street and other avid readers of the sports pages" and awarded a $500 cash prize for the "best" story in a newspaper or magazine (Marsh & Ehre, 1944, p. 9). They put together a panel of three male judges and the first edition of *Best Sports Stories* was born.[22] The first female to be recognized in the volume was *Los Angeles Times* reporter Jeane Hoffman in 1959. "The Chinese Spirit" is her feature story about the new box seat of Dodger owner Walter O'Malley, a mounted wooden platform directly behind the home plate screen, which reminded Hoffman of a pagoda. During the 45 years that *Best Sports Stories* was published, 15 women newspaper sportswriters appeared in 10 volumes of the book. Five female sportswriters were included in the first two editions of a more recent series titled *The Best American Sports Writing* (Stout, 1991). According to the new series' editor, Glenn Stout, he seeks the best *writing about sports* rather than the best *sportswriting*, which is writing that convinces him "after reading it once, to read it again and again" (p. xiii) (see Table 4.3).

A "Mary Garber Female Sportswriter of the Year Award" was established in 1978 at California State University-Northridge and presented through 1983 when funding ran out (Myers, 1984). Winners were: Kathy Maxa, *Washington Star*, 1978; Robin Herman, *New York Times*, 1978; Lesley Visser, *Boston Globe*, 1980; Stephanie Salter, *San Francisco Herald Examiner*, 1981; Pam King, *Los Angeles Herald Examiner*, 1982; Linda Kay, *Chicago Tribune*, 1983 (Myers, p. 226).

The Women's Sports Foundation started an award program in 1986 to recognize and encourage the coverage of women's sports. The awards are presented annually in six categories: daily newspaper,

TABLE 4.3   Sportswriting Awards Won by Women Newspaper Reporters

From *Best Sports Stories*, 1944-1989
1959 Jeane Hoffman, *Los Angeles Times*
1976 Joan Libman, *Wall Street Journal*
1977 Betty Cuniberti, *San Bernardino Sun Telegram*
      Jane Gross, *Newsday*
      Kathleen Maxa, *Washington Star*
1978 Tracy Dodds, *Milwaukee Journal*
      Sheila Moran, *Los Angeles Times*
      Jenny Kellner, *The Record* (Bergen County, NJ)
1979 Amanda Bennett, *Wall Street Journal*
      Betty Cuniberti, *Washington Post*
      Jill Lieber, *Milwaukee Sentinel*
1980 Tracy Dodds, *Milwaukee Journal*
1984 Jane Leavy, *Washington Post*
      Teri Thompson, *Rocky Mountain News*
1985 Jane Leavy, *Washington Post* (2 stories)
1987 Molly Dunham, *Baltimore Evening Sun*
1989 Sally Jenkins, *Washington Post*
      Beth Barrett, *Los Angeles Daily News*

From *Best American Sports Writing*, 1991-1992
1991 Linda Robertson, *Miami Herald*
      Johnette Howard, *National Sports Daily*
      Florence Shinkle, *The St. Louis Post-Dispatch*
1992 Karen Uhlenhuth, *Kansas City Star*
      Linda Robertson, *Miami Herald*
      Donna St. George, *Philadelphia Inquirer*

NOTE: Gross won the top prize in the 1977 news feature category. She was the third woman so honored; the others were magazine reporters.

weekly newspaper, magazine, column, local television and network television. The competition is open to male and female journalists. Judging criteria for the print categories are listed as: uniqueness, accuracy, timeliness, quality of writing and overall presentation of the female as a performer and achiever in sport (St. James & Lopiano, 1992). Judges for this contest are a panel of journalists, chaired by Thomas Hartmann of Rutgers University's Department of Journalism and Mass Media. Among the female sportswriters who have won awards are: Suzanne Haliburton and Shelly Sanford of the *Austin American-Statesman*, 1991; Joan Ryan, *San Francisco Examiner*; Toby Smith, *Albuquerque Journal*; Arlene Schulman, *The Village Voice*, 1992.[23]

Nancy Scannell's work with the *Washington Post* on the legal-business side of sports won awards from the Washington-Baltimore Newspaper Guild and the American Education Writers Association in 1975 ("Women in Sports Journalism," 1976). Women sportswriters have also been honored in the Associated Press Sports Editors writing and editing contests. In 1992, for example, Joan Ryan of the *San Francisco Examiner* won a first place for enterprise reporting for papers with a 50,000 to 175,000 circulation, a second in the event story category and a third in the feature writing category.[24] A team of reporters under the direction of the *Seattle Times*'s Cathy Henkel won in the investigative reporting category.

Increasing Numbers and Education

In the early 1970s, the Associated Press estimated that only about 25 women were sportswriters and about five women were involved in sportscasting on radio and television ("Associated Press Estimate," 1975). By 1975, the estimate had quadrupled (Lapin, 1975). Theberge and Cronk (1986) suggested that the most frequently cited reason for the underrepresentation of women's sports in the media is "the dominance of the journalism profession, especially, sports journalism, by men." Nearly 80% of the female sportswriters in a recent study said there were not enough women in newspaper sportswriting (Eberhard & Myers, 1988).

Certainly, the number of women entering sports journalism has not been nearly as dramatic as the increase in women's participation in sport. One study that looked at the sports departments of the nation's 109 largest daily newspapers found that only 63% employ women as sports reporters (Eberhard & Myers, 1988). Moreover, of the 69 newspapers in the study that did employ women sports reporters, only 9% (96) of the estimated 1,061 sports department employees were female. The number of women working as sports columnists or in management ranks is minuscule. Cyndi Meagher of the *Detroit News* was one of the nation's few female columnists in 1976 ("Women in Sports Journalism," 1976). When the Associated Press named Terry Taylor as its sports editor in 1992, she became one of only a handful of newspaper women with the title in the United States ("The Associated," 1992).[25]

To assist in supporting, retaining and recruiting women in the sports journalism ranks, the Association for Women in the Sports Media was formed in 1987 with 115 members. Christine Brennan of the *Washington Post* served a two-year term as its first president and was followed by Michele Himmelberg of the *Orange County* (CA) *Register* from 1990 to 1991, Tracy Dodds of the *Austin American-Statesman* in 1992 and Cathy Henkel of the *Seattle Times* in 1993. AWSM (acronym pronounced "awesome"), which had grown to 250 members by 1989, has provided an annual scholarship/internship award since 1990 with the help of *Sports Illustrated* and the Gannett newspaper organization.

Although the paths to a sports reporting career are myriad, journalism education could play an increasing role in changing these percentages.[26] Sportswriting is taught as a separate course at 55 U.S. schools of journalism and mass communication and about 34% of course enrollment is female (Creedon, 1993). When this finding is compared with statistics compiled by AWSM, which show that only 3% of the nation's 10,000 print and broadcast sports journalists are women, there may be cause for some cautious optimism. If only a portion of these female students who have shown an interest in sports reporting enter the profession, they could easily double or triple the number of women sportswriters in the United States before the new millennium.

The 1990s may prove that Genevieve Boughner, author of *Women in Journalism: A Guide to the Opportunities and Manual of the Technique of Women's Work for Newspapers and Magazines,* was only about three quarters of a century premature with her prediction in 1929: "Any girl [sic] who takes an intelligent interest in sports and who carefully follows the branches in which she is interested can prepare herself for a place in the sports department of almost any newspaper" (pp. 269-270).

Notes

1. According to Mott (1962, p. 298), the first sports paper in the United States was the *American Turf Register* (1829-1844), which was followed by the *Spirit of the Times* (1831-1902). For the purposes of this chapter, however, the development of the sports page in the mass circulation press is of primary interest.

2. On its masthead, the *New York Clipper* described itself as "The oldest American sporting and theatrical journal" (Stevens, 1987). One of the *Clipper* reporters was Henry Chadwick, considered the first American sportswriter (Betts, 1953; McChesney, 1989; Stevens, 1987). He is often cited for his efforts to popularize baseball.

3. Elizabeth Cochrane chose the pen name Nellie Bly for her first story as a reporter for the *Pittsburgh Dispatch* (Belford, 1986). Because her first story advanced a "revolutionary" theory that women could be as efficient as men in their careers, and because she had decided to write a story in favor of divorce for her second article—also a highly controversial topic at the time—her editor decided she should use a pen name (Jakes, 1969). He reportedly chose it as he heard a copy boy whistling the popular Stephen Foster song: "Nelly Bly, Nelly Bly, bring de broom along" (Belford, p. 119), and she reportedly changed the spelling of the first name.

4. While Nellie was circling the globe west to east, Elizabeth Bisland was dispatched by a rival paper in the opposite direction (Ross, 1965). Bisland also completed the journey, but in 76 days (Brown, 1984).

5. I want to thank Janet Fry Schneider for sharing her work on Mary Bostwick with me, which she completed under the guidance of her advisor Dr. Jonas Bjork at the University of Indiana, Indianapolis campus. I think that her interest in Bostwick is illustrative of the type of work that needs to be done in order to document the existence of many more pioneer women sports journalists.

6. It wasn't until 1973, more than half a century after Bostwick's ride, that the first female reporter was "officially" allowed into the pits at the Indianapolis 500. She was Karol Stringer of the Associated Press ("Associated Press," 1973).

7. I want to thank Susan Birrell for the suggestion that stunts by Bly and Bostwick could be seen as participatory sports journalism.

8. Julia Harpman may also have been a regular sportswriter in Chicago during this period, but she is not mentioned in the text list because the only reference to her work is in the volume *The Greatest Sports Stories From the Chicago Tribune* (Ward, 1953), and no biographical information is included.

9. Hardesty continued in sportswriting for more than 20 years. In 1944, her idea for a "galloping poll" gained her some attention in the journalism community (Duke, 1944). She interviewed more than 100 bettors at the Garden Race Track in Camden, NJ, to assess their opinions on the honesty of horse racing. It ended up as a three-column, front-page story in the *Philadelphia Record* that overshadowed war news of the day.

10. Hickok's work as a political reporter has been the subject of at least five articles written by Maurine Beasley. Her work and relationship with Eleanor Roosevelt has been the subject of several books (see Cook, 1992, and Faber, 1980).

11. The spelling of Hofmann's name is problematic. I have used the spelling from the 1944 article carrying her byline in *Editor & Publisher*. However, it is spelled Jeanne Hoffman in the 1959 edition of *Best Sports Stories*.

12. Some confusion exists with the career of a sportswriter or sportswriters named Mary Flannery. I found references to two Mary Flannery's, both who whom worked in Philadelphia and one of whom is the daughter of another female sportswriting pioneer Rosemary McCarron (see Flannery, 1992; Hardesty, 1944; Lannin, 1987).

13. The apparent tension between feminist scholarship and sport is discussed in Chapter 1 of this book.

14. Although Melissa Ludtke was a magazine reporter at the time, the case is included in the newspaper history chapter because it helps to illustrate the develop-

ment of the locker room issue for print reporters. More detailed history about the involvement of women's sportswriters in magazines is found in Chapter 5.

15. Interestingly, Angell chose to describe the event as the night the "locker rooms became officially heterosexual" (1982, p. 129). He also describes the locker room issue as a "parade float of classical postures in which noble-visaged representations of Propriety, Wholesome Sports, and the Innocence of the American Family are seen to be under attack by similarly admirable figures of Social Mobility, Equal Opportunity, and Freedom of the Press" (p. 129).

16. One study of newspaper stories written about the incident from September 17 through 30, 1990, conducted by Ohio State student David Golden for my graduate seminar in winter 1991, found that the *Boston Globe, Washington Post* and *New York Times* covered the incident as a sports story with a pro-Olson bias.

17. The rumor abounds that the fines have never been paid. Although Kiam apologized to Olson in a full page newspaper ad following the orignial incident, he was forced to apologize to Olson a second time in February 1991 following his remarks at Stamford Old-Timer's Athletic Association meeting. According to reports, Kiam told the following "joke" to the audience: "What do the Iraqis and Lisa Olson have in common? They've both seen Patriot missiles up close" (Garber, 1992).

18. The relationship of sexual and athletic performance is a theme that surfaces often in athletic discourse. Some argue that the relationship between the two created a modern athletic hero starting with Joe Namath. One could argue that Mike Tyson used it as his defense "strategy" in his rape trial in Indianapolis in 1992. Kane and Disch (1993) argue the point from a sociological perspective in a fascinating article in the *Sociology of Sport Journal.*

19. The *Globe* investigative team had no women involved in the analysis. Olson was scheduled to return to the United States for an appearance at the May 1993 Association for Women in Sports Media convention in Minneapolis to respond to questions about the report.

20. Shortly before the incident, Olson had returned to the United States to visit her ill father in Arizona. The Australian paper suggested that she had returned to stir things up in the locker room again. Most recently Olson returned to the United States for the May 1993 Association for Women in Sports Media convention held in Minneapolis, Minnesota.

21. The issue of access to women's locker rooms is sometimes brought up as a counterpoint. Because women's sports coverage has lower value on the arbitrary hierarchy of news, the issue is largely a philosophical one. In cases where there has been reporter interest in post-game interviews, such as at the NCAA Division I women's basketball tournaments, all reporters are allowed access to the locker room for a limited time period immediately following the game (Lederman, 1990). In other cases, separate interview areas have been set up.

22. There was no volume in 1981, but in 1982 the *Sporting News* took over publication of the volume, expanding the writing award categories to four: newspaper features, commentary, reporting and magazine reporting, as well as two categories of photography—black and white and color. The prize money remained $500 for the entry judged best of a category. Judges for the contest since 1982 have been a five-man panel from the University of Missouri School of Journalism. The 1989 volume of *Best Sports Stories* was the last in the series. It has been replaced by another series titled *The Best American Sports Writing,* published by Houghton Mifflin beginning in 1991. Editor Glenn Stout described the criteria for selection for the first

edition: "A story must have been written during 1990, be more than one thousand words long, and must have convinced me, after reading it once, to read it again and again" (p. xiii) (see Table 4.3).

23. In spite of numerous requests, I was unable to secure a complete list of award winners.

24. Two Joan Ryan's have been involved in sportswriting. One began her career in 1964 and was reporting for the *Washington Post* by 1976. The other started her career in 1985 at *The Orlando Sentinel*.

25. Some of the papers that have employed female sports editors include: *The Wichita Eagle*, the *Star-Gazette* (Elmira, NY), *The News Journal* (Wilmington, DE), the *Seattle Times*, the *Austin American-Statesman* and the *News-Gazette* (Champaign, IL).

26. A study by Garrison and Salwen (1989) suggests that newspaper sports journalists have mixed feelings about the value of journalism education, particularly in terms of preparation for sportswriting careers. About 39% of all working journalists are graduates of journalism and mass communication programs (Weaver & Wilhoit, 1992).

References

Angell, Roger. (1979, April 9). Sharing the beat, women sportswriters in locker rooms. *New Yorker*, pp. 46-96.

Angell, Roger. (1982). *Late innings*. New York: Simon & Schuster.

Associated Press estimate. (1975, July 1). *Media Report to Women*, 3(7), 2.

The Associated Press has named. (1992). *Media Report to Women*, 20(4), 9.

Associated Press woman writes sports. (1973, August 25). *Editor & Publisher*, 106(34), 16.

Beasley, Maurine & Silver, Sheila. (1977). *Women in media: A documentary source book*. Washington, DC: Women's Institute for Freedom of the Press.

Belford, Barbara. (1986). *Brilliant bylines*. New York: Columbia University Press.

Bennion, Sherilyn. (1976-77). Fremond Older: Advocate for women. *Journalism History*, 3(4), 124-127.

Bennion, Sherilyn Cox. (1991). Nellie Verrill Mighels Davis: The "spirit of things achieved." *Nevada Historical Society Quarterly*, 34(3), 400-414.

Betts, J. R. (1953). Sporting journalism in nineteenth century America. *American Quarterly*, 5, 39-46.

Bostwick, Mary E. (1922, May 21). Ride in Howdy Wilcox's Peugeot cures desire to be a mechanician [sic]. *Indianapolis Star*, p. 1.

Bostwick, Mary E. (1950). I was a stunt girl. *Page One Program*. Indianapolis, IN: Indianapolis Newspaper Guild.

Boughner, Genevieve Jackson. (1929). *Women in journalism: A guide to the opportunities and a manual of the technique of women's work for newspapers and magazines*. New York: Appleton-Century.

Boutilier, Mary A. & SanGiovanni, Lucinda. (1983). *The sporting woman*. Champaign, IL: Human Kinetics.

Boyle, Robert H. (1963). *Sport: Mirror of American life*. Boston, MA: Little, Brown.

Brenner, Marie. (1993, April 5). Girls of summer. *The New York Times*, p. A17.

Brown, Lea Ann. (1984). Elizabeth Cochrane. In Perry J. Ashley (Ed.), *American newspaper journalists, 1901-1925* (pp. 58-64). Detroit, MI: Gale Research.

Calhoun, Donald W. (1987). *Sport, culture, and personality* (2nd ed.). Champaign, IL: Human Kinetics.

Chance, Jean C. (1984). Adela Rogers St. Johns. In Perry J. Ashley (Ed.), *American newspaper journalists, 1926-1950* (pp. 310-312). Detroit, MI: Gale Research.

Collins, Jean E. (1980). *She was there: Stories of pioneering women journalists.* New York: Julian Messner.

Cook, Blanche Wiesen. (1992). *Eleanor Roosevelt: Volume one, 1884-1933.* New York: Viking.

Creedon, Pamela J. (1993). Training women as sports reporters. *Journalism Educator, 48*(1), 46-51.

Duke, Charles W. (1944, September 2). Girl writer's "galloping poll" hits front page. *Editor & Publisher*, p. 63.

Eberhard, Wallace B. & Myers, Margaret Lee. (1988). Beyond the locker room: Women in sports on major daily newspapers. *Journalism Quarterly, 65*, 595-599.

Emery, Edwin. (1954). *The press and America.* Englewood Cliffs, NJ: Prentice Hall.

Faber, Doris. (1980). *The life of Lorena Hickok: ER's friend.* New York: William Morrow.

Fegan, Lois. (1990, November 24). Advice from a woman sportswriter who's been there. *Editor & Publisher*, pp. 37, 48.

Feud flares over girl sports writer. (1944, April 8). *Editor & Publisher*, p. 43.

Flannery, Mary. (1992, November). Women sportswriters of the 1940s needed a lot of ingenuity. *ASNE Bulletin*, p. 29.

Garber, Angus G. (1992). *Sports scandals and controversies.* New York: Smithmark.

Garrison, Bruce. (1985). *Sports reporting.* Ames, IA: Iowa State University Press.

Garrison, Bruce & Salwen, Michael. (1989). Newspaper sports journalists: A profile of the profession. *Journal of Sport and Social Issues, 13*(2), 57-68.

Gentry, Diane K. (1991). *Interview with Mary Garber.* Women in Journalism Oral History Project of the Washington Press Club Foundation, August 28, 1990.

Gibboney, Douglas. (1975). Female sportswriters are here to stay. *PNPA Press, 48*(3), 7.

Gordon, Alison. (1984). *Foul balls: Five years in the American League.* Toronto: McClelland and Stewart.

Hardesty, Betty. (1944, May 27). Another girl sports writer enters arena. *Editor & Publisher*, p. 60.

Heath, Harry E. & Gelfand, Louis I. (1951). *How to cover, write and edit sports.* Ames, IA: Iowa State College Press.

Henkel, Cathy. (1993, February). A word from the president. *AWSM Newsletter.* Association for Women in the Sports Media.

Henry, Susan. (1990). *Near-sightedness and blind spots in studying the history of women in journalism.* Paper presented at the American Journalism Historians Conference, Coeur d'Alene, Idaho.

Hofmann, Jeane. (1944, April 22). Takes issue with "For men only" on sports page. *Editor & Publisher*, p. 44.

Hollander, Phyllis. (1976). *100 greatest women in sports.* New York: True Books.

Jackson, Derrick Z. (1990, September 28). Thumbs down on Kiam act. *The Boston Globe*, p. 17.

Jakes, John. (1969). *Great women reporters.* New York: G. P. Putnam.

Jenkins, Sally. (1991, June 17). Who let them in? *Sports Illustrated*, pp. 78-90.

Kane, Mary Jo & Disch, Lisa. (1993). Sexual violence and the reproduction of male power in the locker room: A case study of the Lisa Olson "incident." *Sociology of Sport Journal, 10*(4).

Kay, Linda. (1985, November). In defense of sportswriters. *Women's Sports and Fitness*, p. 60.

Lady football writers get mixed reaction. (1947, October 25). *Editor & Publisher*, p. 24.

Lannin, Joanne. (1987, March). Assignment: Sports. *Women's Sports & Fitness*, pp. 77-78, 95.

Lapin, Jackie. (1975). A new generation of sportswriters in the press box. *Matrix*, 60(4), 5-6.

Layne, Patricia. (1989, November 15-21). Sports writer: Karen Hunter-Hodge. *City Sun*, Brooklyn, NY, p. 22.

Leavy, Jane. (1990). My book tour diary. *Gannett Center Journal*, 4(2), 58-67.

Lederman, Douglas. (1990, October. 17). Furor over access to locker rooms reaches colleges in incident at U. of N.C. *The Chronicle of Higher Education*, p. A41, A44.

LeUnes, Arnold D. & Nation, Jack R. (1989). *Sports psychology*. New York: Nelson-Hall.

Logie, Iona Robertson. (1938). *Careers for women in journalism*. Scranton, PA: International Textbook.

Long, Barbara. (1975, May). Memoirs of a feisty sportswriter. *womenSports*, pp. 20, 21, 41-42.

Luckett, Margie H. (1942). *Maryland women*. Baltimore, MD: King Brothers Press.

Ludtke, Melissa. (1990, Oct. 15). They use bathrobes. *Time*, p. 97.

Marsh, Irving T. & Ehre, Edward. (1944). *Best sports stories of 1944*. New York: E. P. Dutton.

Marsh, Irving T. & Ehre, Edward. (1959). *Best sports stories of 1959*. New York: E. P. Dutton.

Marsh, Irving T. & Ehre, Edward. (1977). *Best sports stories of 1977*. New York: E. P. Dutton.

Marsh, Irving T. & Ehre, Edward. (1978). *Best sports stories of 1978*. New York: E. P. Dutton.

Marsh, Irving T. & Ehre, Edward. (1979). *Best sports stories of 1979*. New York: E. P. Dutton.

Marzolf, Marion. (1977). *Up from the footnote*. New York: Hastings House.

McChesney, Robert W. (1989). Media made sport: A history of sports coverage in the United States. In Lawrence A. Wenner (Ed.), *Media, sports & society* (pp. 49-69). Newbury Park, CA: Sage.

Media women object to inconsistent use of Mrs./Miss/Mr. in new AP-UPI stylebook. (1976, November 1). *Media Report to Women*, p. 1.

Mills, Kay. (1988). *A place in the news*. New York: Dodd, Mead.

Moran, Sheila. (1976). The media's getting the message: Newspapers. *womenSports*, 13(9), 41.

Mott, Frank Luther. (1962). *American journalism* (3rd ed.). New York: Macmillan.

Myers, Margaret Lee. (1984). *The female sportswriter in America: A national survey and profile of women sportswriters at large metropolitan daily newspapers*. Unpublished master's thesis, University of Georgia, Athens, Georgia.

Nan O'Reilly dead; editor and author. (1937, March 1). *New York Times*.

Nelson, Kevin. (1981, February). Meet Adeline Daley, one of the first female sportswriters. *Women's Sports*, pp. 16-17,

The New York Times. (1978, November 20). *Newsweek*, p. 133.

Owen, Janet Valborg. (1930, Feb. 15). Women in sports. *New York Evening World*, p. 12.

Owen, Janet Valborg. (1930, March 1). Women in sports. *New York Evening World*, p. 10.

Plimpton, George. (1961). *Out of my league.* New York: Harper.

Plimpton, George. (1966). *Paper lion.* New York: Harper & Row.

Rayne, M. L. (1884). *What can a woman do? Or her position in the business and literary world.* Detroit: F. B. Dickerson.

Ricchiardi, Sherry & Young, Virginia. (1991). *Women on deadline.* Ames, IA: Iowa State University Press.

Rice, Grantland. (1948). The golden panorama. In Allison Danzig & Peter Brandwein (Eds.), *Sport's golden age* (pp. 1-7). New York: Harper & Row.

Richwine, Keith M. (1983). *Mrs. Miller's Maryland.* Westminster, MD: Western Maryland College.

Robertson, Nan. (1992). *The girls in the balcony.* New York: Random House.

Ross, Ishbel. (1936). *Ladies of the press.* New York: Harper & Brothers.

Ross, Ishbel. (1965). *Charmers and cranks.* New York: Harper & Row.

Sabo, Donald & Jansen, Sue Curry. (1992). Images of men in sports media: The social reproduction of the gender order. In Steve Craig (Ed.), *Men, masculinity, and the media* (pp. 169-184). Newbury Park, CA: Sage.

Schneider, Janet Fry. (1992, December). *She didn't want to miss anything: Mary Bostwick, a noteworthy reporter.* Unpublished paper. School of Journalism, Indiana University at Indianapolis.

Scott, Jim. (1973, January 11). The sports page. *Editor & Publisher, 106*(2), 24.

Shah, Diane K. (1978, January 16). Locker-room lib. *Newsweek,* p. 86.

Should women be barred from locker rooms? (1990, October 29). *Jet,* pp. 53-54, 56.

Simmons. (1991). *Study of media and markets.* Simmons Market Research Bureau, New York.

Smith, Wendy. (1990, January 12). LeAnne Schreiber. *Publishers Weekly,* pp. 40-41.

Sparhawk, Ruth M., Leslie, Mary E., Turbow, Phyllis Y. & Rose, Zina R. (1989). *American women in sport: 1887-1987, a 100-year chronology.* Metuchen, NJ: The Scarecrow Press.

St. James, Lyn & Lopiano, Donna. (1992, June 3). *Miller Lite Women's Sports Journalism Awards.* New York: Women's Sports Foundation.

Stevens, John. (1987). The rise of the sports page. *Gannett Center Journal, 1*(2), 1-11.

Stout, Glenn. (Ed). (1991). *The best American sports writing 1991.* Boston: Houghton Mifflin.

Theberge, Nancy. (1981). A critique of critiques: Radical and feminist writings on sport. *Social Forces, 60*(2), 341-353.

Theberge, Nancy & Cronk, Alan. (1986). Work routines in newspaper sports departments and the coverage of women's sports. *Sociology of Sports Journal, 3,* 195-203.

Thomas, Dawn F. (1977). Sarah Kneller Miller, 1867-1920. In Winifred C. Helmes (Ed.), *Notable Maryland women.* Cambridge, MD: Tidewater Publishers.

Turner, Renee D. (1991, February). Black women sportswriters and the locker room wars. *Ebony,* pp. 170, 172-174.

Twyman, Lisa. (1983, September 5). Mileposts; Died. *Sports Illustrated,* p. 67.

Vacek, Rick. (1993, February). Study: Press access getting a runaround. *AWSM Newsletter.* Association for Women in Sports Media, Mililani, HI.

Vare, Robert. (1974). *Buckeye.* New York: Popular Library.

Ward, Arch. (Ed.). (1953). *The greatest sports stories from the Chicago Tribune.* New York: A. S. Barnes.

Watson-Rouslin, Virginia. (1987, January). The men's room. *The Quill,* pp. 20-24.

Weaver, David & Wilhoit, G. Cleveland. (1992, November 17). *The American journalist in the 1990s: Preliminary report*. Arlington, VA: The Freedom Forum.

Whitaker, Leslie. (1990, October 15). Trouble in the locker rooms. *Time*, p. 97.

Williams, Linda D. (1988). *An analysis of American sportswomen in two Negro newspapers: The* Pittsburgh Courier, *1924-1948 and the* Chicago Defender, *1932-1948*. Eugene, OR: Microforms Publications, College of Human Development and Performance, University of Oregon.

Woman sportswriter sues to open locker room. (1978, January 14.) *Editor & Publisher*, p. 11.

Woman writes sports for Albany daily. (1929, April 6). *Editor & Publisher*, p. 48.

Women in sports journalism: Newspapers. (1976, October). *womenSports*, pp. 40-41.

Women: Not welcome in the locker room. (1991, January). *Women's Sports Pages*, 4(1), 6-7, 13.

5

From Whalebone to Spandex

Women and Sports Journalism in American Magazines, Photography and Broadcasting

Pamela J. Creedon

> I suddenly had a passion to *be* that ordinary girl. To be that good little housewife, that glorified American mother, that mascot from *Mademoiselle*, that matron from *McCall's*, that cutie from *Cosmo*, that girl with the *Good Housekeeping* Seal tattooed on her ass and advertising jingles programmed in her brain.
>
> Erica Jong, *Fear of Flying* (1973, pp. 277-278)

Women's sports have had a tight and often exploitative economic relationship with beauty and apparel norms in America. Nowhere is this more evident than in the highly visual media of magazines and television. In order to see how this relationship developed and understand why it is so powerful today, in this chapter I will pull the whalebone stays from the corsets of the 1800s and stretch the spandex of the 1990s. I will look at magazine journalism, photojournalism and sports broadcasting and the relationship of these fields

AUTHOR'S NOTE: I received a number of valuable comments on various portions of this chapter. I wish to thank Beverly Bethune, Judy Cramer, Marlaine Francis, Jim Harless, Sammye Johnson, Susan Kaufman, Ken Metzler, Lisa Rubarth and Linda Steiner.

to women's sports and to fashion and beauty standards. Along the way, I will also take a first step toward recovering some of the many contributions made by American women journalists in sports magazines and photography as well as in radio and television sports announcing and broadcasting.

Ever hear of Phillip K. Wrigley? Sure. Well then, how about Judith Cary Waller? Never? She was just as important to baseball as he was. Did you know that sportswomen had their own prime-time television show on NBC in 1948 hosted by a female sportscaster? No? It would be easy to fill an entire volume with the material about women in sports journalism squeezed into this chapter. Its four major sections —magazines, photography, radio and television—are presented in order of their development in the context of sports journalism. Each section briefly outlines the history of sports journalism in the field and the role of women in it. Newspaper sports journalism is covered in Chapter 4.

Magazines: From Whalebone to Bloomers

Magazines brought the first news of amateur sport to Americans in the early 1800s and played a very important role in popularizing sport in America. Frederick Cozens and Florence Stumpf (1953) argue that a "substantial part of the total answer as to why sports are such a vital part of American culture lies in the persistent campaign of publicity, promotion, and propaganda which has been carried on through the medium of the periodical press" (p. 127). By tracing their development, we can learn a good deal about American attitudes toward women's sports coverage.

When the first sport stories began to appear in magazines in the 1820s, many Americans considered sports a vulgar and distasteful pastime. Early magazine writers covering sports often used pen names to protect their identities (Berryman, 1979; Heath & Gelfand, 1951; McChesney, 1989). However, increasing industrialization created more leisure time, which helped to loosen the grip of puritan prescriptions against sport. Between 1820 and 1835, seven sporting magazines started publishing (only two of these survived more than three years), by the 1860s there were nine and in the 1890s some 48 sports magazines were publishing (Betts, 1953; McChesney, 1989).

The *American Turf Register and Sporting Magazine* is most often cited as the first periodical devoted exclusively to sport (Berryman, 1979; Mott, 1966). A weekly horse racing journal, it first appeared in September 1829. The monthly *Turf Register* was a spin-off from the "Sporting Olio" section of the *American Farmer*, an eight-page weekly first published in 1819 (Berryman, 1979). The "Sporting Olio" section first appeared in 1825, covering a broad range of sports news such as fox hunting, horse racing, fishing and hunting (Berryman, 1979; Berryman & Brislin, 1982). Heath and Gelfand (1951) argue that "as the first magazine inclined to give space to sports, the *American Farmer* is the real forerunner of the hundreds of sports periodicals in this country today" (p. 29).[1] In any event, magazine historians do agree that John Stuart Skinner is the "Father of American Sports Journalism"; he started both magazines.

Skinner's *American Farmer*, published until 1897, may have been the first magazine in the sporting genre to advocate exercise in the form of sport for women. Nine months after the "Sporting Olio" section debuted, "The Ladies Department" was added (Berryman & Brislin, 1982). Although the column maintained an aura of tradition by including recipes and household tips, it regularly included materials pertaining to women's and children's physical health and exercise (Berryman & Brislin, 1982). In particular, it pointed out the health and mobility problems associated with corsets made of whalebone stays laced tightly around a woman's midsection:

> Strong stays, which do the duty of the muscles placed by nature around the spine, cause the muscles to dwindle from inaction. . . . A healthy young woman . . . if braced up in tight stays, according to town fashions will frequently exhibit, at the end of a short time, such a wasting of the flesh, that the points of bone in the spine may be counted in the eye. (*American Farmer*, April 18, 1828, p. 38, cited in Berryman & Brislin, 1982)

Sports coverage in the *American Farmer* paled, however, when compared with *The National Police Gazette*, which began publishing in 1845 in New York City. The connection between sports journalism and the objectification of women as sex objects began, perhaps, with the *Gazette*. It was a new breed of sports magazine, featuring "buxom showgirls, scandals, hangings, red-tinted paper, and spicy stories" (Betts, 1953, p. 50). The coupling of beauty, sport and sensation in the *Gazette* was surely no coincidence.

Printed on shockingly pink paper and distributed at discount rates to such all-male preserves as barbershops, livery stables, saloons, private men's clubs, and volunteer fire departments, the notorious weekly exploited to the fullest the nation's racial bigotry, secret sexual lusts, and thirst for the sensational. Repeated libel suits and efforts by postal authorities to suppress the *Gazette* only served to increase its circulation (Rader, 1983, p. 19).

With the *Gazette* leading the pack, sports magazines competed with newspapers in yellow or sensational journalism by sponsoring contests and awarding prizes for boxing matches, teethlifting, hog butchering, clog dancing and female weightlifting. The *Gazette* boasted a nationwide weekly circulation of 150,000 in the late 1800s; newsstand sales of one issue in 1880 reached a record 400,000 copies (Betts, 1953).

The *Gazette*'s impressive circulation figures helped to awaken the newspaper and magazine industry to the economic value of sports news (see Chapter 4). Readers of sports news could be sold as a potential market for products to a growing advertising industry. National interest in sports also prompted advertisers to incorporate sports images in their general circulation magazine ads in the early 1900s. A 1905 Coca-Cola ad in *Harper's*, for example, shows "a young man in golfing costume carrying his clubs and a young woman dressed for tennis with her racket in hand" (Cozens & Stumpf, 1953, p. 140). And the use of sports images by advertisers prompted an increase in news about sporting activities, outdoor living and the playground movement in the general circulation magazines.

A new genre of magazine focusing exclusively on field sports was launched in the last three decades of the 19th century. *Field and Stream*, which debuted in 1873, is the most prominent survivor of the nearly 30 magazines that entered the fray (Betts, 1953). *Outing*, first published in 1882, was the most significant of the group for women, particularly because it boldly endorsed the "shedding of corsets before a round" of golf (Schinto, 1977).[2] Described as "the most responsible magazine for acquainting the public with the wonders of life in the mountains, the lakes, the forests, and the streams," *Outing* refused to carry baseball news for nearly a decade after the national pastime was rocked by scandals in the 1890s (Betts, 1953, p. 48). Libraries and public schools responded to *Outing*'s ethical image and good writing by subscribing, and its circulation reached nearly 90,000 in the late 1800s. Its excellent circulation figures also contributed to the increased coverage of outdoor sports by general circulation magazines such as *Collier's* and the *Saturday Evening Post* (Betts, 1953, 1974).

In all of the literature reviewed for this chapter, the only mention of a contribution by a woman in the early sport magazine industry is found in the centennial history of *The Sporting News*. Marie T. Spink, involved with the publication from its inception, worked as vice president and treasurer of the publication from 1914 until her death in 1944. The first issue of the eight-page journal in 1886 contained stories on baseball, driving, bicycling, boxing, hunting, horse racing and the theater (Reidenbaugh, 1985). Her obituary in the magazine said that she "exerted a greater influence on baseball and baseball journalism than any other woman in the history of the game" (p. 71).[3]

The "Bloomer Girls"

Many early nonsports periodicals advocated women's participation in sport and exercise. *The New York Mirror* and *Ladies' Literary Gazette*, founded as a fashionable society journal in 1823, advocated some forms of physical activity for women in its editorial columns throughout the 1830s (Mott, 1966). In 1829 the *Journal of Health* advocated exercise for men and women, and in 1832 another periodical, the *Casket: Flowers of Literature, Wit and Sentiment*, printed some woodcuts illustrating women in corsets and pantalets exercising while holding onto a swing (Mott, 1966).

Women wrote about sports and exercise in their own magazines as well. Subscriber-supported women's magazines first appeared in the 1790s, but they were designed for upper-class, wealthy readers (Zuckerman, 1991). However, increasing literacy brought new readers to magazines by the 1830s. In January 1849, the first issue of *The Lily*, considered by some scholars to be America's first woman's suffrage periodical, appeared (Steiner, 1989). Steiner (personal communication, May 25, 1993) suggests that editor and publisher of the magazine,

Amelia Bloomer, advocated for a "new" woman, a sensible woman, one who was active, did exercise, rode a bicycle and ate healthful foods. The significance of the publication for the sporting woman is the fact that Bloomer wore—and editorially defended—"bifurcated trousers" as a healthy form of dress for this new kind of woman. According to Marzolf (1977), "Bloomer and Elizabeth Cady Stanton were among the first women . . . to adopt the costume of long, full Turkish trousers worn under a short, below-the-knee skirt" (p. 223). Although Bloomer did not invent the trousers, they were dubbed "bloomers" because of her role in publicizing them in *The Lily*. She printed daguerreotypes (early metal photographs) of herself wearing them, instructions for making them and advertisements for purchasing them in her magazine.[4]

In their first appearance on the fashion scene, bloomers did not pull the stays out of women's corsets. Instead, they became a symbol used to trivialize the women's rights movement by the mainstream media (Hole & Levine, 1989). Health reformers did not drop the issue of dress reform, however, and by the 1890s "bloomer girl" baseball teams had sprung up across the country (Gregorich, 1993). Some of these teams continued to compete into the 1930s, eventually wearing more traditional baseball clothing.[5]

Other magazine articles promoting the value of exercise influenced socially prominent women. *Godey's Lady's Book*, for example, encouraged leisure-class women to play sports including golf, tennis and swimming. Anne O'Hagan wrote a lengthy article in *Munsey's Magazine* in August 1901 declaring that aside from improvements in legal status, the best things that had happened to women in the previous century were dress reform and the bicycle (O'Hagan, 1901). When bloomers were accepted as the proper attire for girls and women to wear *indoors* for exercising, women started playing basketball and an estimated 30,000 American women—including many female journalists—owned and rode bicycles in the closing decade of the 19th century.

In the early 1900s, Emma E. Walker, M.D., wrote a column in *Ladies' Home Journal* titled "Good Health for Girls" that covered golf, tennis and rowing among other sports. In the March 1902 issue, for example, she "discussed the latest fad among New York girls, the use of the punching bag to solve the problem of indoor exercise" (Cozens & Stumpf, 1953, p. 134).

Fitness became a national priority when it was revealed that one third of the men drafted into the armed forces in World War I were physically unfit (Edwards, 1973). Government funding poured into the educational system to support the development of physical education programs—for women and men—during the economic boom after the war.

Stephanie L. Twin (1979) describes the postwar period as the first wave of athletic feminism. American women entered Olympic competition in 1920 and participated in the Women's World Games in 1922 (Twin, 1979). Agnes R. Wayman of Barnard College wrote regularly about sports in the official Girl Scout magazine, *The American Girl*, in the 1920s (Henry, n.d.). The first "Women as Athletes" category in the *Reader's Guide to Periodical Literature* appeared in 1922 (Twin, 1979, p. xxx).

The boom period of the 1920s was also known as America's Golden Age of Sports, or at least the Golden Age of Sportswriting (Lipsyte, 1975). The media seized on the national interest in sports to capture readers by creating national heroes out of the likes of Babe Ruth, Jack Dempsey and Knute Rockne (see Chapter 4). Women athletes such as tennis stars Helen Wills and Glenna Collett, however, were portrayed as feminine and fashionable, health conscious in their leisure pursuits, as goddesses rather than as athletic heroines. Wills, the top female tennis player between 1923 and 1935, for example, "was praised for 'upholding the wonderful womanhood that uses sports to enhance its womanly charm instead of to affect an artificial masculinity' " ("Sketches from," 1926, p. 66, cited in Twin, 1979, p. xxx). One study of ads in the 1928 issues of *Ladies' Home Journal* and *Cosmopolitan*, for example, found more women shown participating in physical activity or sport than in issues of the same magazines in 1956 or 1972 (Poe, 1975).

Tensions, however, between female physical educators and civic leaders over the participation of women in competitive athletics surfaced.[6] Concerns about physiological differences between men and women and the reification of competition in men's athletics were at the heart of the controversy. Men's athletics were characterized as "joyless, elitist, exploitive, money-making enterprises without educational value" (Twin, 1979, p. xxxii). Although the Girl Scout movement directed by its president Lou Henry Hoover (aka Mrs. Herbert Hoover) had helped to popularize interest in physical activity for women, it opposed the idea of equal physical standards for men and women. Later as First Lady, Lou Hoover, who had played —in bloomers—on Stanford University's first women's basketball team sometime between 1896 and 1898, presided over the Women's Division of the National Amateur Athletic Federation, which promoted anti-competition initiatives (Messenger, 1977).[7]

The country's attention turned to the economy in the 1930s. Sportswriters turned away from the "Gee Whiz" approach that had created superhuman male sports idols to the "Aw Nuts" school (Lipsyte, 1975). Readers wanted more than fake heroes, and editors demanded better reporting. Professional sports remained a national diversion, but sport fashion and leisure time activities became largely the province of the wealthy again.

As the country came out of the Great Depression, opportunities for women to participate in competitive athletics increased and in some cases involved the commercialization of their bodies. Roller Derby, for example, started in 1935 by Leo Seltzer, included women as a publicity gimmick with the intention of building gate receipts (Twin, 1979). Opportunities for women of all socioeconomic classes in sports expanded even more during World War II because few men were available to play professional sports such as baseball (for a discussion of the All-American Girls Baseball League, see Chapter 9).

On the media front, when the economic situation in the United States improved near the end of World War II, the sports magazine industry experienced another growth spurt, much as it had after the Civil War. *Sport* began in 1946, *Sports Digest* in 1944, *Sports Graphic* in 1946, *Sports Album* in 1948, *Sports Leaders* in 1948, *Sport Life* in 1948 and *Sports World* in 1949. Henry Luce introduced *Sports Illustrated* in 1954. Specialty sports periodicals such as *Golf Digest*, *World Tennis* and the *Daily Racing Form* began publication.

A number of women, who were not regular sports reporters, wrote sports feature stories for the *Saturday Evening Post*, *Liberty* and others. Carol Hughes's article, "Heart of a Ballplayer," which ran in *Coronet* in June 1945, was the first story written by a woman selected for *Best Sports Stories* (Marsh & Ehre, 1946). Hughes, a contributing

editor at *Coronet* at the time, profiled Pete Gray, a one-armed baseball player.

> Professional baseball, like any other business, grants no favors. There's
> more money for the winners, and the way to win is to learn your
> opponent's weaknesses and play to them. Pete likes it that way. He
> asks no quarter and he certainly gives none. He expects batters to
> hit high flies in his direction knowing that the split seconds it takes
> him to let the ball roll out of his glove and onto his arm while he sticks
> the glove under the nub of the right arm and gets the ball into his
> hand ready for a throw— that extra time might let a runner score or
> advance a base. (Hughes, 1945, as cited in Marsh & Ehre, 1944, p. 26).

Jeane Hoffman was executive editor of the *Police Gazette* between
1949 and 1951 (Marsh & Ehre, 1959). Jane Perry's work at *Sports Illustrated* was included in the 1956 volume of *Best Sports Stories*, and
Barbara Heilman, who started as a secretary at *SI* in 1956 and was
reporting for the magazine by 1959, had her work included in *Best
Sports Stories* by 1962. Nancy Williamson, considered by some as the
first modern woman sportswriter, started at *SI* in 1959. She would
later make "sociological as well as sports history . . . [e]xposing the
discrimination and exploding the myths that oppress female athletes"
in a three-part series in the magazine in 1973 (Hogan, 1976, p. 49).[8]
Jane Gross started as a researcher and sports reporter at *SI* after gradu-
ating from Skidmore College in 1969 (Marsh & Ehre, 1977). See Table
5.1 for a list of outstanding women magazine sportswriters.

The Emergence of Women's Sports Magazines

The earliest women's sports magazine may have been *The Sportswoman* published from 1924 to 1936 by the U.S. Field Hockey Association, an organization of women physical educators (Twin, 1979).
The magazine had its own staff of college students and teachers and
used contributions from high school students as well. It reported
standings and results of tournaments and meets and ran profiles of
athletes. The editorial philosophy of the magazine "energetically
promoted play days, minimized Olympic coverage, and denounced
professionalism and scholastic 'semi-professionalism'" (Twin, 1979,
p. xxxiii).

TABLE 5.1 Sportswriting Awards Won by Women Magazine Writers

From Best Sports Stories, 1944-1989

1945	Carol Hughes, *Coronet*
1949	Mary Stuhldreher, *Saturday Evening Post*
1950	Maurine Neuberger, *Liberty*
1954	Margaret Lawrence Cosgrove, *Outdoor Life*
1955	Edith Roberts, *Coronet*
	Jean Butts Jones, *Saturday Evening Post*
1956	Jane Perry, *Sports Illustrated*
1957	Joan Flynn Dreyspool, *Sports Illustrated*[a]
1962	Barbara Heilman, *Sports Illustrated*
1966	Doris DeCleene, *Outdoor Life*[b]
1975	Catherine Bell, *Tennis Magazine*
1976	Catherine Bell, *Tennis Magazine*
1977	Jolee Edmondson, *Golf Magazine*
1983	Susan Brenneman, *Women's Sports*
1984	Kim Cunningham, *World Tennis*
1987	Judy Mills, *Women's Sports & Fitness*
1988	Candace Lyle Hogan, *Women's Sports & Fitness*
	Joan Mellen, *Philadelphia Magazine*

NOTE: *Best Sports Stories* was an annual volume of sports writing from 1944 to 1990. See Chapter 4 for more detail about the contest criteria and judging.
[a]Dreyspool's story about Babe Didrikson Zaharias and her husband won first place in the magazine category. A freelance magazine writer, Dreyspool published her unique "conversation piece" stories in many magazines, including at least eight in *Sports Illustrated*.
[b]DeCleene is described in the book's biography section as a "nonprofessional writer and the first lady we've had in this volume in years" (Marsh & Ehre, 1966, p. 308).

Ironically, *The Woman Bowler* started publishing the same year that *The Sportswoman* ceased publishing. Now 58 years old, it's the oldest continuously published women's sports consumer magazine. The first 16-page issue of *The Woman Bowler* in May 1936 featured a logo spelling "Woman" in bowling pins (Karcher, 1991). In 1947, Georgia E. Veatch was named its first female editor. Helen Latham, editor from 1972-1979, was among the first group of women to be admitted to the male-only Bowling Writer's Association of America in 1976. The official publication of the Women's International Bowling Congress since 1939, *Woman Bowler* (it dropped the article in 1986) has a circulation of 100,000 and is published eight times a year at a subscription cost of $6 in a four-color, 62-page format ("Magazine Directory," 1992).[9]

Aside from *Woman Bowler*, no new women's sports publications of any lasting significance were started from the late 1930s until the 1970s. This coincides with the end of what is considered to be the first wave of athletic feminism in the 1920s and 1930s and the beginning of the second wave in the 1970s, which once again pushed at the boundaries of appropriate physical competition for women (Twin, 1979).

Combining both the crusade for physical activity for health reasons in early women's magazines and the physical activity for fitness push in magazines during the post-World War I era, sports for health and fitness became "chic" for women in the 1970s:

> *Glamour* now includes a sports report in its monthly "How to Do Anything Better" column. *Ms.*, *Playgirl*, and *Seventeen* run monthly sports columns. *Ladies' Home Journal* has sponsored the women's portion of the superstar's competition for the last three years; *Redbook* presents annual awards at the Amateur Athletic [sic] Union Track and Field Championships; and *Seventeen* now promotes its own "Teen Tennis Tourney." (Leavy, 1977, p. 53)

The actual amount of editorial space devoted to sports events in these magazines remained very low. Often the stories focused on personalities, how to's, fashion, beauty, fitness or sex discrimination, instead of sport event coverage.

In the spring of 1973 about 85 sports magazines were publishing, most of which featured male sports written for male audiences. A few specialty magazines dealt exclusively with women's sports, such as *The Lady Golfer*, written and published by Dorothy Pease beginning in the 1950s (Glenn, 1991). Several sports organizations published their own magazines for women, such as *The Eagle* for field hockey and *Crosse Checks* for lacrosse (Bateman, 1977). In addition, about 360,000 women were reading *Golf Digest* and about 110,000 subscribed to *Sports Illustrated*. Into this environment came a new women's sports magazine, using the same title but as one word—sans the article—as the earlier field hockey publication. *Sportswoman*, a 30-page quarterly, covered local and regional sporting events, interscholastic and intercollegiate competition, amateur athletics and other non- marquee sports (Boutilier & SanGiovanni, 1983).[10] Editor

Marlene Jensen and her staff tied their coverage to the feminist agenda, including pay equity and Title IX discrimination issues:

> Every issue featured prominent sportswomen. . . . But coverage wasn't limited to the Superstars. Every issue gave descriptions and results of the major collegiate and amateur championships that had taken place that month. The events weren't covered as phenomena but as sports events, and readers were addressed not as neophytes but as knowledgeable sportswomen. (Tyson, 1976b, p. 4)

Jensen started the magazine as a grassroots operation in Los Angeles with an $11,000 investment and charged $225 for a full-page ad (Bateman, 1977).[11] Plagued by limited financial resources, *Sportswoman* temporarily ceased publication in October 1975. A change in publishers revived the magazine for a brief time with Molly Tyson as editor, followed by Lorraine Rorke, but it ceased publication for good in 1977 (Boutilier & SanGiovanni, 1983; "Sportswoman," 1977).

Competition from a second magazine targeting women's sports fans undoubtedly contributed to the demise of *Sportswoman*. Ironically, tennis star Billie Jean King, featured on the first cover of *Sportswoman*, was the founder of the new magazine. She and her husband, Larry W. King, premiered their magazine in June 1974.[12]

> The idea for *womenSports* crystallized as Larry and I were driving across the Bay Bridge to San Francisco. . . . I was paging through a *Sports Illustrated* complaining, as I usually did, that *SI* rarely wrote stories about women, and when they did, it was because they had nice legs rather than because they were accomplished athletes. (King, 1974, p. 4)

In June 1974, the first issue of *womenSports* magazine hit the newsstands.[13] It was billed as a woman's magazine about sports to advertisers of beauty, health, travel, nutrition, alcohol and tobacco products. The editorial department believed its mission was to produce a magazine for all women who cared about sports and physical culture. (See Table 5.2 for an overall view of the magazine's volatile history.)

Rosalie Muller Wright, the first editor of *womenSports*, had worked in magazine journalism in Philadelphia for several years but had no

TABLE 5.2 Editors and Publishers of *womenSports* magazine,1974-1993

Years	Editor	Publisher
6/74-7/75	Rosalie Muller Wright	WomenSports Publishing (Billie Jean & Larry King, plus limited partners) San Mateo, CA
8/75-12/75	Larry King	WomenSports Publishing (Billie Jean & Larry King, plus limited partners) San Mateo, CA
1/76-3/76	JoAnn Finnegan	WomenSports Publishing (Billie Jean & Larry King, plus limited partners) San Mateo, CA
4/76-11/76	Pamela Van Wagenen	Charter Publishing Company (Billie Jean King, Publisher) New York, NY
12/76-1/78	LeAnne Schreiber	Charter Publishing Company (Billie Jean King, Publisher) New York, NY
2/78-12/78	Publication suspended	
1/79-4/80	Margaret Roach	Women's Sports Publications, Palo Alto, CA, Douglas H. Latimer
5/80-10/80	Greg Hoffman Sue Hoover	Women's Sports Publications, Palo Alto, CA, Douglas H. Latimer
11/80-12/81	Sue Hoover	Women's Sports Publications, Palo Alto, CA, Douglas H. Latimer
1/82-5/85	Amy Rennert	Women's Sports Publications, Palo Alto, CA, Douglas H. Latimer
6/85	Amy Rennert Martha Nelson	Women's Sports Publications, Palo Alto, CA, Douglas H. Latimer
7/85-12/87	Martha Nelson	Women's Sports Publications, Palo Alto, CA, Douglas H. Latimer
1/88-7/88	Nancy Crowell	World Publications Inc., Winter Park, FL Douglas H. Latimer
8/88-5/89	Lewis Rothlein	World Publications Inc., Winter Park, FL, Douglas H. Latimer
6/89-3/90	Lewis Rothlein	World Publications Inc., Winter Park, FL, Terry L. Snow
4/90-12/90	Jane McConnell	Women's Sports & Fitness, Inc., Boulder, CO, Priscilla P. Macy
1/91-4/93	Marjorie McCloy	Women's Sports & Fitness, Inc., Boulder, CO, Jane McConnell

NOTE: Data for this table were compiled from information appearing in mastheads in *women-Sports*, *Women's Sports* and *Women's Sports & Fitness*. Monthly issues of *womenSports* were published for Volumes 1-5 from 1974 to 1978. When publication resumed as *Women's Sports* in January 1979, the numbering started with Volume 1 again. *Women's Sports* was published monthly through 1984. Only 11 issues of Volume 7 were published in 1985, but 12 issues were published in 1986 and 1987. The number of issues was reduced to 10 in 1988 and 1989, and reduced again to eight in 1990, which continues to be the frequency listed for Volume 15 in 1993. In some cases, the titles of editor, managing editor or senior editor were used.

sportswriting experience. She hired Candace Llyle Hogan, who had been sports editor at the *Livermore* (CA) *Independent* for about a year, as her assistant editor (Bateman, 1977).

From the outset, *womenSports* struggled with its philosophy of sportswriting. Hogan left *womenSports* after several months, complaining that she was the only staff member who knew anything about sports. She was not replaced. Staff writers quickly found that being a woman writer was no guarantee of being able to write successfully about women athletes.

> You may have all the consciousness in the world, but there's a matter of craft and art to presenting women in nonsexist terms, because sportswriting has been so traditionally like that. . . . [We] have to keep searching for new vocabularies, keep searching for new ways. (Interview with Jon Carroll, 1975, cited in Bateman, 1977)

Women athletes also contributed to the problem. According to Bateman (1977), former Olympic shot-putter Olga Connolly insisted on being identified as "a mother of four" and jockey Mary Bacon asked a staff reporter what "woman reads about other women unless she's queer?" Lesbian readers in turn criticized the magazine for its apparent homophobia, while, according to one staff writer, the lesbians who were interviewed asked the magazine not to write about their sexual preference (Bateman, 1977, p. 193). Editor Wright believed "that the letters from lesbians represented 'the most negative reaction we got across the board' " (Bateman, 1977, p. 192) and responded to readers' concerns in an editor's note that appeared only to beg the question.

> *womenSports* takes a humanistic attitude toward the gay movement —that is to say, one's sexual preference is one's own business. We have yet to be convinced that sexual preference has any direct relationship to athletic performance. ("One for the Road," May 1975, p. 6)

Wright also had to fend off pressures from the advertising director to use clients' story ideas and to run promotional copy supplied by advertisers. From the outset, advertisements from tobacco and alcohol manufacturers were welcomed, perhaps because of their traditional sponsorship of sports events and the particular association of Philip Morris (Virginia Slims) with Billie Jean King and women's tennis. On several occasions the editorial staff protested the visual or copy content of ads accepted for the publication. A March 1975 Speedo swimsuit ad was particularly offensive to the editorial staff. Wright maintained that the magazine was not created to reinforce the ideal that beauty was something women should strive to attain (Bateman, 1977). She was fired in July 1975, and eight members of the original editorial staff also quit. The Kings sold the magazine in 1976 to the publisher of *Ladies Home Journal, Redbook* and other magazines but retained an interest in it.

Financial problems continued to plague the magazine, and it ceased publication after the January 1978 issue. The magazine reemerged with a new editor, publisher and title, *Women's Sports*, in January 1979. Over the next 14 years, it experimented with a number of logotype designs and name changes to help define its identity. The most significant of these changes occurred in May 1984 when the word *fitness* was added to the title. This signaled a conscious editorial change for the magazine, a desire to produce a magazine that would appeal to advertisers and fitness consumers (Endel, 1991). By July 1986, *fitness* had become an equal partner with *sports* in the magazine's title (see Figure 5.1).

Almost as fast as the logotype design changes came and went, the editorial offices moved: from New York City to Palo Alto, California, then to Winter Park, Florida, and finally to Boulder, Colorado. From 1979 to 1993, nine editors and four publishers passed through the revolving door at the magazine's editorial offices. And somewhere along the way, its ideology changed, too. Endel (1991) suggests that the magazine's content from 1974 to 1978 concerned strength, political activism and cultural resistance. Endel characterizes the content during the period from 1978 to 1989 as apolitical, passive and encouraging the viewing of women's bodies as objects.[14]

The effect of the ideological change did not escape the magazine's faithful. Letters constantly arrived asking what happened to the *Sports Illustrated*-type magazine that Billie Jean King had envisioned. In a December 1988 editorial readers were told that for "those of you with a thirst for more" a new monthly publication named *WomenSports Newsletter* would debut in February 1989.[15]

An eight-page newsletter had already started publication in November 1988 with an eye on filling the gap felt by readers of *Women's Sports & Fitness. Women&Sport* billed itself as a "monthly newsletter for those who care about women's sports." Lisa Rubarth, an athlete and former coach, held the titles of editor and publisher.

> I felt a newsletter (without advertising) devoted to women and sport could focus on what was important without having to cater to any advertiser or anyone else. The independence would permit us to put an informative product in the hands of women who really care about sports. We wouldn't look for what was cute or slick or fashionable, but what was real. (Rubarth, 1988, p. 1)

The publication featured coverage of women's collegiate and professional sport, columns on sports psychology and sports medicine and articles about legislation and court decisions affecting women athletes. The tone of the editor's column was reminiscent of the early columns of Billie Jean King in *womenSports.*

The two-color newsletter suspended publication for several months in 1990 but reappeared with a new name, *Women's Sports-PageS* in January 1991. Rubarth, then managing editor, explained the name change: "Our new name tries to reflect the real condition of reporting about women and sports. The daily newspaper sports pages despite their minuscule coverage of major women's sports are really the men's sports pages" (Rubarth, 1991, p. 2). In its second iteration, the newsletter used a magazine cover-type format and expanded to 16 pages an issue. Five issues were published in 1991, but the funds ran out and it ceased publishing in February 1992.[16]

Because *Women's SportsPageS* did not accept advertising, it did not face the same content and ideology struggles that *womenSports, Women's Sports* and *Women's Sports & Fitness* did. Yet from a marketing standpoint, all faced a similar uphill battle. In magazine-marketing jargon, they were *diagonal* magazines, which are the most difficult to start (Eva Auchincloss, personal communication, December 11, 1992). *Horizontal* magazines, such as *Good Housekeeping* and *Redbook,* appeal to a general and identifiable segment of the population— women. *Vertical* magazines, such as *Woman Bowler,* focus on a specific

Figure 5.1. Name and Logotype Changes for *womenSports* Magazine, 1974-1990

interest of a segment of the population. Since only about one out of five new magazines survive five years, vertical magazines often stand the best chance because they can survive with a comparatively small subscriber base. Diagonal magazines have to convince potential subscribers that they share a common interest and potential advertisers that subscribers will buy their products. In short, they must create their own markets.[17] *Sports Illustrated*, which is considered a diagonal magazine, took 11 years to achieve any measure of financial stability.

A number of vertical publications (magazines, newsletters and member-only periodicals) targeting specific sports for women started publishing in the 1980s and 1990s. Among those still publishing in 1991 were: *American Woman Motorsports*, started in 1989, edited by Jamie Elvidge in 1991 with a circulation of 25,000; *Fighting Woman News*, 1975, Debra Pettis, 4,100; *Golf for Women*, 1988, Debra Dottley Brumitt, 241,000; and *Harley Women*, 1985, Linda Jo Giovannoni, 20,000 (Ulrich's, 1992). *Fans of Women's Sports*, a newsletter begun in 1992, is a volunteer-staffed publication, edited by Winifred Simon and published in Austin, Texas. It provides bimonthly assessment of media coverage of sporting events and encourages its readers to write to networks and sponsors by including addresses.

Three women's sports magazines (*Golf for Women*, *Woman Bowler* and *Women's Sports & Fitness*) are included in the list of 1992 consumer sports magazines, but none is listed in the Top 20 for circulation or ad revenue. *Women's Sports & Fitness*, unfortunately, did make the consumer magazine Top 20 list of circulation losers, down 31.5% from 240,194 to 164,598 ("Circulation Losers," 1993).[18]

The readership loss for *Women's Sports & Fitness* may simply reflect the tumultuous environment for national sports magazines in the 1990s. The country's first sports daily, *The National*, lasted only 18 months on the newsstands and closed its doors in mid-June 1991 after reaching a circulation of 200,000 (Brown, 1991). The industry's lone sports centurion, *The Sporting News*, plagued by subscriber and advertising losses, abdicated its role as the "Bible of Baseball" and entered the 1990s by broadening its focus (Brown, 1991, p. 9). The switch at *The Sporting News* also may have been partly a response to the start-up of a new vertical publication, *USA Today's Baseball Weekly*.

Declining advertising budgets and increasing audience fragmentation, coupled with the sluggish economy in the early 1990s, have not been kind to magazines. Weekly tabloid-style magapapers covering regional or specialized markets such as the Evansville (IN) *Indiana Sports Journal* or the Columbus, Ohio, free distribution *Buckeye Sports Bulletin* are providing stiff competition to national sports magazines and doing a fair amount of women's sports coverage. Which, if any, of the national periodical pack will be around to report on sport in the new millennium is a major question. One of the keys to survival may be increasing female readership. Studies have shown that magazine readership has declined steadily for men while rising for women. Today, for example, nearly 25% of *Sports Illustrated* readers are women ("Briefs," 1989). Further research, however, is needed to gain a better understanding of what women are interested in reading about sports and how to best present it.

"Kodak Girls" and Female Photojournalists

Photography, sport and the media were made for each other. When the circulation of Joseph Pulitzer's *New York World* dropped after it cut back on the use of illustrations, the message was clear—readers wanted to see what they were reading about (Kobre, 1991). In 1897, the high-speed presses at the *New York Tribune* made it possible to print photographs successfully; by 1910, major papers around the country carried photos in each issue, and the photojournalist was born (Bethune, 1991).

Advertising helped to popularize an acceptable image for 19th-century women who wished to become photographers.

> George Eastman [owner of the Kodak Company] saw in the nation's women a vast market potential, and he stressed the simplicity of the Kodak camera. Advertising in women's magazines he aimed his message at the middle class woman with her new-found leisure brought by the Industrial Age. The "Kodak girl," wholesome and all-American, photographing everywhere, was featured in advertisements and stretched the still-Victorian society's definition of "lady-like" behavior. (Bethune, 1991, p. 297)

Aided by an advertising gimmick that became a symbol of middle-class freedom, more than 3,500 "Kodak girls" listed photography as their occupation in the census of 1900 (Gover, 1988). These women were also among the pioneers in photojournalism (Bethune, 1991; Kobre, 1991).[19] An early woman photographer, perhaps the first woman to be involved in sports photography, was Sadie K. Miller of Baltimore (see Chapter 4). Miller is best known for her writing and photography that appeared in *Leslie's Illustrated Weekly* from 1900 to 1918. In the manner of "stunt girl" newspaper reporters, Miller, barely five feet tall, traveled by dogsled to the Yukon in

1906, climbed 100 feet up a steel girder to photograph the construction of the Panama Canal in 1908 and flew over Berlin in a zeppelin in 1913—each exploit designed to provide the magazine with a story and a picture (Thomas, 1977).

Although action photography wouldn't be perfected until the mid-1930s, Miller, who "took up photography to help me with my baseball stories," was one of the first photographers to experiment with sports action photos (Miller, 1907).

> A field that Mrs. Miller has been singularly successful in has been the photography of moving objects, particularly of athletes running or jumping. One photo that she made recently of three cadets at West Point just clearing hurdles in a high hurdle race is considered one of the best instantaneous photographs ever made. ("Hurdle jumping," 1907)

Miller took hundreds of sports photos between 1902 and 1918 of Naval Academy, West Point and Ivy League teams (Keith Richwine, personal communication, December 21, 1992). As a precursor of her modern-day counterparts who would be part journalist, part photographer and part athlete, Miller proved that women had the mettle to be sports photographers.

Very little else is known about the contributions of other women photojournalists in sports until the late 1960s. No doubt other women were photographing or filming sports events during these decades. The work of documentary German filmmaker Leni Riefenstahl in the 1930s supports the theory that women's absence from the record is simply the result of a lack of research. Riefenstahl filmed the 1936 Nazi Olympics and produced the film *Olympia* (Graham, 1986).

Contemporary women photojournalists have been winning awards in sports photography for at least 25 years. Linda Wheeler of the *Washington Post* was the first woman photographer to be included in *Best Sports Stories* (Marsh & Ehre, 1969). Her 1968 photo captioned "Miss Bardahl Gives In" featured Billy Shumacher sitting disconsolately in the water on his disabled speedboat—dubbed Miss Bardahl—watching as another boat wins the race (p. 336). Melissa Farlow of *The Louisville* (KY) *Courier-Journal* was the first woman to win first place in the sports action photo category of *Best Sports Stories*. Her 1978 photo captioned "Uneasy Rider's Nightmare" captured a

TABLE 5.3   Sports Photojournalism Awards Won by Women, From *Best Sports Stories*, 1944-1989

1969	Linda Wheeler, *The Washington Post*
1976	Karen Engstrom, *The Portland Oregonian*
1978	Stormi L. Greener, *Minneapolis Star*
	Lil Junas, *Log Cabin* (AR) *Democrat*
1979	Melissa Farlow, *The Louisville* (KY) *Courier-Journal*[*]
	Nancy Mangiafico, *Atlanta Journal Constitution*
1980	Melissa Farlow, *The Louisville (KY) Courier-Journal*
	Judy Griesedieck, *Hartford Courant*
1982	Judy Griesedieck, *Hartford Courant*
	Stormi Greener, *Minneapolis Star*
	Adrienne Helitzer, *The Louisville* (KY) *Courier-Journal* and *Times*
	Jayne S. Kamin, *Los Angeles Times*
1985	Mary Butkus, *United Press International*
	Jayne S. Kamin, *Los Angeles Times*
	Mary Schroeder, *Detroit Free Press*
1987	Paula Nelson, *Dallas Morning News*
1988	Judy Walgren, *Dallas Morning News*[*]
	Marcia Rules, *Daily* (Elgin, IL) *Courier-News*
	Arlene Schulman, *The Village Voice*

NOTE: *Best Sports Stories* was an annual volume of sports writing and sports photojournalism from 1944 to 1989. See Chapter 4 for more detail about the contest criteria and judging.
[*]Melissa Farlow's 1979 contest entry won the Best Action Photo category. Judy Walgren's 1988 entry was also named as a prize-winning photo but was left out of the table of contents so that category could not be determined.

rider about to take a plunge, after losing control of his horse while attempting a water jump (Marsh & Ehre, 1979, p. 245). See Table 5.3 for a list of prize-winning sports photos by women photojournalists.

In 1976, *womenSports* featured interviews with three women sports photojournalists: Ellen Griesedieck, Cary Herz and Laurie Usher (Miller, 1976). Photographs from the trio had appeared in newspapers and national magazines, including: *Golf, LaCrosse Today, Motor Trend, Road and Track, Sports Illustrated, Sportswoman, women-Sports* and *World Tennis*. Marlene Karas, staff photographer for the *Atlanta Journal-Constitution*, has photographed men's professional hockey, baseball and Division I football since 1976 (Rabinowitz, 1993). Several female photographers were also operating broadcast equipment in the late 1970s. They included: Cathy Cavey and Anita Fein at KCRA-TV in Sacramento; Leslie David at KOUR-TV in Sacramento; Susan Utell at KTSF-TV in San Francisco (Trueman, 1979).

What may be a first, a book of sports photography featuring *only* the work of women sports photographers was published in 1993. *At the Rim* is a 184-page book featuring photos of women's intercollegiate basketball by 30 women sports photographers. The publisher? The Eastman Kodak Company and Thomasson-Grant. But the female photojournalist in sports today is a far cry from her "Kodak girl" predecessor. "Sports photographers are like athletes. They must have the aim of the football quarterback, the reflexes of a basketball guard, and the concentration of a tennis player" (Kobre, 1991, p. 99).

Recognizing and supporting the achievements of women in sports photojournalism is important. Two unresolved issues remain, however. One is acceptance—by colleagues and athletes. The other is perspective.

Possession of a camera does not protect a woman photographer from sexism. For example, 17-year veteran Karas says she's not taken seriously by her male colleagues.

> They thought they had to tell me how many outs there are in an inning or how many downs a football team gets. . . . I don't think to this day that they respect my opinion, but it doesn't bother me the way it used to. (Rabinowitz, 1993, p. 16)

Gaining access to locker rooms has been a problem for female photographers (see Chapter 4 for a detailed discussion of the locker room issue). Mary Schroeder, sports photographer for the *Detroit Free Press* since 1979, was barred from the Detroit Lions' locker room in 1983 ("No Intimidation," 1993). Later she was a plaintiff in a suit brought by her paper against the Lions. The result: the Lions denied locker room access to all reporters and photographers—women and men—until the 1990 season. In an interview in 1993 Schroeder said female photographers are still subjected to taunts and lewd comments when they enter the locker room.

Possession of a camera by a trained sports journalist—male or female—does not eliminate the possibility of a sexist perspective. Many consumers assume that a photograph is a completely unbiased, objective, truthful source of information. They assume that it projects realism, naturalness and authenticity (Barthes, 1977; Berger, 1982; Duncan, 1990). However, photographs, like news stories, are never completely neutral. The image can be mechanically altered, digitally retouched or computer-enhanced. The image is also framed by a photographer and that frame is influenced by the photographer's own personal and professional value system. Sports photographers interpret the game, the event, the contest, and record their versions of its reality; they are trained to seek a moment of emotion or conflict that symbolizes the journalistic "essence" of the event or activity.

Consciously or unconsciously, photographic images in sports often rely on stereotypical understandings of gender values and gender relationships when capturing this "essence" (see Chapter 2). Numerous studies examining photographs in magazines have found that females are portrayed as "the other" or less than their male counterparts (e.g., Ferguson, 1978; Luebke, 1989; Miller, 1975). Two recent studies of sports event photography have found some evidence of change, although neither study examined the relationship of the sex of the photographer to the content of the photograph. The conclusion of a study of 1984 Olympic photos was that "the number of strong, competent, powerful women like Florence Griffith Joyner and Jackie Joyner-Kersee [pictured] constitutes an assault on this [gender stereotypes] stronghold" (Duncan, 1990, p. 40). Another study looked at wire service photos from the 1987 Wimbledon tennis tournament and found that photographers did not reinforce the stereotype that women are more emotional than men, and they did not depict women in helpless or dominated positions more than men (Wanta & Leggett, 1989).[20]

Radio and Sports: A Marriage Made in Consumer Heaven

The first wireless (Morse code) broadcast in the United States involved a sports spectacular. The *New York Herald* sponsored the transmission of the America's Cup race, which provided the newspaper with reports of the finish before the ships reached port (Barnouw, 1975). Voice transmissions quickly followed, and on the eve of World War I, the airwaves were a "chaos of crackling codes, voices, and music" (p. 17).

WWJ, a radio station owned by the *Detroit News*, announced the World Series results on August 20, 1920 (Cozens & Stumpf, 1953). A little more than a month later, the Joseph Horne department store ran an ad in the *Pittsburgh Sun* offering "Amateur Wireless Sets at $10 and up" (Barnouw, 1975, p. 30). In October, KDKA of Pittsburgh received its license and broadcast presidential election results to several thousand listeners that November.

Only 100,000 receivers were sold in 1922, but by March 1, 1923, more than half a million sets were sold as the number of licensed stations increased to more than 500 (Sterling & Kittross, 1978, p. 61). Consumer interest in purchasing receivers put radio broadcasting in an entirely new light; it had commercial value. Stations, often owned by the companies that manufactured radio receivers such as Westinghouse and General Electric, competed for listeners. Sports provided a way of attracting them. Radio astonished sports fans with its ability to "be there" at the scene of the action. Boxing quickly emerged as the sports event best suited for the developing medium and its fledgling sports announcers. Early fight broadcasting permitted the listener to hear the roar of the crowd, interviews with celebrities and descriptions of the pre- and postmatch festivities and to get caught up in the "excitement school" of announcing (West, 1941).

From Blow-by-Blow to Play-by-Play

KDKA of Pittsburgh aired the first radio blow-by-blow account of a boxing match on April 11, 1921 (Archer, 1938; Sterling & Kittross, 1978). Three months later, 200,000 "ear-witnesses" heard the broadcast of the world's heavyweight championship prizefight between Jack Dempsey and "Gorgeous" George Carpentier over WJY, a station created for the event (Archer, 1938; West, 1941). In August, KDKA broadcast the first play-by-play description of a baseball game with an announcer in a box behind the home plate screen (Pittsburgh Pirates versus Philadelphia Phillies) and reports of the Davis Cup tennis matches (Archer, 1938; Smith, 1987). In October 1922, accounts of a football game between Princeton and the University of Chicago were broadcast via long-distance telephone lines (Sterling & Kittross, 1978).[21]

New York Herald sports editor "Bill" McGeehan announced the first three games of the 1923 World Series for WEAF but lost his job to Graham McNamee, who would become the first of a new breed of dramatic announcers, who took over the play-by-play microphone for the final four contests (Archer, 1938). Commercial sponsors discovered radio that year, and the fashion-beauty complex discovered the magic of marketing to women over the airwaves.

> The cosmetic Mineralava sponsored a talk by actress Marion Davis on "How I Make Up for the Movies." An autographed photo of her was offered free to listeners, and brought in mail in the hundreds. The news suddenly brought other advertising agencies and their clients: Goodrich, Eveready, Lucky Strike, Happiness Candy. (Barnouw, 1975, p. 47)

Women in Radio Journalism

One female radio pioneer, Judith Cary Waller, understood the power of the relationship. Waller, who had worked for J. Walter Thompson advertising agency in Chicago and New York, was asked in 1922 by the *Chicago Daily News* to run WMAQ, its newly acquired radio station (Marzolf, 1977). Although there was no money for programming and no advertising as we know it, Waller promised performers that they would receive publicity in the *Daily News* in exchange for providing programming for the station (Williamson, 1976/1977).

She also recognized the value of sports programming. Waller has been credited with producing the first play-by-play coverage of a college football game—Chicago versus Brown in 1924 (Packer, 1989).[22] Her major gift to the marriage of radio and sports was in baseball. Most baseball teams at the time disliked the idea of radio play-by-play broadcasts, fearing that they would hurt attendance figures. As the story goes, Waller received a letter from the mother of a handicapped boy who loved baseball asking if WMAQ could broadcast more baseball for her son. Prompted by the letter, Waller convinced Chicago Cubs' owner William Wrigley, Jr., to grant her permission to broadcast the team's home games in 1925 (Williamson, 1976/1977, p. 112). That season the Cubs boasted the best paid attendance in the league, despite a fourth-place finish (Williamson, 1976/1977).[23] The broadcasts also interested women in the games, so much so that Wrigley established a Women's Day at the ball park in 1926, a practice that quickly gained widespread popularity with all baseball clubs.

Baseball and radio still owe Waller a debt of gratitude as baseball continues to be the most popular sport on American radio with about 11% of the public listening to an occasional game (Simmons, 1989).[24]

By the Depression, two thirds of the nation's homes had radios, and the Golden Age of Sports Chatter was in full swing (Towers, 1981). Mrs. Harry Johnson, dubbed the "First Lady Baseball Reporter" in radio, got her break in 1937 when she pleased the sponsor on KFAB in Lincoln, Nebraska (West, 1941).

> It so happened that when Harry [her husband and KFAB sports announcer] turned the microphone over to her for one inning during a game between Brooklyn and St. Louis, the fans were so pleased with the lady's performance that they called, wired and wrote for more. KFAB's baseball sponsor, General Mills, approved the feminine angle and authorized a repeat broadcast. (West, pp. 443-444)

Aside from Waller and Johnson, very little else has been recorded about women's contribution to radio sports from 1940s through the mid-1960s, until 1966 when Anita Martini began her radio career in Texas with KTRH (Barr, 1987). She cohosted a four-hour, sports call-in program on Houston station KRPC for eight years in the 1970s and from 1986 to 1991 (Ryan, 1991).[25] In 1973 Martini was reportedly the first woman journalist to cover an All-Star Game and in 1974 the first to enter a major league baseball locker room (Wizig, 1993). In 1975, she was quoted in *Sports Illustrated* as saying, "I want to do the color on Monday night baseball. If they have the guts to hire me, I'll be great" (Kirkpatrick, 1975, p. 94). In the late 1980s, Marge Petrocelli of WARA in Attleboro, Massachusetts, became the first and only woman sports director of a radio station in New England (Rothlein, 1988).

Since 1987, when WFAN (AM) in New York debuted as the first all-sports radio station, some 27 all-sports radio stations have begun broadcasting (Edelson, 1992). Mixing play-by-play, sports talk and personalities, they have provided some additional opportunities for women in radio announcing (see Chapter 6). Janet Prensky, for example, became the first woman to host a call-in sports show on all-sports radio WEEI-AM in Boston in 1991 (Craig, 1991).

Nanci Donnellan, described as the "only female to have a full-time radio sports talk show" in 1993, is heard on KJR in Seattle (Henkel,

1993, p. 2). Donnellan, who has been in the radio business for 15 years, refers to herself as "The Fantastic Sports Babe," combining sarcasm with her vast knowledge of sports:

> [Her] audience is pure male sports nerd. Females call her rarely, but stop by to offer her support when she's out and about. "Hey give me a call," she tells them. "I'm an equal opportunity offender." (Henkel, p. 2)

The increasing popularity of women's intercollegiate basketball has also provided opportunities for women in local and regional radio markets. For example, on WOSU-AM in Columbus, Ohio, Kristin Watt has been doing color commentary for the home and away Ohio State University women's basketball games since the late 1980s.

Television and Sports: Build It and They Will Come

The first televised sports event in the United States took place on May 17, 1939 (Rader, 1983). The scene was Columbia University's baseball diamond, and the game action, recorded by a single camera for W2XBS (an experimental NBC station), was not a dazzling success.

> Several hundred people at the RCA pavilion [New York City] watched the strange spectacle on a little silver screen. The baseball players . . . looked like "little white flies. The ball was seldom seen except on bunts and infield plays." (Rader, p. 17)

In August of the same year, Red Barber did the first NBC "network" play-by-play for a major league baseball game telecast "over a few dozen primitive receivers scattered around New York" (Powers, 1984, p. 31). Because of the cost of the sets and the quality of pictures, few individuals had television sets, but many taverns did. Experiments with sports telecasts continued with one goal: "If it sells sets, put it on" (Neal-Lunsford, 1992, p. 60). Selling sets was the goal because, paralleling the development of commercial radio, the television networks (NBC, DuMont and later CBS) also manufactured television sets.

The Gillette Razor Company, a major sponsor of radio sports programs, was one of the first commercial sponsors to believe in the commercial potential of television and to back televised sporting events. Gillette "promoted the Joe Louis-Billy Conn heavyweight fight of June 1946—the first interconnected 'network' program" (Sterling & Kittross, 1978, p. 272). Networks relied heavily on sports for prime-time programming from 1946 to 1950, and sales of television sets jumped—from 14,000 to 172,000 from 1947 to 1948 (Neal-Lunsford, 1992). Fully one third (27 of 83 hours) of network programming in 1948 was sports (Neal-Lunsford, p. 65). Boxing, bowling and basketball were the most popular television sports programs through the late 1940s, but commercial television was still a field of dreams. Something seemed to be missing from the mix.

> Baseball was that something, in the late 1940s and early 1950s, and other sports soon followed. "We had to have the rights to carry baseball games," said General David Sarnoff, head of RCA, . . . "in order to sell enough sets to go on to other programming" (Koppett, 1981, p. 58)

Television sports offered the fan a better seat than she or he had ever had. So much so that in the 1950s, newspaper sportswriters were scrambling to find new angles for their traditional game coverage. Movie theaters and most sports events experienced life-threatening declines in attendance. Restaurants were affected. Americans were staying home to watch television. Gillette switched channels from NBC to ABC in 1960 and brought along $8.5 million in advertising revenue (Rader, 1983). The Gillette bonanza—and some help from R. J. Reynolds Tobacco Company—enabled ABC to launch *Wide World of Sports* in 1961 (Rader, 1983; Spence, 1988).

NBC and ABC initially assigned television sports to their news departments. As a result, a CBS news anchor hosted the first television broadcast of the Winter Olympics from Squaw Valley, Idaho, in 1960 (Klatell & Marcus, 1988, p. 212). Technological improvements provided more reasons to watch sports on television. When the instant replay became a standard technique in 1964, viewers were visually vamped (Barnouw, 1975).

Brutal collisions became ballets, and end runs and forward passes became miracles of human coordination. Football, once an unfathomable jumble on the small screen, acquired fascination for widening audiences. (Barnouw, p. 348)

The Federal Communications Commission adopted rules for cable or pay television in 1968, which included "anti-siphoning" provisions, banning pay-TV use of network-produced sporting events (Sterling & Kittross, 1978). Howard Hughes established the first cable sports network, HSN in late 1968, offering sports programs to various station affiliates (Sterling & Kittross, 1978). ABC's *Monday Night Football* began in 1969 (Cosell, 1985b; Spence, 1988). Public interest in televised sports was so enormous by the 1970s that Congress took time to pass legislation banning blackouts for football games if sold out three days in advance (Sterling & Kittross, 1988). The 1980s brought bidding wars for broadcasting rights to major sporting events such as the Olympics, the likes of which were beyond comprehension (see Chapter 1). Television, which had received a big boost from sports to get off the ground only four decades earlier, either bought, sold or owned most marquee sports by the 1990s.

Television and Women's Sports: In Its Own Image

In 1948, a first—a network program featuring women athletes with a woman sportscaster—debuted (Neal-Lunsford, 1992, p. 68). NBC's 15-minute *Sportswoman of the Week* featured interviews with outstanding women athletes. Sarah Palfrey Cooke, who had won 13 national women's and mixed doubles tennis titles between 1930 and 1941, hosted the show. Cooke, described as a "beautiful" Boston socialite, was no stranger to show business either (King, 1988, p. 55). After leaving tennis during the war to start a family, she burst back onto the court in 1947 as a tennis entertainer and promoter. Cooke teamed up with Pauline Betz, U.S. champion from 1942 to 1944, to tour the country and "sell" tennis to schools and colleges.

Pauline, alias "Susie Glutz," would appear on the court dressed in sloppy men's clothes (size 40 shorts) and a rain hat, with a warped racket in her hand. Sarah, the straight woman, would iron out poor Susie Glutz's problems. (King, p. 62)

The pair also spent a month in Europe touring with none other than tennis star Bobby Riggs, who would play Billie Jean King in the infamous 1973 "Battle of the Sexes" (see Chapter 11). Despite Cooke's name recognition and athletic expertise, *Sportswoman of the Week* was not a part of the NBC program listings for 1949.

Aside from occasional glimpses of women on ABC's *Roller Derby*, which was popular from 1949 to 1951, women athletes were essentially invisible on television throughout the 1950s (Neal-Lunsford, 1992). In the early 1960s, however, ABC's *Wide World of Sports* began to do some features on women's sports. CBS brought female athletic competition into American homes as part of the first televised Olympic games in 1960 from Rome and then Squaw Valley. Outside of these two venues, however, very few other women's sports events were televised until the 1970s.

The first "nationally" televised women's intercollegiate basketball game occurred on January 21, 1975; it was a regular season contest between Immaculata College and the University of Maryland (Trekell & Gershon, 1991). The game was picked up by ABC affiliates in Washington and Baltimore as part of a three-game package produced by the Mitzlov Television Network (Dragana McFadden, personal communication, June 10, 1993). The tournament championship game that year between Immaculata and Delta State University was also broadcast—by Channel 53, a local station from the tournament site in Harrisonburg, Virginia—on the Wednesday following the game (Hutchinson, 1991, p. 314)!

In 1976, NBC agreed to tape the final between Maryland and UCLA and rebroadcast segments of it *the next day* on *SportsWorld*. The basketball final was broadcast live for the first time in 1979 by NBC. In that same year, the Association of Intercollegiate Athletics for Women, governing body of women's intercollegiate competition from 1972 to 1982, signed a four-year contract for $225,000 with NBC to broadcast its basketball championships, and a two-year, six-figure contract with independent television (TVS) to broadcast its track and field, swimming, diving, tennis and golf championships (Uhlir, 1984). The National Collegiate Athletic Association took over the governance of most women's intercollegiate sports programs in 1982 and has negotiated the television contracts as package deals with men's sports ever since. (See Creedon, 1993, or Hult & Trekell, 1991, for more detail on the NCAA takeover.) In 1988/1989, only about 100 NCAA women's games were televised, compared with about 1,300 men's games (Becker, 1989).

The power of economic relationship between television and sports in the 1990s has become so great that no one even dares to cry foul as women's sports are transformed in the image of television (see Chapter 7).

Women as Sportscasters

Other than the brief appearance of Sarah Palfrey Cooke on NBC in 1948, women's on-camera roles as sportscasters were extremely limited until the 1970s, when—to keep their licenses—stations reached out to hire women and minorities. Billie Jean King insisted that a woman commentator be hired for "The Battle of the Sexes" in 1973, so ABC hired tennis great Rosemary Casals. The spectacle's producer told Casals not to be afraid to speak out as a "women's libber," but her remarks about Bobby Riggs during the match created a furor (Cosell, 1974). Two years later, skier Suzy Chaffee announced the 10-week *Battle of the Sexes*, for CBS, which pitted professional male and female athletes in head-to-head competition (Tyson, 1976a). Final score of the synthetic events: Men 10, Women 5. In the late 1960s and early 1970s, a few other female athletes such as figure skater Carol Heiss Jenkins and swimmer Donna de Varona also appeared on network sports programs as commentators. See Table 5.4 for a list of milestones for women in sports broadcasting.

Lee Arthur, a veteran of soap operas and a Broadway chorus line, entered sportscasting on a scoreboard show in New York and by 1973 was working in sports for KDKA in Pittsburgh (Kirkpatrick, 1975). Arthur shocked Pittsburgh viewers when she wore "a tank top and a short, short skirt" during live interviews from the 1973 U.S. Open at Oakmont (Kirkpatrick, p. 91). According to Arthur, "Athletes are physical types. . . . Not wearing a bra seems to make somebody interesting to them" (p. 91). Twenty-year-old college student Elizabeth (Liz) Bishop also started a career in sports as a columnist for the *Albany* (NY) *Times Union* in 1973 and by 1975 was a sports columnist at the paper and weekend sports announcer on WRGB-TV in Schenectady while a junior at Albany State University (Kirkpatrick, 1991).

TABLE 5.4   Milestones for Women in American Sports Broadcasting

1924	Judith Carey Waller produces radio play-by-play of a college football game for WMAQ in Chicago.
1937	Mrs. Harry Johnson broadcasts baseball for KFAB radio in Lincoln, Nebraska.
1948	Sarah Palfrey Cooke hosts NBC's *Sportswoman of the Week* program.
1965	Donna de Varona is an ABC sport commentator.
1973	Eleanor Riger is a producer at ABC Sports.
	Anita Martini and Nelda Pena cover the baseball All-Star game in Kansas City.
1974	Jane Chastain broadcasts NFL games on CBS.
	Anita Martini enters the Los Angeles Dodgers' locker room in the Houston Astrodome.
1975	Phyllis George cohosts *NFL Today* for CBS.
	Jane Chastain of CBS and Jeannie Morris for NBC appear at the Super Bowl.
1977	Jayne Kennedy hosts a CBS sports event.[*]
	Mary Shane does major league baseball on television play-by-play in Chicago.
1982	Mary Carillo and Andrea Kirby provide the first all-female tennis tournament coverage at the USA Network.
1983	Gayle Gardner is ESPN *SportsCenter* anchor.
1987	Cheryl Miller is a sports commentator on ABC.[*]
	Andrea Joyce is sports anchor in a Top 10 market (WFAA-TV in Dallas).
1988	Gayle Gardner is an NBC Sports anchor.
	Gayle Sierens is play-by-play announcer of an NFL game for NBC.
1990	Robin Roberts is an anchor/reporter at ESPN.[*]
1991	Nicole Watson is a producer at TBS Sports cable.[*]
	Mimi Griffin broadcasts on-air analysis of a men's NCAA basketball tournament game.
1992	Robin Roberts is an Olympic commentator for ESPN.[*]

NOTE: This is intended to be a list of "firsts" for women in broadcast sports reporting. Where I have found citations from other authors claiming that an individual was "first," I have made that claim explicit in the text. However, I welcome challenges to this list because the more one learns about history, the more one learns that it is never safe to say "first."
[*]These are firsts for African-American women. Research on firsts for other women of color is sorely needed.

She was described as a "Venus in blue jeans," and TV sports announcer Curt Gowdy reportedly said, "If this is what the new wave of announcers looks like, get out the white flag" (Kirkpatrick, p. 91).

Jane Chastain, however, is considered the true pioneer among female sportscasters. She started her television sports career just two years after high school by predicting football results for an Atlanta television station (Kirkpatrick, 1975). After 12 years of television sportscasting experience in Atlanta, Raleigh and Miami, she was hired by CBS Sports in 1974. Her first assignment was as an analyst for women's bowling. Then CBS gave her the job of sideline reporter or color commentator on some NFL football broadcasts, including the 1975 Super Bowl (Gilman, 1976b). She lasted one season.

> I didn't want to be in the [broadcast] booth right away. I would have preferred to start with features and work my way up gradually. I'm not a star type; I'm a sports reporter. But I was just put in there and never really given a job—just a list of things *not* [italics in original] to do—"Don't be cute, don't be funny, don't rely on statistics." The director constantly talking in my earpiece made me sound like I was reading what I was saying at first. The crowd noise threw me off too. (Gilman, 1976b, p. 37)

For the record, Chastain was not alone as the first woman sportscaster at the 1975 Super Bowl. Jeannie Morris, author of *Brian Piccolo: A Short Season*, who began her sports television career in 1969 with WMAQ in Chicago, was also at the game working for NBC (Kirkpatrick, 1975). Morris appeared in the postgame show and interviewed the crowds outside the players' locker rooms.

After Chastain, CBS created "hostess" roles to address its lack of women sportscasters. They hired Phyllis George, a former Miss America and occasional cohost of *Candid Camera*, to do short sports features and interviews in 1975. George became the first female cohost of the *NFL Today* show doing pregame, halftime and postgame spots; she ended the season by cohosting the Super Bowl (Gilman, 1976b). In 1977, CBS hired former *Playboy* cover girl Jayne Kennedy to replace George as cohost of *NFL Today* (Jones, 1985). Kennedy became the first black woman network sportscaster but was fired from her role when she signed a contract with NBC to cohost *Speak Up America* in 1980 (Davis, 1980).[26]

ABC's approach was to hire former athletes. According to Jim Spence (1988), a former senior vice president of ABC Sports, it reflected the need of ABC Sports President Roone Arledge to surround himself with celebrities.[27] Skater Peggy Fleming did expert commentary during the 1964 National Figure Skating Championships for ABC and a segment called *Girl Talk* (Spence, 1988). Arledge signed Billie Jean King in 1974 for a record salary of $100,000 but never took the time to teach her the broadcasting business. ABC also hired swimmer Diana Nyad, gymnast Cathy Rigby Mason and figure skater Peggy Fleming for event commentary; speed skater Anne Henning, track star Wyomia Tyus and swimmer de Varona to help cover the 1976 Olympics (Gilman, 1976b).

De Varona had started by doing event commentary in 1965 for ABC's *Wide World of Sports*. She has laid claim to the title of "first female sports broadcaster on network television" (Rennert, 1985) or at least to "first woman to cover a men's event" (swimming) on network television (Briska, 1993). After winning two gold medals in swimming at the 1964 Tokyo Olympics, de Varona "told ABC I could bear to quit [swimming] if I knew I could still go to swimming meets. I wanted them to give me a chance," (Briska, p. 21). She is credited with helping to change the broadcast look of the 1968 Olympic Games by suggesting that ABC show the athletes "up close and personal" because she knew that viewers were unfamiliar with amateur athletes (Briska, 1993). Her idea has become an integral part of nearly all amateur and professional broadcast sports coverage. She left television to work for the President's Commission on Olympic Sports after the 1976 Olympics, then joined NBC in 1978 where she stayed until 1983. She moved back to ABC in 1984, working as a special assistant to Arledge. After nearly three decades of sports broadcasting experience, ABC's Emmy award-winning de Varona now covers everything from the annual Iditarod in Alaska to the Special Olympics and has written a book and narrated a video about fitness and swimming.

Ann Myers, the first woman drafted by a National Basketball Association team, didn't make the Indiana Pacers' team roster in 1979 but started her broadcasting career as a color commentator for them that season (*At the Rim*, 1993). In 1980, ABC hired Diana Nyad, who had done Olympic event commentary for the network in 1976, to cover water sports and endurance events, later expanding her responsibilities at the Sarajevo and Los Angeles Olympic games (Greenspan, 1985). In 1983, Mimi Griffin started her broadcasting career as a color analyst for women's basketball games.

The networks also hired a few women with some previous journalistic experience. Rhonda Glenn, a former editor of *Woman Golfer* magazine and a leading amateur golfer, joined ABC as women's golf commentator in 1978 (Glenn, 1991). For the 1984 Olympics, Arledge hired NBC's Kathleen Sullivan, then a news anchor, as the daytime cohost in Los Angeles with Frank Gifford (Calio, 1984). Following the

Olympics, Sullivan left for a news position at CBS ("Enjoying Smaller," 1990). In 1987, ABC hired black basketball star Cheryl Miller, who majored in communications at the University of Southern California, as a sports feature commentator to cover football, basketball and rodeos (Kort, 1987; Paige, 1989). Her first assignment was to interview her former Olympic teammate Lynette Woodard, the first woman to play for the Harlem Globetrotters ("Cheryl Miller," 1986). Andrea Kirby, who had previous experience as a sportscaster in Florida and Baltimore, worked at ABC from 1977 to 1981 and spent a couple of seasons with Dave Diles on ABC's college football scoreboard show (Jenkins, 1991). Her broadcast network downfall? Viewers supposedly lit up the network switchboard to express their outrage after she announced the football scores braless one afternoon (Spence, 1988, p. 185). In 1982, she and Mary Carillo made history on the USA Network as the first all-women team to broadcast a women's tennis tournament (Jenkins, 1991). In 1992, Kirby started her own business, Sports Media Workshop, offering workshops in which she shared her expertise about the media with professional athletes (Rosenberg, 1992).

Lesley Visser is perhaps the most notable of those hired for journalism and sportswriting experience rather than beauty or athletic recognition. After 14 years as a *Boston Globe* sports reporter with experience covering most marquee sports and their championships, Visser joined CBS in 1988. In 1990, she became the first woman on its *The NFL Today* program since George and Kennedy (Jenkins, 1991). According to Visser, "I wasn't at the dawn of women covering sports . . . . But I made the breakfast" (Jenkins, 1991, p. 82).

Two other women who had paid their journalistic dues made sportscasting history in the football broadcast booth in the late 1980s: Gayle Sierens of NBC became the first female play-by-play announcer of an NFL game in December 1987, and Gayle Gardner, then of NBC, became the first woman network sports anchor on New Year's Day 1988 (Olson, 1988). Sierens, who tired of waiting for network executives to provide a female journalist rather than a beauty queen with an opportunity to do sports, had switched from sportscaster to newscaster at Tampa's WXFL-TV before she was offered the network sports job (Shuster, 1986), but she returned to news shortly after her NFL play-by-play "experiment" (Jenkins, 1991).

Many women in the industry consider Gardner a role model, even the "dean of women sportscasters," although her career points out the perils of life as a female sportscaster. Gardner, who has a master's degree in broadcasting/film from Boston University, started in broadcasting in 1971. She was a three-time Emmy winner and sports anchor, producer and reporter at television stations in Boston, New York, Detroit and Baltimore when she "got her break." ESPN sportscaster Randy Blair died of a heart attack in 1983, and the cable network hired Gardner to anchor its *SportsCenter* program (Freeman, 1991; Jenkins, 1991). In an interview in the mid-1980s while at ESPN, she said that television sportscasting was 25 years behind television news in terms of providing opportunities for women (Tabacsko, 1987).

> I've done everything right as far as putting my career together. What purpose would it serve after all those years to go to the [broadcast] networks as some silly token? I guess I'll just have to be satisfied knowing that I cover the nation's top sporting events. I'm in 40 million homes, and a lot of people who know sports know who I am. (Gardner, quoted in Tabacsko, 1987, pp. 26-27)

Despite her comment, Gardner did join NBC in 1988. She anchored three football bowl games her first year with them. In the midst of contract negotiations two years later, she was exiled to the sidelines for six weeks, where she did "little more than interviews with twitchy coaches and players" (Freeman, 1991, p. 14). Not surprisingly, the network let the rumor float that she was temperamental and difficult to work with. Gardner responded that she didn't like being treated "like a piece of meat" and wanted to have some say in what was done at the network (Freeman, p. 14). In December 1990, she was back on the air in an anchor role on NBC's *Prudential Update*, a scoreboard show seen 45 weekends a year. Then in May 1991, she signed a multiyear contract with NBC for $300,000 a year, making her the country's highest paid woman sportscaster. Her salary, however, pales in comparison to those of network "celebrity" sports anchors such as Al Michaels of ABC and John Madden of CBS, who earn more than $2 million a year (Jenkins, 1991).

Disappointingly, the addition of the first all-sports cable station, ESPN, in 1979 didn't put many more female sportscasters on the screen, although it put the first women at network sports anchor desks (Jenkins, 1991). Eight women had stints at anchoring ESPN's *SportsCenter* between 1981 and 1991, but in 1987, for example, ESPN had a total of two women sportscasters: Gardner and Sharon Smith (Jenkins, 1991; Shuster, 1986). Kerry Ross joined ESPN in 1988, and Carla Dunlap provided weightlifting and bodybuilding commentary in 1989 (Greenwood-Robinson, 1989). CNN also hired Hannah Storm as its first female sports anchor in 1989 (Jenkins, 1991), but she switched to NBC where she reportedly tripled her salary to $200,000 as late night coanchor for the 1992 Olympics (Baker, 1992).

In 1990, ESPN hired former women's collegiate basketball star Robin Roberts after two years as sports anchor at WAGA-TV in Atlanta, where she was known as the "Bo Jackson of Atlanta sportscasting" because she had worked in radio and television (Prentis, 1989, p. F2). At ESPN she moved quickly from a late-night anchor spot to anchor/host of a two-hour Sunday show (Ryan, 1991) and helped with the ESPN Olympic coverage in 1992. Roberts told *Sports Illustrated*'s Sally Jenkins, "My ambition is just to stay for a while. We've never had [a woman] stay before" (1991, p. 88).

At ESPN *and* the three broadcast networks combined, women held less than 20% of the on-camera sports jobs in 1991 (Jenkins, 1991). The percentage would be considerably lower if women who commented on Olympic events were removed from the figures. Aside from those network sportscasters already mentioned, among the women doing broadcast network sports in the 1980s and 1990s were: Becky Dixon on ABC's *Wide World of Sports* and *Monday Sportsnite*; Beth Ruyak at ABC Sports; Ann Simon who did sideline work for ABC's NCAA football telecasts for a season and some gymnastics interviews at the 1984 Olympics; Dorothy Lucey on CBS's *SportsWorld*; Andrea Joyce and Ann Butler, CBS sports correspondents (Barr, 1987; Jenkins, 1991; Olson, 1988; Spence, 1988).

Former golf professional Carol Mann started in television as an event commentator shortly after her retirement from golf in 1981 and continued to appear regularly on NBC women's golf coverage in the 1990s (Mann, 1981; "Standing Tall," 1991). Another former golfer who joined the ABC golf commentary team in 1985, Judy Rankin is described as "the first woman to make a living covering golf on television" (Sampson, 1990, p. 68). But it wasn't until June 1993 on cable's Prime Network that the first all-woman golf commentary crew of four covered an LPGA event ("LPGA TV Coverage," 1993). Unfortunately, the event was marred by the fact that the live third-round coverage ended while the two leaders were still on the course with one putt remaining as well as the fact that the final round was shown on a tape delay.[28]

The opportunities for women to broadcast men's games since Sierens broke ground in 1988 have also remained sparse. CBS steadfastly refuses to allow women to broadcast Professional Golf Association events (Hiestand, 1991). Mary Carillo, a former professional tennis player, who started her broadcasting career at Wimbledon in 1980 for the USA Network, was the first female TV commentator to cover men's Davis Cup tennis in 1988 and the first woman to call men's tennis on a consistent basis (Reed, 1992; Shmerler, 1989). She moved to ESPN and then to CBS in 1985 where she remains. Carillo is known for her incisive, frank and often abrasive commentary, and NBC's tennis commentator Chris Evert has said, "I'm trying to be as good as she is" (Reed, p. 68). In the early 1990s, CBS employed Carillo, Mimi Griffin and Ann Myers to announce and report on collegiate women's basketball and other women's sports. In 1991, Griffin became the first woman to broadcast on-air analysis of a men's NCAA basketball tournament games (*At the Rim*, 1993).

At the network affiliate level, where there are an estimated 630 stations, there were fewer than 50 women working as sportscasters in 1991 (Jenkins, 1991). A number of women, however, have had the chance to be pioneers as sports anchors or reporters for local stations.[29] Mary Shane, for example, is thought to have been the first woman to announce major league baseball on television when she took the play-by-play mike in Chicago in 1977 (Sparhawk, Leslie, Turbow & Rose, 1989). Although Anita Martini had done some television sports for Houston's KPRC-TV in the late 1970s and 1980s, a story in the *Houston Post* in 1992 declared the city's first two female sportscasters to be Pam Oliver and Lisa Malosky (Roberts, 1992).

Nearly every major market station across the country can now cite a "first" woman sportscaster. These pioneers have included: Lee Arthur, WTVJ, Miami; Barbara Borin, WNAC, Boston; Lisa Burkhardt, KENS, San Antonio; Carolyn Burns, WMAQ, Chicago; Anne Doyle, WJBK, Detroit; Rhonda Glenn, KXAS, Fort Worth, TX; Andrea Joyce, WFAA, Dallas; Andrea Kirby, WJZ, Baltimore; Karen Kornacki,

WBNS, Columbus, OH; Jackie Lapin, KTTV, Los Angeles; Maggie Linton, WTTG, Washington, DC; Maria Mannion, WHAS, Louisville, KY; Anne Montgomery, WROC, Rochester, NY; Jeannie Morris, WBBM and WMAQ, Chicago; Marcia Neville, KNKC, Denver; Carol Sadler, WTVT, Tampa; Gayle Sierens, WXFL, Tampa (Barr, 1987; Gilman, 1976b; Sanz & Carter, 1991; Shuster, 1986; Spence, 1988; Trueman, 1979).[30]

Important firsts for women in sports broadcasting have occurred off camera too. Eleanor Sanger (aka Riger and Keys), who won seven Emmy awards, was reportedly the first woman network television sports producer ("Passages," 1993). Described as the first woman at ABC sports "to pound more than a typewriter," she started as Manager of Client Relations in 1965, a glorified title for her sales promotion and award presentation responsibilities (Gilman, 1976a, p. 52). A journalism major in college, she was quickly frustrated with her job and moved to news after little more than a year; she returned when Arledge asked her to be an associate producer for the 1968 summer and winter Olympics. When she was assigned to editing and sales following the Olympics, she left the network to do freelance documentaries. After the National Organization for Women leveled charges of discrimination at ABC Sports in 1972 because they had no women on staff, Arledge called her again. This time she rejoined ABC Sports as the first woman full producer in the history of televised sports (Spence, 1988).

> Finally dealing from strength, she put together two highly acclaimed hour-long "Women in Sports" specials in 1974 and 1975. The first illustrated a full gamut of participants in women's sports from Olga Korbut to Princess Anne [of England], the second was built around and narrated by Billie Jean King, with added emphasis on amateur athletics. (Gilman, 1976a, p. 52)

Sanger, who left ABC in 1985 to move to London, died of uterine cancer on March 7, 1993 at age 63 ("Eleanor Sanger," 1993).

Several other women made inroads in network sports production. Starting as an assistant in the accounting department, Carol Lehti became an associate director at ABC Sports in 1972 and won an Emmy for her work at the 1976 Winter Olympics (Gilman, 1976b; Spence, 1988). Joan Richman, who started in television in 1962, became executive producer of CBS *Sports Spectaculars* in the early 1970s (Gilman, 1976b). At NBC, Ginny Seipt spent 10 years in the NBC Sports Department before being named an associate producer in 1975; later Linda Jonsson made a number of significant contributions to the coverage of women's sports as coordinating producer of *Sports-World* (Gilman, 1976b; Mandel, 1981; Spence, 1988).

In the early 1980s, Hilary Cosell—Howard's daughter—produced several Emmy-nominated *Sports Journal* segments of *SportsWorld* (Cosell, 1985a). Cathy Barreto directed her first National Football League telecast at CBS on December 20, 1987 (Hiestand, 1993). Nicole Watson, who began work as an associate producer at TBS Sports in 1988, became the first black woman to produce cable television sports (Schulman, 1989). In 1991 at ESPN, Libby King headed the program acquisitions department, with women's sports accounting for 20% of the overall coverage (Ryan, 1991). Lydia Stephans was ABC's director of sports programming in 1991 (Ryan, 1991).

Beyond Whalebone, Bloomers and Spandex

The struggles of *Women's Sports & Fitness* discussed earlier in this chapter provide three extremely valuable lessons that stretch throughout the sports media/marketing complex described in Chapter 7. First, advertisers ultimately won control over the editorial content of the magazine. From this we learn how powerful the fashion-beauty complex is. It provides the advertising revenue needed by the media/marketing complex for survival.

Second, the economic pressures that forced the ideological shift that transformed *womenSports* magazine to *Women's Sports & Fitness* is also transforming women's sports. The woman of the 1990s is restricted once again in a form-fitting girdle—only now it's made of spandex. Media messages featuring spandex-wrapped models tell women across the country to shape up in order to attract men. The annual spandex swimsuit issue of *Sports Illustrated* sells almost 2 million extra copies—at $2 over the regular price—and brings in millions extra with spin-offs such as calendars and videos. We know that bikini volleyball has enough wiggle for television, and that women's professional basketball players have been squeezed. To attract spectators and television viewers with their bodies, they donned unitards, form-fitting spandex uniforms designed by their sponsor, Danskin. League organizer Jim Drucker believed that the spandex outfits would "at least slow the men down" who might tune in to see women playing basketball ("New Pro BB League," 1991, p. 4).[31]

Third, women who were writing about women athletes at the magazine faced many of the same challenges and criticisms leveled at male sportswriters. This suggests that fundamental concerns about sexist portrayals in sports journalism may not be addressed by merely adding more traditionally trained women sportswriters or sportscasters to the mix or by increasing coverage of women's sports. As we have seen in previous chapters, today's brand of sports journalism has roots reaching back to the end of World War II and to a value system inherited from millennia before that.

The experience of women's sports with sports broadcasting also provides some lessons. Sportscasters have a significant impact on audience perception (see Chapter 1). Several studies have shown that the two predominant frames used by sportscasters to describe female athletes on network television and radio are trivialization and abnormality:

- At the 1987 Pan Am basketball games, as U.S. player Jennifer Gillom brought the ball upcourt, CBS commentator Billy Packer turned to his colleague and said, "Doesn't Gillom remind you of a lady who someday is going to have a nice large family and is going to be a great cook?" (Halpert, 1988, p. 36).
- At the opening of the women's downhill skiing competition in Calgary, as a montage of female athletes flashed on the screen, ABC's Al Trautwig chose to observe, "At some point these women were all normal little girls. Somewhere along the way they got sidetracked" (Halpert, p. 36).

Empirical research by professors Margaret Carlisle Duncan and Cynthia Hasbrook (1988), in which they analyzed transcripts of televised events, confirmed the pervasiveness of these frames (see Chapter 2). Harris (1991) found a particularly disturbing pattern of racism in her empirical study of television commentary of women's sports events. She examined commentary during women's intercollegiate basketball games on ESPN, CBS and HSE from 1989 to 1991. She found that commentators portrayed black women as exceptional athletes, not because they had worked hard to refine their skills but because they had been bred to excel in physical activities.

Taken together, these media lessons from sport present a loud, clear and visible message. Women journalists who fight for access and acceptance and female athletes who battle for acceptance of their physicality are struggling, just as their foremothers in whalebone corsets, for control of their own bodies and destinies.

Notes

1. *Spirit of the Times*, first published in December 1831, has been called the first "all-around sporting journal" in the United States (Mott, 1966) and the "bellwether sports periodical" (Stevens, 1987). However, its first issues devoted a little less than one quarter of their space to sports, much of which consisted of printed columns of race schedules and results (Stevens, 1987).

2. Stephanie Twin (1979) wrote that *Outing* first appeared in 1900 as "America's first mass circulation magazine" (p. xxi). This is inconsistent with my findings.

3. Her husband, Charles C. Spink, was the brother of the founder of the magazine, Alfred H. Spink. Charles started work on *The Sporting News* in 1886, and his wife became involved in the early 1900s as the bookkeeper. Reidenbaugh (1985) explains that she "helped collect payments. Those collections frequently consisted of shoes for the children and groceries for the table" (p. 70).

4. The publicity effort boomeranged causing women's rights advocates to be ridiculed as "bloomers." Because of widespread backlash, leading feminists abandoned bloomers in the late 1850s, but efforts of the Dress Reform Association emphasizing the health benefits of dress reform were eventually successful and bloomers were popular by the 1890s (Kesselman, 1991). Amelia Bloomer also abandoned the "bloomer" cause and returned to a more conventional dress style, but the controversy served to increase the circulation of the magazine from about 500 to 4,000 (Steiner, 1989).

5. "Bloomer girls" teams often had at least one male player—the catcher (Gregorich, 1993). "In the earliest days, male bloomer players were called toppers and occasionally wore wigs and skirts in order to pass as women. But after ballplaying women discarded their skirts and bloomers and stepped into traditional baseball pants, males stopped posing as females—although as late as the 1930s ballpark announcers and sports reporters thought it humorous to call a male player by a female name. Thus a Charles Smith would be announced as 'Miss Charlotte Smith, catcher' " (p. 12).

6. For a complete discussion of the controversy over women's participation in competitive athletics, see Twin, 1979, or Hult and Trekell, 1991.

7. Messenger's (1977) account of Mrs. Hoover's collegiate basketball experience is particularly revealing. "The players were in bloomers and midy blouses, and scrimmaged modestly behind high board fences since there was no girl's gym yet. In their one intercollegiate game, they played the University of San Francisco. No

men were allowed. Doorkeepers, janitors, ushers, spectators, and reporters were all women. Even so, the very nature of the enterprise caused such a stir that the faculty forbade a rematch" (p. 12).

8. The series, coauthored by Bill Gilbert, won *SI* the 1974 National Magazine Award for Outstanding Educational Achievement in Service to the Individual. Williamson also coauthored *Whatta-Gal: The Babe Didrikson Story* (1977) with William Oscar Johnson.

9. For this chapter, I examined the four most recent issues of the publication from 1993 (November/December, January, February and March/April). The covers and lead stories featured Asian, African-American, senior and physically and mentally challenged bowlers, respectively.

10. The number of charter subscribers listed for the magazine varies, ranging from 500 (Boutilier & SanGiovanni, 1983) to 5,000 (Bateman, 1977).

11. By contrast, *Sports Illustrated* charged $16,310 for a black-and-white full-page ad in 1972 based on a circulation of 2.1 million (Bateman, 1977).

12. According to Bateman (1977), Larry King had contacted *Sportswoman* publisher Marlene Jensen in 1973 and attempted to buy a controlling interest in her magazine before starting *womenSports*.

13. Initial media reports suggested that the magazine would be called *Ms. Sports*, but according to Bateman (1977), *Ms.* magazine objected to the name on the grounds that magazine buyers might confuse the two publications.

14. According to Endel (1991), 90% of the *womenSports* covers from 1974 to 1984 presented sportswomen who were actual athletes in their appropriate sports environments. Between 1984 and 1989, 23 covers used white female models, who were not athletes.

15. In 1979, the magazine was designated as the membership publication of the Women's Sports Foundation. Today, subscribers automatically become affiliate members of the foundation with no voting status (Donna Lopiano, personal communication, October 15, 1992). The foundation also issues a bimonthly newsletter to members that covers activities of the foundation and issues of concern in women's athletics.

16. Lisa Rubarth planned to start up again with a four-color, glossy magazine tentatively titled *Winning Women* in late 1993 (Rubarth, personal communication, April 1, 1993).

17. The short-lived *Gladiator Sports Magazine* started in 1989 is another example of a diagonal magazine. Published by Flo Anthony and edited by Vinette K. Pryce, it was a bimonthly sports publication devoted to bringing out the human side of black athletes and to featuring their achievements (Montas, 1989).

18. The only sports magazine found in the circulation Top 20 among consumer magazines was *Sports Illustrated*, with combined subscription and newsstand sales of 3,297,493 ("Circulation Leaders," 1993).

19. According to Bethune (1991), women did not enter the field of photography until the 1880s because the "bulky, heavy" equipment and the "complexity of the wet-plate process combined with intense social pressures" discouraged their interest (p. 297). By the turn of the century, several thousand women were working as professional photographers.

20. Sports editors, however, *did* over-sample emotional photographs of women and over-select photos of women in helpless poses (Wanta & Leggett, 1989).

21. Game details were provided over the telephone in some cases and play-by-play descriptions were manufactured by announcers who could not see the game.

Bill Stern, an early NBC radio sports celebrity, reportedly told his spotters "if we have a man with the ball on his way to a touchdown and we discover at the five yard line that we have the wrong man, *we will have him lateral to the right man* [italics in original] (Powers, 1984, p. 38).

22. There are many conflicting versions of radio sports "firsts" in the literature. Harold Arlin, for example, reportedly announced a University of Pittsburgh versus West Virginia University game on October 8, 1921 (Smith, 1987, p. 7). Most accounts of the history of baseball broadcasting credit William Wrigley with realizing radio's potential; Waller is not even mentioned (cf. Smith, 1987).

23. She also produced the first successful television program for preschoolers, *Ding Dong School* (Williamson, 1976/1977).

24. In 1946, as Director of Public Service for NBC, Waller wrote a textbook on radio for the NBC Radio Institute titled *Radio: The Fifth Estate*. The institute was set up to train broadcasters, and Waller's book was used in the program held at Northwestern University. Sports programming at the network level in radio involves "special events" such as the Kentucky Derby, the World Series, some prizefights and professional football. As Waller explained: "Unless the sports event has wide national appeal there is no object on the part of the advertiser in sponsoring it" (p. 134).

25. Reports said that Martini was removed from her cohost position in 1991 to "help her with her recovery" (from surgery on a malignant brain tumor that took place two years earlier). Martini, however, claimed not to "need any help with my recovery, thank you" (Ryan, 1991, p. 49). Martini died on July 10, 1993, of cancer. Coincidentally, she died on the day of baseball's annual All-Star Game, a game that she and former colleague Nelda Pena were reportedly the first female journalists to cover in 1973 (Wizig, 1993). Martini also reported on sports for ESPN and KPRC television.

26. There is debate about whether or not the sports "hostess" roles that George and Kennedy held qualify them to be considered sportscasters. George left sports in the early 1980s to coanchor the *CBS Morning News*, which she left in 1985 (Hall, 1984). She now lives in Kentucky with her husband, former Kentucky governor John T. Brown, and their two children and markets a line of easy-to-cook marinated chicken called Chicken by George (Houtchens, 1991). Kennedy left television in 1985, married actor/model Bill Overton and had two children (Johnson, 1985). She recently signed on as a spokesperson for "The California Diet" and formed a company with her husband to market the work of black artists (Randolph, 1992).

27. Sanders and Rock (1988) discuss a meeting about the "women problem" in sports that was held at ABC with Arledge in 1977. The topics reportedly discussed were employment, promotions and sexual pressures on the road. "The route for promotions for female production assistants was well known in the department: a liaison with a sports vice president" (p. 167).

28. Male outrage at a network decision to leave an American Football League game between the New York Jets and the Oakland Raiders in 1968 before it ended resulted in the creation of the Heidi Awards for the best and worst in sports TV by *Sports Illustrated*'s William Taaffe. The annual awards are named in honor of "the little Alpine brat whose movie bumped a thrilling AFC game off the air" (Taaffe, 1986, p. 144). If only it had been *Batman* or *Dirty Harry*!

29. A survey in 1979 of the top 50 television markets in the United States by Deborah Nan Trueman found 35 women working in sports broadcasting. Eight of the individuals who responded to her survey were sportscasters, 16 worked in sports

production, five worked as sports photographers, two as sports directors and four in other sports-related capacities.

30. Game announcing is also a facet of sports broadcasting. In March 1993, the San Francisco Giants made history by selecting the first woman to serve in a full-time capacity as a stadium announcer in major league baseball history ("Attention," 1993). Sherry Davis, a legal secretary for a San Francisco law firm, beat out 500 candidates—including eight other women—for the $75-a-game job (Bagnato, 1993). Women such as Wendy Craver of WSYX-TV in Columbus, Ohio, have made inroads in the collegiate ranks as well. Craver has announced Ohio State women's home basketball games and high school girls' tournament games for years. However, her selection to announce the 1993 Women's Basketball Final Four from Atlanta caused a little controversy. Iowa's coach Vivian Stringer criticized the choice of Craver as announcer for the semifinal game between Ohio State and Iowa because her voice might give Ohio State a slight "comfort zone" (Monroe, 1993).

31. In 1991, Liberty Basketball Association had television contracts with ESPN for some games and several of its six teams had contracts with local stations, but the league folded after a little more than a season. Two earlier attempts to start a U.S. women's professional basketball league, the Women's Basketball League (1978-1981) and the Women's American Basketball Association (1984), had no television contracts.

References

Archer, Gleason L. (1938). *History of radio*. New York: The American Historical Society.

At the rim: A celebration of women's collegiate basketball. (1993). New York: Professional Imaging Division of Eastman Kodak Company and Thomasson-Grant Publishers.

Attention, Giants fans! (1993, March 22). *Time*, p. 26.

Bagnato, Andrew. (1993, June 27). Giants' announcer gives new meaning to term "high pitch." *Chicago Tribune*, Sec. 3, p. 3.

Baker, Jim. (1992, August 4). Women's hoop: The other dream team. *TV Guide*, p. 22.

Barnouw, Eric. (1975). *Tube of plenty: The evolution of American television*. New York: Oxford University Press.

Barr, Barbara. (1987, November). Women in sportscasting. *RTNDA Communicator*, pp. 28, 30.

Barthes, Roland. (1977). *Image, music, text* (Stephen Heath, Trans.). New York: Hill & Wang.

Bateman, Janis K. (1977). *Billie Jean King's publishing adventure: A documentary on the evolution of* womenSports *magazine from March 1973 through May 1975*. Unpublished master's thesis, University of Oregon, Eugene.

Becker, Debbie. (1989, January 31). Coaches also play saleswomen. *USA Today*, pp. C1, C2.

Berger, Arthur A. (1982). *Media analysis techniques*. Beverly Hills, CA: Sage.

Berryman, Jack W. (1979). The tenuous attempts of Americans to "catch up with John Bull": Specialty magazines and sporting journalism, 1800-1835. *Canadian Journal of History and Physical Education, 10*(1), 33-61.

Berryman, Jack W. & Brislin, Joann. (1982). The ladies department of the *American Farmer* 1825-1830; A locus for the advocacy of family health and exercise. In Reet Howell (Ed.), *Her story in sport* (pp. 57-69). New York: Leisure Press.

Bethune, Beverly M. (1991). A brief history of photojournalism. In Greg Lewis (Ed.), *Photojournalism: Content and technique*. Dubuque, IA: William C. Brown.

Betts, John R. (1953). Sporting journalism in nineteenth-century America. *American Quarterly, 5,* 39-46.

Boutilier, Mary A. & SanGiovanni, Lucinda. (1983). *The sporting woman*. Champaign, IL: Human Kinetics.

Briefs. (1989, January/February). *Media Report to Women*, p. 9.

Briska, Ellen. (1993, April). Competitive edge. *Northwest Airlines World Traveler, 25*(4), pp. 20-22, 24.

Brown, Curt. (1991, July/August). Taking a plunge. *The Quill*, p. 7-9.

Calio, Jim. (1984, August 20). ABC gets a big splash from its gorgeous new anchor at the Los Angeles games. *People Weekly*, pp. 126-127.

Cheryl Miller hopes to score as TV commentator. (1986, December 15). *Jet*, p. 48.

Circulation leaders. (1993). *Folio: Special sourcebook issue 1993, 21*(10), pp. 159-160.

Circulation losers. (1993). *Folio: Special sourcebook issue 1993, 21*(10), p. 163.

Competitive media factbook. (1992). New York: Radio Advertising Bureau.

Cosell, Hilary. (1985a). *Woman on a seesaw*. New York: G. P. Putnam.

Cosell, Howard. (1974). *Like it is*. Chicago: Playboy Press.

Cosell, Howard. (1985b). *I never played the game*. New York: Avon.

Cozens, Frederick W. & Stumpf, Florence S. (1953). *Sports in American life*. Chicago: University of Chicago Press.

Craig, Jack. (1991, September 4). WEEI All-sports smooths out after crude start. *Boston Globe, 26,* p. 1.

Creedon, Pamela J. (1993). Acknowledging the infrasystem: A critical feminist analysis of systems theory. *Public Relations Review, 19*(2), 157-166.

Davis, Ed. (1980, July 10). CBS drops Jayne. *Los Angeles Sentinel*, pp. A1, A11.

Duncan, Margaret Carlisle. (1990). Sports photographs and sexual difference: Images of women and men in the 1984 and 1988 Olympic games. *Sociology of Sport Journal, 7*(7), 22-43.

Duncan, Margaret Carlisle & Hasbrook, Cynthia A. (1988). Denial of power in televised women's sports. *Sociology of Sport Journal, 5,* 1-21.

Edelson, Matt. (1992, June). Radio plays (all sports radio). *Sport*, p. 8.

Edwards, Harry. (1973). *Sociology of sport*. Homewood, IL: Dorsey Press.

Eleanor Sanger dies; TV producer was 63. (1993, March 7). *New York Times*, p. B10.

Endel, Barbara L. (1991). *Working out: The dialectic of strength and sexuality in* Women's Sports & Fitness *magazine*. Unpublished doctoral dissertation, The University of Iowa, Iowa City.

Enjoying smaller things: After soaring to the top of her profession, Kathleen Sullivan takes stock of life and golf. (September/October, 1990). *Golf for Women*, pp. 52-54.

Ferguson, M. (1978). Imagery and ideology: The cover photographs of traditional women's magazines. In Gaye Tuchman, Arlene Kaplan Daniels & James Benet (Eds.), *Hearth & home: Images of women in the mass media* (pp. 97-115). New York: Oxford University Press.

Freeman, John. (1991, December 29). Gayle Gardner back on track as part of NBC sports team. *The Columbus Dispatch Televiewplus*, p. 14.

Gilman, Kay. (1976a, August). TV sports producer Ellie Riger. *womenSports*, pp. 52-53.

Gilman, Kay. (1976b, September). The media's getting the message: Women in sports journalism, television. *womenSports*, pp. 37-39.

Glenn, Rhonda. (1991). *The illustrated history of women's golf*. Dallas, TX: Taylor.

Gover, C. Jane. (1988). *The positive image*. Albany, NY: State University of New York Press.

Graham, Cooper C. (1986). *Leni Riefenstahl and Olympia*. Metuchen, NJ: Scarecrow Press.

Graham, Cooper C. (1989). *Leni Riefenstahl and Olympia*. Metuchen, NJ: The Scarecrow Press.

Greenspan, Emily. (1985, March). Out of the water and onto the airwaves: The obsessions of Diana Nyad. *Ms.*, pp. 74-78.

Greenwood-Robinson, Maggie. (1989, June). Carla Dunlap: More than muscle. *Women's Sports & Fitness*, p. 62.

Gregorich, Barbara. (1993). *Women at play: The story of women in baseball*. San Diego, CA: Harcourt Brace.

Hall, Jane. (December, 1984). A CBS new morning star, Kentucky's Phyllis George. *People Weekly*, pp. 54-55.

Halpert, Felecia E. (1988, October). You call this adorable? *Ms.*, pp. 36-39.

Harris, Johnnie Frances. (1991). *Nobody knows her name: The depiction of the black female athlete in national sports telecasts*. Unpublished master's thesis, University of Texas, Austin.

Heath, Harry E. & Gelfand, Louis I. (1951). *How to cover, write and edit sports*. Ames, IA: Iowa State College Press.

Henkel, Cathy. (1993, May). Dialing in: It's okay to call her The Babe. *AWSM Newsletter*, p. 2.

Henry, Elliott P. (n.d.). What do girls read? Letter from the office of the advertising manager of *The American Girl* magazine. Available from the Lou Hoover Collection of the Hoover Presidential Library Archives, West Branch, IA 52358.

Hiestand, Michael. (1991, August 6). CBS producer won't let women do PGA telecast. *USA Today*, p. C3.

Hiestand, Michael. (1993, February 21). Women play down roles as TV pioneers. *USA Today*, p. 3C.

Hogan, Candace Lyle. (1976, June). Sportswriter Nancy Williamson. *womenSports*, p. 49-50.

Hole, Judith & Levine, Ellen. (1989). The first feminists. In Laurel Richardson & Verta Taylor (Eds.), *Feminist frontiers II* (pp. 437-444). New York: Random House.

Houtchens, C. J. (1991, February). Southern comfort. *Harper's Bazaar*, p. 160-165.

Hult, Joan S. & Trekell, Marianna. (Eds.). (1991). *A century of women's basketball*. Reston, VA: American Alliance for Health, Physical Education, Recreation and Dance.

Hutchinson, Jill. (1991). Women's intercollegiate basketball: AIAW/NCAA. In Joan S. Hult & Marianna Trekell (Eds.), *A century of women's basketball* (pp. 309-334). Reston, VA: American Alliance for Health, Physical Education, Recreation and Dance.

Jenkins, Sally. (1991, June 17). Who let them in? *Sports Illustrated*, pp. 78-82, 85-90.

Johnson, Robert E. (1985, August 5). Jayne Kennedy, Bill Overton: Newlyweds talk about love, marriage, baby and careers. *Jet*, pp. 54-56, 58.

Johnson, William Oscar & Williamson, Nancy P. (1977). *Whatta-Gal: The Babe Didrikson Story*. New York: Little, Brown.

Jones, Gwen. (1985, April). Jayne Kennedy. *Essence*, pp. 70-71.

Jong, Erica. (1973). *Fear of flying*. New York: Holt, Rinehart & Winston.

Karcher, A. W. (1991). *WIBC: The first 75 years*. Greendale, WI: Women's International Bowling Congress.

Kesselman, Amy. (1991). The "Freedom Suit": Feminism and dress reform in the United States, 1848-1875. *Gender & Society, 5*(4), 495-510.

King, Billie Jean (with Kim Chapin). (1974). *Billie Jean King*. New York: Harper & Row.

King, Billie Jean (with Cynthia Starr). (1988). *We have come a long way*. New York: McGraw-Hill.

Kirkpatrick, Curry. (1975, April 21). Getting into the picture. *Sports Illustrated*, pp. 84-87, 91-96.

Klatell, David A. & Marcus, Norman. (1988). *Sports for sale*. New York: Oxford University Press.

Kobre, Kenneth. (1991). *Photojournalism: The professionals' approach* (2nd ed.). Boston, MA: Focal Press.

Koppett, Leonard. (1981). *Sports illusion: Sports reality*. Boston: Houghton Mifflin.

Kort, Michele. (1987, June). Cheryl Miller: Calling the shots. *Women's Sports and Fitness*, p. 56.

Leavy, Jane. (1977). Sports chic. *womenSports*, pp. 53-57.

Leslie's Illustrated Weekly. (1906, August 16), p. 160.

Lipsyte, Robert. (1975). *SportsWorld*. New York: Quadrangle.

LPGA TV coverage. (1993, June-July). *Fans of Women's Sports, 1*(7), 8.

Luebke, Barbara F. (1989). Out of focus: Images of men and women in newspaper photographs. *Sex Roles, 20*(3/4), 121-133.

Magazine directory. (1992). *The 1992 Media encyclopedia: The working press of the nation*. Chicago, IL: National Research Bureau.

Mandel, Bill. (1981, April). Behind the screens. *Women's Sports*, pp. 26-30, 32.

Mann, Carol. (1981, July). The girl next door grows up. *Women's Sports*, p. 6.

Marsh, Irving T. & Ehre, Edward. (1946). *Best Sports Stories*. New York: E. P. Dutton.

Marsh, Irving T. & Ehre, Edward. (1959). *Best Sports Stories*. New York: E. P. Dutton.

Marsh, Irving T. & Ehre, Edward. (1966). *Best Sports Stories*. New York: E. P. Dutton.

Marsh, Irving T. & Ehre, Edward. (1969). *Best Sports Stories*. New York: E. P. Dutton.

Marsh, Irving T. & Ehre, Edward. (1977). *Best Sports Stories*. New York: E. P. Dutton.

Marsh, Irving T. & Ehre, Edward. (1979). *Best Sports Stories*. New York: E. P. Dutton.

Marzolf, Marion. (1977). *Up from the footnote*. New York: Hastings House.

McChesney, Robert W. (1989). Media made sport: A history of sports coverage in the United States. In Lawrence A. Wenner (Ed.), *Media, sports & society* (pp. 49-69). Newbury Park, CA: Sage.

Messenger, Janet Graveline. (1977). The first ladies. *womenSports, 8*(8), pp. 12-14.

Miller, Anne. (1976, September). Photography. *womenSports*, pp. 41-42.

Miller, Sadie K. (1907, Dec. 22). Hurdle jumping by cadets at West Point Military Academy. *Baltimore Sun*.

Miller, Susan H. (1975). The content of news photos: Women's and men's roles. *Journalism Quarterly, 52*, 70-75.

Monroe, Derek. (1993, April 3). Buckeyes, Hawkeyes feel the pressure of big game. *Columbus Dispatch*, B1.

Montas, Phillippe R. (1989, Nov. 15-21). Magazine publisher: Flo Anthony. Supplement to the *City Sun*, Brooklyn, NY, p. 23.

Mott, Frank Luther. (1966). *A history of American magazines: 1741-1850.* Cambridge, MA: Harvard University Press. (Fourth printing, original in 1930)

Neal-Lunsford, Jeff. (1992). Sport in the land of television: The use of sport in network prime-time schedules, 1946-1950. *Journal of Sport History, 19*(1), 56-76.

New pro BB league makes debut. (1991, March). *Women's SportsPages,* p. 4.

No intimidation from flying pucks, lewd comments. (1993). *News Photographer, 48*(4), 15.

O'Hagan, Anne. (1901, August). The athletic girl. *Munsey's Magazine,* pp. 729-738.

Olson, Wendy. (1988, March). Tubin' it: Women break into network sportscasting. *Women's Sports and Fitness,* p. 102.

One for the road. (1975, May). *womanSports,* p. 6.

Packer, Cathy. (1989). Judith Cary Waller. In Joseph P. McKerns (Ed.), *Biographical dictionary of American journalism* (pp. 721-722). New York: Greenwood Press.

Paige, Anthony Carter. (1989, November 15-21). TV reporter: Cheryl Miller. Supplement to the *City Sun,* Brooklyn, NY, p. 23.

Passages. (1993, August). *Women's Sports and Fitness,* p. 20.

Poe, Allison. (1975). Active women in ads. *Journal of Communication, 26*(3), 185-192.

Powers, Ron. (1984). *Supertube.* New York: Coward-McMann.

Prentis, Roger. (1989, October 26). Roberts: Bo Jackson of Atlanta sportscasting. *Atlanta Constitution,* F2, F5.

Rabinowitz, Allen. (1993). Marlene Karas: In a league of her own. *News Photographer, 48*(4), 12-14, 16.

Rader, Benjamin G. (1983). *In its own image: How television has transformed sports.* New York: The Free Press.

Randolph, Laura B. (1992, October). I was over 200 pounds, devastated and embarrassed. *Ebony,* pp. 68-70.

Reed, Susan K. (1992, September 14). Telling it straight. *People Weekly,* pp. 67-68.

Reidenbaugh, Lowell. (1985). *The Sporting News: First hundred years, 1886-1986.* St. Louis, MO: The Sporting News.

Rennert, Amy. (1985, March). Up close and personal with athletic activist Donna de Varona. *Women's Sports & Fitness,* pp. 29-32, 50-51.

Roberts, Raequel. (1992, March 25). Second female sportscaster will join Houston TV scene. *Houston Post,* p. D2.

Rosenberg, I. J. (1992, February 27). Adviser gives tips on media. *Atlanta Constitution,* pp. E1-2.

Rothlein, Lewis. (1988, December). Interview with woman sportscaster M. Petrocelli. *Women's Sports and Fitness,* p. 52.

Rubarth, Lisa. (1988, November). A note from the editor. *Women & Sport,* p. 1-2.

Rubarth, Lisa. (1991, January). We're back. *Women's SportsPageS,* p. 2.

Ryan, Joan. (1991, August). Making headlines: In radio, television and print, these top reporters are covering all the bases. *Women's Sports & Fitness,* pp. 44-49.

Sampson, Curt. (1990, May/June). Home on the road: From fairways to air waves with Judy Rankin. *Golf for Women,* pp. 68-72.

Sanders, Marlene & Rock, Marcia. (1988). *Waiting for prime time.* Urbana, IL: University of Illinois Press.

Sanz, Cynthia & Carter, Alan. (1991, May 6). Anchors in love. *People Weekly,* pp. 67-69.

Schinto, Jeanne. (1977, April). A fashion history of golfing. *womenSports,* pp. 41-43, 55.

Schulman, Arlene. (1989, November 15-21). TV producer: Nicole Watson. *City Sun,* Brooklyn (NY), p. 22.

Shmerler, Cindy. (1989, June). Working girl. *World Tennis,* pp. 66-67.

Shuster, Rachel. (1986, February 14). Burden of the beat: Women look for equality on networks. *USA Today,* p. 3C.

Shuster, Rachel. (1986, February 14). ESPN's Gardner is role model. *USA Today,* p. 3C.

Simmons Market Research Bureau. (1989). *Study of media & markets.* Author.

Sketches from Helen: A novel from Suzanne. (1926, April 17). *Literary Digest, 89*(3), p. 66.

Smith, Curt. (1987). *Voices of the game.* South Bend, IN: Diamond Communications.

Sparhawk, Ruth M., Leslie, Mary E., Turbow, Phyllis Y. & Rose, Zina R. (1989). *American women in sport, 1887-1987, a 100-year chronology.* Metuchen, NJ: The Scarecrow Press.

Spence, Jim. (1988). *Up close & personal: The inside story of network television sports.* New York: Atheneum.

Sportswoman Lorraine Rorke becomes editor of "Sportswoman." (1977, March 1). *Media Report to Women,* p. 11.

Standing tall in her sport. (1991, March). *Women's SportsPages,* p. 6.

Steiner, Linda. (1989). Amelia Bloomer. In Sam G. Riley (Ed.), *American magazine journalists, 1850-1900* (pp. 64-68). Detroit, MI: Gale Research.

Sterling, Christopher H. & Kittross, John M. (1978). *Stay tuned: A concise history of American broadcasting.* Belmont, CA: Wadsworth.

Stevens, John. (1987). The rise of the sports page. *Gannett Center Journal, 1*(2), pp. 1-11.

Taaffe, William. (1986, December 22-29). It's Heidi duty time. *Sports Illustrated,* pp. 144, 146-147.

Tabacsko, Ken. (1987, January). Gayle Gardner's lament. *The Quill,* pp. 25-28.

Thomas, Dawn F. (1977). Sarah Kneller Miller. In Winifred G. Helmes (Ed.), *Notable Maryland women* (pp. 234-237). Cambridge, MD: Tidewater.

Towers, Wayne M. (1981). *World Series coverage in New York City in the 1920s.* Journalism Monographs No. 73. Lexington, KY: Association for Education in Journalism and Mass Communication.

Trekell, Marianna & Gershon, Rosalie M. (1991). Title IX, AIAW, and beyond—A time for celebration. In Joan S. Hult & Marianna Trekell (Eds.), *A century of women's basketball* (pp. 401-426). Reston, VA: American Alliance for Health, Physical Education, Recreation and Dance.

Trueman, Deborah Nan. (1979). *Who are the women sports broadcasters in the top fifty television markets in the United States?* Unpublished master's thesis, University of Georgia, Athens, Georgia.

Twin, Stephanie L. (1979). *Out of the bleachers.* Old Westbury, NY: The Feminist Press.

Tyson, Molly. (1976a, March). Challenge of the sexes: Here we go again. *womenSports,* pp. 46-49.

Tyson, Molly. (1976b, March/April). Editorial. *Sportswoman,* p. 4.

Uhlir, Ann. (1984). The wolf is our shepherd: Shall we not fear? In D. Stanley Eitzen (Ed.), *Sport in contemporary society: An anthology* (2nd ed., pp. 374-384). New York: St. Martin's Press.

Ulrich's International Periodicals Directory, 31st ed. (1992). New Providence, NJ: Bowker.

Waller, Judith C. (1946). *Radio: The fifth estate.* Boston: Houghton Mifflin.

Wanta, Wayne & Leggett, Dawn. (1989). Gender stereotypes in wire service sports photos. *Newspaper Research Journal, 10*(3), 105-114.

West, Robert. (1941). *The rape of radio*. New York: Robin Publishing.

Williamson, Mary E. (1976/1977). Judith Cary Waller: Chicago broadcasting pioneer. *Journalism History, 3*(4), 111-115.

Wizig, Jerry. (1993, July 14). Martini's love of baseball is remembered: Sportscaster bids fond farewell. *Houston Chronicle*, Sports Section, p. 3.

Zuckerman, Mary Ellen. (1991). *Sources on the history of women's magazines: An annotated bibliography*. New York: Greenwood Press.

6

Conversations With
Women Sports Journalists

Judith A. Cramer

> Sports remains a bunch of boys observing what a bunch of boys do together.
>
> Sally Jenkins, *Sports Illustrated*

With few exceptions, women are missing from the pages of sports journalism history. Although the women's movement and Title IX and Affirmative Action policies have contributed to an increase in the number of women entering the field, their numbers remain comparatively small, their professional contributions minimized or unrecognized (Poe, 1978). In short, the field continues to be regarded as a male domain.

A handful of women sports journalists in 1987 founded the Association for Women in Sports Media (AWSM). Its membership is now estimated to include some 500 women who work in sports media and women and men who are supportive of them (Tracy Dodds, personal communication, February 3, 1992). The group's activities include annual conferences, research into such areas as sexual harassment and salary disparity and the awarding of an annual scholarship to a young woman pursuing sports journalism as her profession.

AUTHOR'S NOTE: I would like to thank Lane Smith, Richard Weber, Finnegan Cooper, Melanie Hauser and Robin Roberts for their helpful suggestions.

159

Nineteen of the most highly visible and experienced women working in a wide range of media, many of whom are members of AWSM, were interviewed for this chapter.[1] Five African-American women are included in this group. The interviews focused on job perceptions dealing with such areas as responsibilities, the locker room and supervisory support. They also addressed the coverage of men's and women's sports with such topics as sports coverage hierarchy and the impact of women sports journalists on coverage.

Description of Women Interviewed

Eleven of the women work for newspapers, five for television stations, two for radio stations and two for sports magazines. They range in age from 27 to 46, their average age 35. All have at least an undergraduate degree, and two have graduate degrees; half of these women majored in journalism. All but three have participated in sports either recreationally or at the high school, collegiate or professional level. Their sports journalism experience ranges from one to 17 years, with an average of 11 years in the sports journalism field. Eight of the women earn annual salaries from $25,000 to $49,999, and three earn between $50,000 and $74,999 a year. Three have annual salaries between $75,000 and $99,999, five earn in the $100,000 to $124,999 range and one earns more than $150,000 annually.

Entering and Working in Sports Media

Several of these women sports journalists discovered early on that they loved sports and writing and found that sports journalism was a great way to combine the two. Lesley Visser is one of them. She has spent 19 years working as a sports journalist, the first 14 as a college basketball and professional football beat reporter for the *Boston Globe*, the past five as a correspondent for CBS Sports. Visser believes there are two kinds of people who become sports journalists—those who have a love for the sport and those who love writing. Visser had both. "I had a passion. I loved the games. I read *Sports Illustrated*—I loved to read it from cover to cover. I loved the language."

Thirty-two-year-old Sally Jenkins was a four-sport athlete in high school. She spent 13 years working as a sports reporter for the *San Francisco Chronicle, San Francisco Examiner, Los Angeles Times* and *Washington Post* before becoming senior writer for *Sports Illustrated* in 1991. Jenkins had writing in her blood. "My dad worked for *Sports Illustrated* for 25 years. I knew I wanted to be a writer."

Christine Brennan, 34, spent two years as the Washington Redskins beat reporter for the *Washington Post*; she now works their Olympics beat. Brennan thoroughly enjoys her career. "It's a dream come true. To get paid to cover sports. . . . The negatives are so minor compared to the positives."

More than five of these women did not actively choose sports journalism. Thirty-five-year-old ABC-TV Sports producer Emilie Deutsch's first choice was news. "My first offer was as a sportscaster so I took it. I still find myself more interested in the newsy topics that relate to sports." Thirty-one-year-old Barbara Barker, the New York Jets beat reporter for *The* [Bergen County] *Record*, says sports reporting was not her goal either. "I don't think I had an overriding sports interest. I just kind of slipped into it. The people in the sports department were more fun."

Thirty-seven-year-old African-American Annette John-Hall of the *San Jose Mercury News* considered sports journalism a stepping stone. "There were lots of openings. I wanted to use it as a way to get my foot in the door to do news. But once I did, I wanted to stay."

John-Hall stayed because of the benefits she derived from her job. "I've gotten to write and travel, meet lots of nice people, learn how to organize my time, and learn to be a proficient, creative writer." John-Hall is quick to point out, however, that there is a downside to the job: "It is stressful, eliminates a private life, and as a black woman, you need to be very, very careful about how you conduct yourself—you need to be above reproach."

Like John-Hall, most of the women interviewed have mixed feelings about their career choice. For Visser, a career in sports journalism has taken her places she never imagined going. But, says Visser, it's also a profession in which "you have to be very flexible, have a lot of stamina and a great sense of humor. This business is as much about stamina as it is about talent."

Sports Illustrated's Jenkins comments, "It's the life of a total vagabond. It's a great adventure. We're basically paid to recreate. But it can be pretty lonely. Your social life just suffers tremendously. It's why a lot of the women leave the business. You can't be married and have kids—very few do. I think it's a helluva lot easier for a guy [in this business] to be married and have kids." The marital status of the women interviewed appears at least partially to support Jenkins's comment. Eleven of the women have never married, three are divorced and six are married. Only three have children.

Work Routines in the Sports Department

The sports media devote the greatest amount of time and space to those sports believed the most interesting, newsworthy and accessible (Fishman, 1980; Tuchman, 1978).

In newspaper sports departments, reporting responsibilities increasingly are based on the beat system, in which journalists report regularly on a sport or team (Garrison, 1985). Currently, more than 19% of the newspaper reporters in the United States have sports beat assignments, more than any other individual beat ("What the Numbers Say," 1987). *The New York Times* employs this system. As the national baseball writer/columnist for that paper, 39-year-old African-American Claire Smith devotes all of her time to writing and reporting on that sport. This is not the case, however, for Melanie Hauser, 37, the Houston Oilers' beat reporter for the *Houston Post*. She writes about golf and does some general assignment reporting during the off-season.

A similar situation exists in broadcasting. WFAN (New York City) is an all-sports radio station that has a beat system in place. Suzyn Waldman, 46, is WFAN's beat reporter for the New York Knicks and New York Mets. Waldman hosts the pre- and postgame shows for those two teams. In contrast, WMAQ (Chicago) has no beat system, so Cheryl Raye, 37, is a general assignment sports reporter. And although Leah Secondo may fill in as sports anchor on WTNH-TV in New Haven, CT, her primary responsibilities are as a general assignment sports reporter.

Thirteen of the 19 women are beat reporters. Of those, eight say that although they have writing/reporting/producing responsibilities for more than one sport, their primary responsibility is to cover a college or professional football beat. Six cover college or professional basketball, three cover professional baseball and one covers Olympic sports.

The Locker Room

The locker room— a necessary evil in the sports journalism field. All of the women interviewed say it is paramount to beat and/or game coverage. And yet all say it is the place where they spend the least amount of time, between 1% and 5% of their work week. Without the locker room, without access to it, women sports journalists are at a disadvantage with their male counterparts and can't do the jobs they've been hired to do.

Helene Elliot, 36, is the *Los Angeles Times*'s California Angels' beat reporter. Elliot states, "Far less time is spent there [in the locker room] than sensationalistic stories would have you believe. After a game you spend a brief period, 10 to 15 minutes. It's a must for the job because it offers the immediacy of the event."

Smith says there is only one reason a woman would want to go into a men's locker room—to get information. "It's a smelly, stinky, nasty place. Some of these guys wouldn't wear a robe even if they were paid a bonus to do so. My personal standard: if I can avoid it, I will at all costs not interview an athlete who's naked."

The Columbus Dispatch's Marla Ridenour, 37, who covers the Cleveland Browns' beat, looks for other ways to get interviews. "I will avoid the locker room if I have time. My best interviews this year were done after practice, not in the locker room."

The rationale for locker room access differs between media. Although the need for access is ongoing for newspaper and magazine beat reporters so that they can offer "regular" coverage of a particular team that includes pre- and postgame quotes and background information, television and radio reporters want access for additional reasons. "Historically what you get in the locker room," says Entertainment Sports Network (ESPN) National Correspondent

Andrea Kremer, 34, "are a lot of clichés. But pictures are everything. I would rather do a one-on-one interview outside the locker room. But if I want to capture the moment then I have to be in the locker room."

Almost all of the women interviewed can tell a story about the difficulties they've had in men's locker rooms either at the collegiate or professional levels. It is an uncomfortable place for these women to conduct business, made all the more so when they're harassed. Jill Lieber, now 36 and a senior writer for *Sports Illustrated*, was sexually assaulted: "I was four months out of college when it happened. It was a professional baseball player. I didn't complain." She didn't complain because she felt it would hold her back in her career. She says that if it happened today, she would complain because she's more comfortable as a woman and because times have changed. Lieber says she's also been verbally harassed. But she says her male colleagues are harassed too and that's part of the job.

Granted, their male colleagues may be verbally harassed, but not because of gender. Verbal harassment of women sports journalists can include anything from what Brennan terms "the whoops, hollers and jokes," to the refusal of some male athletes to even speak to a woman reporter. Waldman has run into the silent treatment: "There's a guy on the Yankees who refuses to talk to me in the locker room. In Toronto, there was a really bad situation a while ago but another player came to my defense. I talk back now and once they get used to you, it generally stops."

To forestall any locker room difficulties, these women often approach their jobs differently than their male counterparts. This might entail, for example, telephoning Notre Dame's sports information director to let him know a woman will want access to their locker room, or giving advance warning that a woman is entering the locker room. Ridenour was told to do this when she took over the Cleveland Browns' beat. "I was told I had to yell 'Woman in the locker room' before going in. Finally, someone told me what the guys did when they heard it—they dropped their towels, but I never saw it."

Many of these women go to great lengths not to give athletes a wrong impression. WTNH-TV's Secondo says "I go in there, do what I have to do and get the hell out. I make sure my eyes don't stay anywhere too long so people don't get the wrong idea." *Sports Illustrated*'s Jenkins says "You don't linger. A lot of times I'll leave and come back just so people don't think I'm looking for something I'm not."

The women sports journalists interviewed generally agree that women encounter the fewest locker room difficulties covering National Hockey League (NHL) and National Basketball Association (NBA) teams. One thinks women might feel less intimidated entering these locker rooms because there aren't as many players as on football and baseball teams. Some black women reporters say black athletes seem to have a special understanding of just how difficult it is for women journalists to enter the locker room (Turner, 1991). "Often, they feel a special bond, and at times a protectiveness and camaraderie, stemming from their common struggle and triumph over odds" (Turner, 1991, p. 175).

Few of the women sports journalists interviewed for this chapter have encountered problems in women's locker rooms, either because they haven't reported on women's sports or because women's locker rooms are not open. Hauser, who has reported on women's golf, says "I have very seldom been in a women's locker room. The LPGA [Ladies Professional Golf Association] used to have an open door policy for their locker room. No more. I think it's been a negative for them." According to Hauser, locker room access means the reporter and public can become more familiar with athletes. She believes lack of access to women's locker rooms is one of the reasons reporters are more familiar with male athletes.

Visser tried to conduct a locker room interview in 1986 with Hana Mandlikova, the defending U.S. Open tennis champion. Mandlikova had just lost her match to Wendy Turnbull. Visser calls it one of her most embarrassing moments as a reporter. "The U.S. Open locker rooms are open to the media; it's the only Grand Slam event where that happens. I went into the locker room because I wanted to talk with her. She started yelling at me, telling me to get out, that she didn't want to talk to me, that I had no business being there." Visser left the locker room and Mandlikova later came out and granted Visser the interview.

These women sports journalists say women athletes generally make themselves available in places other than the locker room. Most often, interview rooms are set aside or women individually move outside the locker room into a hallway to be interviewed.

More than three-quarters of the women sports journalists interviewed say their supervisors (i.e., editor, sports director, producer), who are mostly men, are supportive of them when they encounter on-the-job difficulties. The *Washington Post's* Brennan says that when she asks for help she gets it. According to her, "Behind every good woman sports writer is a man with guts somewhere along the way." Although CBS's Visser has received support throughout her years at that network and the *Boston Globe,* she says, "The worst thing is that no one teaches you how to be humiliated. A lot of women just absorb the blows along the way. Women develop scar tissue."

A few, like John-Hall, say they handle their own problems because they don't want to create unnecessary conflicts. According to her, "Women in this business are their own best support system. We let each other know who to watch out for."

Women who would not have asked for support from their supervisors a few years ago do so now. Waldman is one of them and says a little notoriety doesn't hurt either: "I'm now relatively famous. Once you get minor celebrity or credibility, people listen to you more. Once people know who you are, it's difficult not to have someone support you. If something happens to me in a locker room it's in every paper and on television."

News Values

The sports events and topics deemed to have news value are the result of the personal values held by journalists and the convergence of several factors: "professional ideologies, rules or goals (themselves sometimes taken to define news in a narrower sense); social attitudes, economics of news gathering and transmission; organizational psychology and sociology; habit and so on" (Pingree & Hawkins, 1978, pp. 120-121).

Women athletes and women's sports must contend with a related problem, namely the media organization's need to be economically efficient. The beat system is one solution (Pingree & Hawkins, 1978, p. 122). If the organization can assign reporters to topical and geographic areas where, according to past experience, news is most likely to happen on a regular basis, then it can attain economic efficiency. Unfortunately, this system makes it more difficult for women athletes and women's sports to obtain coverage, because sports media organizations traditionally have determined that women's sports are an area where news is least likely to be made.

Similarly, sports reporters, editors and directors base news value decisions on their perceived audience and that audience's interests. According to Pingree and Hawkins, "Audience interest is usually not directly assessed, but only presumed to be known and news selections are made on the basis of those assumptions" (1978, p. 123). Sports reporters, editors and directors by and large are white men. Their subconscious tendency in most cases is to treat as newsworthy those sports topics with which they are most familiar and, therefore, most comfortable. They then project those values onto their audience. Women's sports coverage, as a result, is badly neglected.

Information subsidies provided to the sports media on a regular basis also influence the athletes and sports that reporters, editors and directors consider valuable. Established sports information personnel who make information readily accessible by media release and/or telephone help strengthen the ties between athletes and sports and the media. Lack of organizational resources generally prevents women's sports from establishing this formal ongoing relationship (Cramer, Creedon & Granitz, 1990). Few women's sports beats exist, breeding a lack of media familiarity with women's sports. Most coverage of women athletes and women's sports, therefore, is the result of extra effort put forth by individual sports reporters, editors and directors and the individual efforts made by women athletes and coaches to reach out to the media in an effort to develop some informal ties.

Eleven of the women sports journalists interviewed say they rely more heavily on publicists for women's sports. ESPN anchor/reporter Robin Roberts, 32, an African-American who was a scholarship athlete in college, says the media know more about male athletes and tend not to know much about the women, so that they have to rely more on women's sports information. Barker says, "I would not have done a story on women athletes in the past if the publicist hadn't searched me out. It's sad to say."

Forty-year-old Tracy Dodds, now the sports editor of the *Austin American-Statesman*, distinguishes between the degree of reliance and the amount of information used: "We don't staff as many women's events so I guess we depend more on them [women's sports publicists]. But as far as how much we use, we use more of the men's."[2]

Three of the women interviewed say that although they don't rely more heavily on organized women's sports information efforts, they do recognize that women athletes and coaches "go the extra step," making individual efforts to get the attention of the media. Four say there is no difference in the degree to which they rely on publicists for information on men's and women's sports, and three of the women sports journalists do not cover women's sports and so could not respond to this issue.

Hierarchies of Sport

The importance attributed to the level of competition and the sport itself often depends on the geographic location, market size, fan interest and commercialism. "For it is the commercial sports, including professional but also amateur spectator sports such as the Olympics and some university sports, that have the greatest need for media coverage" (Theberge & Cronk, 1986, p. 198). The minor, non-commercial sports, including most women's sports, aren't revenue-producing and so don't have the money to spend on obtaining coverage.

According to the Miller Light *Report on American Attitudes Toward Sports* cited in a 1983 *New York Times* article, football, baseball and basketball garner the most media coverage (Garrison, 1985, p. 4). And the responses of these women sports journalists concur. The amount of coverage given to professional, college, high school and recreational sports depends on the number of sports competing for that coverage and on the size of the radio and television audience— and on newspaper and magazine circulation (Garrison, 1985, p. 5).

"Equally important, the news net is a hierarchical system of information gatherers, and so the status of reporters in the news net may determine whose information is identified as news" (Tuchman, 1978, p. 4). Since media institutions rely on the beat system, those who cover beats tend to report on the sports topics traditionally considered most newsworthy and those who cover the most newsworthy beats achieve the most status in their profession. Clearly then, the journalists who report on the sports that receive the most coverage (football, baseball, basketball) have the most prestigious beats.

Because women's sports on the whole receive the least amount of coverage, being deemed not very newsworthy, having a women's sports beat carries almost no weight for professional advancement. John-Hall, the Stanford University football beat reporter, says, "If you want to succeed in sportswriting, you don't want to cover women's sports. Women sportswriters get pigeonholed into women's sports and when that happens, your career stalls." Visser agrees with John-Hall: "Women who get into sports journalism don't want to cover women's sports. They want to cover sports that lead to success."

Ridenour, who has been working as a sports reporter for 14 years, began her career covering high school girls sports. In fact, says Ridenour, "I wrote a weekly girls sports column for the *Lexington (KY) Herald*. In my last year I told the editor I wanted to report on other sports as well but he said he didn't believe women could cover men's sports."

Economics of Sport

The sports department of a broadcast station or newspaper until fairly recently was often jokingly called the Toy Department by those working in other editorial departments (Fensch, 1988). Attitudes toward the sports department are changing, albeit slowly. Women sports journalists such as *The New York Times*'s Smith still feel sports departments don't get due respect: "They're really trying to get past the view that it's [the sports department] a stepchild. I marvel at the resources when it comes to coverage of the war [Gulf] or Kennedy Smith."

More and more people are spending increasing leisure time engaged in or watching sporting activity. For many of the women sports journalists interviewed who are employed by newspapers, the sports department has risen in stature since they started their careers. Expanded sports sections in newspapers such as *The New*

York Times and the creation of ESPN and WFAN, all-sports cable television and radio stations, respectively, are recognition of the revenue-producing potential and reality of sports and sports coverage.

Brennan believes her sports department gets a lot of respect from those working in other news editorial departments: "The *Washington Post* probably has more page 1 sports stories than any other paper in the country. Internally, it's important."

Ridenour says hers is the most important editorial department at The *Columbus Dispatch*: "I think we're selling the paper. I don't think as many people would buy it. I think we're the most important staff but we're not treated like that."

The seriousness granted the sports department may well depend on the sport and season. WTNH-TV's Secondo says, "The only time the sports department is of primary importance is when UCONN [University of Connecticut] basketball is in season. Other than that, sports is definitely secondary."

The importance of the sports department to a media organization is often reflected in the size of its staff. According to The *Record*'s Barker, "The editors outside of sports pay attention to us. When we had cutbacks they didn't cut much in sports."

Coverage Trends

Competing media, namely radio, television and *Sports Illustrated*, with its mix of "literacy and leisure," have been major players in the changing coverage of sport (Anderson, 1985, p. 7). With its immediacy, television, more than any other medium, has influenced the content and form of sports coverage. It has caused the print media to offer more insightful and interpretive reporting that places less emphasis on the *who, what, when* and *where*'s of sporting events and much more on nonevent sports coverage in the form of features, investigative pieces and columns in which opinions are expressed (Garrison, 1985).

In addition, newspapers and magazines have responded to the electronic media's growing influence by offering more and better coverage of women's and participant sports. Sports news now accounts for at least 20% of the editorial content in metropolitan daily newspapers (Stevens, 1987). In the past 15 years, television has stepped up its event coverage of women's tennis and golf tournaments. That has meant larger purses for the participants and, as a result, better players and greater fan interest (Garrison, 1985).

Participant sports such as local basketball and softball leagues rarely were accorded coverage before the mid- to late-1970s, until newspaper management realized this was an area being neglected by the electronic media, an area they could report on to attract and increase readership.

Although all-sports electronic media outlets such as ESPN and WFAN have played significant roles in changing the coverage of sport, so too has the newspaper *USA Today*, which has set a trend of more stories but less depth. It also has set a new standard for graphics. John-Hall says "newspaper coverage has become much more visual with its charts, pictures and reader phone-in polls."

The advent of specialist national writers/columnists also has changed the newspaper coverage of sport. According to Smith, herself a national baseball writer/columnist, "They were killing the beat reporters, asking them to write this stuff [columns and in-depth investigative pieces]. It's increased the emphasis on sports news like lock-outs and contracts." *Sports Illustrated*'s Jenkins says sportswriters now "cover teams like business writers cover corporations. You have to be fairly well-versed in labor and contract law." According to Hauser, a good sportswriter "is part accountant, part lawyer."

Sports coverage also has become more personality-oriented, in large part the result of more resources devoted to feature reporting in all media. The molding of media personalities, however, stretches beyond the sports page/sportscast into advertising and public appearances. Lieber says athletes don't need the press anymore: "They'll create images through Nike ads or bogus charity events." Other changes have brought a rise in the sheer number of journalists and an explosion of women's sports coverage that now includes large-scale annual coverage of the women's NCAA Final Four basketball tournament.

Thirty-one-year-old African-American Donna Carter, the Denver Nuggets beat reporter for the *Denver Post*, says the coverage of sport has indeed changed to include more women's sports but doesn't believe the amount of women's sports coverage has changed appreciably. "There's been a very gradual infusion of women's sports on the pages. A large portion of the sports articles on women in the *Post* have made it there because of me, my efforts."

Differences in Men's and Women's Sports Coverage

Although the coverage of women's sports has increased over the last 15 years, it sadly lags when compared with the increases in women's sports participation and the overall media time and space accorded sport. The women's sports coverage that does exist can be categorized in three ways: less coverage than men's sports, greater coverage devoted to "feminine" sports such as tennis and golf and coverage of athletes according to sex-role stereotypes rather than sports roles (Boutilier & SanGiovanni, 1983).

Sports and sporting events need to meet certain standards to be awarded coverage. Those who've majored in journalism in college during the last quarter-century have learned there are six criteria for determining what events are newsworthy (not necessarily in the order that follows): importance, interest, proximity, timeliness, controversy and the unusual (Stephens, 1993). In sports, more often than not, underlying the "importance" of an event and its audience "interest" is how much money the sport earns for the team(s) and the media institution itself. The more revenue the sport and sporting event produces, the more likely it is to receive more significant media coverage. Those sports that don't earn money and don't have television exposure or male interest, receive little or no media coverage. Deutsch says, "It has to be able to make money to be sold to a sponsor. It has to be attractive to advertising people. It also has to be an interesting sport."

A track record for revenue producing and at least the perception of significant fan interest, according to many of the women sports journalists, are the bases for determining whether a sport or sporting event is newsworthy enough to cover with any regularity. On a more local level, the proximity of the sporting event is an additional criterion for determining newsworthiness. These underlying qualities hold true for all levels of sports competititon.

Men's sports earn the largest sums of money and have the highest attendance. It follows, then, that they receive the lion's share of media coverage. What media coverage women's sports receive is at best sporadic and at worst nonexistent. It has often taken the form of single-event coverage—the television broadcasts of two women's intercollegiate basketball games in one afternoon (a requirement built into the NCAA's men's television contract with the network broadcasting the games) and the final round or two of the Ladies Professional Golf Association's (LPGA) events with the biggest purses. Television and print media coverage might entail start-to-finish coverage of prestigious women's tennis tournaments such as Wimbledon, the U.S. Open, and Family Circle Cup, or the U.S. and World figure skating championships. These are sex-appropriate individual events, *not* team sporting events, that offer the biggest prizes, attract large audiences and generate significant advertising revenues.

Women athletes and women's sports frequently are fit into "the unusual" category for determining newsworthiness. Thirty-three-year-old Sandy Keenan, a sports copy editor for *Newsday*, believes this happens because the staffing is so much smaller for women's sporting events. According to Keenan, "It has to be a better story" to grab the attention of the media and to focus it on someone or something the media would not ordinarily deem newsworthy. The story of a female playing goalie for an all-male ice hockey team, the two girls who were the kickers for their high school football teams and Heidi and Heather Burge, six-foot-four-and-a-half-inch twins who played for the 1992 nationally ranked University of Virginia women's basketball team, are three such examples.

According to many of the women sports journalists interviewed, physical performance and appearance, and whether a woman athlete is engaged in an individual or team sport, are important criteria for determining how much women athletes are covered, if at all. Women who play team sports are often overlooked in favor of those who participate in individual sports such as tennis, golf, figure skating and gymnastics. Those women athletes, according to Jenkins, Elliot and Barker, who are physically attractive and perform well stand a much better chance of receiving media coverage. Lieber says, "Women always seem to be described [as to appearance], not the guys."

Because female athletes perform and compete in what still is fairly widely regarded as a male domain, a female athlete's physical appearance is often equated with her sexual orientation by reporters and fans. According to Kremer, a female athlete's appearance and sexuality matter when it comes to media coverage. But for at least one of these women sports journalists, the sexual orientation of female athletes is not much of an issue anymore. "Back when it was all men reporting sports, and they didn't cover women's sports at all except for every once in a while," says Dodds, "they'd get all hot about Olga Korbut or Peggy Fleming and there was something to that [sexuality], but I think that with the wider range of women's sports and their increased competitiveness, people take them more seriously. I think it's dropping by the wayside." Dodds says that tennis player Martina Navratilova's sexual orientation has not had an impact on the amount of media coverage she's received over the years. And Dodds believes that that's because people like and respect her. Dodds' comments, although hopeful, run contrary to documentation that Navratilova's earning power off the court has been affected by the public knowledge of her sexual orientation (Nelson, 1991, p. 149).

Job Perceptions and Impact

In May of 1992, 14 years after Melissa Ludtke, then a reporter for *Sports Illustrated*, was a plaintiff in a federal lawsuit that challenged Major League baseball's exclusion of women sportswriters from locker room interviews,[3] Ludtke addressed the members of AWSM at their annual convention. Ludtke, who'd spent the year as a Nieman Fellow at Harvard University, alluded to work done by noted feminist scholar Carol Gilligan and sociologist Nancy Chodorow,[4] telling the women that when they aren't allowed in the locker room or are made to feel unwanted and uncomfortable there, the public misses out on a different sports perspective (Cramer, 1992, p. 3).

Ludtke feels women see things differently than men because they experience life in a relational way (Cramer, 1992, p. 3). She related a conversation she'd had some years before with Johnny Bench, catcher for the Cincinnati Reds. Bench told her that male sports reporters are more concerned with the kind of pitch that is thrown to strike out a batter. Women, however, said Bench, would rather know about the nine-inning conversation that takes place between the catcher and the umpire (Cramer, p. 3). According to Ludtke, women bring a humanistic perspective to the coverage of sport (p. 3).

Nearly half ($N = 9$) of the women sports journalists interviewed, however, believe an increase in their numbers would have little, if any, impact on sports coverage. Kremer would like to think that women sportswriters aren't going to write like women sportswriters but like sportswriters.

There are those, however, who appear to subscribe to Ludtke's way of thinking. Ridenour thinks more women sports journalists "might make it [coverage] more human." One interviewee, who requested anonymity, says, "Women are more sensitive . . . they bring a different point of view." Jenkins says that women and men write differently: "Stephanie Salter once wrote that Rick Barry 'flounced across the basketball floor.' Men don't use color in their prose." According to Waldman, women cover sports the way they think a man wants them to instead of doing what they want to do. "I think a lot of women have it in their heads that to be emotional or to take something to a different level is wrong because the men aren't doing it."

Keenan and Hauser say the impact that more women sports journalists might have on the coverage of sport won't be felt until there are more women filling the top level (i.e., editor and columnist) positions. But some, such as Carter and Secondo, believe that an increase in the number of women sports journalists is bound to mean more space and time will be devoted to the coverage of women's sports. Dodds says it already has: "People don't understand the degree to which the assigned reporter influences what stories are written. If a reporter can see possibilities, then a story develops. The more women who are on that staff, the wider the network for the possibility of stories. Now sure, they can get shot down. But if they don't come into this office in the first place, it's not going to happen."

Brennan views any increase in the coverage of women's sports as a total process. She says, "As more women become involved in sports at a young age, more will write about them and move up the ranks. More women will read about sports and more women's sports coverage will come about."

Jenkins isn't sure of the effect more women sports journalists would have on the general coverage of sport and the coverage of women's sports in particular. She says, though, that she isn't going to shy away from reporting on women athletes and women's sports: "When I got to *Sports Illustrated* there was a lack of women's sports coverage. I'm going to do the women's stories. If they're good stories, why not do them? I feel a responsibility and an obligation." Jenkins has "made it" in sports journalism and that, aside from her interest in sports and her empathy for women athletes, may be one reason why she's willing to report on women's sports.

The Future

For most of these women, working as a sports journalist is what they've always wanted to do and has offered them opportunities to meet people and to go places they'd never have dreamed of. But sadly, very few see themselves making sports journalism, as they now know it, their life's work. Waldman, who spent several years work- ing on Broadway before going to work for WFAN seven years ago, is one who does. "It's the first time in my whole life that I feel I'm giving something back to the world, and at the same time, getting what I want out of it. I really love this."

The tremendous demands of the beat and the difficulties associ- ated with sports reporting have taken their toll (Cramer, 1992; Kettmann, March/April 1989). Changes in career emphasis lie ahead for three quarters of these women. The responses of some suggest that their love for writing takes priority over any interest in sports. A few want to remain in journalism but are actively looking to leave the sports department in favor of reporting news. Others say they want to make sports journalism their lifetime career but can't imag- ine themselves covering a sports beat for the rest of their lives. Kremer says, "I don't want to be 40 and in a locker room," and Smith notes, "It's very easy to be 65, male and a sports reporter." Although Kremer isn't sure what the future holds, she does think it could include moving into local television, writing or teaching. Smith eventually wants to "move inside" and work as a copy editor, and

Roberts sees the possibility of moving out of her sports anchor/reporter chair and into a production or programming role.

Ridenour, Hauser, Smith and Barker are less hopeful than they used to be about the future for women in sports journalism. These women have worked as newspaper sportswriters an average of 12 years. They say that five years ago they felt that women were making great strides but now realize that although their numbers may have risen, their progress into management positions has been limited. Hauser says women have moved up into the ranks of beat reporter and assistant editor but not beyond in any appreciable numbers. In addition, according to Barker and Smith, more women need to be working the more highly coveted beats such as professional football.

Several of the women, though, see a bright future. Roberts points to the increasing number of women producers and correspondents in network television sports as reason for her optimism, and Jenkins and others note that *The New York Times* and *Washington Post* now have deputy sports editors who are women. Dodds is one of the few who has risen to the rank of sports editor. She says there was a high turnover rate when women first entered the field. "I've been around 20 years and women on the staff have been around 12 or 13 years. You're going to see more of that and so there will be more women in management. The fact is there haven't been enough trained with experience. We all started in the '70s."

Many of the women interviewed for this chapter, however, have worked in sports journalism a decade or more, yet say they expect to change careers or at least change their career emphasis. Most are now in positions that suggest they have attained at least a modicum of "success" as it traditionally has been defined (beat reporter, assistant sports editor, network sports correspondent, columnist). They are at a point where their years of experience and positions seemingly command some respect and power. And they may, as gatekeepers of the sports value system, have the opportunity now or in the near future either to maintain the status quo of placing minimal value on the significance of women sports journalists and coverage of women's sports or to change it, making the working conditions for women sports journalists more favorable and the coverage of men's and women's sports more equitable. Although it is important that the number of women sports journalists increases at all levels in all sports media, it is not enough. According to Waldman, "Women have to *want* to be in positions of making a difference."

Notes

1. The majority of the information contained in this chapter was obtained from personal interviews with the individual sports journalists. A listing of the dates of these interviews can be found at the end of this chapter.

2. At the time of this interview, Tracy Dodds was assistant sports editor of the Orange County *Register*. Dodds took over as sports editor of the *Austin American-Statesman* in August of 1992.

3. In 1978, Melissa Ludtke, together with her employer, *Sports Illustrated*, won their suit against the New York Yankees, giving women sports journalists equal access to interview players in the locker room. See Chapter 4 for more detail.

4. The work of Carol Gilligan (1982) and Nancy Chodorow (1978) has found that girls and boys are taught different skills and that they have different goals and different personality characteristics, which lead to two different approaches to the world.

References

Anderson, Douglas A. (1985). *Contemporary sports reporting*. Chicago: Nelson-Hall.

Boutilier, M. A. & SanGiovanni, L. (1983). *The sporting woman*. Champaign, IL: Human Kinetics.

Chodorow, Nancy. (1978). *The representation of mothering: Psychoanalysis and the sociology of gender*. Berkeley, CA: University of California Press.

Cramer, Judith. (1992, September). Ludtke: Not enough has changed. *Newsletter of the Association for Women in Sports Media*. (Available from Ann Miller, AWSM, P.O. Box 4205, Mililani, HI 96789.)

Cramer, Judith, Creedon, Pamela & Granitz, Elizabeth. (1990, August). *The role of the collegiate sports information officer in promoting media coverage of women's sports*. Paper presented at the annual conference of the Association for Education in Journalism and Mass Communication. Minneapolis, MN.

Fensch, Thomas. (1988). *The sports writing handbook*. Hillsdale, NJ: Erlbaum.

Fishman, M. (1980). *Manufacturing the news*. Austin, TX: University of Texas Press.

Garrison, Bruce. (1985). *Sports reporting*. Ames, IA: Iowa State University Press.

Gilligan, Carol. (1982). *In a different voice: Psychological theory and women's development*. Cambridge, MA: Harvard University Press.

Kettmann, Steve. (1989, March/April). Making it easier to stay in the game. *Columbia Journalism Review*, pp. 14-15.

Nelson, Mariah Burton. (1991). *Are we winning yet?* New York: Random House.

Pingree, Suzanne & Hawkins, Robert. (1978) News definitions and their effects on women. In Laurily Keir Epstein (Ed.), *Women and the news* (pp. 116-135). New York: Hastings House.

Poe, Randall. (1978). The writing of sports. *Esquire, 82*(4), pp. 173-176, 373-374, 376-379.

Stephens, Mitchell. (1993). *Broadcast News* (rev. ed.). New York: Holt, Rinehart & Winston.

Stevens, John. (1987, Fall). The rise of the sports page. *Gannett Center Journal, 1,* 1-11.

Theberge, Nancy & Cronk, Alan. (1986). Work routines in newspaper sports departments and the coverage of women's sports. *Sociology of Sport Journal, 3,* 195-203.

Tuchman, Gaye. (1978). *Making news.* New York: The Free Press.

Turner, Renee. (1991, February). Black women sports writers and the locker room wars. *Ebony,* pp. 170-176.

What the numbers say: A statistical look at the sports-media connection. (1987, Fall). *Gannett Center Journal, 1,* 76-77.

Interviews

Barker, Barbara. Sports reporter for *The* [Bergen County] *Record.* Telephone communication, 30 January 1992.

Brennan, Christine. Sports reporter for the *Washington Post.* Telephone communication, 27 January 1992.

Carter, Donna. Sports reporter for the *Denver Post.* Telephone communication, 1 May 1992.

Deutsch, Emilie. Sports producer for ABC Sports. Telephone communication, 3 April 1992.

Dodds, Tracy. Sports editor for the *Austin American-Statesman.* Telephone communication, 3-4 February 1992.

Elliot, Helene. Sports reporter for the *Los Angeles Times.* Telephone communication, 12 March 1992.

Hauser, Melanie. Sports reporter/columnist for the *Houston Post.* Telephone communication, 5 February 1992.

Jenkins, Sally. Senior writer for *Sports Illustrated.* Telephone communication, 9 March 1992.

John-Hall, Annette. Sports reporter for the *San Jose Mercury News.* Telephone communication, 10 February 1992.

Keenan, Sandy. Sports copy editor for *Newsday.* Telephone communication, 15 January 1992.

Kremer, Andrea. National correspondent for ESPN. Telephone communication, 12 February 1992.

Lieber, Jill. Senior writer for *Sports Illustrated.* Telephone communication, 12 February 1992.

Raye, Cheryl. Sports reporter for WMAQ. Telephone communication, 12 February 1992.

Ridenour, Marla. Sports reporter for *The Columbus Dispatch*. Telephone communication, 31 January 1992.

Roberts, Robin. Sports anchor/reporter for ESPN. Telephone communication, 19 February 1992.

Secondo, Leah. Sports reporter for WTNH-TV. Telephone communication, 15 February 1992.

Smith, Claire. National baseball writer/columnist for *The New York Times*. Telephone communication, 14 February 1992.

Visser, Lesley. Correspondent for CBS Sports. Telephone communication, 4 March 1992.

Waldman, Suzyn. Sports reporter/anchor for WFAN. Telephone communication, 5 February 1992.

7

Pandering or Empowering?

Economics and Promotion of Women's Sports

Pamela J. Creedon
Judith A. Cramer
Elizabeth H. Granitz

> [Women's sports] won't attain overall equality. Nor will that third generation of true-bred women fans alter the situation when they come of age. To the extent that they become mass fans (and therefore important factors in television ratings and ticket sales), they will develop the tastes males already have, and become just as captivated by the "best" illusion.
>
> Leonard Koppett, *Sports Illusion, Sports Reality* (1981, p. 214)

Hype is an integral part of the sports world. It sells tickets, fills stadiums and pays athletes' multimillion dollar salaries. It creates the illusion that the outcome of the sporting event matters (Koppett, 1981). Although the press has long been a willing accomplice, sports marketers keep the illusion alive.

Promoting sport in America today is big business. Sport ranks in the Top 25 of the largest U.S. industries, ahead of the auto, lumber and airline industries with an excess revenue of $63 billion (Helitzer, 1991). In 1990, companies spent $1.7 billion on sports sponsorships

(Shell, 1991). On the consumer side, nearly three quarters of Americans consider themselves sports fans (*Sports Illustrated*, 1986). Fans paid just under $3 billion during 1991-1992 seasons to attend regular and postseason professional contests, paying an average of $11.86 for a ticket (Sports Law Center, 1992).

The relationship between the woman athlete and promotion is a struggle between empowerment and pander. Although media images of women athletes can provide empowering role models, athletes must find ways of satisfying the media's obsession with sex, winners, conflict and controversy. At the root of this relationship is the sports/media/marketing complex, a largely invisible, hegemonic economic structure that makes it impossible to earn a living as an athlete in America without bowing to its demands.[1]

This chapter explores some dimensions of that economic structure, particularly as they relate to the promotion of women's sports. The Ladies Professional Golf Association is used as an example of how the structure affects women's professional sport. The role of the collegiate sports information director in promoting amateur sport is also examined. The chapter uses a liberal feminist or reform approach to provide descriptions of the current economic structure and a radical feminist or transform approach to discuss alternatives to the "best" illusion (see Chapter 1 for a discussion of various feminisms and sport).

Sport and Economics

The economic structure of U.S. professional sports is at once very simple and very complicated. Revenue is generated from two primary sources: ticket sales and the sale of rights to media outlets and sponsors. Profits increase relative to the size of the crowd or audience. How tickets are sold and what configurations are used to sell broadcast rights begin to complicate the picture. Suffice it to say that these decisions in the United States are largely guided by the heuristic "Whatever the marketplace will bear" (see Jhally, 1989).

Although the media have made us keenly aware of expenses such as players' salaries, other and more complicated aspects of the commercial nature of sport in our culture are not well covered. In this environment, for example, "it almost goes without saying that violence—should it function as an audience attraction—will be exploited" (Bryant & Zillmann, 1983, p. 204). Particularly troubling is the absence of substantive discussion of the symbiotic relationship between sport and the mass media.

> The media without sports lose an enormous amount of their advertising revenue, as well as a significant percentage of their programming content in television and space allocated in daily newspapers. Sports, by the same token, have reshaped themselves to please the media audience; they need media revenues for survival, and they depend on print and broadcast coverage to give their people and organizations identity and credibility. (Dennis, 1988, p. 1)

Many believe that the future of sport is closely tied to television (e.g., Klatell & Marcus, 1988; Staudohar & Mangan, 1991). During the average week, more than 80% of Americans can be found viewing televised sporting activities (*Sports Illustrated*, 1986). During a year, "more than 8,000 sports events are televised, an average of 22 a day. . . . Of the 10 highest-rated TV shows of all time, five have been SuperBowl telecasts. ESPN [is] . . . avidly watched in over 52 million homes" (Helitzer, 1991, p. 5.).

Major league baseball has a $1.1 billion broadcasting contract with CBS and a $400 million cable deal with ESPN (Shapiro, 1993). The three broadcast networks shelled out an additional $3.6 billion in their four-year package with the NFL signed in 1990. ESPN is paying the National Football League $1.4 billion for three years of broadcasting rights (McClellan, 1992).

Network bidding wars for American television rights to the Olympics escalated steadily through the 1980s. CBS paid $394,000 for the rights to the first televised Olympics in 1960 from Rome and $50,000 for the winter Olympics from Squaw Valley (Thottam, 1988). ABC paid $309 million for rights for the 1988 winter Olympics from Calgary; losing nearly $65 million on the deal (Thottam, 1988). The 1992 summer games from Barcelona cost NBC a record $401 million.

And colleges have long been cashing in. While other universities debated the advisability of radio broadcasts of their sporting events, Yale sold the rights to six home football games for $20,000 in 1937 (West, 1941, p. 382). A little more than a half century later, the NCAA signed a seven-year, $1 billion contract with CBS to televise its championships, an average of $143 million a year (Lederman, 1992).[2]

How does this work? Modeling a system developed by radio, most television stations buy broadcast rights to sporting events and then sell commercial time during the broadcasts. Premium sports channels, superstations and pay-per-view cable stations have also entered the fray. Commercial rates are based on ratings: the more viewers, the higher the cost for a commercial spot; the higher the cost of the spot, the more income generated for the station. For example, the average price for a 30-second commercial during the 1993 Super Bowl was $850,000 (Mandese, 1993).

As early as 1985 the World Wrestling Federation promoted its syndicated shows by paying stations in some cities more than $100,000 to air them (Taaffe, 1985). Some stations now routinely sell airtime to teams that produce their own games. At least one team—the Boston Celtics—owns its own radio and television stations ("The Greening," 1989). And a few station owners own their own professional teams (i.e., Ted Turner, owner of several cable channels, owns the Atlanta Braves and a controlling interest in the Atlanta Hawks).

Sponsorship is another way in which revenue is generated by the sports/media/marketing complex. Sponsors, often corporations, provide money to teams and events to associate their names with particular activities. Television stations, for example, require sponsors for golf events; that is, they require a sponsor to pay for the airtime in exchange for some commercial time during the event and the association of the sponsor's name with the event. Perhaps the most blatant example of this commercial relationship was the "hamburger" Olympics, so nicknamed because of the sponsorship arrangements made with the McDonalds Corporation.

> The auctioning off of the Los Angeles [1984] Olympics was perhaps the most spectacular example to date of this linking of the spheres of commerce and sports. . . . Indeed, given the prevalence of brand names in the athletic events themselves and the use made of sporting themes in the advertisements that appeared between the events, the blurring of the line between the two realms was so complete that, at times, it was difficult to tell exactly what one was watching. (Jhally, 1989, p. 79)

The proliferation of sporting events on television, increasing fragmentation of the viewing market because of cable, and the recession have brought about many of these new approaches. By 1991, there were three national rights holders and 75 local rights holders in Major League baseball alone ("Searching for," 1991). Some networks lost more than $10 million on the 1990-1991 National Football League season ("First Down," 1991). Attendance at NFL and major league baseball games was down during 1991-1992 (Sports Law Center, 1992). Rather than take a 55% cut in network rights fees because of declining viewership, major league baseball owners formed a partnership with NBC and ABC to share profits from advertising and sponsorship sales begining with the 1994 season (Smith, 1993).

What might these changes mean for women's sports? The coverage debate has always revolved around this question: How large must the audience interested in women's sports be? The splintering and fragmentation caused by these new economic realities could help to redefine how large is large enough. " 'Narrowcasting,' the televising of program material that interests small segments of the population" could mean that instead of needing 40 to 50 million viewers for traditional sports programming, an audience of only a few million may be enough to bring an event to television (Mandel, 1981, p. 27). Ironically, in the 1950s, boxing, bowling and wrestling were moved from prime time to weekends *because* they didn't have a broad enough appeal among female viewers (Neal-Lunsford, 1992).

In this new environment, women's sports fans would presumably be considered a viable market segment; thus, women's sports could attract advertising dollars and corporate sponsorships.

Sports Promotion

In addition to the economic changes in the media environment that promise to affect women's sports coverage, sports marketing is playing an increasing role in creating a demand for coverage.

In the 1930s and 1940s, these promotion specialists were known as press agents or publicity men [sic]. Now in professional sports, the title may be PR director, press director, director of communications,

media director, or director of community relations. . . . In colleges,
their equal is the sports information director. (Helitzer, 1991, p. 55)

There is considerable confusion in many fields today about the
relationship of public relations, marketing, advertising and fund-
raising. In public relations theory, marketing is a selling function and
public relations is a broader management function. Public relations
is concerned with each of an organization's publics—employees,
stockholders, customers, and so on—whereas marketing focuses on
one public—the consumer. Advertising is viewed as a tool of public
relations or marketing, and fund-raising is an activity that can be
administered by either function and uses a number of tools such as
advertising, promotion and media relations.

Sports promotion in public relations theory is called *press agentry*
(Grunig & Hunt, 1984). The historical figure associated with this
model in public relations is P. T. Barnum, the preeminent circus promoter. Like Barnum, press agents seek ways of getting free publicity.
They measure their success by how many tickets are sold for the
show or game.

Media relations or public information is a second model in public
relations theory that involves sports. Top management of sports
organizations most often select the media as their primary strategic
public (Helitzer, 1991; Maymi, 1987; NCAA, 1985). The media also
rely heavily on public relations sources for information subsidies
such as press releases, statistics, and the like (Turk, 1985, 1988).

Several books have attempted to describe the overall role of
public relations in sports. Helitzer (1991), for example, produced a
comprehensive "how to" book titled, *The Dream Job: $port$ Publicity,
Promotion and Public Relations.* Focusing almost exclusively on media relations, he details publicity fundamentals including writing
press releases and backgrounders, placing feature stories on print
and broadcast media and planning a press conference. He also covers
promotional techniques including creating the news through special
events, interviews and speeches as well as crisis communication.

The National Collegiate Athletic Association produced a *Public
Relations and Promotion Manual* in 1985 for staff at member institutions. Divided into sections on public relations and promotion, its
primary emphasis is also on media relations. The manual describes

advertising, marketing and athletic fund raising as related and often overlapping functions.

Bronzan (1977) provided a more comprehensive look at the role of public relations in sports in a book titled *Public Relations, Promotions, and Fund-Raising for Athletic and Physical Education Programs.* The book is divided into three parts: public relations (including publicity), promotions and fund-raising.

Promoting Women's Professional Sports

In the professional ranks, women's sports have struggled to get and keep television contracts despite the fact that they are a "good buy" (read cheap) in today's high-priced sports marketplace. The most successful (read lucrative) women's professional sports are those that feature sponsored tour events such as the Ladies Professional Golf Association and have contracts with network and cable stations. Women's professional sports leagues featuring team play between cities have not fared well. For example, high Olympic TV ratings and college popularity helped Major League Volleyball get a contract with ESPN for tape-delay broadcasts of 10 of its games in both 1987 and 1988. The six-team league died mid-season in 1989, however. In contrast, the Women's Professional Volleyball Association, started in 1987—featuring two-person beach volleyball teams, a tournament rather than a league schedule and bikinis as team uniforms—has been more successful.[3] Minimum prize money for a televised tournament is $40,000, and 12 of the 18 WPVA tournaments in 1991 were televised by ESPN ("WPVA Kicks," 1991). The showcase television event for bikini volleyball is the World Championship held on a sand court at the Flamingo Hilton in Las Vegas, sponsor of the event. The tournament is also a dubious first for women's sports; it involves gambling. Spectators are encouraged to place bets on the winning team in the Hilton's casino.

What does the success of bikini volleyball portend? To attract the television revenue needed to support player salaries or athletic department budgets, women's sports promoters are following the path of least resistance. If women's sports need to be sold as part of a package, sell them. If women need to change the rules of their games to make them more exciting, change them. If sex sells, then sell it. Call it pandering, call it fruitful ambivalence:

- The NCAA sells the broadcast rights to women's collegiate sports as part of a "little sister" package deal. They tell the networks, if you want the men's championships, you must broadcast the women's too. The 1993 CBS coverage of the NCAA's "little sister" championship between Ohio State and Texas Tech outdrew NBC's coverage of Michael Jordan and the Chicago Bulls (Hiestand, 1993).[4]
- Without the help of a "big brother," women's professional basketball remade itself in the image of television and failed miserably after one season. The Liberty Basketball Association reduced the length of the court to 90 feet (instead of 94), used a ball with a smaller circumference (25 inches instead of 28), and lowered the basket to nine feet, two inches (eight inches lower than regulation)—in a futile effort to make women's professional basketball "more interesting" for television.[5]
- The Ladies Professional Golf Association keeps trying the "If sex sells, sell it" approach. After several years of steady growth with Nancy Lopez and Jan Stephenson charging male batteries, the LPGA started losing contracts from sponsors and television in the late 1980s. To help boost its image, several members posed in swimsuits for a controversial advertising supplement prepared by the LPGA and published in the February 1989 *Golf* magazine ("Photos Suit," 1989).

As suggested in Chapter 5, the power of the economic relationship between television and sport in the 1990s has transformed sport in the image of television.[6]

Selling the LPGA: Personalities and Sex Appeal

Why is selling the right "image" of the LPGA so important? Unlike sports in which players are under contract for one or more years, financial rewards in golf are directly tied to performance. The amount of reward is directly tied to the size of the tournament purse (Theberge, 1978). Attracting sponsors to fill these purses and to buy the television time for the event is the paramount marketing goal.[7]

Women in sports have long been blamed for lacking self-promotion and marketing skills (Kay, 1985). Except, that is, for the flamboyant Babe Didrikson Zaharias, who was criticized for being too full of self-promotion. Babe had a great flare for publicity. "The press saw her as a female version of Will Rogers, a blunt-speaking Texan going up against the genteel snobbism of country club golfers" (Sochen, 1987, p. 123). But when she, golfer Patty Berg, husband George Zaharias, agent Fred Corcoran and Wilson Sporting Goods put together the "proette" (a press term for women golfers) tour in 1949, only 11 women signed up. Why? At least one reason was that the concept of playing for pay ran afoul of the class-based notions of amateurism that permeated American sport at the time.

Babe died in 1956, but the tour did not. It continued a slow and steady pace. A decade later, 30 to 35 players were playing. The first televised event was the 1963 U.S. Women's Open (Whitworth, 1990). By 1967, the number of players had grown to 50-55. Kathy Whitworth was the leading money winner on the tour in 1966 and earned $33,500.

In 1975, advertising executive and hockey marketer Ray Volpe was hired as the LPGA's first commissioner. In 1976, the first publicity director, Bob Basche was hired (Aubin, 1976). Depending on whose version of history you believe, Volpe's hiring was a response to competition for sponsorship dollars from the women's tennis tour, players' dissatisfaction with low prize money, the result of a war between straight women and lesbians on the golf circuit about the image of the tour or some combination of these factors (Glenn, 1991; Kaplan, 1979).

> Volpe thought he'd found his savior in Laura Baugh, a pretty, shapely young player who hadn't won any of the major tournaments but did wear tight T-shirts and colorful hats while she played. (Kaplan, 1979, p. 91)

Baugh also pleased male sportswriters. In 1974, *Sports Illustrated*'s Barry McDermott described her as: "The tour's bonafide starlet and a delight for entrenched chauvinists. Wearing daisy earrings, the petite, honey blonde chipped in for an eagle on the ninth hole, her second in two days" (p. 31). With Baugh titillating the crowd and the writers, Volpe went about the work of selling the association to sponsors, aided in no small way by public involvement of golfer, TV show host and Colgate-Palmolive celebrity spokesperson Dinah Shore, described as "a non-threatening missionary for women's sports" (Kaplan, 1979, p. 5). CP chipped onto the LPGA golf green because their soap opera commercials were getting lost under those of Procter & Gamble, which had a much larger advertising budget (Kaplan, p. 4). By 1976, tour purses totaled $2.5 million for 31 tournaments, including four sponsored by CP.

In 1977, Judy Rankin became the first LPGA golfer to earn six figures in a season, and in 1978, NBC telecast the LPGA championship from Kings Island, Cincinnati. Purses had risen to $5 million by 1980. Then,

> The LPGA made giant steps into the realm of big money because of one individual—a charismatic young brunette with a dazzling smile: Nancy Lopez. It's no coincidence that from Miss Lopez's rookie year, 1978, through her last year as the tour's number-one player, 1985, LPGA purses jumped to $9 million. (Glenn, 1991, p. 280)

Lopez was on the cover of *Sports Illustrated* and the front page of *The New York Times*.[8] Newspaper headlines from tournament events were as likely to feature Lopez's finish as they were to announce the winner (Glenn, 1991). She appeared on television programs, including, of course, *The Dinah Shore Show*. With Nancy Lopez smiling to the crowd on the tour, the LPGA had the charismatic individual it needed to offset "the image problem."

When Lopez took a maternity "leave" in 1983, no one emerged to take her place. A new commissioner, John Laupheimer, was hired in 1985. Then uncertainties in the economy caused sponsored tour events such as Elizabeth Arden, Uniden, Mazda and J&B Scotch to be canceled. The men's senior tour also started up with big names and plenty of nostalgia to sell. Faced with the loss of tournaments and sponsors, Laupheimer resigned in mid-1988 (Barrett, 1988). Operating without a commissioner, the "image" issue reared its ugly head again among players. It became a public feud after the special swimsuit insert in *Golf* magazine ("Photos Suit," 1989).

In November 1988, Bill Blue, a mix of "slick public presentation with a brusque interpersonal style," was hired as commissioner. Wrestling with the question of whether to market the LPGA on looks or on the talents of the golfers, Blue openly suggested that the tour needed to tackle the public perception that the pros were lesbians

(Diaz, 1989, p. 6). Ultimately, his leadership style was so divisive that he alienated many sponsors and players and was forced to resign in 1991.

Charles S. Mechem, a lawyer and former chairman and chief executive of Taft Broadcasting, was named the fourth commissioner in LPGA history in February 1991. Mechem has said he doesn't believe in a Roman candle-type promotion; instead he thinks that he can market the LPGA as the best women golfers in the world and still bring sponsors and stability to the tour.

> Years ago, I read a speech by the chairman of Procter and Gamble which said the only effective form of marketing is superior product performance. If that's true for a bar of soap, it's certainly true of a professional sports organization. (Mechem, cited in Allen, 1993, p. 46)

Mechem seems less inclined to emphasize sex appeal to sell the tour than his predecessors and more inclined to "be open about things like how far the women actually hit the ball" (Diaz, 1989, p. 6). The LPGA had never released such statistics! (The average is 215 yards.) Nineteen LPGA tournaments (10 on the commercial networks) were televised in 1992 (Allen, 1993). The television commercials promoting the tour presented golf as a sport for everyone, especially women and their children.

The Sports Information Director

Clearly, the goal of professional sports promotion is raising funds to pay players' salaries and provide institutional profits. Ostensibly, fund-raising is not the goal at the collegiate level. However, the publicity and promotional duties performed by the Sports Information Director (SID) at least help to sell tickets and presumably affect the image of the school, which has an impact on its ability to attract students and donations.[9] The College Sports Information Directors Association (CoSIDA) was formally organized in 1957, as an outgrowth of the American College Public Relations Association (Schulthess, 1985). Today, it hosts workshops and a national conference and publishes a monthly newsletter. When initially formed, CoSIDA focused its attention almost exclusively on men's intercollegiate sports. However, with the passage of Title IX of the Education Amendments Act of 1972, which prohibited sex discrimination in programs receiving federal funding, women's sports entered the competition for support services such as sports information.

The SID's duties can, and generally do, include several or most of the following: press releases, media relations, promotions of special events/tournaments, hometown contact, photography, publications, programs, score reporting, budgeting, supervising office help and attending events both home and away (Smith, 1980). A study by Cramer found that SIDs play a significant gatekeeping function in the coverage and portrayal of athletes, particularly women athletes (Cramer, 1981). Two other studies examined the qualifications necessary to become an SID (Driver, cited in Smith, 1980; Flarup, 1980) and a third investigated why SIDs leave the field (Wolff, cited in Smith, 1980). The third study also asked respondents about the impact of Title IX and nearly 71% indicated that it had affected the athletic structure at their institution. For many this caused an increase in employment of student assistants in sports information and in some cases the creation of separate offices for women's sports information.

The role and duties of SIDs in promoting women's sports have been examined in two studies conducted a decade apart.[10] The first was undertaken in 1980 by Karen Smith, then Women's Sports Information Director at the College of William and Mary. Her study grew out of the formation of a Publicists for Women's Sports Committee, which was established at the 1980 CoSIDA convention.

The formation of this committee coincided with the NCAA's successful move to take over governance of women's intercollegiate sports, in which it offered to pay for transportation to women's championship events and to provide lucrative television contracts to colleges and universities who signed up (Uhlir, 1984). The purpose of Smith's survey, administered to schools that were members of the Association for Intercollegiate Athletics for Women (which governed women's intercollegiate athletics at the time), was to develop a demographic profile of publicists for women's sports. She sent surveys to the 961 AIAW member institutions and had a response rate of 38.4% or 369 surveys (Smith, 1980, p. 17).

Nearly 71% of her respondents were men and more than a third of all respondents were between ages 25 and 29. More than 80% of her respondents had five years or less experience. The majority of respondents in Smith's study—both men and women—earned between $10,000 and $15,000. Many of the respondents were former news or sports reporters with degrees in journalism, English and public relations. The most popular job title was that of Director of Sports Information (48%), with 11% of her respondents called Director of Women's Sports Information (WSID) with primary responsibility for publicizing women's sports. The majority (63.4%) of her female respondents had the title of WSID. Most Directors of Sports Information reported to Men's Athletic Directors and most of the Directors of Women's Sports Information reported to Directors of Women's Athletics.

In terms of job assignments, more than 60% of her respondents were responsible for publicizing both women's and men's sports teams. She found that more than 80% spent less than 25% of their time on fund-raising and promotion. Nearly 91% reported generating press releases for women's sports. About two thirds of the respondents did not have a separate budget for women's sports publications.

Smith also asked her respondents whether they thought women's and men's sports should be governed by one administrative body. More than 70% of her respondents favored one organization.

Since Title IX and the NCAA takeover, the average number of sports offered for women at the intercollegiate level has risen: 7.24 per school as compared with 5.61 in 1980 (Acosta & Carpenter, 1990). The number of women participating in intercollegiate sport has grown from 16,000 in 1972 to nearly 140,000 today (Ditota, 1992). However, by 1990, the number of female head coaches of women's sports teams had declined by 43% from the pre-Title IX era and the number of athletic programs headed by women stood at 15.9%, compared to the 90% of coaching and administrative jobs held by women before Title IX (Acosta & Carpenter, 1990).

The primary purpose of the second study was to examine the role of the college or university sports information director responsible for women's intercollegiate sports, particularly during a time when opportunities for women to participate in male-directed intercollegiate athletics had grown and women's leadership roles had declined (Cramer, Creedon & Granitz, 1991). Specifically, the study sought to provide a demographic profile of the individuals, to examine the techniques that they were using in their efforts and to attempt to discover the extent of these efforts.

Surveys were mailed to 1,452 members of CoSIDA in early 1990, with a final response rate of 44% or 613 usable surveys. Overall, 83% of the respondents were male and 17% were female. The mean age for female SIDs was 30 and 34 for men. The mean experience for women was six years as compared with nine years for men. Almost all of the respondents were college graduates and 45% of the sample had a graduate degree or some graduate credits. As undergraduates, more than half of those surveyed majored in journalism, communications or public relations. More than 90% of the respondents were Caucasian. Eighteen were African-American and four of these respondents were women. The mean salary range for both men and women in the study was $20,000 to $29,999. The most significant factors in determining salary were school enrollment, market size, NCAA division, age and experience.

The most popular job title of respondents (N = 406) directing women's sports was that of Sports Information Director. A variety of other job titles were used: Assistant SID, 118; Director of Women's Sports Information, 14; Men's Sports Information Director, 2; College Information Director, 8; Public Relations Director, 9; Public Information Director, 10; Graduate Assistant, 11.

At most schools, the women's sports information budget was found to be part of the general sports information budget. The mean percentage of the total sports information budget spent on women's sports was 31%. Although many SIDs reported to another individual in athletic administration, they reported retaining a fairly high degree of autonomy in terms of deciding which sports would be publicized. At 43% of the schools, the primary decision maker with regard to which sports are publicized was the SID. At 13% of the institutions, publicity decisions were shared, usually with an athletic director, and at 17% of the schools, the athletic director was the primary decision maker. NCAA Division I schools employed half of all the respondents.[11] Forty-nine percent of female survey respondents (62) and 49% of male survey respondents (247) worked for Division I schools.

The respondents reported performing four primary functions. These were: writing news releases, making phone calls to the media, running sports event promotions and advertising. Thirty-eight percent of the schools use all four methods and another 38% use three types, usually omitting advertising. Twenty-nine percent use only two methods, typically writing news releases and making media phone calls. The larger the enrollment of the school, the more likely respondents were to use a variety of promotion and publicity techniques.

In keeping with the post-Title IX averages, respondents' schools offer slightly more than seven sports for women. Women's basketball ranked the highest among those sports promoted with 80% of all respondents selecting it as the sport they publicize the most. Volleyball was ranked second and softball third. According to three quarters of the schools, newspapers provide 70%-100% of their women's sports coverage. Television ranked second and radio third.

More than 10% of those surveyed provided unsolicited comments on the issues they faced in promoting women's sports. Survey respondents listed a number of structural variables that constrained their ability to successfully promote women's sports. These included: media news values, media format, revenue versus nonrevenue sport status and the role of the NCAA in conferring status on certain sports to the exclusion of others. Other constraints on sports information office efforts to promote women's sport included: lack of public interest, a media system interested solely in "winning" teams and the role of the coach in the sports information effort. The largest group of comments focused on news values and market constraints:

- Sports editors tell me that with the exception of football and men's basketball, *all* my teams must do two things to warrant more coverage: (1) win; (2) attract fans.
- We provide effort greater than the reward (relative to men) to get the coverage we enjoy. To expect coverage to be equal is blatantly unrealistic. The sporting public dictates coverage and the sporting public does not consider them [men's and women's sports] equal.
- The lack of media coverage of women's athletics is the result of an ongoing vicious circle—few in the public care, so less is covered, which makes it more difficult for people to take an active interest.

- In order to have penetration in media markets you need to have at least 2 of the following: (1) consistent winners on a national basis; (2) charismatic coach or players; (3) area with traditional fan support or lack of entertainment alternatives.

- I have worked at two schools (Houston and SMU), both in large metropolitan areas (poor coverage) and at Texas [Austin] where media coverage is outstanding. Obviously, size of the market is important.

A second group of responses dealt with quality of play and image:

- In the town where I work, women would get loads of media coverage—if they were good enough to play in the NFL.

- The public is used to seeing athletes make impossible plays look routine. Women aren't capable of many of those things, and fans want slam dunks and 490-foot home runs.

- And then there's the femininity problem. The average fan doesn't want to see women who wish they were men play. Sports that allow women to be women (tennis, gymnastics, volleyball, track) enjoy some support. One's that don't (lacrosse, field hockey, basketball, soccer, softball) aren't supported. Rightly or wrongly, this is the perception people have.

Another set focused on institutional constraints:

- To put it bluntly, our AD [athletic director] has negated women's sports. . . . [O]ne coach has commented, "At this school, there's basketball and then there's women's basketball." All in all, we're in the dark ages in equality.

- With an increased staff, we could provide more information on women's sports to the media and better publicize upcoming events—but that doesn't mean the local media will give us more coverage. Our university is located in a major metropolitan area and we compete for coverage with six other colleges and three professional teams within a 30-mile radius.

- We are starting football at our college next fall, and I can offer horror stories already about the contrast in attention given to that sport and our women's sports by the media as well as by our school administration.

- This university does not classify sports by men's/women's teams; rather [we use] revenue (football, men's basketball, women's basketball) and nonrevenue.

Comparing these two studies shows that today's SID is a few years older, with a couple of years more experience, and is more likely to have a degree in journalism, communication or public relations than his counterpart a decade ago. Yet contrary to the overall trend in the public relations field in which women are becoming the majority of practitioners, men are assuming increased responsibility for promoting and publicizing women's sports at the collegiate level. In the 1990 survey, 83% of those responsible for promoting women's intercollegiate sport were men, as compared with only 71% in 1980.

The significant decline in the percentage of females responsible for women's sports promotion—from 29% in 1980 to 17% in 1990—is disheartening. The title of Women's Sports Information Director has nearly disappeared. Whereas 11% of Smith's sample used the title WSID, only 2.3% of the 1990 survey respondents did. Overall, women constitute less than 10% of those in top promotions or media relations jobs in the sports industry (Helitzer, 1991).[12]

Pandering or Empowering?

Women's sports promise to become increasingly attractive to the sports/media/marketing complex. Why? They are a relatively cheap buy. They are nearing a critical audience mass in an era of narrowcasting. They are eager to please. But remember we are not talking about equity here; this is a commercial transaction. Something will need to be exchanged. What might that be?

As male athletes assault the corporate bank in salary negotiations, women athletes could become an attractive low-cost alternative. When she organized the LPGA, Babe Didrikson discovered the class-based notions of amateurism that pervade the economic structure of sport. The amateur shill game called college athletics provides another example. What value would be assigned to women working as athletes? What concessions would be necessary? What lifestyle compromises would be demanded by the sports/media/marketing complex?

The image struggle in the LPGA and the structural changes in women's intercollegiate sports information relate to the economic shocks being felt throughout the sports/media/marketing complex. Yet the persons responsible for promoting women's intercollegiate and professional sports, the majority of whom are men, appear to be parroting traditional news values and modeling the status quo when the conditions argue for a much more strategic perspective. Both surveys found that the primary function of the SID is perceived to be that of media relations. Until the hiring of Mechem, each of the three previous LPGA commissioners had concentrated his attention on television contracts.

Constrained by this press agentry/media relations perspective, women's sport is promoted from the same economic, social and cultural context as men's sport. It has become a product to be packaged, promoted, sold and distributed to an audience expecting to see men's sport. As a commercial commodity with its value determined in the marketplace, promoted through traditional channels and in traditional ways, the "product" will always be perceived as lesser than or of inferior quality.

Beyond the reformist strategies designed to achieve equity and attract more media attention, more fundamental change in women's sports promotion may be possible, even advisable. Although the economics of sports promotion are changing somewhat, the new configuration promises to retain the underlying values of the sports/media/marketing complex. The story of the NCAA takeover of women's sports is ample proof that equity simply means women's sports must conform to established norms.[13]

What if, in the interactive media age just around the corner, promoting women's sports meant something totally different? What if, instead of marketing the outcome of the event and comparing the quality of play to that of men, the focus was shifted? What if we rejected packaging women's sports in the image of the sports/media/marketing complex? What if the "best" in sport were no longer determined solely by commercial values, but rather by a variety of values?

What if the LPGA gave up striving for a uniform, acceptable, feminine image? What if it simply reflected what is? "There are cover girl types, the jocks, the gays, the divorcees, the Bible-study faction, the married women, and the single mothers" on the tour (Edmondson, 1987).[14] There is yet another model in public relations theory that may provide a basis for a new approach to balancing commercial and other values in the promotion of sport (see Creedon, 1993).

Communication in this model values differences. Its goal is not to achieve homeostasis or to minimize differences. It values dissymmetry, which is symmetry or balance in different directions.

It can work. Pam Highlen describes a Co-Essence Model of Sport in Chapter 13 based on these principles. She illustrates how it has contributed to the success of the Stanford women's basketball program under head coach Tara VanDerveer. The new model is not about hype or media coverage. Sanford's success does not come from external sources; they find it in values of self-esteem, trust, respect and love. And they sell plenty of tickets, have numerous sponsors and command the respect of their opponents. They often get more coverage than the men's team. Oh yes, and they're winners, and the sports/media/marketing complex loves a winner.

Notes

1. Jhally (1989) uses the term *sports/media complex*. I prefer *sports media/marketing complex* because it explicitly acknowledges the central role of marketing (commercialization) in the sports world. Jhally's cultural studies analysis of sport is fascinating but unfortunately lacks a critical feminist perspective.

2. Prior to 1984, the NCAA negotiated broadcast network television rights contracts for all 509 of its member schools (Eastman & Meyer, 1989). Since then, Division IA schools (Ohio State, UCLA, Maryland, etc.) and some others have negotiated their own rights to regular season contests. In some cases, the schools assign the rights to a production syndicate who then sells the rights to cable networks, local stations or the broadcast networks. Currently, the NCAA gets nearly three quarters of its annual budget from television contracts (Helitzer, 1991).

3. However, sponsor problems and controversy challenged the WPVA in 1993. Coors, the WPVA's main sponsor, was forced to reduce its ubiquitous marketing signage on ESPN telecasts, so the tour moved to Prime Network, which reduced sponsorship revenues for the league ("Women's Pro," 1993). And PowerBurst, one of the league's top sponsors, filed for bankruptcy causing a reduction in the number of events and in tournament prize money from $40,000 in 1991 to $20,000 in 1993. Not surprisingly, the expectation that beach volleyball will become an Olympic event in 1996 or 2000 has brought about a power struggle for control of the sport with the men's league, the Association of Volleyball Professionals ("Women's Pro," 1993). Eight former WPVA players signed with the APV for the 1993 season, and the top two WPVA players—Karolyn Kirby and Liz Masakayan—suggested that competing as a supporting event with the men's tour was an insult.

4. In 1980, NBC's coverage of the Association of Intercollegiate Athletics for Women's basketball championship game also outdrew an NBA game. However, both programs were beaten in the ratings by CBS's "The Battle of the NFL Cheerleaders" (Mandel, 1981)! The highest rated women's basketball game to date was the CBS

coverage of Louisiana Tech versus Cheyney (PA) State in 1982, which drew a 7.3 rating or 5.5 million viewers.

5. Men's sport has not been immune from the television transformation flu. Professional basketball instituted the 30-second shot clock to speed up the pace of the game for television audiences. In professional football, we are all too familiar with the "official's time out," which means a break for commercial message. In the broader context, professional franchises are often determined on the basis of media market size.

6. Jhally (1989) suggests that the "argument that because media revenues are so important to their functioning, professional sports have been *transformed* and changed . . . detracts from the fact the sports have *always* been based on commercial relations" (p. 80). His argument is problematic because it suggests that women's sports have *always* had commercialization as a core value (see Chapter 13).

7. Women golfers incur expenses whether or not they win. The cost of travel on the tour, tournament entry fees, caddie fees and so forth must be covered by the golfer. Consequently, many have auxiliary income sources such as sponsorship (an agreement by which an individual or group gives a player financial support in exchange for a percentage of her winnings), fees from lessons and clinics, product endorsements and so on (see Theberge, 1978).

8. Between 1956 and 1992, only eight women golfers made the cover of *Sports Illustrated* (Allen, 1993).

9. Helitzer (1991) suggests that the pronunciation of the acronym SID produces a symbolic association of the role with the Spanish folk hero, El Cid.

10. Except in the case of the specific descriptions of job titles, the acronym SID is used broadly to mean all survey respondents working in sports information capacities.

11. According to the NCAA, Division I status equates to offering at least six sports and full-tuition scholarships; Division II and Division III schools must offer at least four sports and various scholarship money.

12. Susan Waks became the first female public relations director in the National Hockey League in 1977, Susie Mathieu its first sports information director in the same year (Helitzer, 1991, p. 61). In the mid-1980s, Robin Monsky sued the Atlanta Braves for sex discrimination when denied a promotion in the media relations department because the team's management "didn't want a woman traveling with the team" (Fornoff, 1993, p. 200). Several women now hold such positions in Major League baseball, including Monique Giroux, media relations director for the Montreal Expos, and Robin Carr-Locke, assistant director of public relations for the San Francisco Giants. But getting the job does not guarantee acceptance. The harassment faced by Carr-Locke, who joined the Giants' organization in 1985, is detailed in Susan Fornoff's book *Lady in the Locker Room* (1993). Perhaps a light on the horizon is Sports Media Workshop, created in 1992 by former sportscaster Andrea Kirby to train athletes to better deal with the media (Rosenberg, 1992). The Atlanta Braves were her first client. A *Directory of Women in Sports Business* is available from Women's Sport Guide, Box 1417, Princeton, NJ 08542.

13. The most recent round of Title IX equity battles presents an interesting case study. After more than a decade of controlling women's athletics, an NCAA-sponsored gender equity study—conducted at the urging of the National Association for College Women Athletic Directors—led to vague recommendations about problems in funding and participation ratios. Equally unsurprising, the media, whose wallet

stands a good chance of being picked by equity, are using this frame for the findings: equity means cutting men's programs.

14. All types, however, are very white.

References

Acosta, Vivian R. & Carpenter, Linda J. (1990). *Women in intercollegiate sport: A longitudinal study—Thirteen year update 1977-1990.* Brooklyn, NY: Brooklyn Colleges.

Allen, Debbie. (1993, March/April). Aiming for quality and equality. *Golf for Women,* pp. 42-45.

Aubin, Carol. (1976, May). The LPGA's new image makers. *womenSports,* pp. 32, 50.

Barrett, David. (1988, October). A tour in trouble. *Golf,* p. 24.

Bronzan, Robert T. (1977). *Public relations, promotions, and fund-raising for athletic and physical education programs.* New York: Wiley.

Bryant, Jennings & Zillmann, Dolf. (1983). Sports violence and the media. In Jeffrey H. Goldstein (Ed.), *Sports violence* (pp. 270-289). Newbury Park, CA: Sage.

Cramer, Judith A. (1981). Athletic heroes and heroines: The role of the press in their creation. *Journal of Sport Behavior, 4*(4), 175-185.

Cramer, Judith A., Creedon, Pamela J. & Granitz, Elizabeth. (1991, February). The role of the SID in promoting women's coverage. *Cosida Digest, 41*(2), 14-20.

Creedon, Pamela J. (1993). Acknowledging the infrasystem: A critical feminist analysis of systems theory. *Public Relations Review, 19*(2), 157-166.

Dennis, Everett C. (1988). *Media economics and sports coverage: A conference report.* New York: Gannett.

Diaz, Jaime. (1989, February 13). Find the golf here? *Sports Illustrated,* pp. 58-60.

Ditota, Donna. (1992, June 21). Women in sports: After 20 years of Title IX, equality remains a dream. *Syracuse Herald American,* pp. 1, A 12.

Eastman, Susan Tyler & Meyer, Timothy P. (1989). Sports programming, scheduling, costs, and competition. In Lawrence A. Wenner (Ed.), *Media, sports & society* (pp. 97-119). Newbury Park, CA: Sage.

Edmondson, Jolee. (1987, February). The troubled tour. *Golf Digest,* pp. 50-53, 232-235.

First down and $1 billion in 4th quarter. (1991, August 12). *Broadcasting,* p. 38.

Flarup, Tamara. (1980, June 30). *SID salaries from CoSIDA meeting.* Kansas City, MO.

Fornoff, Susan. (1993). *Lady in the locker room.* Champaign, IL: Sagamore.

Glenn, Rhonda. (1991). *The illustrated history of women's golf.* Dallas, TX: Taylor.

The greening of the Celtics. (1989, October 16). *Newsweek,* p. 60.

Grunig, James E. & Hunt, Todd. (1984). *Managing public relations.* New York: Holt, Rinehart & Winston.

Helitzer, Melvin. (1991). *The dream job: $ports$ publicity, promotion and public relations.* Athens, OH: University Sports Press.

Hiestand, Michael. (1993, April 9). Women's hoops final's rating tops NBA. *USA Today,* p. 3A.

Jhally, Sut. (1989). Cultural studies and the sports/media complex. In Lawrence A. Wenner (Ed.), *Media, sports & society* (pp. 70-93). Newbury Park, CA: Sage.

Kaplan, Janice. (1979). *Women and sports.* New York: Viking.

Kay, Linda. (1985, November). In defense of sports-writers (women). *Women's Sports and Fitness*, p. 60.

Klatell, David A. & Marcus, Norman (1988). *Sports for sale: Television, money and the fans*. New York: Oxford.

Koppett, Leonard. (1981). *Sports illusion, sports reality: A reporter's view of sports journalism and society*. Boston: Houghton Mifflin.

Lederman, Doug. (1992). Men get 70% of money available for athletic scholarships at colleges that play big-time, new study finds. *The Chronicle of Higher Education, 38*(28), 1, A45, A46.

Mandel, Bill. (1981, April). Behind the screens. *Women's Sports*, pp. 26-31.

Mandese, Joe. (1993, February 8). Super Bowl '94 has tough act to follow. *Advertising Age, 64*(6), 34.

Maymi, Rosa A. (1987). *Public relations in sports firms: Models, roles, dominant coalition, horizontal structure and relationship to marketing*. Unpublished master's thesis, University of Maryland.

McClellan, Steve. (1992, April 6). Networks come up short on football goal. *Broadcasting, 122*, 14-15.

McDermott, Barry. (1974, April 29). One for the money, two for the show. *Sports Illustrated*, pp. 26-31.

National Collegiate Athletic Association. (1985). *Public relations and promotion manual*. Mission, KS: NCAA.

Neal-Lunsford, Jeff. (1992). Sport in the land of television: The use of sport in network prime-time schedules 1946-1950. *Journal of Sport History, 19*(1), 56-76.

Photos suit LPGA just fine. (1989, June 5). *USA Today*, p. 2C.

Rosenberg, I. J. (1992, February 27). Adviser gives tips on media. *Atlanta Constitution*, p. E1.

Schulthess, Dave. (1985). CoSIDA: A leader in public relations. In *NCAA Public relations and promotion manual* (p. 7). Mission, KS: NCAA.

Searching for diamond success in rough time. (1991, March 11). *Broadcasting*, pp. 29-30.

Shapiro, Walter. (1993, April 12). The last great season. *Time*, pp. 60-65.

Shell, Adam. (1991, July). Firms try to pitch the perfect game. *Public Relations Journal*, pp. 10-11.

Smith, Claire. (1993, June 3). TV contract spurs soul-searching. *The New York Times*, p. B 15.

Smith, Karen M. (1980). *Descriptive profile of the publicists for collegiate women's sports: A survey of demographic characteristics, job descriptions and publicist's needs unrecognized by the collegiate athletic governing organizations*. Unpublished master's thesis, University of Minnesota.

Sochen, June. (1987). *Enduring values: Women in popular culture*. New York: Praeger.

Sports Illustrated. (1986). *Sports Illustrated Sports Poll '86*. New York: Time.

Sports Law Center. (1992). *Sports attendance GNP*. San Francisco, CA: Sports Law Center.

Staudohar, Paul D. & Mangan, James A. (Eds.). (1991). *The business of professional sports*. Chicago: University of Illinois.

Taaffe, William. (1985, April 29). How wrestling got TV in its clutches. *Sports Illustrated*, p. 38.

Theberge, Nancy. (1978). The world of women's golf: Responses to unstructured uncertainty. In Michael Salter (Ed.), *Play: Anthropological perspectives* (pp. 226-239). West Point, NY: Leisure Press.

Thottam, George. (1988). *The economic impact of American television on the Olympics.* Paper presented at the International Association for Mass Communication Research, Barcelona, July 23-28.

Turk, Judy V. (1985). Information subsidies and influence. *Public Relations Review,* *11*(3), 10-25.

Turk, Judy V. (1988). Public relations' influence on the news. In R. Hiebert (Ed.), *Precision public relations.* New York: Longman.

Uhlir, Ann. (1984). The wolf is our shepherd: Shall we not fear? In D. Stanley Eitzen (Ed.), *Sport in contemporary society: An anthology* (2nd ed., pp. 374-384). New York: St. Martins' Press.

West, Robert. (1941). *The rape of radio.* New York: Rodin Publishing.

Whitworth, Kathy. (1990, May/June). A history lesson. *Golf for Women,* pp. 25-27.

Women's pro beach v-ball tour threatened. (1993, June/July). *Fans of Women's Sports,* *1*(7), 4.

WPVA kicks off beach volleyball season. (1991, March). *Women's SportsPageS,* p. 5.

PART II

Cultural Contexts and Gender Values

c. 1940

Double Fault

Renée Richards and the Construction and Naturalization of Difference

Susan Birrell
Cheryl L. Cole

In July, 1976, a reporter covering a local tennis tournament in La Jolla, CA, became suspicious when the defending champion in the women's division was soundly thrashed by a six-foot-two-inch newcomer by the name of Renée Clarke. Searching further, the reporter discovered that Renée Clarke was actually Renée Richards, a "constructed-female transsexual"[1] who less than a year before had been Richard Raskind, a man ranked highly by the United States Tennis Association in the 35-and-over men's division. The media clamor that ensued might have died down had Richards not accepted an invitation to play in a national tournament in South Orange, New

AUTHORS' NOTE: This chapter was written during a developmental leave provided by the University of Iowa and generously supported by the staff and colleagues at University House. The senior author gratefully acknowledges this collegial support. We would also like to thank Nancy Theberge, Linda Yanney and Nancy Romalov and the reviewers for the *Sociology of Sport Journal* for bringing important sources to our attention and for useful critical feedback.

SOURCE: From "Double Fault: Renée Richards and the Construction and Naturalization of Difference" by S. Birrell and C. L. Cole, 1990, *Sociology of Sport Journal* (vol. 7, No. 1), pp. 1-21. Copyright © 1990 by Human Kinetics Publishers, Inc. Reprinted by permission.

Jersey, that his/her[2] old friend Eugene Scott was organizing as a warm-up to the United States Open. The United States Tennis Association (USTA) and the Women's Tennis Association (WTA) promptly withdrew their sanctions from the South Orange tournament. In protest of Richards's participation, 25 of the 32 women originally scheduled to play in South Orange withdrew to enter an alternative tournament hastily arranged and sanctioned by the USTA and the WTA. Undaunted, the 41-year-old Richards advanced through three rounds before losing in the semifinals to 17-year-old Lea Antonopolis. Thus begins one of the more sensational and most illuminating incidents in contemporary sport.

A few days later, Richards announced his intention to play women's singles in the 1976 U.S. Open at Forest Hills, and the antagonism between Renée Richards and the women's tennis world was formalized. The USTA, the WTA and the United States Open Committee (USOC) responded by requiring that all women competitors take a sex chromatin test known as the Barr body test. Richards refused, and the U.S. Open went on without him/her. One year later, s/he took the case to the New York Supreme Court, which ruled that "this person is now female" and that requiring Richards to pass the Barr body test was "grossly unfair, discriminatory and inequitable, and violative of her rights" (*Richards v. United States Tennis Association [USTA]*, 1977, p. 272). The court's decision cleared the way for Richards to play in the women's singles at the 1977 U.S. Open where s/he lost in the first round to Virginia Wade, 6-1, 6-4. Richards's modest professional career continued until 1981 when s/he retired from competition at age 47. After a successful year as Martina Navratilova's coach, s/he left professional tennis and returned to his/her ophthalmology practice.

The entrance of Renée Richards into women's professional tennis created confusion and controversy for the players, the fans, organized tennis and the public. Adding drama to the general controversy over the sexual status of transsexuals was Richards's decision to participate as a woman in a cultural activity still accepted as legitimately divided into two sex categories. The confusion that followed Richards's action illuminates sport as an important element in a political field that produces and reproduces two apparently natural, mutually exclusive, "opposite" sexes.

The controversy over Richards's contested entrance into women's sport was addressed at length in the press and later reexamined in Richards's autobiography *Second Serve* (1983) and the television movie, *Second Serve*. These sources framed the Renée Richards story within traditional liberal rhetoric as a story about fairness and human rights focused around the problematic status of the transsexual. By focusing on the question of individual sex legitimacy, that is, whether Renée Richards is a man or a woman, the media obscured the broader political and social issues.

The purpose of our analysis is to show how our culture constructs women and produces particular notions of gender, sex and difference by examining a case in which these ideological processes are literally enacted: the construction of a "woman," Renée Richards, from a man. In Richards's rather spectacular case, the construction can be examined on two dimensions: the relatively private technical construction of Richards accomplished by an array of medical and legal experts; and the more public construction of Richards accomplished through the discursive practices of the print media and the autobiographical construction offered by Richards in the book and television movie *Second Serve*. In this chapter, we examine the media's construction of the controversy surrounding Renée Richards; we offer a critical reading of discursive practices that construct and control transsexualism, sexuality, sex and gender; and we explore the particular problem posed by Richards's entrance into the highly gendered world of professional sport. Moreover, by asking how it is possible to "change" sexes, what it means to want to change and what it means to be able to change, we argue that transsexualism simultaneously illuminates and mystifies the cultural constructions of woman and man by positioning a seemingly anomalous case within hegemonic discourses of sex difference, sex and gender identity and the gendering of bodies.

Although initially Renée Richards appears to be newsworthy because s/he is a sexual anomaly who challenges taken-for-granted assumptions about sex and gender, our critical reading suggests how the various media frames invoked to explain the meaning of Renée Richards reproduce rather than challenge dominant gender arrangements and ideologies, specifically the assumptions that there are two and only two, obviously universal, natural, bipolar, mutually exclusive sexes that necessarily correspond to stable gender identity and gendered behavior. And although the media coverage of the controversy surrounding Richards's desire to play women's professional tennis is seemingly confined to the immediate event, we will suggest that the media enter into and depend on a broader discourse produced by a constellation of institutions empowered to enforce boundaries between woman and man based on essential conceptualizations of gender, sex and difference.

Transsexualism and the Technological Construction of Woman

Within the dominant discourse of sex research, the category of *transsexual* is assigned to a person who believes that he or she was born into the wrong body, a belief Jan Morris describes as "a passionate, lifelong, ineradicable conviction" (1974, p. 8). The anatomical structure of the body that indexes sex, particularly the genitals, is in direct conflict with the preoperative transsexual's sense of self as a gendered individual. In contrast to transvestites, who habitually cross-dress, "true transsexuals feel that they belong to the other sex, they want to be and function as members of the opposite sex, not only to appear as such" (Benjamin, 1966, p. 13). Such an identity depends on the belief that there are two neatly distinct and absolute categories of sex-gender. As Jan Morris understands it, "I was born into the wrong body, being feminine by gender but male by sex, and I could achieve completeness only when the one was adjusted to the other" (1974, p. 26).

Anxieties constructed through sex, gender and sexuality in our culture reside ultimately in the body and our attitudes toward our own body as well as the bodies of others. Foucault (1979) suggests, "The body is directly involved in a political field; power relations have an intimate hold upon it: they invest it, train it, and torture it, force it to carry out its tasks, to perform ceremonies and emit signs" (pp. 25-26).

The gender dysphoria that transsexuals suffer often drives them to seek "sex reassignment," a lengthy process that requires the services of a number of experts in normalizing disciplines: surgeons, gynecologists, endocrinologists, plastic surgeons, psychiatrists, speech therapists and lawyers. These experts enact a discourse that legitimates sex reassignment by working together to alter what is presented as the unalterable. In this sense, gender dysphoria and transsexualism are not neutral categories but elements in a social system that controls and regulates the body and sex.

For the constructed-female transsexual—estimated as comprising about 80% to 90% of the 10,000 transsexuals in the United States (Grimm, 1987)—the sex reassignment process begins with extensive psychotherapy to ensure that surgery is advisable. This is followed by a lengthy period during which the preoperative transsexual must live as a member of the opposite sex as proof of his or her ability to accomplish appropriately gendered behavior. Finally, a series of operations are performed during which the sex signifiers are exchanged: male sex organs are removed and an artificial vagina is constructed and implanted. Massive doses of female sex hormones, breast implants, cosmetic plastic surgery on the face and Adam's apple and speech therapy further sustain the apparent change.

The knowledge that organizes our understanding of transsexualism has been divided into two major approaches (Bolin, 1987): clinical approaches that characterize the psychiatric and psychological research and are based on a medical model in which transsexualism is constituted as an individual problem, "a syndrome subject to treatment" (p. 41); and sociocultural approaches taken by ethnomethodologists and anthropologists, which focus on "the relationship of . . . transsexualism to the culture at large" (p. 47).

Clinical approaches (e.g., Benjamin, 1966; Money & Ehrhardt, 1972; Money & Tucker, 1975; Stoller, 1975) are concerned with transsexual etiology or the biological and/or psychological variables that have caused transsexualism.[3] They subscribe to some form of sexual essentialism while locating the problem within the individual and the dysfunctional family, "with the family as the largest unit of external etiological influence" (Bolin, 1987, p. 59). However, by focusing on the individual as the pathological victim of a disconcerting sexual syndrome, the body and transsexualism are removed from the technologies of gender[4] and the broader network of social relations in which we live and understand our lives. In this view, the transsexual is blamed for failing to adjust to a rigid system of gender stereotypes. Therapeutic management programs designed to create gender reversal and surgical treatment, though an object of some dispute, are viewed as legitimate treatments to cure transsexuals. Gender dysphoria is represented as a state that can be most effectively corrected through the combination of biomedical and legal authorization of the exchange of the material signifiers that reconstitute sex status.

Sociocultural approaches view transsexualism not as an individual malady but an epiphenomenon that can be understood only within the context of a particular culture. Sociocultural researchers (e.g., Bolin, 1988; Garfinkel & Stoller, 1967; Kando, 1973; Kessler & McKenna, 1978; Williams, 1986) are interested in "what transsexualism reveals about the cultural construction of gender and the sex/gender system" (Bolin, 1987, p. 47). For example, although a disproportionate number of transsexuals are male to female, historically the reverse was true (Bullough, 1975), testimony to the cultural and historical specificity of transsexual emergence.[5] And the ethnocentricity of our two-sex/two-gender paradigm is revealed through analyses of different sex/gender arrangements in other cultures such as the berdasch and the amazonia (Williams, 1986).[6]

The existence of transsexualism is discomforting because it simultaneously disrupts and confirms our common sense about the nature of sex, gender and the relationships between them. Transsexualism unravels and rebinds our cultural notion that there are two and only two, mutually exclusive, naturally occurring, immutable, opposite sexes. The acute gender dysphoria that impels a transsexual to consider surgical remedy suggests that radically reconfiguring the body through the removal and construction of sex signifiers is easier than living in a culture in which rigid gender ideologies do not permit men to act in stereotypically female ways.

The transsexual's solution to gender dysphoria is to change sexes: an individual solution to a systemic problem. Gender dysphoria is the personal manifestation of a larger cultural problem, in this case, the institutionalization of a system that reduces sex to two mutually exclusive, natural categories. By seeking surgical remedy, the transsexual acquiesces to a system that locates individuals as either male or female subjects. Ironically, the transsexual's personal relief reinforces the very system that produces transsexualism.

Contesting Sex: The Legal Construction of Woman

In her critique of the "transsexual empire," Jan Raymond (1979) raises important critical issues: Who is empowered to legitimate transsexual surgery as a valid medical procedure and treatment? Who is authorized to decide who qualifies for sex reassignment and what will the "proof" of qualification be? Who will determine the legal status of the postoperative transsexual? Raymond bases her argument on the cultural construction of gender identity and transsexualism.[7] The successful male candidate for sex reassignment surgery, for example, must demonstrate stereotypical female behavior patterns and attitudes to the men who hold the power to reconstruct his body.

By conceptualizing transsexualism within a scientific-clinical discourse as an exceptional pathological condition traceable to early childhood abnormalities, and by dealing with it on a case-by-case basis, those who control the technologies of gender, especially the transsexual empire, give themselves license to offer a technological solution to the cultural problem of inflexible gender-role prescriptions. For a culture organized around rigid gender roles and for the individuals most discomfitted by those demands, the transsexual empire prescribes the small but expensive Band-Aid of reconstructive surgery.

The Renée Richards case offered a particularly public opportunity to examine Raymond's thesis, but the power of the transsexual empire is one of the major issues obscured by the news media in that case. The coverage of Richards's entrance into women's tennis fails to acknowledge the existence of the male-dominated transsexual empire of surgeons, lawyers and psychologists whose technological and discursive practices make it legally and, Raymond would argue, morally possible to change one's body/sex. Although medical technology makes sex reassignment possible, the legal system insists on and is the final arbiter of sex identity.[8] Renée Richards was positioned as a woman through legal discourses and was granted the legal right to play tennis as a woman because the New York Supreme Court accepted as its criterion of womanhood a female-appearing phenotype brought about by cosmetic surgery and sustained by massive amounts of female hormones.

In formulating their decision, the court was persuaded by the argument of the expert witnesses Richards called on his/her behalf: the surgeon who performed the sex reassignment operation; the gynecologist; and John Money, a psychologist from Johns Hopkins considered the most prominent sex reassignment expert in the United States and a major architect of the transsexual empire. In effect, the court accepted as voices of legitimation those very people responsible for producing Richards as a postoperative transsexual in the first place.

Opposing Richards in court were the defendants—the USTA, the WTA and the USOC—who argued that "there is a competitive advantage for a male who has undergone 'sex-change' surgery as a result of physical training and development as a male" (*Richards v. USTA*, 1977, p. 269). To support their case, they submitted affidavits from an expert witness defending the validity of the Barr body test; from three women professional tennis players—Françoise Durr, Janet Newberry and Kristien Shaw; and from the Director of Women's Tennis for the USTA, Vicki Berner. Those who would articulate oppositional discourses, however, lacked access to both the institutions and the means of challenging them directly. Thus, the Renée Richards case offers literal and dramatic evidence that when an individual's sex is contested, and when the discourses of womanhood are contested, male-dominated institutions have disproportionate power to decide what is and is not a woman. Acting in concert, the medical and legal institutions have the power to authorize, regulate and control the body and sex.

Media Conventions and Frames, and the Construction of Woman

The construction of Renée Richards began with the transformation of Richard Raskind to Renée Richards through extensive psychological and medical procedures. Thus, Renée Richards exists as Renée Richards at least partially because it is technologically possible. The construction continues more publicly in the news media's coverage of the controversy and in Richards's autobiography *Second Serve* (1983) and the made-for-television movie adaptation of the autobiography that aired in 1985. By drawing on examples from both the news media and the autobiographies, we will show how dominant liberal conventions shape the narrative and thus public understandings of Renée Richards and transsexualism.[9]

The media produce news, not truth. Although the media appear simply to report "what happened," they actively construct news through frames, values and conventions. Having made the initial decision that an incident is worthy of treatment as news, reporters and editors make a number of choices that foreground some elements of the potential narrative and obscure others, and they define and delineate issues through a series of choices including headlines, descriptive word choices, photographs, who to authorize with an interview and what to report (Hartley, 1982). Gitlin (1980) suggests that the hegemonic frames, codes and conventions in U.S. news include an emphasis on elements of drama and personality; conventions of "balance," brevity and stereotyping in which the complexity of an event is collapsed into two opposing positions and authorities representing each side are offered the opportunity to comment; temporality; and suspicion of difference and disorder as threat. In the production of news, the frame constructed and choices made offer a preferred reading of the events. As Hall (1977) summarizes the effect:

> It is masked, frequently by the intervention of the professional ideologies—those practical-technical routinizations of practices (news values, news sense, lively presentation, "exciting pictures," good stories, hot news, etc.) which, at the phenomenal level, structure the everyday practices of encoding and set the encoder within the bracket of a professional-technical neutrality which, in any case distances him [sic] effectively from the ideological content of the material he is handling and the ideological inflections of codes he is employing. Hence, though events will not be systematically encoded in a single way, they will tend, systematically, to draw on a very limited repertoire: and that repertoire . . . will have the overall tendency of making things "mean" within the sphere of the dominant ideology. (p. 344)

Following convention, the newspapers recognized the tennis controversy as news because its immediacy and finiteness marked it as newsworthy within the media's ideological code. The coverage of the Renée Richards story began in the national news media on

July 24, 1976, the first news mention of Richards during the South Orange tournament, and it ended on August 18, 1977, the date the papers reported the court decision that granted Richards the right to participate as a woman in the 1977 U.S. Open. By using the official proclamation of the law to provide closure for the story, the newspapers implied that the end of the tennis controversy marks the logical resolution to the issue of transsexualism itself.

To the newspapers, the threshold of newsworthiness had passed. Indeed, only Richards's intentions to enter women's sports had qualified the story as news in the first place: the mere existence of a transsexual in society has not been news since Christine Jorgensen (1967). Thus, the newspapers focus on what seems to be a concrete event: the controversy surrounding Renée Richards's decision to enter women's tennis. But by isolating the event in the present, the historical and cultural context and significance are excluded from the frame. In other words, the ideological codes that journalists follow in their apparent impartiality actively mystify the ideological determinants of the story.

The media identified two issues that guided their coverage: Is it fair to allow Renée Richards to play women's professional tennis? and, Is Renée Richards a man or a woman? Both issues are clearly embedded in ideological frames of liberalism and sexual essentialism. The central narrative was constructed around liberal notions of human rights, and fairness clearly was defined in terms of Richards, not in terms of the women players who had to accommodate him/her as one of them. Richards was represented as the central character within a drama of heroic confrontation between an individual and the tennis bureaucracy. Richards was thus positioned within a familiar cultural discourse of heroic narrative, a story worthy of Frank Capra, about an individual's struggle to prevail against the tyranny of the system.

Generally obscured in the newspapers' construction of this drama of human rights were any serious consideration of the women players' case, particularly the social and historical context within which sport in North America has developed as an activity that privileges males; the meaning of the sex test ordered by the USTA; the meaning of the antifeminist sentiment that was packaged as pro-Richards rhetoric; and the wider implications of the Richards controversy, including the cultural meaning of transsexualism, sex and gender and the power of the male-dominated medical and legal professions to construct and legitimate the female.

The news coverage and the autobiographies differ in the relationship between the issues of whether Richards should be allowed to play women's tennis and whether Richards is a man or a woman. The news media focused on the former and implicated the latter, whereas the autobiography and film used the former as an occasion to focus on the latter. The news media clearly defined the issues in terms of tennis, and the Renée Richards story unfolded as news almost entirely on the sport pages of newspapers and the sport sections of magazines. In contrast, the autobiographies rely on the familiar autobiographical convention of exposing personal truths to address broader issues of transsexualism. In the entire book of 373 pages, tennis comprises only 46 pages, a proportion that is matched in the film as well. Tennis, it is clear, is merely the occasion for the unfolding of a deeper personal narrative.

Yet even taken together, the news media's exposition of the tennis controversy and the autobiographies' analyses of transsexualism as personal history do not offer a critical understanding of transsexualism. Both accounts work within the constraints of a dominant discourse that constructs two essential, universal and opposite sexes. By maintaining a tight frame around Richards and by presenting Richards as an isolated case, they endorse an individualistic, clinical model, and they neglect the larger cultural context of gender arrangements. Beneath the surface of their narratives, the ideology of gender relations lies undisturbed, and important questions go unasked: What is a woman? On what basis should we make our decision? Who shall be empowered to decide? How have women been constructed? What is the connection between sex and gender, since transsexual gender identity makes it clear that one cannot necessarily be mapped from the other? These issues are not centralized in the narrative; they are too controversial and complex to be treated within the media conventions of balance, immediacy, objectivity and appeals to authority.

The Gendering of Renée Richards

The news media focused primarily on whether Richards should be allowed to play women's tennis, but the issue of whether Richards is a man or a woman formed an implicit frame for their narratives. Indeed, the most significant framing device the papers used in their construction of the story was the gendering of Richards as a female. The framing of Richards as female was accomplished through their choice of personal pronouns and through the descriptions of Richards they drew for their readers.

Although there was some doubt in their minds about what sex category Richards belonged in and whether Richards was a transvestite or a transsexual (*New York Times [NYT]*, July 24, 1976), in fact they resolved the problem for themselves and their readers by referring to Richards as "she" from the very first day of coverage. This choice of personal pronoun was made a full year before a legal decision was made,[10] and it is one of the primary ways that the public came to know Richards. By framing Richards as "she," the press resolved the very issue it was purporting to cover: the contest over his/her sex. In a similar manner the casting of Vanessa Redgrave to portray Richards in the television movie tells viewers from the very first minute that Renée Richards is truly and naturally a female.

An individual contesting his or her sex creates a linguistic dilemma in cultures where pronouns and adjectives denote gender. The dilemma is reflected in the quotes from women protesting Richards. Glynnis Coles was quite consistent: "I don't think he should be playing. . . . As far as I'm concerned he's just a man who's had an operation" (*Washington Post [WP]*, January 1, 1978). But Diane Fromholtz's complaint captured the ambiguity most protesters could not work through: "People are laughing at us, at the way she walks on and acts like a female" (*WP*, January 1, 1978). With the very act of refuting Richards's claims to be female, Fromholtz genders Richards female. The most telling statement was Roz Reid's protest on behalf of his wife, Kerry Melville Reid: "We don't believe Renée is a woman. Kerry will never play her again" (*WP*, January 1, 1978).

Officials also had difficulty with the ambiguity. Early in the controversy W. E. Hester, vice president of the USTA, stated, "I don't know on what grounds we could admit her and on what grounds we can refuse to admit him" (*Los Angeles Times [LAT]*, August 12, 1976). The USTA first described Richards as "a man [who had] won a woman's tournament" (*NYT*, July 24, 1976) and "a biological male" (*NYT*, August 14, 1976) and then, as more sophisticated discourses developed, as a "person not genetically female" (*NYT*, August 15, 1976). Phillippe Chatrier of the International Tennis Federation, determined to bar Richards from international competition, said "Mr.- Miss Richards should not be allowed to play" (*Winston Salem Journal*, October 22, 1977).

Richards was also gendered by the press in terms of the descriptions they offered of him, many of which captured the ambiguity the press and the public were trying to resolve. The *Times* noted: "Dr. Richards displays traits associated with both sexes. The soft husky voice is mostly male but the high cheekbones, shapely legs, graceful gold pierced earrings and peach nail polish . . . are distinctly female" (August 19, 1976). And Neil Amdur reported Richards's declaration that "I'm as much a woman as anyone on the U.S. tour" and added:

> At 6 feet 2 inches, Dr. Richards who weighs 147 pounds is considerably taller than most women, even women athletes. She has tight muscles in her calves, the kind you might expect to see on a male sprinter or a halfback in football. Yet her facial features, the high cheekbones, the brown eyes and the sharply defined eyebrows—are distinctly feminine. She carries herself considerably smoother than many female athletes. . . . Her voice is soft, somewhat raspy but firm in the manner of a confident professional. (*NYT*, August 21, 1976)

Elsewhere the press followed their convention of mentioning details of physical appearance of women athletes they generally ignore in male athletes. By reporting on physical appearance, the press legitimates physicality as a valid means of assessing one's sex status, thus confusing the issue of the sex/gender relationship and obscuring the cultural production of such relationships.

Richards's autobiography makes even more explicit the cultural confusion about sex, gender and sexuality. Throughout the book Richards dwells on his/her appearance and the confirmation of his/her true female self, his/her "success as a girl," that is reflected in male attention to his/her female-appearing body: "Renée fed on

[the attention] because [it] represented a casual and ready acceptance of her femaleness. Men held doors open for me, young boys
and sometimes older men looked me over appreciatively" (p 31).
On a trip to Casablanca, Richards was mistaken for a woman and
picked up for the first time. His/her suitor had "eyes that appraised
me with obvious interest. This was the first time I had ever been
openly, unreservedly ogled by a man. I quite liked it. . . . The more
he appreciated me the more I felt like a girl" (p. 220).

Elsewhere in the autobiography Richards enacts male-defined
conceptions of feminine behavior. These include the almost total
objectification of his/her new body, an exhibitionism evident throughout the book and symbolized by sitting naked for an hour in the locker
room while being interviewed by reporters after the South Orange
tournament (*WP*, August 22, 1976), and his/her desire to relate to
men in submissive ways. Of one male friend who had known him/
her only as Renée, s/he says, "He'd always treated me with overtones of male superiority, and I loved it, considering this treatment
a compliment of my validity as a woman" (p. 321).

His/her submission to men is most marked in his/her accounts
of intimacy in which s/he clearly equates sexuality, specifically sexual
passivity and submission, with being a woman. In his adolescent
years, for example, he enacted mock rapes with a male high school
friend under the guise of wrestling naked on his bed.

> Eventually I would have to surrender to his compelling strength.
> There was something about this situation that pleased me. . . . I
> struggled like hell because that was crucial to my feeling. I had to
> know that his dominance was real. . . . It was very sensual to sur-
> render like that. (p. 45)

His/her trip to Europe was full of sexual encounters with strange
men: a truck driver who helped him/her by scraping ice off the wind-
shield of his/her Maserati and then made sexual advances ("After
all, he had done me a favor and deserved something for his trouble. . . .
It's not every day that a truck driver gets to make out with a classy
dame in a Maserati," p. 237); a dangerous episode with a stranger in
Marrakech; and a ménage à trois in Majorca. Finally, after the reconstructive surgery, Richards "waited three months, resigning myself to

a lengthy virginity" (p. 287) before being "deflowered" by a former homosexual lover:

> I got a real sense of satisfaction out of being the object of his desire. . . . Tremendously exciting also were his encompassing size, the smell of him, his hairiness, and his weight pressing down on me . . . . [H]e finished quickly, and I loved that as well. I was warmed by his sense of urgency and the forceful thrusts that accompanied his climax. I didn't have an orgasm myself. . . . Nonetheless, I loved it. I was at last fully capable of the woman's role. (pp. 294-296)

By offering his/her body as a source of sexual pleasure for men, Richards apparently believes s/he has been re-sexed as a woman. S/he has clearly incorporated the dominant cultural discourse on femininity, gendered bodies and femaleness into his/her consciousness.

Constructing the Oppositions

Because conventions limit journalists' abilities to deal with the complexity of the issues posed by controversy, and because reporters are required to cover and present only two sides of a story, the controversy over Renée Richards's entrance into women's professional tennis was reduced and assembled into two mutually exclusive and opposing positions. Support for Richards came from his old male tennis friends, such as Gene Scott and Bobby Riggs, and from two prominent women, Gladys Heldman, who provided several opportunities for Richards to play on a women's tour she was promoting, and Billie Jean King, who invited Richards to play women's doubles with her on that tour.

Opposition came from the rank and file of the women's tour, some of whom refused to play Richards. Their position was represented by Beth Norton in a letter to the WTA quoted in the *Winston-Salem Journal* in which she protested

> the unfairness of forcing young girls to compete with a middle-aged transsexual who previously has been a nationally ranked men's player . . . [and who had] 30 years experience playing men's and boy's tennis. . . . It is only fair that her rights should not impose

upon the rights of girls earning a professional living in the women's
tour. The rights of all of us as individuals should be taken into
consideration. (February 14, 1978)

However, the voices of the individual women tennis players
who opposed Richards were generally silenced by the media,[11] who
represented opposition to Richards as "the tennis establishment,"
"organized tennis" or most often by the impersonal device of initials: the WTA, the USTA, the USOC. The use of initials and the fact
that most spokespersons for these groups were men not only deper-
sonalized the opposition, it obscured sex and gender in a situation that
is in fact about sex and gender. Richards's sex status was constantly
foregrounded while the sex of his/her opposition was obscured.

The autobiographies obscure the opposition even more, never
acknowledging adverse reaction from anyone other than the USTA
and the WTA. Richards claims "most of the women . . . were on my
side" (1983, p. 346). S/he reports receiving 40,000 letters after the
La Jolla tournament, of which "nine-tenths was positive" (p. 324),
and s/he notes a pattern of support from the fans: "I was treated
respectfully and if there were hecklers I never heard them" (p. 350).
The newspapers confirmed this impression (*NYT*, August 28, 1976).

Thus, opposition to Richards was framed as organizational impulses to protect the carefully nurtured image of women's tennis by
protecting the women players from unfair competition.[12] What might
have been reported as a series of individual dramas that paralleled the structure of the sport itself—Richards versus Antonopolis,
Richards versus Smith, Richards versus Evert—was instead packaged as Richards versus The Establishment. The controversy was
framed within the classic American liberal tradition of the heroic
struggle of one individual against the bureaucracy. Given such a
plot, the American tradition is to root for the beleaguered underdog.

Richards solidified his/her role as an underdog by positioning
himself/herself as a spokesperson for a minority group. S/he first
discovered this possibility at the La Jolla tournament when a woman
of color said

Renée . . . I don't want you to withdraw. I am a member of a minority myself. . . . I've found that when people don't know what pigeon-
hole to put you in, your only alternative is to show them what you

are and act as if you have the right to be that. You won't be doing
yourself a favor if you run away from this tournament. You'll be
giving in to stupidity. Hold your head up and play. (p. 317)

Richards noted, "This was the first time anybody had ever put the
issues in broader perspective," and s/he began to consider him-/her-
self "a kind of standard bearer" (p. 317). S/he was deluged with letters
of support from "people who were members of minorities. Among
others, I heard from blacks, convicts, Chicanos, hippies, homosexuals, people with physical handicaps and, of course, transsexuals"
(p. 325). Notably absent from his/her list of oppressed groups is
women. The support surprised Richards who admitted

> I've never even been political [but] . . . I was susceptible to this
> flood of sentiment. Until you have pawed through thirty thousand
> letters pleading with you to stand up for your rights and, in so doing,
> stand up for the rights of the world's downtrodden, you don't know
> what pressure is. Left to my own devices, I probably would have
> resolved my personal pique at being summarily barred from com-
> petition—but, my god, the whole world seemed to be looking for
> me to be their Joan of Arc. (p. 325)

The broadened support an identity as Joan of Arc could provide
him/her was not lost on Richards, who returned to that theme
throughout the book and regularly spoke to it during interviews
with the press. In a story headlined "Renée Richards Pursuing
Tennis Career for a Cause" (August 19, 1976), the *Times* positioned
Richards as a champion for all transsexuals, and later they broadened Richards's underdog status by quoting him/her: "[The USTA]
have done the same thing with me that they've done with every
other minority" (September 1, 1976).

However, Richards's inability to recognize women as a political
group whose interests must be protected, or whose interests might,
indeed do, interfere with his/her own, undermines his/her stance
as a spokesperson for human rights. Richards acknowledged in the
autobiography that much as s/he desired to live life as a woman, s/he
had little sensitivity to the political implications of that life: "My
idea of how a lady is treated was formed prior to women's liberation"
(p. 291). Like many transsexuals, s/he displays an exaggerated,

stereotypical notion of feminine behavior drawn from male-defined notions of gender. This attitude was exacerbated by the requirement that s/he prove to male psychiatrists and medical experts that s/he was ready for the drastic surgical step of sex reassignment by demonstrating almost hyperfeminine behavior.

Moreover, Richards is clearly unaware of the advantages of Raskind's life of male privilege, including attendance at a boys' prep school, graduation from Yale, completion of medical school, a successful surgical practice, the thrill of being approached by a scout from the New York Yankees and access to highly competitive tennis, which s/he took as his/her natural right as a male. His/her own sister, who so longed for such opportunities, was summarily denied them. Yet Richards never acknowledges the implications for women of his/her entrance into their world. As one colleague has suggested to us, "Renée Richards should have had his consciousness raised before he had his sex changed."

Support for Richards as Suspicion of Women

Richards's apparent inability to recognize the political position of women problematizes the media's construction of him/her as a symbol for human rights. But although Richards was being positioned by the press as a symbol of human rights, support for him/her can be read for meanings overlooked by the media: Indeed, it is difficult to read the support for Richards as anything other than opposition to women. Richards's entrance into women's professional sport occasioned an outburst of antifeminist sentiment that was unexamined by the press.

The vehemence of this opposition to the women players can be read within a Foucauldian (1979) context of anxiety, suspicion and surveillance. Terry (1989) has argued that "we witness daily technological developments designed to keep a watchful eye on those entities considered suspicious . . . in an effort to contain 'danger' and restore 'security' "(p. 14). Given the challenges transsexuals pose to the dominant gender system, medical and legal surveillance systems work together to contain what they consider to be dangerous. In a similar manner, growing anxiety about changes in women's social positions and participation in traditional masculine practices such as sport have intensified suspicion of women.

The historical struggles of women and sport are particularly important in locating the sources of the tension around the women players, since Richards entered women's sport in the wake of the women's liberation movement and dramatic gains for women and for women in sport throughout the 1960s and 1970s. Billie Jean King's defeat of Bobby Riggs in "The Battle of the Sexes" (1974) and the success of Gladys Heldman and King in organizing resistance to male control of the women's tennis circuit in the early 1970s marked the end of men's complete dominance in tennis. Ironically, Richards's desire to play on the women's tour depended on the recent struggles of women players and organizers whose successes gave the tour increased economic viability. Thus, Richards stood to benefit directly from the hard-won opportunities for women in sport at the very moment he was challenging them.

Although the media's narratives make general references to the history of sex discrimination in tennis and to past confrontations, in effect they provided space for male voices to frame women's successes within an atmosphere of suspicion, and readers were not given a context in which to understand these challenges to the women's integrity. By directing attention to the event's immediacy and presenting the controversy apart from its historical context, the origins of opposition are obscured. Jameson (1983) notes:

> The disappearance of a sense of history, the way in which our entire contemporary social system has little by little begun to lose its capacity to retain its own past, has begun to live in a perpetual present and in a perpetual change which obliterates traditions of the kind which all earlier social formations have had in one way or another to preserve. . . . One is tempted to say that the very function of the news media would thus be to help us forget, to serve as the very agents and mechanisms for our historical amnesia. (p. 125)

The support for Richards can be read within a context of anxiety and suspicion of women's recent successes in sport. Gene Scott's support of Richards was particularly revealing of this suspicion: "The women players are always talking about sex discrimination but when it comes to a real issue they run and hide. If we followed them we'd still be reading by candlelight" (quoted in Kennedy, 1976, p. 19).

Although Scott's comments allude to a history of struggle around women and sport, to him the "real" issue is not the hard-won rights of the women players but the rights of constructed-female trans-sexuals. Equally telling was Scott's comment to the Washington Post:

> I think the women players today are basically sheep followers. They have worked hard and gotten a terrific recognition factor and lots of spectators. The prize money has escalated out of all proportion. But they did all this by cultivating a reputation of being in a mood of change and imagination. [Their reaction to Renée Richards] shows this is all bunk. They're actually afraid of new ideas. (August 21, 1976)

This quote betrays Scott's feelings about women's equality when he complains that "the prize money has escalated out of all proportion." He dismissed the women players' opposition to Richards as childish whimpering: "I've heard the women whine for years about Chris Evert's dominating on clay" (*WP*, August 21, 1976).

Ilie Nastase's comment also reveals more disdain for the women players than support for Richards: "If she wears a dress, why not? Now you see how strong the women players are. She could be their mother, yet they complain. They're afraid" (quoted in Kennedy, 1976, p. 18).

Richards was proud to report that Nastase "was one of my earliest supporters; he once made a remark that I was more feminine than some of the women already on the tour" (p. 332). Such comments cast suspicion on the women players as imperfect women and belittle the historical struggles of women in sport. Through similar homophobic comments about the women players Richards attempted to establish his/her own claim to female status. Explaining why s/he refused to take the sex chromosome test, for example, Richards argued, "in my case such tests were irrelevant. Of all the potential competitors my sex was the least in doubt. It was a matter of public record based on legal documentation" (p. 343). Admitting that at six feet, one inch "I looked so damn fearsome," Richards continued, "still Betty Stove was six feet tall and hefty besides. So were some lesser known pros, yet their *sexuality* had never been questioned" (our emphasis, p. 344). Throughout the autobiography, Richards used the concepts *sex status* and *sexuality* interchangeably. That confusion reveals the homophobia that also forms the basis for the men's anxieties. Elsewhere the confusion can be understood as a central feature in Richards's construction of him-/herself as a gendered being.

In all the coverage of the Renée Richards controversy, not one mention was made of a male player who did not support Richards, a rather extraordinary detail that may indicate either the press's reluctance to report opposition among male players or the depths of antiwoman sentiment on the tour. As one woman player who opposed Richards complained, "They want to see anybody beat us, even a transsexual" (quoted in Steinem, 1977, p. 85). Thus, "support" for Richards came in a form that simultaneously cast suspicion on or discredited the women players. Steinem pointed out the tactic as well:

When the women players themselves questioned the fairness of their facing someone trained physically and culturally for 40 years as a man, they were ridiculed as poor sports, anti-civil libertarians, or cowards who feared they couldn't win. (p. 85)

The press sometimes joined in the trivialization of the women's opposition. The *Washington Post* acknowledged: "Few on Tour Support Richards" and "Opposition to Richards Apparently Growing" (January 1, 1978). They estimated that 80% of the women opposed Richards: "some of it friendly, some impersonal, some viciously hostile." Yet in one of the few stories dealing with the reactions of individual women players, the *Post* chose to report instances of "downright cruel" behavior, including two British players who appeared at a tournament wearing T-shirts with the message, "I am a real woman."

A final example of producing sympathy for Richards by casting suspicion on or blaming women can be found in Richards's autobiography. The book is an extended narrative of personal etiology in which Richards recounts in detail the anguish of gender dysphoria, his/her analysis of the causes and his/her 41-year search for remedies, including the mutilation of his/her penis in a denial of the signifier of manhood, vivid accounts of sexual adventures into hyper-heterosexuality, transvestism, homosexuality and quasi-lesbianism and the cruel series of promises and rejections from the medical establishment, the psychiatric community and family and friends as s/he finally sought sex reassignment.

In the book and movie a major focus of blame and suspicion was Richards's mother. The book begins, for example, with the words, "My mother was a headstrong woman" (p. 1) and within two pages the reader has been acquainted with the sex role reversals tradition- ally believed to be the root of transsexualism and male homosexu- ality: the domineering mother, the submissive father. Richards paints a picture of a childhood full of gender confusion—an older sister named Michael who wanted to be a boy, and his mother and sister's habit of dressing him in girl's clothes, including a traumatic incident at age four when he was humiliated by being made to appear in public dressed as a girl. Richards argues that "my early life is strewn with unsubtle touches that beg to be seen as reasons for my sexual confusion. If they aren't the true cause they ought to be" (p. 5).

Most of these incidents are depicted in the film as well, and a rather foreshortened analysis is offered by his/her psychiatrist mother (Louise Fletcher in a tight performance reminiscent of her portrayal of Nurse Ratched in *One Flew over the Cuckoo's Nest*). When confronted by her son's admission of deep sexual confusion, she prescribes psychiatric therapy and states simply, "Maybe it's my fault. . . . You probably identified with me instead of your father. Quite *natural* really. I was so strong" (our emphasis). To underscore her strength, she is portrayed in her first scene as a feminist, and her first line, de- livered to someone on the phone while her son awaits her attention, is, "But women have always had to fight." In both the book and the film, strong women come in for more than their share of blame for Richards's condition while cultural constructions of rigid gender and sex ideologies go unaddressed.

Competitive Equality and the Natural Inferiority of Women

Opposition to Richards was framed in terms of the issues of com- petitive equality and the domino effect. As the USTA saw it, "The entry into women's events . . . of persons not genetically female would introduce an element of inequality and unfairness into the championships" (*NYT*, August 15, 1976). USTA counsel Peter Leisure argued in court, "It would be unfair to have women who have worked hard and prepared for this tournament beaten by a person who is *more than woman*" (our emphasis, *NYT*, August 11, 1977). Added to the fear that Richards's male body provided an insurmountable natural advantage over the women players was the fear that Richards would "open the way to problems in the future from young male players with transsexual tendencies" (*NYT*, December 31, 1976). As Richards viewed the issue:

> If I was allowed to play, then the floodgates would be opened and through them would come tumbling an endless stream of made-over Neanderthals who would brutalize Chris Evert and Evonne Goolagong. . . . Some player who was not quite good enough in men's tennis might decide to change only in order to overpower the women players. (p. 345)

These debates over fairness were translated into issues related to the body and power. The body, one of the most seemingly natural elements of social life, was foregrounded by the press. Descriptions emphasizing Richards's/women's physical appearance and women's physical inferiority were presented uncritically and circulated by the media. The logic they employed seemed to say that if Richards is weaker than s/he was or if s/he adorns his/her body in stereotypical feminine ways, then Richards is weak enough and feminine enough to be allowed to play.

Because the media focused on men's "natural" ability rather than the years of privileged access to sport that Richard Raskind had enjoyed, they foregrounded physical definitions of sex and gender and obscured cultural ones. Richards also constructed the argument in physiological and biomechanical terms. S/he noted with characteristic humor, "They think of me as a bionic woman" (*NYT*, August 18, 1976), but s/he refuted this view. Noting the changes in his/her body as the result of hormonal treatments, s/he said, "The tone of the muscles . . . seemed to be softer now" (p. 172). Of his/her tennis game s/he remarked, "I didn't notice much decrease in my general abilities though I was definitely less strong. After six months of hormone therapy I estimate that I had about four-fifths of my previous strength" (p. 178). In fact, Richards argued that his/her heavier male bone structure and hormonally reduced muscle mass actually meant "I was playing with a handicap" (p. 344). S/he argued that his/her losses proved a point: "They served to inform the public that I was not an unbeatable behemoth out to prey on helpless little girls" (p. 350).

The discourse on bodies within the Richards's controversy demonstrates the cultural significance of constructing women's bodies as different from and representing them as physically inferior to men's bodies. The challenge of Richards's presence in women's sport works to naturalize women as physically inferior, and that assumption of the natural inferiority of women is evident in Richards's thinking throughout the autobiography. Playing social tennis in Europe while undergoing hormonal treatment preliminary to his/her operation, Richards was pleased at his/her partners' reaction to his/her superior skill but "when I missed a ball, they were quick to blame it on my being a woman. I didn't mind these jibes because they affirmed my womanliness" (p. 238).

Richards's mediocre performances on court were also used by the press to suggest his acceptability as a woman. After Richards lost to Antonopolis in South Orange (August 28, 1976), the *Times* asked, "So what was all the fuss about?" Billie Jean King argued in Richards's defense, "She does not enjoy physical superiority or strength so as to have an advantage over women competitors in the sport of tennis" (*Richards v. USTA*, 1977, p. 272). And the USTA eventually decided against an appeal because Richards "did not represent the physical threat that officials and players once feared" (*NYT*, August 18, 1977). Richards himself noted that "none of the fears that drove them to ban me ever proved warranted. I certainly haven't dominated the world of women's tennis" (p. 365).[13]

Richards's inability to "dominate" women's tennis is offered as proof of his/her status as a woman. Radically reconfiguring his/her body through the exchange of material sex-signifiers has apparently cost Richards his/her natural superiority as a (former) male. Through reference to his weakened condition, the news media and Richards construct Richards as less-than-male and thus an acceptable challenge for women players.

Representation and Constraint

In this chapter we have tried to show how meanings of sex, gender and difference are literally inscribed onto the body and then how that body is represented through the discourse of news and the autobiographical constructions of individual subjectivity. The ambiguity of Richards's constructed-female transsexual body triggered a crisis in representation in terms of sport and the body. However, the media not only ignored the contradictions posed by Richards but positioned him/her as a hero and a signifier of resistance while women as a group became targets for the exercise of power through criticism. Homophobic and sexist discourses were constructed to contain women as suspicious. Dyer (1982) reminds us:

> A major legacy of the social and political movements of the Sixties and Seventies has been the realization of the importance of representation. The political chances of different groups in society—powerful or weak, central or marginal—are crucially affected by how they are represented, whether in legal and parliamentary discourse, in educational practices, or in the arts. The mass media in particular have a crucial role to play, because they are a centralised source of definitions of what people are like in any given society. How a particular group is represented determines in a very real sense what it can do in society. (p. 43)

The Renée Richards case provides a dramatic moment for examining these issues.

Our examination of the media's representation of the controversy around Renée Richards is an attempt to illuminate the everyday practices of the media and the processes through which representations define femininity. In this case, the media accepted as unproblematic the assumptions of liberalism, dominant images of femininity and ideologies of sport. Although the contradictions embedded in and through the processes of transsexualism potentially trigger a crisis in representations of sex and gender, the conventions of the media make it difficult to articulate and interpret the controversy outside of dominant discourses.

This is not to suggest that all readings are symmetrical with encodings or preferred readings. The varied and complex lived experiences of social actors no doubt produce readings that depart from the frame constructed by the commercial media. But the tight frame and the narrative constructed around the controversy combined with a neglect of the historical position of women and sport, the meaning of the possibility of transsexualism and the technologies of gender work to constrain the possibility of alternative readings. These conventions produce what Hall (1977) has suggested is the endemic tendency of the media: support of the status quo.

Renée Richards, Sport and the Production of Difference

Renée Richards's determination to enter women's sport, the support and opposition to that move and the representation of the controversy that the media constructed provide fascinating insight into our cultural understandings of sex difference, gender behavior and the role that sport plays in their production and reproduction.

The entrance of a transsexual into women's sport posed an interesting dilemma that was symbolized by the fact that Richards had to sue to gain the legal right to enter sport as a woman. After all, Jan Morris did not have to sue to be allowed to be a writer, Christine Jorgensen did not have to sue to become an entertainer and Richards continued his/her career as an ophthalmologist. The particular difficulty of this dilemma reveals sport not only as a gender-producing, gender-affirming system but as a difference-producing system. For sport works to differentiate winners from losers, the men from the boys, the men from the women. As a significant gendering activity, sport not only reproduces gender and sex differences but produces a logic of differentiation.

Because sport celebrates physicality within a competitive frame, working to determine winners based on physical superiority, it is a major site for the naturalization of sex and gender differences. Moreover, sport's logic continually reproduces men as naturally superior to women (Connell, 1983; Willis, 1982). The sex test instituted for the 1968 Olympic Games is a clear example of the manner in which sex categories are vigilantly maintained in sport. The sex test arose from the suspicion that superior female athletic performances, such as those of Ewa Klobukowska, were actually accomplished by women who were not truly women or by craftily disguised men. The implication is that superior athletic prowess is the natural domain of males.

The prestige of athletic victory, the "natural" inferiority of women constructed through sport's power as metaphor and thus the easier competition assumed in the women's division all lead to the logical conclusion that enterprising men might try to pass as women. Renée Richards represented one form that challenge might take. Although Richards asked, "How hungry for tennis success must you be to have your penis chopped off in pursuit of it? How many men would do it for a million dollars?" (1983, p. 345), in fact the U.S. obsession with sport makes it not at all unlikely that some man would willingly sacrifice his penis for victory; drug abuse, steroid use, blood doping, urine transplants, overtraining and ignoring life-threatening or crippling injuries are all a part of the modern sport scene.

A critical reading of the Renée Richards incident illuminates the part sport plays in the reproduction of an ideology of sex difference/power, gender and sex identity and the regulation of the body. As Willis and others argue, sport is a central site for the naturalization of sex and gender difference; that is, sport produces a narrative structured around physical superiority in which sex differences are understood as, and thus reproduced as, real and meaningful. Transsexualism appears to challenge the neatness and logic—indeed the "reality"—of a sex/gender system marked by biological difference. This reveals not only the social construction of gender but the social construction of the sex-gender connection. Moreover, transsexualism demonstrates that it is not only the categories of difference that are culturally produced but the notion of difference itself.

It would seem as though the re-sexing of an individual such as Richards deconstructs notions of natural sex identity, but in fact, by remaining gendered, Richards reaffirms the concept of difference. By apparently changing sex, Renée Richards appears to upset our dominant ideology of gender relations, but in fact he stabilizes that ideology by merely shifting categories, by demonstrating dramatically that we must have a gendered home and that the "mistakes of nature" can be technologically corrected by man.

As Joan Scott and other poststructuralists point out, "meaning is made through implicit and explicit contrast" (1988, p. 36), through antithesis and difference. Primary among these binary oppositions that structure our discourses and thus our consciousness, indeed the archetype of that ideological practice, is sexual difference. When sex difference is contested, the entire ideological enterprise of meaning through difference is shaken. Although Renée Richards demonstrates the disproportionate power that male-dominated institutions have in the construction and legitimation of woman, even more profound is the illumination the Renée Richards incident casts on our cultural mandate to maintain difference. There are no alternative categories for Richards or other nonconforming subjects to inhabit in the law, medical science, language or sport. Their order depends on the maintenance of the familiar binary opposition of male/female. The Renée Richards case is not only about tennis and transsexualism, not only about the construction of woman, but about the construction of difference itself.

Notes

1. A major purpose of this chapter is to problematize concepts that form the discourse of transsexualism, particularly the assumption that sex reassignment or sex change is possible. We note our objections to these terms with the use of quotation marks at first mention and through the use of the rather awkward phrase "constructed-female transsexual."

2. As we will suggest in our analysis of the media framings of Richards, the pronoun used to describe Richards is a significant political move. After much debate we have opted to refer to Renée Richards as s/he to denote Richards bisexual lived experience and his/her difference from those who have lived only one sexual identity or known only one biological sex. We might have chosen to counter the mainstream positioning of Richards as female by repositioning him as male; however, the choice of a singular pronoun would deny either Richards's past or present positioning.

3. This is true, as well, of the autobiographies of transsexuals (e.g., Jorgensen, 1967; Martino, 1977; Morris, 1974; Richards, 1983), which struggle to comprehend their own personal etiology, which dwell on the personal anguish of gender dysphoria and which end on a note of personal triumph.

4. According to deLauretis (1987), the concept of technologies of gender "takes . . . its conceptual premise from Foucault's theory of sexuality as a 'technology of sex' and proposes that gender, too, both as a representation and self-representation, is the product of various social technologies, such as cinema, as well as by institutional discourses, epistemologies, and critical practices; [meaning] not only academic criticism, but more broadly social and cultural practices" (p. ix).

5. According to Bullough (1975), strict religious sanctions and "a kind of mystic view of the inferiority of the female" made it almost impossible for men to assume the female role without harsh reprisals. Thus, the majority of preoperative transsexuals, or transvestites, prior to the 19th century were women.

6. We persist in our two-sex/two-gender paradigm despite the existence of counterexamples in our own culture: tomboys and sissies, transvestites, female impersonators, drag queens, gay men, lesbians, gender-blending women (Devor, 1987). These anomalies are repositioned within dominant discourse through a variety of cultural practices: labeling homosexuals as queers whose behavior "goes against human nature," refusing to take transvestites and drag queens seriously, patiently waiting for tomboys to grow out of their inappropriate behavior and completely misunderstanding the meaning of the berdasch by imposing an ethnocentric model on them (Williams, 1987).

7. Raymond's book clearly makes an important contribution to sociological understanding of transsexualism through its illumination of the relationship between sex stereotypes and the medical empire's understanding and treatment of transsexuals. Although Raymond's argument is based on an understanding of the cultural constructedness of gender, she contradicts her explanation of the sociocultural construction of gender identity and transsexualism when she argues that female transsexuals can never be real women because women's biology makes females unique. This clearly is a weakness in her argument.

8. Whereas a number of criteria traditionally have been available to distinguish between the sexes—including chromosomes, anatomy or morphological structure, genital or gonadal evidence, endrocrine or hormonal balances and psychological factors (Money & Ehrhardt, 1972)—the law accepts genital anatomy as its means of "official sex designation" (Dunlap, 1979, p. 1132).

9. Our analysis of the news frame is an analysis of three metropolitan newspapers of national reputation: the *New York Times* (*NYT*), the *Washington Post* (*WP*) and the *Los Angeles Times* (*LAT*). Included in the analysis are all news stories, editorials, photographs and cartoons featuring Renée Richards that appeared between July 24, 1976, the first news mention of Richards during the South Orange tournament, and August 12, 1982, when Richards returned to medical practice. However, only occasional articles on Richards appear after August 18, 1977, the date papers reported the court decision that granted Richards the right to participate as a woman in the 1977 U.S. Open. In addition, we included articles in major popular magazines during the same period. These included *Sports Illustrated, Ms., Time, Newsweek*, and the like.

10. The legal system also accomplished gendering through language. In the very case that was to determine Richards's legal sex status, the court referred to Richards as "she" in the very first sentence: "A professional tennis player who had undergone sex reassignment surgery which allegedly changed her sex from male to female" (*Richards v. USTA*, 1977, p. 267).

11. Reactions of feminists outside of tennis were not covered by the news media. Writing in *Ms.* magazine, Gloria Steinem (1977) noted the deeper cultural meaning of transsexualism underlying the Richards story and she decried the diversionary effect that attention to Richards had on women's issues. Marcia Seligman (1977), by focusing on the promotional efforts launched in Richards's behalf and the opportunism s/he displayed, raised serious doubts about his/her sincerity and commitment.

12. The Renée Richards incident illuminates the centrality of economic and commercial interests within sport. Why does the mostly male, clearly conservative tennis establishment oppose Richards? The answer is not to be found in their consciousness of women as a culturally oppressed group: nowhere in any of these narratives are the interests of women as a cultural group foregrounded. Rather they opposed Richards because it was economically irrational to do otherwise. Although their

position was represented as being "for the good of the tour," it represented male protectionism not of women's rights but of commercial profit and economic interest. The economic rationality of the tour depends on a clear division of competitors by sex, because one tenet of profit maximization is to provide a product that clearly differentiates itself from the competition (Jones, 1976). Renée Richards had to be challenged because s/he challenged the division of sport into two separate markets, each open to individual entrepreneurial manipulation.

13. What neither Richards nor the USTA seems to realize is that dominating the game is not the point. None of the top players ever lost to Richards, but many of the younger, less experienced, or lower ranked players did, and their interests should have been seen as equally worthy of protection. In order for Richards to play in the U.S. Open in 1977, for example, some woman player had to stay home. It was not King or Evert or Wade or Navratilova, but it was a professional woman tennis player. It appears that the USTA, assured that its top stars and thus its economic vitality were not in serious jeopardy, abandoned the defense of the rank-and-file players. Their image as protectors of the women players is again seriously compromised by their apparent concern for economic interest.

References

Axthelm, Pete. (1977, September 12). Only human. *Newsweek*, pp. 77-78.

Benjamin, Harry. (1966). *The transsexual phenomenon*. New York: Julian.

Bolin, Anne. (1987). Transsexualism and the limits of traditional analysis. *American Behavioral Scientist, 31*, 41-65.

Bolin, Anne. (1988). *In search of Eve: Transsexual rites of passage*. South Hadley, MA: Bergen & Garvey.

Bullough, Vern L. (1975). Transsexualism in history. *Archives of Sexual Behavior, 4*(5), 561-571.

Connell, Robert. (1983). *Which way is up?* Sydney: George Allen and Unwin.

de Lauretis, Teresa. (1987). *Technologies of gender: Essays on theory, film, and fiction*. Bloomington: Indiana University Press

Devor, Holly. (1987). Gender blending females: Women and sometimes men. *American Behavioral Scientist, 31*,12-40.

Dunlap, Mary C. (1979). The constitutional rights of sexual minorities: A crisis of the male/female dichotomy. *Hastings Law Journal, 30*(4), 1131-1149.

Dyer, R. (1982). The celluoid closet. *Birmingham Arts Lab Bulletin, 1*, 43.

Foucault, Michel. (1979). *Discipline and punish: The birth of the prison*. New York: Vintage.

Garfinkel, Harold & Stoller, Robert J. (1967). Passing and the managed achievement of sex status in an "intersexed" person. In H. Garfinkel (Ed.), *Studies in ethnomethodology* (pp. 116-135). Englewood Cliffs, NJ: Prentice Hall.

Gitlin, Todd. (1980). *The whole world is watching*. Berkeley: University of California Press.

Grimm, David E. (1987). Toward a theory of gender. *American Behavioral Scientist, 31*, 66-85.

Hall, Stuart. (1977). Culture, the media and "ideological effect." In James Curran, Michael Gurevich & Janet Woollocott (Eds.), *Mass communication and society*. London: Edward Arnold.

Hartley, John. (1982). *Understanding news*. New York: Methuen.

Jameson, Frederic. (1983). Postmodernism and consumer society. In H. Foster (Ed.), *The anti-aesthetic: Essays on postmodern cultures* (pp. 111-125). Port Townsend, WA: Bay Press.

Jones, J. Colin. (1976). The economics of the NHL revisited. In Richard Gruneau & John Albinson (Eds.), *Canadian sport: Sociological perspectives* (pp. 249-258). Don Mills, Ontario: Addison-Wesley.

Jorgensen, Christine. (1967). *Christine Jorgensen: A personal autobiography*. New York: Bantam.

Kando, Thomas. (1973). *Sex change: The achievement of gender identity among feminized transsexuals*. Springfield, IL: Charles C Thomas.

Keerdoja, Eileen (with Jennifer Foote). (1978, October 23). Tennis transsexual. *Newsweek*, pp. 28, 33.

Kennedy, Ray. (1976, September 6). She'd rather switch—and fight. *Sports Illustrated*, pp. 16-19.

Kessler, Suzanne J. & McKenna, Wendy. (1978). *Gender: An ethnomethodological approach*. New York: Wiley.

Kroll, Jack. (1976, November 22). The transsexuals. *Newsweek*, pp. 104-105.

Los Angeles Times. Selected articles, August 12, 1976 to August 12, 1987.

Martino, Mario. (1977). *Emergence: A transsexual autobiography*. New York: Signet.

Money, John & Ehrhardt, Anke. (1972). *Man and woman, boy and girl*. Baltimore, MD: Johns Hopkins University Press.

Money, John & Tucker, P. (1975). *Sexual signatures: On being a man or a woman*. Boston, MA: Little, Brown.

Morris, Jan. (1974). *Conundrum*. New York: Henry Holt.

New York Times. Selected articles, July 24, 1976 to August 18, 1977.

Raymond, Jan. (1979). *The transsexual empire*. Boston, MA: Beacon Press.

Richards, Renée (with John Ames). (1983). *Second Serve*. New York: Stein & Day.

Richards v. United States Tennis Association (USTA), 400 N.Y.S. 2nd 267 (1977).

Scott, Joan W. (1988). Deconstructing equality-versus-difference: Or, the uses of poststructuralist theory for feminism. *Feminist Studies, 14*, 33-50.

Seligman, Marcia. (1977, February). The packaging of Renée Richards. *Ms.*, pp. 74-76, 85.

Steinem, Gloria. (1977, February). If the shoe doesn't fit, change the foot. *Ms.*, pp. 76, 85, 86.

Stoller, Robert. (1975). *Sex and gender. Vol. 2: The transsexual experiment*. New York: Jason Aronson.

Terry, Jennifer. (1989). The body invaded: Medical surveillance of women as reproducers. *Socialist Review, 19*, 13-45.

Washington Post. Selected articles, August 12, 1976 to January 1, 1978.

Williams, Walter L. (1986). *The spirit and the flesh: Sexual diversity of American Indian culture*. Boston, MA: Beacon.

Williams, Walter L. (1987). Women, men, and others. *American Behavioral Scientist, 31*, 135-141.

Willis, Paul. (1982). Women in sport in ideology. In Jennifer Hargreaves (Ed.), *Sport, culture and ideology* (pp. 117-135). London: Routledge & Kegan Paul.

Winston Salem Journal. Selected articles, August 5, 1977 to February 14, 1978.

9

Baseball and the Social Construction of Gender

Karlene Ferrante

> And then the boos began. [Roseanne] Barr, who said later she was parodying the way baseball players scratch themselves, scratched at her crotch three times and spit before she left the field [after singing *The Star Spangled Banner* on July 16, 1990, prior to a San Diego Padres' game]. . . . President Bush called it "disgraceful."
>
> Garber (1992, p. 99)

There is nothing more American than motherhood, apple pie and baseball. These cultural symbols are about the American experience. Baseball, in particular, is ostensibly about wholesomeness and fairness. As we will see, it is also an expression of the naturalness of a patriarchal order that regularly associates positive meanings with men and negative meanings with women. In this poststructural feminist analysis, I will take a look at how baseball as an institution constructs woman. I will argue that baseball embodies a nostalgia for a pure and perfect experience of individual, masculine achievement and that the sacredness of that ideal is protected against the mundane by a taboo against women.

AUTHOR'S NOTE: The author acknowledges gratefully all the baseball players who have participated in her classes and Joli Jensen, whose guidance and feedback have been invaluable.

The Social Construction of Gender

The basis of this critique is Lana Rakow's idea that gender is a dynamic social process. Rakow has argued that "gender should be seen as a verb, that is, work that we do to construct and maintain a particular gender system, and as a meaning system, that is, organizing categories used to make sense of the world and experience" (Rakow, 1986, pp. 12-13). She asserts that *masculine* and *feminine* are more than normative groups of characteristics for socialized males and females. These concepts constitute a dualism used to classify objects, both animate and inanimate. Gender is a classification system that men have used to "think the world with."

Some instances of this structuring principle are more obvious than others. The colors pink and blue, for example, are directly associated with baby girls and boys. However, in the case of baseball, we no longer have such a simple correspondence. Rather, as an extension of structural changes in family life, baseball became an arena for the renewal of a masculine ideology of individual competition.

The early history of baseball reveals that, some time around the middle of the 19th century, baseball was transformed from just a random, idle pastime into a national institution. This transformation began in the cities of the Northeast around the time of the Industrial Revolution. Ann Douglas sets the scene when she describes, in *The Feminization of American Culture* (1977), the economic and cultural "disestablishment" of middle-class women. With the coming of textile mills, men went off to earn wages. Women were no longer engaged in the production of homespun.

Woman's new role would focus more on fashion and the *consumption* of textiles than on her productive role in the home.

> Formerly an important part of a communal productive process under her direction, [the home] had become a place where her children stayed before they began to work and where her husband rested after the strain of labor. Once her family had looked to her quite literally to clothe and feed them; now they expected a complex blend of nurture and escape from her "voluntary" care. (Douglas, 1977, p. 48)

According to Douglas, this structural change resulted in women's loss of influence and gain of compensatory deference. Women lost legal privileges, including, in some places, *the right to vote*. They were gradually excluded from a variety of occupations. At the same time, flattery and finery were increasingly at the center of women's lives.

> Finery symbolized the flattery which was their due. Expensively educated, well-treated, and well-dressed, they could both advertise male earnings and compensate themselves for their own lost productivity. They did not make homespun; they displayed fine cottons and silks. Fashion was the back door through which middle-class northern women re-entered the American economy. . . . The self-involved style favored by the Victorian lady—pinched waist, swelled bosom, and proliferating profusion of hooped skirts and lacy petticoats—both obliterated and exaggerated the female body; it objectified and enforced the feminine function as euphemism. (Douglas, 1977, p. 61)

It is not coincidental that professional baseball and a cult of femininity developed at roughly the same time. It stands to reason that separate and corresponding masculine/feminine cultural rituals would develop in relation to the Victorian preoccupation with gender.

The Reification of Baseball

Both professional baseball and women's fashion are products of a symbolic mystification process or reification. As conceptualized by Frederic Jameson (1979), *reification* describes a reorganization and fragmentation of human activity resulting in a separation between means and ends. Jameson adapted the concept from its earlier emphasis on production and applied it to the consumption of mass culture. In this case, reification transforms any utopian impulses of the audience into identification with, for example, a tragic hero or, in the case of baseball, the home team. A fan may go to a baseball game feeling vaguely dissatisfied with his lot; but he will leave either elated over a home team victory or disappointed and waiting for revenge. Thus, Jameson argues, any revolutionary impulse is transformed and channelled into predictable and politically impotent responses to cultural commodities.[1]

Jameson argues further that reification obscures the means of production. It leads to a forgetting of history. In terms of the institution of baseball, reification may lead to a lack of questioning of a number of assumptions: for example, that baseball originated in America, that baseball has always existed in its present form, that baseball has always been a man's game. To see how the reification of baseball from a pastime to a spectator sport has involved the construction of gender, we need to look at the history of baseball.

The institution of baseball named itself in the constructed origin of the sport in Cooperstown, New York. M. Hirsh Goldberg explains in a case study in *The Blunder Book* (1988): According to Goldberg, as baseball became increasingly popular, most people just assumed that it had originated in America. Goldberg reports that, in 1903, Henry Chadwick, America's first baseball reporter, who had grown up in England, wrote in a *Baseball Guide* that baseball resembled rounders, a game he had played as a boy. The article caused a storm. Goldberg goes on to explain how the controversy was settled.

> Albert G. Spalding, a famous baseball player of the nineteenth century and founder of a sporting goods manufacturing company, proposed establishment of a committee to "learn the real facts concerning the origin and development of the game."

A seven-member committee, chaired by Abraham G. Mills, president of baseball's National League, studied the subject over several years. In 1907 the committee issued its findings: Baseball had been invented by Abner Doubleday as a youth in Cooperstown in 1839 and was clearly American in origin. The only basis for this finding, however, appeared to be the testimony of Abner Graves, who had once lived in Cooperstown and who said he remembered seeing Doubleday organize a game of baseball in a field during the summer of 1839 (Goldberg, 1988, p. 163).

Most sports historians agree that baseball did, in fact, derive from the English game of rounders. But this shows how important it had become by the turn of the century for baseball to be American and not English. I believe that a similar kind of dissociation was made in relation to women. As baseball was transformed from a mere pastime to an important cultural (and patriarchal) symbol, it was necessary that it be defined as completely masculine.

Women as Players

The process through which baseball became almost exclusively masculine has been documented by David Voigt in a 1977 article in the *Journal of Popular Culture*. Voigt argued that there is a taboo against women in baseball, and that this taboo has not always been as well defined as it is today.[2] He found documentation of the existence of a professional women's baseball team during the 1880s managed by a Mr. Freeman. Voigt notes that the team was likened to a bunch of whores by sportswriters. And then, he goes on to say that "a decade later when Ed Barrow employed Lizzie Arlington (Lizzie Stride) to pitch exhibitions against minor league men's clubs to boost receipts, the events smacked of a Barnum freak show promotion" (Voigt, 1977, p. 393).[3]

Nevertheless, women *did* play baseball during the Victorian era. According to Debra Shattuck (1991), baseball was popular for many years among college women. Shattuck reports further that numerous male entrepreneurs organized ladies' exhibition teams during the 1870s and 1880s. Shortly after the turn of the century, a number of "bloomer girls" teams formed throughout the country, again only for exhibition play against men's teams. In addition, a number of women distinguished themselves by playing with otherwise all-male teams. We know that Miss M. W. Phelan offered to play center field for the Flora Baseball Club of Indiana in 1903, that Alta Weiss was the first woman to finish college essentially on a baseball scholarship and that "Lizzie" Murphy, the "Queen of Baseball," played semiprofessional baseball from 1915 to 1935 (Shattuck, 1991).

The first recorded protest against women in baseball occurred in 1928. According to Shattuck,

> Fourteen-year-old Margaret Gisolo helped her Blanford, Indiana, American Legion men's baseball team win county, district, sectionals, and state championships. In seven tournament games she had 9 hits in 21 at bats. She scored 10 putouts and 28 assists in the field, with no errors charged against her. A protest against her participation filed by opposing teams went all the way to the American Legion's National Americanism Commission, which referred it to the major league baseball commissioner, Judge Kenesaw Mountain Landis. Landis determined that American Legion rules did not specifically

ban the participation of women and disallowed the protest. (Shattuck, 1991, p. 617)

However, just three years later, Landis ruled against 17-year-old Jackie Mitchell's signing with the Chattanooga Lookouts.

> She became an overnight celebrity on April 2, 1931, when she pitched in an exhibition game against the visiting New York Yankees—and struck out Babe Ruth and Lou Gehrig, back to back. Speculation continues as to whether Ruth and Gehrig were merely putting on a show or really trying to hit Mitchell's pitches. . . . Landis informed Engle (her manager) that he had disallowed Mitchell's contract on the grounds that life in baseball was too strenuous for women. Organized baseball formalized the ban against women signing professional baseball contracts with men's teams on June 2, 1952; the ruling still stands. (Shattuck, 1991, p. 617)

It appears that Landis's decision was made not so much to protect Jackie Mitchell from the strenuous life of baseball as to protect baseball from the active presence of women.

Such a prohibition hardly seems necessary when you consider how many women and girls who wanted to play baseball were diverted to softball instead. In 1923, Gladys Palmer compiled an official set of rules for girls' softball. This "woman's" version of the game was designed to be less strenuous and has been variously called playground ball, diamond ball, indoor baseball and kitten ball (Meyer & Schwarz, 1965). The history of softball, specifically in the context of women's athletics, provides a fascinating feminine parallel to the history of baseball but is beyond the scope of this work. It is, however, significant that early women's athletic programs tended to be grounded in a belief that team sports provided an opportunity for girls to learn about cooperation, whereas baseball was supposed to teach boys about competition. It is clear that baseball is closely interwoven with the construction of gender between the early Victorian period and the present.

It seems that the later Victorian emphasis on extreme gender differences required that women temper public displays of physical power. In her book, *Connotations of Movement in Sport and Dance*, Eleanor Metheny (1965) suggests that it is not culturally acceptable for women to exert as much force as men in overcoming the inertia of mass, either in the form of another person or an object. This would explain why it is culturally acceptable for women to play softball, which uses a larger ball that is (traditionally) pitched slower and hit shorter distances. Thus, the channeling of women into softball would "soften" public displays of women's power, in compliance with the later Victorian ideal.

It is interesting to note that, although baseball may well generate more statistics and official and unofficial records than any other sport, it was, until recently, extremely difficult to find any record that a woman *ever* played professional baseball! Barbara Gregorich's (1993) book *Women at Play: The Story of Women in Baseball* has helped to change all that, yet if it weren't for the feature film *A League of Their Own* (Greenhut & Abbot, 1992), most Americans would not know that women had ever played professional baseball in the United States.

The feature film was also preceded by two documents recording the history of the All-American Girls' Professional Baseball League, which existed from 1943 to 1954. In 1986, Sharon Roepke wrote a pamphlet entitled *Diamond Gals: The Story of the All American Girls Professional Baseball League* (Roepke, 1986). Then, in 1987, Community Television Southern California released a documentary videotape entitled *A League of Their Own* (Wilson & Candaele, 1987) (not to be confused with the 1992 feature film with the same name). This videotape documents a recent reunion of AAGPBL players. Before this time, standard baseball histories tended to gloss over the war years, failing to mention that baseball, like the defense plants, depended to a great extent on women to produce what men could not.

World War II had decimated the ranks of professional baseball, and many Americans, including President Franklin Roosevelt, were concerned about the possible negative consequences for American morale if baseball were to disappear. P. K. Wrigley seized the opportunity to "make a buck while the boys are overseas" (Greenhut & Abbot, 1992), organizing the AAGPBL in 1943. The "girls" played in skirts and were required to attend a charm school to learn how to dress fashionably, to move gracefully and to make small talk.[4]

They played for teams in small cities throughout the midwest. At first, they drew crowds because they were a novelty, but then they built a loyal following of season ticketholders who came to appreciate how well they played. According to Pepper Paire Davis, one of the players,

> In the early part of our league, we used regulation spikes, Louisville sluggers from 32 ounces to 36 ounces, baseball gloves—everything except the hard ball—in the early parts. And we had a tailor-made ball. And then as the years progressed, the pitching mound went back, the bases went back, the ball got smaller, and it became truthfully women's hard ball. (Wilson & Candaele, 1987)

One team owner, Carl Orwant, explains why these changes were made.

> This game was way, way ahead of its time. They began to make the old game look easy and that was what we tried to avoid. We tried to make this look like something unusual—way above average. They had so mastered softball, people would say, "the girls are just playing softball." They could never do it with a hard ball or anything like that. And most of the girls, if you talk to the ones who survived through the last year, '54, they liked it better when the hard ball came in. They made great plays and we had less errors with the hard ball and the scores looked more respectable. They looked like baseball, see? (Wilson & Candaele, 1987)

Players explain that the league dissolved because they began to retire, but there was no more recruiting. One player said, "People had too much to do," so women's baseball faded away, almost without a trace.

Although most traditional histories of baseball do not mention that women played professional baseball during the war, they do describe the euphoria experienced by fans as the troops returned and "real" professional baseball made a comeback. It seems that the scouts stopped recruiting women baseball players because they could once again start recruiting men baseball players.

The fact that the AAGPBL consisted of all-white women's teams does not mean that African-American women were excluded from baseball during this era. Recent research by Linda Williams (1988, 1989, 1991) and Barbara Gregorich (1993) shows that they had their own leagues and teams and several even played on men's teams in the Negro baseball leagues.

Women in Other Roles

The sports histories show that "real" baseball players were men. Women have traditionally been restricted to auxiliary roles. Voigt (1977) reports that women occasionally had a role in running the business, but usually only as appendages to men. Mrs. Helene Hathaway Robison Britton inherited the St. Louis Cardinals from her uncle in 1911. She ran the club for eight years but was reportedly patronized by the other owners. Bessie Langert worked successfully as a scout during the 1920s. In 1869, a Margaret Truman, fiancée of pitcher Asa Brainard, sewed the red stockings for the legendary Cincinnati Red Stocking team. (One is reminded of Betsy Ross.) Mrs. Sally van Pelt worked as baseball editor for the Dubuque *Times*, and Amanda Clement worked as a semipro umpire and Florence Knebelkamp, the sister of the owner of the Louisville Colonels, was the club's traveling secretary (Voigt, 1977). And now Marge Schott, the only female owner, has been temporarily barred from participation for making racist comments. The irony of Schott's suspension underscores both the requirement that women remain "cleaner" than men and the structural interrelationship of sexism and racism (and, as we will see, homophobia).

As of 1993, no woman has ever been hired as an umpire in the major leagues. Pam Postema, who worked in the minor leagues for 13 years, was the woman most likely to make this jump. Her quest gained notoriety because of Houston pitcher Bob Knepper's statement: "As far as her ability for umpiring, she seems fine, but I don't think a woman should be an umpire" ("Knepper Gets No Backup," 1988, p. C2). According to Knepper, the Bible decreed that women should not hold authority over men. Not long afterward, Postema was released from her umpiring contract. Thus forced to confront the reality of the taboo, Postema lost the idealistic expectation of fairness toward—or at least minimal accommodation of—outstanding women that she had once brought to baseball.

> I'll never understand why it's easier for a female to become an astronaut or cop or fire fighter or soldier or Supreme Court justice than it is to become a major league umpire. For Christ sakes, it's only baseball. (Postema, 1992, p. 255)

It has been rare, indeed, for women to hold any sort of official status in relation to professional baseball. These examples show that, for the most part, the only accepted role for women has been on the outside or auxiliary. Thus, woman has been conceptualized or "constructed" within the discourse of baseball as the object rather than the subject, or, in the words of Simone de Beauvoir, "the Other."

She asserts in *The Second Sex* (1983) that subject-object relations tend to be reflexive. That is, the subject is likely to become the object in a different context, and vice versa. "The native traveling abroad is shocked to find himself in turn regarded as a 'stranger' by the natives of neighboring countries" (Beauvoir, 1983, p. xvii). However, she found no such reflexivity in the subject-object relations between men and women. In our culture, man remains fairly consistently the subject, and woman is usually designated the object. She reasoned that this must necessarily reflect a power imbalance.

> No subject will readily volunteer to become the object, the inessential. It is not the Other who, in defining himself as the Other, establishes the One. The Other is posed as such by the One in defining himself as the One. But if the Other is not to regain the status of being the One, he must be submissive enough to adopt this alien point of view. (Beauvoir, 1983, p. xviii)

Baseball as a cultural icon constructs woman as the Other, whose function it is to bring comfort, meaning and identity to the One. There is further evidence that this function is a sexual function. To a great extent, in the world of baseball, "woman" became synonymous with "sex." In fact, Voigt's 1977 article about women and baseball is entitled "Sex in Baseball: Reflections of Changing Taboos." Voigt begins by pointing out the use of baseball terminology as a euphemism in sex talk.

> When describing a female encounter, males of my generation sought to know what "pitch" to use. A "change of pace" might serve, especially if she "threw" me a "curve." "Getting to first base," or "hitting in the clutch," or "going into extra innings" all indicated a kissing relationship which if far gone could earn a player the coveted title of "Ace"! But being "caught off base," or "caught stealing," or "thrown out" described ardor rebuffed, while "striking out" spelled abject failure. (Voigt, 1977, p. 390)

The ambiguity of such terms suggests that all baseball talk may carry a hidden gendered meaning and function. However, only at the sexual level of meaning does men's exclusive ownership and control of baseball become apparent.

The analogy of women and baseball is common. Baseball is a forum in which young men compete and in which the best men may become heroes. It is clear from this analogy that sex and womanhood are objectified into a sort of forum in which young men compete and in which the hero "scores."

The Taboo Against Women and Sex

Voigt points out, however, that women and sexuality have been treated as taboo in professional baseball. According to Voigt, there is a common myth that women and sex are evil because they sap the strength of athletes, who need to be directing all of their energy toward athletic performance. In fact,

> in the case of the 1889 Brooklyn Bridegrooms, a team nicknamed by writers who noticed the number of newlyweds in the ranks, the desperate pennant race of that year called for drastic measures. In the September stretch drive, needing an all out effort to carry the battle the marrieds were persuaded to avoid their wives for the duration. The celibatory sacrifice was applauded by local writers who praised pitcher Bob Carruthers for refusing even to visit his newborn child. (Voigt, 1977, p. 394)

Thus, in order for baseball to retain its power, it was necessary to place a taboo on women and sex. In other words, for the sacred to remain so, it was necessary to isolate it from the profane. This dualistic principle of the sacred and profane is critical to an understanding of gendering in baseball.

It is the same principle identified by Susan Griffin in *Pornography and Silence: Culture's Revenge Against Nature* (1981). Griffin argues that pornography is not an expression of natural sexuality but rather a continually unsuccessful attempt to silence the sexual urge by humiliating and punishing and, she argues, inevitably murdering "sexual" women who have been labeled as "bad." According to Griffin, pornography is the result of dualist thinking that associates the male with the soul and intellect (the sacred) and the female with the body and "base" sexual urges (the profane). Women, she argues, are dualistically divided into "good girls" and "bad girls," the difference being that "good girls" have not yet been raped.

In the case of the Brooklyn Bridegrooms and of pornography as discussed by Griffin, man is destined for powerful and pure activities (e.g., the pennant race), while woman is assigned the role of sexual temptress. If man fulfills his sexual desires, it becomes the fault of the temptress. If man is not successful in his competition against other men, he is justified in blaming not himself but the woman, for it was she who interfered with his pure or godlike state. This story has been replayed countless times and in countless ways throughout history. In a sense, all of these are slightly different versions of Eve tempting Adam to partake of the tree of knowledge.

The association between woman and sex has been reinforced many times throughout the history of baseball. There are countless quotations about "broads" and "dames" from players, managers and sportswriters through the years. For example, Richie Ashburn, announcer for the Philadelphia Phillies, is quoted as once having joked about a rookie, "The Kid doesn't chew tobacco, smoke, drink, curse or chase broads. I don't see how he can possibly make it" (Maikovich, 1984, p. 23). And in 1955, White Sox manager Marty Marion caught and fired four players for dalliances, and afterward the team went into a slump. Marion lost his job, and his response was, "Dames wrecked more teams than bad liquor, big bonuses, or all the sore arms" (Voigt, 1977, p. 402).

Thus, if man wins in the fair forum, he becomes a hero. If he fails, he may blame woman for being such a successful temptress. This is not unlike the pornographer blaming the rape victim for being in the wrong place or looking too sexy. These cases "prove" the need for the taboo by showing how things go wrong when the taboo is not observed.

It would seem that the designated role for women in baseball is as observer. Yet, even in this capacity, women have been harassed and maligned. Voigt (1977) reports that in the early days of baseball women were allowed to watch games only if they were escorted. Unescorted women, and sometimes even escorted women, were harassed by cursing, spitting "mashers." According to Voigt, owners discouraged single women from attending for fear that they would arouse the "beastly instincts" of male fans. (Thus, if the men misbehaved, the women would be blamed.)[5]

Ladies' Days were an innovation of the 1880s. Male fans complained about the "inhibiting presence of gossipy women and their squabbling children" (Voigt, 1977, p. 392). Voigt explains such attitudes in terms of the myth of feminine evil. In this case, women and children are blamed for distracting man from the higher pursuit of watching baseball. Male fans viewed these women as not sexual and also not useful, although the owners felt that their presence had a calming effect on the crowd, so fewer bouncers were needed. Thus, it was the profit motive that opened attendance to women.

Later, when groups of unescorted women became infatuated with particular players, the myth of feminine evil again took on a sexual tone. These women were "bad" girls. They were ridiculed but apparently not discouraged by the players, many of whom seemed to enjoy trying to live up to the myth of the oversexed athlete. According to Voigt (1977), these women, variously known as "Bimbos, Annies, Shirleys, Groupies, and Starfuckers," include sex-starved wives, some stagestruck innocents, some sex thrill-seekers and a few nymphomaniacs. I would add that no such labels have been applied to the players who have had sexual encounters with these women. For the most part, management and the press seem simply to have looked away from sexual adventures of the players so long as they have not interfered with the game.[6]

Another group of women associated with baseball, the wives, are written about almost exclusively in terms of their cliques and pettiness. One angry wife described them as "a bunch of little, spoiled bitches . . . sitting around . . . gossiping . . . drinking coffee all morning" (Voigt, 1977, p. 402). Although woman is by no means always constructed as sexual or even "bad," she is always conceptualized as the Other. For example, on his retirement from baseball, Willie Mays was quoted as saying,

> I remember the last season I played, I went home after a ball game one day, lay down on my bed, and the tears came to my eyes. How can you explain that? It's like crying for your mother after she's gone.

> You cry because you love her. I cried, I guess, because I loved baseball and I knew I had to leave it. (Maikovich, 1984, p. 20)

As one of the earliest accepted black players, Mays could not be associated with sex or "bad" girls, I believe, because the myth of the oversexed black man had played such a powerful role in keeping blacks out of baseball. The first accepted black players had to be particularly "pure." Thus, it is appropriate that Mays should be quoted in comparing his love for baseball with his love for his mother. Both reflect a pure nostalgia for an ideal perfection.

It was the need to maintain an aura of purity around baseball that made it so difficult for black players to break into the game. The story of Jackie Robinson demonstrates the strength of the resistance to breaking the barriers of "racial purity." Although black men no longer face such an absolute racial taboo, racism is still a problem (particularly for women of color, whose presence would have been unthinkable even in the AAGPBL). Similarly, although members of the AAGPBL have finally been honored with an exhibit in Baseball's Hall of Fame in Cooperstown, the continuing absence of women in professional baseball attests to the importance of "gender purity" in baseball as an all-American institution.

The Unspoken Taboo Against Homosexuality

Perhaps the greatest challenge of all to the now standard gendering function of baseball is homosexuality. After all, if we can't keep men clearly separated from women, the "purity" derived from the avoidance of taboo groups is sullied. Openly accepted homosexuality threatens the entire meaning system of baseball (and obviously other sports as well).

Homophobia is expressed through the insistence on clear gender marking of players. The AAGPBL requirement that all players attend charm school reflects a fear that the "girls" might appear too masculine (despite those short skirts they wore). The fear was well articulated when, in the feature film *A League of Their Own* (Greenhut & Abbot, 1992), Miss Mayda Gillespie reads a social commentary on the radio.

Careers and higher education are leading to the masculinization of women, with enormously dangerous consequences to the home, the children, and our country. When our boys come home from war, what kind of girls will they be coming home to? And now the most degrading example of this sexual confusion—Mr. Walter Harvey of Harvey bars is presenting us with women's baseball. Right here in Chicago, young girls, plucked from their families, are gathered at Harvey Field to see which one of them can be the most masculine. Mr. Harvey, like your candy bars, you're completely nuts. (Greenhut & Abbot, 1992)

By "sexual confusion," Miss Gillespie implies lesbianism. If women are supposed to be weak, strong women are suspect. And of course the easiest way to maintain the existing gender ideology is to transform aberrations (gays and lesbians) into "normal" men and women. If that is not possible, they must, at least, be made invisible.

According to Helen Lenskyj (1986), "tomboyism" has long been associated (and sometimes confused) with lesbianism. Coaches for girls' and women's sports have long been advised to minimize any appearances of lesbianism. Lenskyj quotes the advice of Patsy Neal (1969, p. 106) in *Coaching Methods for Women*:

Coaches should put a damper on masculine mannerisms that are not necessary to a girl's performance or that create an undesirable impression . . . (Such) mannerisms are frequently given as reasons for the public's negativism towards athletics for women . . . The coach should seize every opportunity to improve the girl's behaviour. It may not make the woman a better athlete, but it will eventually make the athlete a better woman. (Lenskyj, 1986, p. 99)

Thus, Neal (1969) defines the purpose of women's athletics more in terms of supporting the extant gender system than helping women to pursue athletic excellence, for the very existence of homosexuality raises questions about the validity of that system.

The Meaning of Baseball

The strength of these taboos reflects the importance of the cultural meanings constructed. To understand how important baseball has been in American culture, we need to delve deep into the American psyche. In *The Machine in the Garden* (1964), Leo Marx traces the uses of the pastoral ideal in the interpretation of American experience. Marx describes a powerful metaphor of contradiction that includes both a dread of and fascination for the possibilities of technology in a virgin land. The land or "the garden" is important because it is essential for the rejuvenation of technological man. No one embodies this idea better than Ralph Waldo Emerson. According to Marx,

> Emerson is confident that in Young America mechanical power is to be matched by a new access of vitality to the imaginative, utopian, transcendent, value-creating faculty, Reason. His hope arises from a conviction that men who confront raw nature will ask ultimate questions. He regards the virgin landscape as a source of spiritual therapy, a divine hieroglyph awaiting translation by Americans into aims worthy of their vast new powers. "The land," he explains, "is the appointed remedy for whatever is false and fantastic in our culture." (Marx, 1964, p. 236)

The contradiction lies in the need, on the one hand, for technology and urbanization to cross and transform the natural landscape and the requirement, on the other hand, of a *virgin* landscape to serve as a source of spiritual therapy. This adds new meaning to the vast amount of green in the outfield of baseball diamonds, especially in urban settings. It also explains the transcendental quality of the many famous quotations about the importance of baseball as a spiritual proving ground for the young men of America. It is particularly significant that the word *virgin* is used so often to describe the essence of the pure sphere.

In his book *The Nervous Generation: American Thought, 1917-1930*, Roderick Nash (1970) explains why baseball took on a special meaning as the frontier disappeared. According to Nash, urbanization created a longing for a new expression of the rural values of rugged individualism. The frontier provided, at least in the American imagination, a forum for courageous individuals to take risks, to work hard, to compete fiercely and, ultimately, to become heroes. It mattered not that most Americans had never actually seen the frontier. Rather, it was important for Americans to believe in the existence of such a forum. Nash argues convincingly that the institution of baseball took over at least part of this symbolic function. This would account for the emphasis on individual performance and the traditional hero-worship of baseball fans.

Analyses such as those of Nash and Marx show how it is functional for American culture to transcend urban/modern life through symbolic purifying interactions such as baseball. Such analyses have not shown, however, that a major source of "purity" in the cultural symbol of baseball is the taboo against women's participation and a positioning of woman as the sexual "Other." The fact that baseball—together with motherhood and apple pie—seems so simple, so natural, makes it particularly effective in the gendering process. Rakow emphasizes that it is important for the continuation of the patriarchal order that gendering be presented as *natural*.

> The meaning of gender—in this case of being a woman—seems to be confirmed by the experience of it. Consequently, it is not gender that causes the women's behavior but our gender system, which locates some people as women in a particular organization of social life, making that location appear natural and the result of biology and psychology rather than culture and politics. (Rakow, 1986, p. 24)

Gender *appears* to be a natural organizing principle because it is encoded into the philosophical underpinnings of cultural symbols such as baseball. The reification of baseball into "the" all-American spectator sport obscures the history of baseball as well as its contribution to the continuing process of gendering. As a symbol of equal opportunity, baseball has an aura of simplicity and purity about it, at the expense of women and, some would argue, men. This cultural symbol is actually part of a complex meaning system, structured in a way that validates the correctness and necessity of the patriarchal social order.

Yet women continue to challenge the "masculine" world of sports. Girls and women are increasingly involved in sports, and the result is not only that sports are changing women—women are also changing sports. According to Mariah Burton Nelson (1991), women are gradually changing the ways athletes relate to other athletes and the way men and women relate to each other. If baseball has been the site of the social construction of such extreme gender polarities, then surely the gradual changes brought about by the emergence of women in this all-American sport can again make baseball the site for more positive changes as well. We'll be watching.

Notes

1. The same may be said about women using shopping sprees to meet emotional needs resulting from patriarchal domination.

2. For a more complete discussion of the function of *taboo*, see Frazer (1914) and Freud (1918). The fear of women is discussed in Horney (1932) and Lederer (1968).

3. The Appleton (WI) *Post* reported in August 1892 that a female baseball team from New York lost to a local team (presumably men), 12 to 9. The most newsworthy aspect of this event was not, however, the remarkably close score but rather the unfeminine appearance of the female players. One spectator bet his friend that one base runner was unfeminine enough to break his pocket watch. "Looking at the timepiece he found that it had stopped not a minute before. The laughter the affair created could have been heard a block away" (Mendyke, 1992, p. B-6). Things haven't changed all that much. When Julie Croteau, a pioneer in high school baseball, made a recent television appearance on *Live: Regis and Kathie Lee*, she was made to play a fielding drill with Regis. According to Julie, "It felt like a freak show" (Nelson, 1991, p. 20).

4. Mariah Burton Nelson, one of America's first professional women basketball players, reports a similar situation in women's professional basketball during the 1970s. "The owner of the California Dreams sent us to John Robert Powers' Charm School. The New Orleans Pride hired a cosmetician to apply makeup to 'the girls' before each home game. The league owner was a man; all the head coaches were men" (Nelson, 1991, p. 7).

5. This conception of men as out of control around women is still with us. It was the basis of the defense in Mike Tyson's rape trial.

6. This has certainly been the case with Ervin "Magic" Johnson, whose sexual adventures were legendary. More public concern has been voiced for other players who might be exposed to AIDS via some freak accident than for those multitudes of women already infected by Johnson.

References

Beauvoir, Simone de. (1983). *The second sex*. New York: Knopf.

Douglas, Ann. (1977). *The feminization of American culture*. New York: Knopf.

Frazer, James G. (1914). *Taboo and the perils of the soul*. London: Macmillan.

Freud, Sigmund. (1918). *Totem and taboo: Resemblances between the psychic lives of savages and neurotics*. New York: Moffatt, Yard.

Garber, Angus G. (1992). *Tales from the locker room*. New York: Smithmark.

Goldberg, M. Hirsch. (1988). *The blunder book: Colossal errors, minor mistakes, and surprising slipups that have changed the course of history*. New York: Morrow.

Greenhut, Robert & Abbot, Elliot. (Producers) & Marshall, Penny (Director). (1992). *A league of their own.* [Videotape]. Burbank, CA: Columbia House Video.

Gregorich, Barbara. (1993). *Women at play: The story of women in baseball.* New York: Harcourt, Brace.

Griffin, Susan. (1981). *Pornography and silence: Culture's revenge against nature.* New York: Harper Colophon.

Horney, Karen. (1932). The dread of women.*International Journal of Psychoanalysis, 13,* 348-360.

Jameson, Frederic. (1979). Reification and utopia in mass culture. *Social Text, 1,* 130-148.

Knepper gets no backup: Houston teammate says "male ego" was talking. (1988, March 16). *Austin American-Statesman,* p. C2.

Lederer, Wolfgang. (1968). *The fear of women.* New York: Harcourt Brace Jovanovich.

Lenskyj, Helen. (1986). *Out of bounds: Women, sport and sexuality.* Toronto: The Women's Press.

Maikovich, Andrew J. (1984). *Sports quotations: Maxims, quips, and pronouncements for writers and fans.* Jefferson, NC: McFarland.

Marx, Leo. (1964). *The machine in the garden: Technology and the pastoral ideal in America.* New York: Oxford University Press.

Mendyke, Don. (1992, August 4). Female baseball team a big draw (Looking back). *Appleton Post-Crescent,* p. B-6.

Metheny, Eleanor. (1965). *Connotations of movement in sport and dance.* Dubuque, IA: William C. Brown.

Meyer, Margaret & Schwarz, Marguerite. (1965). *Team sports for girls and women.* Philadelphia, PA: W. B. Saunders.

Nash, Roderick. (1970). *The nervous generation: American thought, 1917-1930.* Chicago: Rand-McNally.

Neal, Patsy. (1969). *Coaching methods for women.* Reading, MA: Addison-Wesley.

Nelson, Mariah Burton. (1991). *Are we sinning yet? How women are changing sports and sports are changing women.* New York: Random House.

Postema, Pam & Wojciechowski, Gene. (1992). *You've got to have balls to make it in this league: My life as an umpire.* New York: Simon & Schuster.

Rakow, Lana. (1986). Rethinking gender research in communication. *Journal of Communication, 36*(4), 11-26.

Roepke, Sharon L. (1986). *Diamond gals: The story of the All American Girls Professional Baseball League.* Marcellus, MI: AAGPBL Cards.

Shattuck, Debra A. (1991). *Total baseball* (2nd ed.). New York: Warner Books.

Voigt, David Q. (1977). Sex in baseball: Reflections of changing taboos. *Journal of Popular Culture, 21*(3), 389-403.

Williams, Linda D. (1988). *An analysis of American sportswomen in two Negro newspapers: The* Pittsburgh Courier, *1924-1948, and the* Chicago Defender, *1932-1948.* Eugene, OR: Microform Publications, College of Human Development and Performance, University of Oregon.

Williams, Linda D. (1989). *American sportswomen for a quarter of a century (1924-1948) through the writings of the* Pittsburgh Courier, *Negro weekly.* Unpublished paper.

Williams, Linda D. (1991). *Before Wilma and Althea: Afro-American women in sports.* Unpublished manuscript.

Wilson, Kim & Candaele, Kelly (Producers). (1987). *A league of their own.* [Videotape]. Community Television Southern California. New York: Filmakers Library.

10

Global Games, Entertainment and Leisure

Women as TV Spectators

Anne Cooper-Chen

> It has long been my conviction that we can learn far more about the conditions, and values, of a society by contemplating how it chooses to play, to use its free time, to take its leisure, than by examining how it goes about its work.
>
> Giamatti (1989, p. 13)

Women and Leisure

A. Bartlett Giamatti, former president of Yale University and, when he died, the commissioner of baseball, didn't get it quite right. "We can learn," he should have added, "about the conditions and values of a society by contemplating who gets awarded free time for play and who gets assigned what kind of work."

Giamatti, by no means the first man to deify play as a basis of culture, can trace his thinking back to Aristotle. Greek philosophers saw wise, productive use of leisure as a measure of one's character. Ironically, this gift of leisure "relied on the intrusion on another's freedom—that of slaves" (Wearing & Wearing, 1988, p. 117). Today, as this chapter will show, the gift of leisure to husbands and children

257

relies to a great extent on the worldwide intrusion on women's freedom.

As a contemporary sports philosopher, Giamatti brings a unique perspective and undeniable eloquence to understanding the cultural meaning of sports and play. Leisure "is so important, as a concept, as an index to a culture's condition, because it is a form of freedom and is about making choices" (Giamatti, 1989, p. 22). He concludes:

> In short, whether classical or Christian, leisure as an ideal was a state of unforced harmony with others; it was, ideally, to live fully amidst activity, which activity has the characteristic of free time. (p. 30)

Paul Weiss (1969, p. 134) echoes the other sports philosophers in seeing in play "the idea of being cut off from the workaday world." According to Guttmann (1978, p. 3), play is any "non-utilitarian physical or intellectual activity pursued for its own sake." Play is in its ideal sense "the most human of activities" (Guttmann, 1978, p. 4). Huizinga (1950, p. 5) believes that "genuine, pure play is one of the main bases of civilisation."

John Huizinga, who wrote in 1938 the seminal work on leisure and play, *Homo Ludens*, dignifies play with these words:

> You can deny, if you like, nearly all abstractions: justice, beauty, truth, goodness, mind, God. You can deny seriousness, but not play. But in acknowledging play you acknowledge mind, for whatever else play is, it is not matter. (Huizinga, 1950, p. 3)

Set these authors' rhapsodic views of play against those who argue that the work/play dichotomy has no meaning for many adult women (Coles, 1980; Deem, 1982, 1986). Moreover, the identification of autotelic play (play as an end in itself) with culture, harmony and a worthy life subtly puts down women who do not (because they cannot) pursue a rich leisure life.

Deem (1982, p. 45), in a study of British women, found that most had "little choice about their leisure patterns and 'space' for leisure"— especially those who had married young, had no car and had little education. Their leisure carried greater constraints than men's, as did other aspects of their lives: "The broader gender power relationships of wider society have been shown by feminist theorists to constrain women's autonomy over their lives to a greater extent than for men" (Wearing & Wearing, 1988, p. 117).

Male and female play worlds, which diverge at adolescence, often rest on opposite sides of a great divide by the time women take on child care and home care tasks. Babies and young children, like puppies and kittens, spontaneously engage in unorganized play, gleefully tumbling, chasing objects and hiding behind curtains. "Animals," points out Huizinga (1950, p. 1), "have not waited for man to teach them their playing."

Rules of the Game

At ages 7 through 11, child developmentalist Piaget (1951) has observed that games with rules appear (see Figure 10.1). Piaget (1951) defines what he calls Stage II play as

> games with sensory-motor combinations (races, marbles, ball games, etc.) or intellectual combinations (cards, chess, etc.), in which there is competition between individuals (otherwise rules would be useless) and which are regulated either by a code handed down from earlier generations, or by temporary agreement. (p. 113)

Noncompetitive games (having rules but no won-lost outcome) do exist but are far less common than competitive games (contests). Leapfrog, ring-around-the-rosie, *kemari* (an ancient Japanese game in which players work together to keep a ball in the air) are all noncompetitive games (Guttmann, 1978).

Most adult games, according to Piaget (1951, p. 113), have "regulations imposed by the group, and their violation carries a sanction." Of course, contests exist outside the realm of play; legal proceedings and wars are competitive but hardly aimed at playfulness, although lawyers and generals may in fact enjoy them (Guttmann, 1978).

According to Guttmann (1978), games

> symbolize the willing surrender of absolute spontaneity for the sake of playful order. One must obey the rules one imposes on oneself. The rules are quite often designedly inefficient. (p. 4)

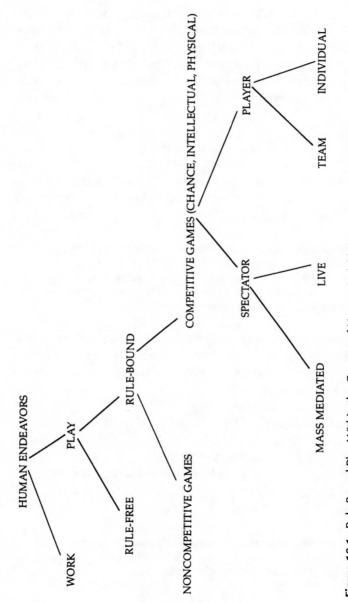

Figure 10.1. Rule-Bound Play Within the Context of Human Activities

SOURCE: Based on ideas from Guttmann (1978), Piaget (1950) and Roberts and Sutton-Smith (1969).

Huizinga (1950, p. 11) concurs that rules "determine what 'holds' in the temporary world circumscribed by play. Indeed, as soon as the rules are transgressed the whole play-world collapses." Sutton-Smith, in his introduction to Stephenson (1988, p. xi), criticizes Huizinga for an emphasis on physicality and rules: "Much play is tenuous, oral, humorous and relatively unstructured. There is little in Huizinga about the kind of daydreaming reverie, wish-fulfillment, and imagining which is more characteristic of women's life and play."

Granted, rules are an integral part of games. "Where its rules begin, there the game begins; where its rules end, there the game ends. When the game is over those rules are left behind," states Weiss (1969, p. 146). Rules (competition) can even benefit players, believes Guttmann (1988):

> Provided the situation is not excessively stressful, subjects in psychological experiments do better when the task is made into a contest. Beyond that, psychologists discovered, nearly a century ago, that the physical presence of a human competitor stimulated subjects to higher levels of achievement than they were able to attain when measured only by a stopwatch or a speedometer. (p. 4)

Roberts and Sutton-Smith (1969), who use large databases to study the relation of games and culture, have isolated three main types of competitive games: (1) games of physical skill, which may involve strategy and chance; (2) games of strategy, which may involve chance; and (3) games of chance. As Weiss (1969) states:

> There is always an element of luck in every game. . . . [I]t could be argued that luck is but a way of describing the overall effect of the contingencies which are essential to the very existence of a game. The athlete is to show what he is and can do in a game as it actually unfolds, peppered with the unexpected. (p. 191)

Weiss (1969, p. 187) adds that for gamblers, unlike athletes, "luck is not a grace note, an addendum to what they are or do. It is an integral part of their lives and of their performances."

Figures 10.1 and 10.2 do not list specific activities because the "right" slot for a sport/pastime varies. Borrowing insights from anthropologist Clifford Geertz (1973, p. 6) regarding culture, we must

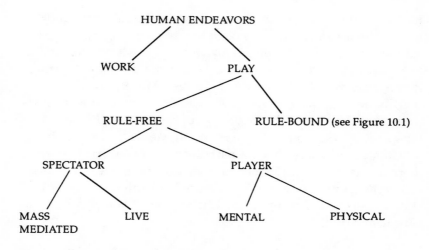

Figure 10.2. Rule-Free Play Within the Context of Human Activities
SOURCE: Based on ideas from Guttmann (1978), Piaget (1950) and Roberts and Sutton-Smith (1969).

likewise give "thick" rather than "thin descriptions" of actions to understand play across gender. For example, Olympic team and individual swimming events are competitive physical games that attract many spectators—some of them on site, but most of them watching on television. Thus a single activity, swimming, can fit in any of the six lower slots on Figure 10.1.

Furthermore, adult swimmers can choose to glide or flop about completely free of any rules (see Figure 10.2), as young swimmers do quite naturally. Finally, under the WORK segments of Figures 10.1 and 10.2, we could place Navy frogmen and Japanese pearl divers. A "thin description" would merely lump all these activities together as *Webster's* does for *swimming*: "to move through the water using arms, legs, fins, etc." A "thick description" requires understanding.

The "thick description" approach of cultural anthropologists, which emphasizes the *activity* aspect of leisure, does not lend itself to quantification. *Time,* another aspect of leisure, is easier to study and quantify. The sportswriters with roots in the Greek tradition emphasize the time element of leisure: work hours versus nonwork hours. As Giamatti (1989, p. 2) points out, the Greek word for *business* ("a-scholia") means literally "un-leisure," implying a division of one's time into two spheres.

Time for Play

Time studies can enlighten us as to the different meanings of "free time" for men and women. Szalai, Converse, Feldheim, Scheuch and Stone (1972), using time diaries from 25,000 subjects in 12 countries in 1965-1966, found people on average had 4.5 hours per day of "free time." On workdays, employed men had 21% of their waking hours free, while employed women had only 15% free. On their days off, the proportions were 56% for men and 40% for women.

Mercer (1985) found a decline of 3% in weekend free time for employed women in Melbourne, Australia, but an increase of 8% for employed Melbourne males. Szalai et al. (1972) found that housewives had about the same amount of free time on weekdays (25%) and Sundays (30%). The very concept of the weekend ("days off") presupposes work outside the home ("days on"). Although free from their regular jobs, employed people may work almost as hard at something else on the weekend: home repairs, gardening or athletics (Rybczynski, 1991).

Kelly (1982, p. 113) considers leisure to include *time* and *activity* but gives priority to *experience*—whether an activity, no matter how mundane, gives "personal satisfaction" and has "meaning." Wearing and Wearing (1988), who focus specifically on women, agree with this emphasis on experience:

> Definitions of leisure as "time" and "activity" do not go far enough in addressing differential access to leisure for men and women. For many women, especially those with young children, these definitions are inappropriate as they do not feel they have a right to time or activity just for their own enjoyment. . . . The concept of leisure as a freely chosen, self-enhancing experience is a concept of leisure that is appropriate for women and also for men. (p. 121)

One need not look far to find women resourcefully carving out leisure experiences—women who belie the " 'squashed ant' model of women's position" while embodying the model of "women as resistant individuals holding back the weight of power" (Wearing & Wearing, 1988, p. 120). Think of Anastasia in Marilyn French's *Her Mother's Daughter* (1988). In her twenties with two preschool children and no money, she took photographs of her friends' children while watching her own, then sold the pictures to buy film. Then think of Joy, Anastasia's divorced sister, who had to cope with three teenage children and a job, while attending school at night to finish college.

If women's leisure lives differ from men's in Western nations such as the United States, the United Kingdom and Australia, they differ even more in non-Western societies. In Japan, for example, differing gender patterns persist even after children have grown and husbands retire "back home." In a survey of older couples (Asahi News Service, 1993), about two thirds of husbands cited going out/traveling with their wives as their favorite activity. However, two thirds of the wives cited going out/traveling with their female friends and "hobbies and lessons" as their favorite activities.

Non-employed, well-to-do women who have grown children or household help exhibit another leisure pattern. They may take *koto* and tea ceremony lessons in Nagoya, Japan; do volunteer work in Berlin, Germany; or haunt the tennis courts in Westchester County, New York.

At the other extreme, in developing countries, such as in much of sub-Saharan Africa, "leisure as non-work time" is not only "an inappropriate concept for women" (Wearing & Wearing, 1988, p. 112)— it has virtually no meaning for them. Besides doing child care and household upkeep, women in Africa prepare and raise the family's food, putting in many more hours of work each day than men.

Worldwide TV Viewing

Women such as Joy and her counterparts around the world who pull double or triple shifts need a flexible relaxation option. Even in developing countries, television fills that role for many women. In the United States and abroad, women watch more than men in every time and program category except one: sporting events. Among specific age groups, females over age 55 outdistance everyone else. The gender gap is most striking in the afternoon, peaking at about

3 p.m. to 4 p.m., after which children take over. During these "women's hours," soap operas, comedy reruns and game shows predominate (Condry, 1989, p. 39).

After prewar experiments in industrialized countries during the 1930s and 1940s, the worldwide ascendance of television from the 1950s to the 1980s makes it "by far the fastest developed medium in human history," according to Ray Browne (1983, p. 118), founder of the Center for Popular Culture at Bowling Green (Ohio) State University. Today, more than 1 billion TV sets dot the globe.

Because two thirds of the world's people live in the Third World, a large number of sets exist in Third World countries, despite a lower percentage of penetration.[1] The Third World's share of the planet's television sets increased from 5% in 1965 to 40% in 1990. Part of the dramatic increase resulted from China's and India's relatively late expansion of television—in China after Mao Zedong's death in 1976[2] and in India[3] after the Satellite Instructional Television Experiment (SITE) broadcasts of 1975-1976.

Television's suitability as an activity one can do at the same time as housekeeping and child care makes it a strong force in women's lives worldwide. In Australia in 1985, TV watching ranked as the top leisure activity among adults aged 25-39. The others were reading, visiting friends/relatives, listening to music, dining out, relaxing/doing nothing, gardening for pleasure, entertaining, arts/crafts and walking for pleasure. Women participated more than men in each activity except "dining out" and "relaxing/doing nothing." As Wearing and Wearing (1988, p. 115) point out, all the activities that women pursue "can be carried out in conjunction with child care."

According to Szalai et al. (1972, p. 177), subjects spent the following percentage of their free time in 1965 viewing television as a primary activity (only communities where more than two thirds of people had a set are included):

100 electoral districts, West Germany	24% of free time
Olomounc, Czechoslovakia	28% of free time
Belgium	28% of free time
Osnabruck, West Germany	25% of free time
Hoyerswerda, East Germany	25% of free time
44 cities, United States	31% of free time

In addition, about 60% more time was spent with television as a secondary activity. Since 1965, television viewing has taken over even more free time.

In a study of adults in five countries—Japan, Korea, the Philippines, Britain and the United States—Newton and Buck (1985, p. 302) found "more differences on specific variables related to gender than to culture." In all five cultures, women watch more than men do. Looking at all males in the study contrasted with all females, Newton and Buck (1985) conclude:

> For men, television is only one of many significant others with whom they interact in a day; therefore, the act of viewing is perceived as positive (entertainment and relaxation after a day of involvement in socially valued occupations) and as an activity shared with other men. This is particularly true for televised football games and other male sporting events. Women showed that their association with television is negative. (pp. 306-307)

Women, Media, Sports: The Global View

Considering the dearth of materials on women, media and sports in the United States (see Chapters 1 and 2), their lack in other countries is not surprising. The global counterpart of the U.S. story must be pieced together from TV ratings data and anecdotal evidence. Unfortunately, only a few countries have reliable, publicly available ratings data, not all of which is divided by gender. But certain conclusions may be safely drawn.

First, worldwide, more men than women watch televised sports. In Norway, for example, 64% of men and 49% of women watch televised sports. In Germany, 75% of men and 52% of women regularly watch televised sports. Sports is the only TV program type that attracts more men than women (Condry, 1989, p. 39).

Second, sex-appropriateness of sports (see Chapters 1 and 2) seems to hold across national borders. Individual sports, especially those with graceful movements and minimal body contact, appeal to female viewers. As in the United States, women elsewhere like to watch ice skating, swimming, diving and gymnastics. According to data from

Norway, for example, women are more likely than men to watch swimming and gymnastics.

Third, given the worldwide similarity of news values, one can safely say that female Olympic champions and winners of competitions (marathons, regional skiing events) receive coverage from their home country's media and may even achieve celebrity status. In Japan, Olympic skating medalist Midori Ito now appears as a TV quiz show panelist.

Fourth, although sports reporting remains largely a male preserve worldwide, women have made inroads. In Japan, for example, the NHK network has a female anchor for the sports portion of its main (7p.m.-8 p.m.) national news program. In England, the number of women sportscasters is growing. Three women (Shelley Webb, Penny Silvester and Estelle Matthews) began work for the London Sports Network in 1993 (Viner, 1993).

Is a TV sports news program as "newsy" as a "real" newscast? Do reality-based televised sports events have more in common with news than with fantasy-based entertainment? Donald Browne (1983, p. 188) categorizes dramas as entertainment and sports as information. However, Kelly (1982), who emphasizes leisure as experience, would probably argue that viewers feel entertained, not like the receivers of information.

In a broad sense, writings on sport form the basis for understanding *all* entertainment enterprises. Greatly influenced by Huizinga (1950), William Stephenson, one of the first mass media scholars to take entertainment seriously, wrote *Play Theory of Mass Communication*, first published in 1967 and reissued in 1988. Stephenson (1967) says that some content deals with work (informational and educational programs), and some deals with play. To date, information theory has been "all about work and not about fun" (p. 198). But the question goes much deeper than that.

TV Entertainment Versus Information

The well-entrenched distinction between entertainment and informational TV programs has bureaucratic roots: first, the institutional division within commercial television; second, the industrywide division between commercial and noncommercial ("educational") television.

In the dual system of the United States, the United Kingdom, Israel, Australia, Japan and other countries, one or more "educational" networks coexist with one or more commercial, entertainment-oriented networks. These "institutional barriers help to . . . encourage departmentalized thinking" (Fischer & Melnik, 1979, p. 145). However, the "myth that 'pure entertainment' exists is one that is slowly but surely being dismantled" (p. xix).

Indeed, the false division of programs into "information" and "entertainment" means little to researchers who study *television*'s (rather than *situation comedies'* or *news shows'*) long-term effects, such as George Gerbner's Philadelphia group. The arguments against separating entertainment from information take three forms.

First, a chorus of voices (e.g., Browne, 1989, p. 58; Singhal, 1990, p. 80) contends that TV entertainment does indeed inform. Viewers may turn to television as a medium of entertainment, relaxation and enjoyment, but inadvertently—and consistently—they learn from it. In sum, in the words of former FCC Commissioner Nicholas Johnson (1978), "All television is educational. The only question is: what does it teach?"

Second, and conversely, *all* media have properties of entertainment" (Fischer & Melnik, 1979, p. xiii). Even the nightly TV news is "entertainment and mythology under the respectable guise of 'reality' " (Kaminsky & Mahan, 1985, p.165). As Fischer and Melnik (1979) note, "A documentary is or can be entertaining. . . . Conversely, entertainment can be informative and can influence" (p. 145).

Third, given its complex nature, TV entertainment has complex effects. "Entertainment fulfills a variety of social functions and hence cannot avoid being political in the widest sense of the word" (Fischer & Melnik, 1979, p. xix). According to Barnouw and Kirkland (1989, p. 102), entertainment "has informational content that usually cultivates conventional themes, outlooks and perspectives."

The dual properties of TV sports further bolster the futility of separating information and entertainment. Indeed, TV sports have two unlikely first cousins, one of them a product of television's informational divisions (news) and the other what has been called the lowest of the low-brow entertainment.

Women Spectators and Mind Games

Instead of limiting the last branch of Figure 10.1 (Competitive Games/Spectator/Mass-Mediated) to stadium sports, we can add made-for-television, nonathletic sports: TV game shows (Cooper-Chen, 1993).

Most television content (e.g., dramas, comedies) falls under the Rule-Free play category in Figure 10.2. TV game shows fall near TV sports and under rule-bound television. TV game shows resemble rule-bound, competitive sports, but some go one step beyond: Some games permit the viewer to "jump into the tube" and play along. Aside from this interactive quality, sports and game shows both share the following characteristics:

> *Immediacy* The action unfolds in real time, unlike drama or comedy, which can compress hours, days or years into minutes.
>
> *Independence* The action unfolds on its own accord, adhering to established rules, beyond the control of sponsors, advertisers, script-writers or producers.
>
> *Purity* The outcome is not predetermined, and when game-fixing scandals do occur, fans feel betrayed.
>
> *Luck* Present in varying degrees, ranging from near absence in chess to paramount importance in a show such as *Let's Make a Deal*.
>
> *Skill* Present in varying degrees, ranging from near absence in a show such as *Card Sharks* to paramount importance in gymnastics.
>
> *Closure* The outcome results in a winning player or team and a loser or losers.
>
> *Escape* The game unfolds without relation to the world's events, only an adherence to internal rules.

Ratings data other than that of sporting events suggests that women may seek more balanced spectating experiences than men. In addition to watching physical contests, women seem to derive satisfaction as well from watching contests based on intellect and chance (see Figure 10.1).

For example, of nine game shows aired in France in fall 1989, all drew more women spectators than men; the French version of *Jeopardy!* had 1.6% of the men watching and 3.0% of the women.

The 1986 Cassandras (for syndicated programs) also revealed age and gender differences in viewing patterns: among the top five shows watched by women aged 25-54 were *Wheel of Fortune, Jeopardy!* and *New Newlywed Game*; by men aged 25-54, the only game show was *Wheel of Fortune*; and by teenagers, the top five were all comedies.

Game shows seem to assume for women—especially older Western women—the role that TV sports holds for men. It seems to take a cultural studies analyst, namely John Fiske, or a female game show fan, namely Maxene Fabe, to see the gender-based hypocrisy of TV game show bashing, cheek-by-jowl with delirious enthusiasm for televised (male) team sports. Fabe (1979) sees sexism in some (males') criticism:

> The critics were *really* condemning the sight of someone (women, maybe?) acting spontaneous and uninhibited while participating in a competition. Why not, I wondered, the same opprobrium for sports fans screaming at a hockey game? (p. xiii)

For his part, Fiske (1990, p. 136) celebrates the freedom game shows give women "to be noisy in public; to escape from demure respectability, from the confines of good sense that patriarchy has constructed as necessary qualities for 'the feminine.' "

Fiske (1990, p. 134) equates the "low critical standing" of women's-interest game shows with "the disciplinary power of patriarchy to devalue anything that resists, threatens, or evades its power" or, by implication, the power to elevate in value anything that confirms its power, such as male team sports.

Notes

1. According to BBC statistics for 1989, television reaches at least 600 million of China's 1.1 billion population (55%); about 125 million of India's 880 million people (15%); and about 70 million of Mexico's 80 million people (87%) (Singhal, 1990, p. 78).

2. The story of China's romance with television in the 1980s shows dramatically the phenomenal pull of the medium most. In 1980, the country had about 630,000

sets. By 1985, there were 12 million sets, and by the end of the decade, about 118 million (about one set for every 10 persons).

3. In India, between 1984 and 1985, the number of TV viewers jumped from 37 to 60 million, then increased again to 90 million in 1988. During that year, sets were sold at the rate of one every five minutes, even though a black-and-white set cost $200 to $250, or about two months' salary. For those who still cannot afford this relatively high cost, the practice of community viewing increases access to television. By the year 2000, India will have an estimated 63 million sets, with an audience of some 378 million people (Singhal & Rogers, 1989, p. 67).

References

Asahi News Service. (1993, February 19). Survey: Spouses should do what they want. *Asahi Evening News*, p. 5.

Barnouw, Erik & Kirkland, Catherine. (1989). Entertainment. In Erik Barnouw (Ed.), *International encyclopedia of communications* (pp. 101-104). New York: Oxford University Press.

Browne, Donald. (1983). Media entertainment in the Western world. In John Martin & Anju Grover Chaudhary (Eds.), *Comparative mass media systems* (pp. 187-208). New York: Longman.

Browne, Donald. (1989). *Comparing broadcast systems: The experiences of six industrialized nations*. Ames, IA: Iowa State University Press.

Browne, Ray B. (1983). The repressive nature of TV esthetics criticism. *Journal of American Culture, 6*(3), 117-122.

Coles, Libby. (1980). Women and leisure: A critical perspective. In David Mercer & Elery Hamilton-Smith (Eds.), *Recreation planning and social change in urban Australia* (pp. 63-73). Malvern, Victoria: Sorrett.

Condry, John. (1989). *The psychology of television*. Hillsdale, NJ: Lawrence Erlbaum.

Cooper-Chen, Anne. (1993). *Games in the global village: A 50-nation study of entertainment television*. Bowling Green, OH: The Popular Press.

Deem, Rosemary. (1982). Women, leisure and inequality. *Leisure Studies, 1*, 29-46.

Deem, Rosemary. (1986). *All work and no play? The sociology of women and leisure*. Philadelphia: Open University Press.

Fabe, Maxene. (1979). *TV game shows*. New York: Doubleday.

Fischer, Hans-Dietrich & Melnik, Stephan. (1979). *Entertainment: A cross-cultural examination*. New York: Hastings House.

Fiske, John. (1990). Women and quiz shows: Consumerism, patriarchy and resisting pleasures. In Mary Ellen Brown (Ed.), *Television & women's culture* (pp. 134-143). London: Sage.

French, Marilyn. (1988). *Her mother's daughter*. New York: Ballantine.

Geertz, Clifford. (1973). *The interpretation of cultures*. New York: Basic Books.

Giamatti, A. Bartlett. (1989). *Take time for paradise: Americans and their games*. New York: Summit Books.

Guttmann, Allen. (1978). *The nature of modern sports*. New York: Columbia University Press.

Guttmann, Allen. (1988). *A whole new ball game: An interpretation of American sports*. Chapel Hill, NC: University of North Carolina Press.

Huizinga, John. (1950/1938). *Homo ludens*. Boston: Beacon Press.

Johnson, Nicholas. (1978). Lecture at Cornell University Law School.

Kaminsky, Stuart & Mahan, Jeffrey. (1985). *American television genres*. Chicago: Nelson-Hall.

Kelly, John R. (1982). *Leisure*. Englewood Cliffs, NJ: Prentice Hall.

Mercer, Darren C. (1985). Australians' time use and preferences. *Australian and New Zealand Journal of Sociology*, 21(3), 371-394.

Newton, Barbara & Buck, Elizabeth. (1985). Television as a significant other: Its relationship to self descriptors in five countries. *Journal of Cross Cultural Psychology*, 16(3), 289-312.

Piaget, Jean. (1951). *Play, dreams and imitation in childhood*. London: Heinemann.

Roberts, John & Sutton-Smith, Brian. (1969). Child training and game involvement. In John Loy & Gerald Kenyon (Eds.), *Sport, culture and society* (pp. 120-131). New York: Macmillan.

Rybczynski, Witold. (1991). *Waiting for the weekend*. New York: Viking.

Singhal, Arvind. (1990). *Entertainment-education strategies for development*. Unpublished PhD dissertation, University of Southern California.

Singhal, Arvind & Rogers, Everett. (1989). *India's information revolution*. Newbury Park, CA: Sage.

Stephenson, William. (1988/1967). *The play theory of mass communication*. Chicago: University of Chicago Press.

Sutton-Smith, Brian. (1988). Introduction. In William Stephenson, *The play theory of mass communication* (2nd ed., pp. ix-xx). New Brunswick, NJ: Transaction Books.

Szalai, Alexander, Converse, Philip E., Feldheim, Pierre, Scheuch, Erwin K. & Stone, Philip J. (Eds). (1972). *The use of time*. The Hague, The Netherlands: Mouton.

Viner, Katharine. (1993, January 4). Calling the shots. *Guardian*, p. 10.

Wearing, Betsy & Wearing, Stephen. (1988). "All in a day's leisure": Gender and the concept of leisure. *Leisure Studies*, 7(2), 111-123.

Weiss, Paul. (1969). *Sport: A philosophic inquiry*. Carbondale, IL: Southern Illinois University Press.

PART III

Developing
a New Sports Model

ca 1990

11

From the Feminine Mystique
to the Female Physique

Uncovering the Archetype
of Artemis in Sport

Pamela J. Creedon

> [W]e should note the way in which inequality among men and women
> was built not only into the language, thought, and philosophy of
> Western civilization, but the way in which gender itself became a meta-
> phor defining power relations in such a way as to mystify them and
> render them invisible.
>
> Gerda Lerner, *The Creation of Patriarchy* (1986, p. 211)

The Ohio State University basketball team played for the NCAA
Division I Championship on April 4, 1993, losing to Texas Tech
by two points. It was the best finish ever for the team, and the first
time that a Big Ten Conference team had made it to the finals. Columbus media riveted the town's attention on the "Lady Buckeyes" during
the tournament, particularly, I suspect, because no men's sports team

AUTHOR'S NOTE: I wish to thank Lynn Buck, Betsy Caprio, Marlaine Francis, Patty
Hickey, Pamela Highlen, Susan Kaufman, Molly Merryman and William Peterson for
their helpful comments, useful suggestions and wonderful insights on various drafts
of this chapter.

in the capital city—or the state for that matter—was still in contention for anything at the time.

At the height of the frenzy, a local television reporter called me for my reaction to all the media attention that the team was receiving. When I explained that although highly competitive, physically strong women might seem odd and unusual to the media in Columbus, Ohio, women had been playing basketball for more than 100 years and women's basketball games had been televised for at least 20 years, she was shocked. She and a camera operator rushed over to my house to get my comments on tape for the evening news.

Her reaction is not surprising. Whenever reporters, or more generally the media, "discover" women's sports and female athletes, they think that they are creating them. Of course, they aren't; instead, they are uncovering a female archetype that has been around a lot longer than American leisure-time sports. It is the archetype of female physicality. In this section of the book, we will take a closer look at the archetype, her acceptance in American culture and her image in the media. We explore the development of the archetype, her appearances in film and her role in developing a new model for sport in the next three chapters.[1]

In this chapter, I trace the emergence of Artemis in Greek mythology, her characteristics (physicality, femininity and sexuality) and her relationship with the Amazons. I will show how Artemis and the Amazons have been—and still are—used as metaphors to illustrate relationships of power in Western civilization and will deconstruct the violence associated with the archetype. I conclude with a discussion of how re-visioning the archetype could cause a rupture in cultural values.[2]

Mythology and Artemis

Myths are cultural glue. They tell stories about the "why" of existence and of nature that are difficult to know directly. Often they are so pervasive and powerful that they frame perceptions in such a way that there is no need to ask the "why" of things because they are "known" at an unspoken level:

The clearest of assumptions in an age are those which are unspoken, which buttress every argument, which form the background of every utterance. (duBois, 1982, p. 18)

Records of myths explaining the "why" of the antagonism between masculine and feminine values, energies or psyches have existed for more than five millennia, ever since writing was invented in Mesopotamia (Lerner, 1986). The roots of understanding in contemporary Eurocentric American culture can be traced to the beginnings of Western civilization.

Early Greek theories about "why" men and women differ actually grew out of myths created to justify an event that had occurred centuries earlier. Somewhere between 1600 and 700 B.C., a process took place in many cultures that shifted the power of creation from the Goddess to more patriarchal gods (Lerner, 1986; Woolger & Woolger, 1989).[3] In Greece, the ancient Mother Goddess, known as Gaia or Earth, was divided and replaced by a supreme male god of war and the hunt (Woolger & Woolger, 1989, p. 24). Six lesser goddesses with specific powers emerged from the division of Gaia: Athena, wisdom and civilization; Aphrodite, love; Persephone, spirit and underworld; Demeter, motherhood; Hera, marriage; and Artemis, physicality and the wild (Woolger & Woolger, 1989). According to Jungian (1969) theory, each of these goddesses represented archetypes, or patterns in thinking, feelings, instincts and behavior.

Who benefitted from the division of Gaia into six lesser goddesses? What purpose was served by establishing six separate female archetypes?

Riane Eisler (1987) describes a "cataclysmic turning point in the prehistory of Western civilization" when societies that worshipped the "life-generating and life-nurturing powers of the universe" were overtaken by people who worshipped the power of the blade "to establish and enforce domination" (p. xvii). A number of scholars believe that the division was the outcome of invasions by early tribes, which needed to reframe differences between men and women in order to justify their patriarchal religions and social structures (duBois, 1982; Lerner, 1986; Tyrrell, 1984). For the purposes of this chapter, *patriarchy* is defined as the institutionalized system "of male dominance over women and children in the family . . . and society in general" (Lerner, 1986, p. 239).

Whatever the reason for the division of Gaia, myths were constructed for each of the six archetypes to teach lessons about the appropriateness of some roles for women and the inappropriateness of others (Woolger & Woolger, 1989). Although each of the goddess archetypes has had an important role in influencing Western culture, two are of particular interest in this book. They were warrior-like. They fought with or like men and had no male consorts or lovers.[4] They were self-sufficient and independent. They were revered and feared by men. One, Athena, is often pictured fully armed with a sword. The other, Artemis (Diana to the Romans), is often shown hunting with bow and quiver accompanied by dogs.[5]

Within the past two decades, Athena's primary strength (intellect) has won reluctant recognition by the "system," whereas Artemis' primary strength (physicality) still struggles for accommodation. In the 1990s, Athena can put on her business suit and head to the office to work for her male boss and earn about two thirds of what her male co-worker does, whereas Artemis remains outside and alienated from the system because she refuses to "play the game" in order to fit in or to be accepted:[6]

> Artemis embodies a profound denial of the world of patriarchy, the world where some persons have power over others, the world of dominance and submission, where one can be hunter *or* hunted. (Downing, 1988, p. 176)

Psychologically, Artemis is alienated from patriarchal society because she is willing to take on the roles of avenger and protectress and because her femininity is not defined by a relationship to a lover, child, father or husband.[7] As a child, she is called a "tomboy," indicating that exhibiting physicality or a preference for outdoor play or activity means acting like a boy, which is, by inference, an inappropriate gender role (Hancock, 1989).[8] The adolescent Artemis is "the athlete, the gymnast, the dancer, the jogger, the tennis player, the swimmer, the skier, the rider, and so on, depending on the resources available to her" (Woolger & Woolger, 1989, p. 106). Later in her life, because of her physical strength and independence, she continues to find herself alienated from the feminine ideal. In essence, she rejects what Betty Friedan (1984) called "the feminine mystique," the identification of womanhood solely with the roles of wife and mother and the qualities of frailty and passivity.

Earlier chapters in this book have explained how the media reflect the gender conformity that defines power relationships in sport. Because sport has long been seen as less important than other venues for gender power struggles, its content remains unrehearsed and its messages relatively unfettered. Power relationships involving the Artemis archetype that are well hidden in more complicated settings and contexts are therefore visible in sport.

Although contrived, one of the more memorable examples of how this archetypal power struggle is played out in the media was the "Battle of the Sexes" in the Houston Astrodome on September 20, 1973.[9] In front of what was then the largest television audience in the United States to view a sport event, 29-year-old Billie Jean King, at the top of her form, was carried onto the tennis court on a litter like Cleopatra (Lumpkin, 1982). She presented her opponent, Bobby Riggs, with a symbolic piglet and he gave her a Sugar Daddy the size of a tennis racquet (King, 1974):[10]

> Built up into the battle of the sexes, Mrs. [sic] King, as the dynamic defender of women's liberation in tennis, found herself matched with the 55-year-old hustler. . . . The queen easily and quickly disposed of the former champion to the glee of feminists and the chagrin of the chauvinists. (Lumpkin, 1982, p. 525)

Artemis: Physicality and Femininity

Woolger and Woolger believe that Artemis may be the oldest of all the Greek goddesses (1989). Known as the Moon Goddess because of her relation to menstruation and the rhythm of life, she ruled over reproduction (Adler, 1986; Spretnak, 1978). In Sparta, Artemis was known as Korythalia and "worshipped in orgiastic dancing" (Monaghan, 1990, p. 34). Bolen (1984) credits her as the archetype behind the feminist movement (p. 50). Scholars describe her as the embodiment of absolute femininity, which is not defined by a relation, positive or negative, to the masculine (Downing, 1988; Harding, 1935; Paris, 1986).

Culturally, however, Artemesian femininity is more likely to be defined in relation to physicality. As such, it is often diminished by the energy of another goddess. Rooted in Aphrodite energy, beauty has replaced the feminine mystique in contemporary culture as the definition of true femininity (Wolf, 1991):

> As soon as a woman's primary social value could no longer be defined as the attainment of virtuous domesticity, the beauty myth redefined it as the attainment of virtuous beauty. It did so to substitute both a new consumer imperative and a new justification for economic unfairness in the workplace where the old ones had lost their hold over newly liberated women. (p. 18)

If she wishes to be accepted in contemporary American culture, a strong, self-sufficient, even muscular Artemis archetype must make offerings to the beauty myth. She can engage in fitness and exercise *for the purpose* of weight reduction and body toning, or she can overemphasize her "femininity." Several authors have described the effect of the beauty myth in athletics in terms of an "apologetic" (Del Rey, 1978; Felshin, 1981). The apologetic refers to the belief that women's sports and female athletes must emphasize that they are feminine in order to reduce cognitive dissonance they experience as a "social anomaly" (Del Rey, 1978). Researchers continue to find that strength, muscularity, assertiveness and competitiveness are still largely defined as "masculine" characteristics and that a female exhibiting them represents an unacceptable side of femininity (Bem, 1974; Matteo, 1988).

Judges in women's body-building competitions, for example, acknowledge that they have a definition of muscles for women restricted by their definition of femininity. Recruited by a movie producer, world champion Australian powerlifter Bev Francis brought the controversy between "feminine" muscle and "unfeminine" muscle to the American movie screen (see Chapter 12). Recognized as the strongest woman in the world, Francis placed eighth out of 15 at the Caesar's Palace World Cup of bodybuilding in 1983—an event conceived solely for the movie *Pumping Iron II: The Women* (McGough, 1993, p. 65). One judge told her: "As a bodybuilder you were the best, but in a women's bodybuilding competition, I just felt that I couldn't vote for you" (Mitchell & Dyer, 1985, p. 97). Francis later made concessions to the beauty myth that included cosmetic surgery, a change in hair color and style, and reduced musculature. Describing herself as "the most 'feminine,' in traditional terms, that I've ever looked," she placed second in the 1990 Ms. Olympia contest (McGough, p. 153).

The dualism of masculine versus feminine is further confounded by the existence of a sex-appropriate ranking schema in sport. An "appropriate" sport is one that does not challenge traditional gender-role expectations. Not surprisingly, individual sport activities such as tennis, ice skating, swimming and gymnastics are ranked as more sex appropriate for women than team sports; graceful, fluid body movements are more appropriate than contests of strength and power; and sports with minimal body contact are more appropriate than sports with heavy contact (Colley, Nash, O'Donnell & Restorick, 1987; Metheny, 1967). Kane (1987), for example, showed that gender-role conformity has a powerful influence on attractiveness ratings for female athletes. Attractiveness ratings from pictures of females matched with a sex-appropriate sport such as volleyball dropped significantly (4.88 to 2.97) when they were compared with ratings from pictures of the same athletes associated with a sex-inappropriate sport such as football.

Lenskyj (1987) linked sex-appropriate physical activities with power dynamics. Her argument is that sex-appropriate rankings, based on male-defined femininity, provide the patriarchal cultures with power over females and their sexuality. "The effective channeling of males into masculine sports and females into feminine sports maximized sex differences and entrenched the masculine/feminine dichotomy" (p. 141). The dichotomy, Lenskyj suggests, leaves the roles of protector and aggressor to the males.

Sexuality and Artemis

Many myths surround the sexuality of Artemis:[11]

What we learn from classical times, when the cult of Artemis was strong, is that sexuality was free and barely constrained by the social institution of marriage and issues of paternity. (Woolger & Woolger, 1989, p. 116)

In our contemporary dualistic sexual framework of hetero- or homosexuality, Artemesian sexuality defies classification. For female athletes, the power struggle over sexuality surfaces in questions about their sexual orientation. At the time of her tennis match with Bobby Riggs, King was "happily married" and competing in an individual sport regarded as appropriate for women. What this young Artemis didn't bargain for was the revenge of the defeated male archetype. Eventually, in the male-dominated sports media across the country, questions about King's sexual orientation surfaced. In typical Artemesian candor, two days after the accusation that she had had an extramarital and lesbian affair with her secretary Marilyn Barnett, she held a press conference to acknowledge the relationship (King, 1982).

More than a decade later, many professional female athletes—heterosexual, homosexual, bisexual or whatever—still express concern about the "Billie Jean King thing." Lesbians cite economic concerns—fears that paychecks, sponsorships, endorsements and the like will be affected if their "secret" is known (Nelson, 1991, p. 135). Their fear is not without justification; Martina Navratilova, for example, who has been open about her lesbianism, has fewer endorsements than Chris Evert did. Consequently, women's fear of not being perceived as heterosexual females functions to increase male control over female sexuality and femininity. The Ladies Professional Golf Association, which has been run by men since its founding in 1950, is a prime example of how this control works (also see Chapter 7):

> Sponsors, LPGA staff, and players attempt to eradicate what they delicately call their "image problem" by publicly denying the existence of lesbians on the tour. To this end they play up marriages and mothers, employ an "image consultant" to serve as hairstylist and makeup artist (people so frequently confuse a traditional feminine image with heterosexuality that hairdos and mascara still serve as effective camouflage), and maintain . . . "a silence so loud it screams." (Nelson, p. 139)

The archetypal power struggle has deteriorated into battle over the media image of Artemis, an image constructed largely by male-controlled organizations using economic fears to constrain female sexuality. It's a battle that only a few female athletes in recent history have had the resources—economic, psychological or physical—to fight publicly.

Artemis and the Amazons

Artemis was a pre-Christian Greek goddess, but her archetype has survived in stories about the legendary Amazons, fierce warrior women who supposedly lived almost entirely without men.[12] Herodotus speaks of an Amazon society in the fifth century B.C. and Homer, Euripides and Aristotle also wrote about a cult of strong and powerful women (Lefkowitz, 1986). Some scholars have linked Artemis' origins to the hunting tribes of Anatolia, where Amazons were said to have dwelt (Woolger & Woolger, 1989, p. 99). Others have described the Amazons as worshippers of Artemis (Downing, 1988).

The Amazons may have been mythic characters; they may have been living, breathing humans. We know that contracts issued in the 1500s to Spanish explorers "frequently included clauses requiring a search for these mythical women" (Leonard, 1944, p. 561). Columbus, Cortes, Magellan, Sir Walter Raleigh and even Marco Polo were among those explorers to record sightings of female warriors (Cavin, 1985). Many scholars argue that the myriad references to them in literature and poetry and the multiple works of art around the world that give them form are not sufficient empirical proof of their existence. Because there has been no major "Amazon dig," we have no absolute archaeological proof of their existence. Of course, as Cavin points out, we have no empirical proof to the contrary either.

Cavin (1985) links the Amazons to societies in which there were extreme high-female/low-male sex ratios. Sobol (1972) has developed several theories about the existence of Amazons. First, they may have been barbarian women who fought beside men against the Greeks. Second, they may have resulted from a case of mistaken identity; they may have been smooth-shaven Hittites from Asia Minor who attacked the Greeks between 2000 and 1200 B.C. To the early Greeks, hairiness was a symbol of masculine strength, so they may have assumed their beardless attackers were women. Third, they may be descendants of the armed Hittite priestesses who sacrificed male victims. Fourth, and most relevant for this book, they may have been contrived from the athleticism of Greek girls.

> Scholars of today tend to overlook the participation of Greek girls in sports. . . . If the Amazons did not stem from armed women . . . they may well have started with a group of high-spirited maidens who took to hardening their bodies with strenuous exercises as, later, the Amazons exercised to keep their battle-edge between campaigns. (Sobol, 1972, p. 127)

We know that the men of Greece did their best to keep women from participating in sports. Women were banned from participating in the Olympics, so they established their own games named in honor of Hera; according to some sources, these predate the Olympics (Monaghan, 1990). We also know that while Greek boys listened to tales of Heracles, Greek girls heard stories of Atalanta. She has been described as "the ultimate delineation of the competitive female. Her beauty and talents incite love and resentment in male champions, whom she outshines at running, hunting, and wrestling" (Sobol, p. 129).[13]

Whether we believe them to be fact or fiction, Amazons are found in European, African, North American, South American and Asian cultures (Cavin, 1985).[14] Writing in the 1860s, Bachofen (1967/1861) saw Amazonism as a "universal phenomenon," not based on the special physical or historical circumstances of any particular people but on conditions characteristic of all human existence.[15]

What is universal about the Amazons across cultures? Amazon stories are found to dominate across cultures in two periods of history: origin and patriarchal transition (Cavin, 1985, p. 78). Chesler (1982) hypothesized that the Amazon archetype as the "Terrible Woman" was needed by early patriarchs to justify their divorce from and division of the Great Mother Goddess and their subsequent domination of her and, ultimately, of women. Some scholars believe that the pervasiveness of the myth points to its utility in patriarchal cultures in the creation of social reality. Cavin (1985) argues that *"patriarchal society is founded on the defeat of Amazons, the defeat of women"* [italics in original] (p. 67).

Tyrrell (1984) charges that the Greek Amazon myth was developed by the "men in charge of the media" in order to develop a gender order in which female was inferior (p. 22). He links the development of Amazon myth in Greek fiction and archaeology to the need to validate patriarchal marriage, to control female sexuality and to justify the expansionist goals of the Athenian government.

DuBois (1982) echoes this theme with her contention that the Amazons were used in fifth-century-B.C. Greek art, poetry and drama to conceptualize difference from the male norm. She believes that the Amazon myth represented the boundary of difference between male and female, much as the centaur myth was used to represent the boundary between man and animal. DuBois argues that this model of gender difference was used until Greek losses in the Peloponnesian Wars led to social upheaval and a greater dependence on slavery. The upheaval necessitated the development of a "new" model of difference in which philosophers expounded the "natural" hierarchy with white men at the top. Aristotle, for example, argued in the fourth century B.C. that woman was a mutilated male and menstrual discharge was impure semen that lacked one ingredient, "the principle of soul" (Lerner, 1986, p. 207). This hierarchical model, which still influences our perceptions, also described inferiorities based on class and race.

Simply put, Amazon mythology was designed to teach women in patriarchal cultures that female physicality, self-sufficiency and power violated gender norms.

Artemis, the Amazons and Violence

Gaia—from whose division Artemis and five other goddess archetypes emerged—was also known as the Great Earth Mother. She had, in the manner of Mother Nature, both a life-giving and a violent, destructive side (Harding, 1935). According to various myths, Gaia invented the sickle for use in harvesting crops but also used it to castrate Uranus (Salmonson, 1991).

Similarly, in many stories Artemis is portrayed as the goddess of midwifery, as well as of the hunt, which may explain why by some accounts her name is thought to be a derivative from *artamos*, meaning "butcher" or "slaughterer" (Smith, 1992). Although she is never seen with sword or ax, she is often pictured with a silver bow and arrows (Salmonson, 1991). In several different myths, Artemis rescues women from rapists and kills the attackers (Bolen, 1984). One of the women she protects is her own mother, Leto. In one myth, she is outraged at being seen naked by Actaeon, so she turns him into a stag that is chased and killed by his own hunting dogs (Downing, 1988). According to Downing, "When Actaeon's glance turns the huntress into the hunted, she naturally makes him experience the same transformation from hunter to victim" (p. 177). In other myths, Artemis kills Koronis and Ariadne when they are unfaithful to their immortal lovers, and "thereby in some profound sense betray themselves" (p. 180).

In nearly every culture, there are also tales recounting how the Amazons fend off various aggressors. Mythology across generations of Greek culture tells of battles being waged against the Amazon menace. The Amazons in these tales, who are often pictured armed with a labrys—a double-edged ax—are not the aggressors. However, in one Greek myth the Amazons are clearly the attackers. When Theseus kidnaps the Amazon Hippolyta to make her his queen, her Amazon sisters set sail for Athens and attack, ultimately losing a bitterly fought battle in which Hippolyta is killed (Schwab, 1974).

The purpose of this chapter is not to chronicle all of the violent myths surrounding Artemis and the Amazons. Instead, it seeks a basic understanding of who benefits from the construction of an image of them as vengeful, uncontrollable warrior women. Kleinbaum (1983) suggests that over time the weapons used to subdue the Amazons simply shifted from the sword to the pen. Deconstructing the general context of their violence is central to understanding it. The violence exhibited in various mythic episodes involving Artemis or the Amazons is almost exclusively associated with one of three values: protecting, avenging or sustaining life, rather than dominating others' lives. The distinction is crucial because it suggests that although the archetype exhibits violent behavior, the violence is not motivated by dominating, expansionist or materialist aims.[16]

American Amazons

Although the Greek mythmakers wove negative meanings about female physicality and self-sufficiency into their stories of Artemesian and Amazonian adventures, women through time have resisted the definition of Amazon as a pejorative. Instead, the archetype has excited women's imaginations and provided images of liberation. Its opposition to the "exchange of women between men of the same kind"—patriarchal marriage—has served many women as a source of inspiration across centuries (duBois, 1982, p. 41).

In her *Encyclopedia of Amazons*, Jessica Amanda Salmonson (1991) filled 280 pages with examples—even though she restricted the listings to women duelists or soldiers that engaged in direct combat with some degree of skill (p. xi). Athletes, as well as many other possible categories of Amazons, are left out of the volume! A convincing argument can be made that women sportswriters and sportscasters deserved to be included in the volume as duelists who have exhibited the physical and mental stamina to battle the sport world (see Chapters 4 and 5).

If one were to compile an *Encyclopedia of Amazon Athletes*, defining Amazons as women with the ability to defeat men in physical contests, we'd start with Billie Jean King. Tennis star Lottie Dod would also need a page. She defeated Wimbledon champion Ernest Renshaw in 1888 (Blue, 1987, p. xi). Ella Hattan, who toured the United States at the turn of the century as Jaguarina, "Champion Amazon of the World," would certainly warrant inclusion (Mrozek, 1987). On horseback with a broadsword, Jaguarina met and defeated many male challengers.

> Newspaper accounts of Jaguarina's efforts lavished attention on her physical features, emphasizing her grace and marking her power and force as quite unexpected. . . . Praise of her beauty conformed to the stereotypes of the time. But her ability to defeat men was provocative. (Mrozek, 1987, p. 290)

Mildred "Babe" Didrikson (later Zaharias) would also deserve an entry. Voted Associated Press Woman Athlete of the Year in 1945 and 1946, she set Olympic records for the javelin, high jump and hurdles, played basketball, baseball and billiards and was instrumental in organizing the Ladies Professional Golf Association (Sochen, 1987). This Artemis pitched one no-hit inning for the Philadelphia Athletics in 1934, struck out Joe DiMaggio in 1950, and equaled men's par more than 50% of the time on the golf course (Sparhawk, Leslie, Turbow & Rose, 1989). Not surprisingly, sportswriters had great difficulty describing her five-foot-six-inch, 145-pound body:

> Reporters portrayed her as a female Samson, a woman whose physique resembled that of a man more than a woman. Therefore, she was hard to categorize; she was too serious, too determined, and too competitive to qualify as the average female athlete. (Sochen, 1987, p. 122)

Another entry from professional tennis would surely be Czechoslovakian-born Martina Navratilova, who defected in 1975 and became a U.S. citizen in 1981 (Navratilova, 1985). Like so many of the other Artemis archetypes, she is known for her sexuality, candor and independence, as well as her athletic skill. Her public palimony case with Judy Nelson was settled out of court for more than $1 million (Faulkner, 1993). She publicly criticized society's double standard, which created a hero out of Magic Johnson after he admitted that he contracted AIDS from heterosexual promiscuity, but which condemns gays with AIDS. Her outrage at the passage of an anti-gay law in Colorado led her to join five others in a court case to challenge its constitutionality.

Basketball's Nancy Lieberman (now Liberman-Cline) would also deserve a page. Lieberman-Cline, who learned basketball with the neighborhood boys in Harlem, was recruited by 100 colleges and became the highest-paid woman in professional basketball at $100,000 a year in 1980 with the Dallas Diamonds of the now-defunct Women's Professional Basketball League (Lieberman-Cline, 1992). She is candid about her relationship with Martina Navratilova in her autobiography, *Lady Magic* (1992). She was the first—and to date remains the only—woman to play men's professional basketball; she played two seasons in the United States Basketball League, following which she played for the Harlem Globetrotters companion team, the Washington Generals.

Jackie Joyner-Kersee would certainly be prominent in the volume. Described as "America's seventh wonder" when she won her second Olympic heptathlon in 1992, Joyner-Kersee has turned in six of the seven 7,000-point performances in the history of the track and field event (Janofsky, 1992). Heptathlon competition involves seven separate events: 100-meter hurdles, high jump, shot put, 200-meter sprint, long jump, javelin and 800-meter run.

The list of names that need to be included in this *Encyclopedia of Amazon Athletes* is extensive, but, because space in this chapter is limited, I'll conclude with two fictional characters that should be mentioned.[17] Gloria Steinem (1972, 1982) wrote about the archetype in *Wonder Woman* stories from the 1940s. The comic book character, who came from an Amazon island ruled by her mother, conceals her true identity by using the name Diana (the Roman name for Artemis) and was drawn as self-sufficient, strong, athletic, courageous and a protector of women out to change "a world torn by the hatreds and wars of men."[18]

> Wonder Woman symbolizes many of the values of the women's culture that feminists are now trying to introduce into the mainstream; strength and self-reliance for women, sisterhood and mutual support among women, peacefulness and respect for human life, a diminishment of both "masculine" aggression and of the belief that violence is the only way of solving conflicts. (Steinem, 1982, p. 117)

A recent fictionalized account of another female Amazon is worth mentioning because it provides a well-researched feminist perspective on Amazon physicality and sexuality (Walker, 1992).[19] In her novel titled *Amazon*, Barbara Walker takes Antiope, a young Amazon warrior, thousands of years through time to find herself in the 20th century, where she mixes her memories of life in an ancient matrilineal society with her experiences in a modern patriarchal culture. She is befriended by a writer, appropriately named Diana, who documents her story in what becomes a best-seller about Amazon culture. She also helps produce *The Amazon Workout* videotape on which the time-traveler Antiope wields her sword and performs warrior-training exercises. The book and tape result in Antiope's "discovery" by the media, an Amazon fashion craze and the formation of female vigilante groups. Throughout the book, Antiope provides insightful commentary on the cultural practices she observes in the United States:

[T]he teevy box almost never showed people pleasuring one another. There were no stroking or massaging and no real sex, although young men and women were shown eating each other's mouths. There was nothing to instruct mothers about massaging their babies, or nursing, or doing midwifery. There were no old wise women in the teevy box. (Walker, p. 39)

If Walker's (1992) fictional Amazon Antiope had provided her observations of American sport on "teevy," she would undoubtedly describe the sexism, racism, classism and heterosexism that continually reappear as norms for determining power relations in sport. If we asked for her perceptions of the dominant media image of today's American athlete, she would describe an elite athlete who is male, functioning as sort of a new urban cowboy, making his own rules, dominating the land and "winning the woman" at the end of the game.[20] Undoubtedly, she would also comment on the audience's reaction to sports violence as Bryant and Zillmann (1983) have:

The spectators need not be ill at ease as they see players go down in pain. In their perception, these players are more than adequately compensated for risking their necks once in a while. (p. 209)

As the chapter has shown, the gender metaphor in sport is based to a large extent on the assumption of inferior female physicality. Yet throughout history some women have actively resisted this assumption. Why were they willing to challenge the assumption? What caused them to ignore the stereotype?

Although there's no simple answer, several patterns emerge from the characteristics common to prominent contemporary athletic examples. Didrikson, Francis, Joyner-Kersee, King, Navratilova and Lieberman were from lower-middle- or working-class backgrounds; moreover, like Artemis, they did not necessarily define themselves by standards of white femininity or compulsory heterosexuality.[21]

The Contemporary Feminine Mystique and the Female Physique

Any discussion of physicality and gender ultimately leads us to the relation between physicality and sexual oppression.[22] A physically strong woman communicates a much different message than a weak one:

> It's threatening to one's takability, one's rapeability, one's femininity, to be strong and physically self-possessed. To be able to resist rape, not to communicate rapeability with one's body, to hold one's body for uses and meanings other than that can transform what *being a woman means*. (MacKinnon, 1987, p. 122)

Myths, and the lessons they teach, describe what being a woman means. As we have seen, they are preserved, even created, using media ranging from epic poems to comic books. For the Greeks, the epic poem was a popular medium of communication for mythmaking. In contemporary culture, the mass media play a major role in framing lessons about values that have been preserved or are being produced.

Powerful women, including Athena archetypes such as Hilary Rodham Clinton, still perplex the media. For example, the February 1993 *Spy* magazine cover shows Clinton's head superimposed onto the body of a leather-bikini clad dominatrix holding a whip. The Artemis "problem" hasn't been solved by the media yet either. The lead paragraph from an article in *The Detroit Jewish News* (Ellenstein, 1991) titled "Sugar & Spice & Takedowns Are Nice" is a good illustration:

> Lauren Wolfe has all the attributes of a normal 14-year-old girl. She plays the violin in the orchestra, is treasurer of her eighth grade class. . . . And Lauren is one of the top mid-Michigan wrestlers for her weight division. That's right, Lauren regularly hits the mats against male athletes in a male-dominated sport. But don't tell that to Lauren. (Ellenstein, 1991, p. 50)

Like Artemis, Lauren becomes the "other." The reporter portrays her as independent and different from other little girls. The "sugar and spice" metaphor sets up the antagonism between the feminine attributes of a "nice" little girl and the masculine attributes of an athlete on the wrestling mat.[23] Because of her 16-0 wrestling record against boys, she must be taken seriously as a wrestler, so she can no longer be a "normal" little girl. In sport, women "get to choose between being a successful girl and being a successful athlete" (MacKinnon, 1987, p. 120).

In a quotation at the beginning of this chapter, Lerner suggested that gender is a metaphor for power relations. Throughout this chapter, sport has been described as a setting in which power relations based on the gender metaphor, along with the various intersections at which race, class and sexuality are joined with it, are played out. Gender values are the cultural products of these intersections. Eisler (1987) summarizes the outcome of the existing model for gender values:

> The underlying problem is not men as a sex. The root of the problem lies in a social system in which the power of the Blade is idealized —in which both men and women are taught to equate true masculinity with violence and dominance and to see men who do not conform to this idea as "too soft" or "effeminate." (p. xviii)

The feminist critique of gender values in sport to date has focused largely on gender difference. It has attempted to dispel the myth of female inferiority in sports as compared with men and to promote the concept that women athletes should have equal opportunity. A growing body of feminist literature calls for women to reject the values of male-dominated sports and to reinstitute a system based on female values.

A third feminist critique urges the development of a new sport model to transform the gender metaphor. It compares sport to the process of developing and accepting one's humanness. Much as Artemis can be viewed as "absolute femininity," that is, femininity not defined in relation to masculinity, the new model values all forms of life as unique manifestations of the spirit; therefore, self-worth is inherent and independent of external, physical realities (Myers, 1988; Myers et al., 1991). The highest value in this model is positive interpersonal relationships among people with self-esteem at the core. The model, described in detail by Pamela Highlen in Chapter 13, drops gender-based distinctions and uses dynamic or expanding and magnetic or opening roles to describe behavior.

Central to popularizing the new sport model and empowering the Artemis archetype are contemporary mythmakers. They are the sportswriters and sportscasters, as well as the media owners, publishers and producers, who, like the storytellers in ancient Greece, are primarily males. In their work, they assume a male norm and compare Artemis with it. They appear to be blind to the constructed nature of gender in our culture and their own role in perpetuating the model supporting it, which was inherited from fourth-century-B.C. Greek culture.

Currently, the most hopeful signs that the old model may be on the verge of rupturing come instead from ecofeminists—and environmentalists—who have had some success in transforming the media's mythmaking. When environmental concerns are taken seriously, the need for alternative values becomes more clear. Not surprisingly, at the core of ecofeminist discourse is the suggestion that "if women counted so would the earth, because the system would have been totally reorganized" (DiPerna, 1989, p. 5). At the core of the earth is Artemis, the goddess of reproduction, often portrayed as a tree, a bear or the moon. Empowering the Artemisian energy associated with the force of creation means re-visioning the energies associated with environmental destruction and pollution.

The suggestion that the environmental movement and an alternative sport model in sport are different sides of the same coin may seem a stretch. The relationship is much clearer if we look at it in terms of the description of Artemis found throughout this chapter. She is the archetype "most directly concerned with the contemporary ecological debate and its related choices" (Paris, 1986, p. 110). Environmental concerns have made the destructive outcome of inequities in gender values visible and immediate; it has provided the stage for speaking of things about which we have long been silent.

Unfortunately, the entertainment context of sport in Western culture has devalued its importance. Yet it is a microcosm of the abuse and unhealthiness that results from gendered power relations. A "re-vision" of the portrayal of the archetype of Artemis in Western culture is clearly in order. One of the most visible places to start re-visioning would be with the media portrayal of the archetype of Artemis in sport.

Notes

1. Jung makes a distinction between an *archetype*—the pattern of energy in the psyche—and the symbol or character embodying, incarnating or personifying the energy. He views the energy of the archetype as asexual. Thus, my references to "her" appearances and "her" role in this sentence would be considered inappropriate by purists in the Jungian sense (personal communication, Betsy Caprio, April 30, 1993).

2. Adrienne Rich (1979) defined *re-vision* in this way: "The act of looking back, of seeing with fresh eyes, of entering an old text from a new critical direction—[this] is for women more than a chapter in cultural history; it is an act of survival. Until we can understand the assumptions in which we are drenched we cannot know ourselves" (p. 35).

3. Lerner (1986) suggests that the division or dethroning of the Mother Goddess "takes place in many cultures at many times, but usually it is associated with the same historical process" (p. 154). According to Woolger and Woolger (1989), other names for the Great Mother Goddess include: Isis (Egypt), Atana (Crete), Astarte (Crete), Inanna (Sumer) and Ishtar (Babylon). For the purposes of this book, we are limiting our examination to Western civilization and its roots in the philosophy of classical Greece.

4. Athena and Artemis are often described as virgin goddesses (cf. Harding, 1935). Woolger and Woolger (1989) explain that this meant unmarried and self-sufficient, not chaste. They explain: "Chastity as a component of virginity is largely an overlaid patriarchal value" (p. 38). Betsy Caprio also prefers to think of Artemis as the virgin archetype, which includes physicality but much more (personal communication, April 30, 1993).

5. Because of her association with hunting dogs, "Great Bitch" was a sacred title of the goddess Artemis; it became an insult when Christianity swept over Europe (Walker, 1988).

6. This statement represents a Western, white, middle-class perspective on the archetype, which is the dominant construction of the female athlete in American media.

7. The Greek mythmakers did not give Artemis high marks on interpersonal relationships. She is portrayed as a loner and as alienated. It is likely that this interpretation may have served some goal of the patriarchal culture in Athens.

8. The archetype of the juvenile Artemis may be the "tomboy." See Hancock (1989) for an interesting discussion.

9. The King versus Riggs match had an element of revenge to it as well. Margaret Court had been defeated by Riggs on Mother's Day in 1973 (Sochen, 1987). Later, a "Battle of the Champions" in which Jimmy Connors defeated Martina Navratilova was played in Las Vegas in 1992 to much less fanfare (Preston, 1992).

10. The pig is a fascinating choice for the "male chauvinist" metaphor because Artemis was often associated with wild boars. Pigs are also goddess animals in other cultures that were degraded by patriarchal religions (cf. Caprio, 1982; Johnson, 1988).

11. In one version of a myth, Callisto was seduced by Zeus in the guise of Artemis, indicating the possibility of a lesbian relationship (Hamlyn, 1967, p. 48). Another version has the maiden turned into a bear by Zeus or Hera, then into the Great Bear constellation. In still another version of the story, Zeus becomes a bear to seduce Callisto. In one version, when Artemis learned of the seduction of Callisto by Zeus, she killed her companion for violating her vow of chastity, but just as plausible as an explanation is jealous rage because of Callisto's unfaithfulness. One interpretation of the myth suggests that Callisto was simply another incarnation of Artemis and that the seduction by Zeus brings divine incest into the story.

Another myth associated with Artemis involves the rescue of Iphigenia, daughter of Agamemnon and Clytemnestra. In this story, Artemis asks for the sacrifice of Iphigenia and promises to provide wind to fill the sails of Agamemnon's fleet, which is stuck in unfavorable winds and can't sail to Troy to wage war. As the story goes, Artemis rescues Iphigenia at the last moment and takes her into her cult where she lives for many, many years. Perhaps, Artemis' ultimate goal in the trade was to satisfy her longing for Iphigenia.

Artemis also was rumored to be in love with Orion, but she killed him by mistake when her brother Apollo deceived her.

12. The term *Amazon* has numerous possible meanings. If it was derived from *Amazosas*, it means "opposed to man." Homer called the Amazons *antianeirai*, which has been translated as both "mannish" and "man-hating." If *Amazon* is derived from *Amastos* or *A-Maso*, it means "those without a breast." Some writers describe a widely disputed Amazon practice of burning off the right lacteal gland in childhood, presumably in order to become better archers or more strongly muscled in the right arm or to avoid injury from the bowstring (Chesler, 1982, p. 103). Another possibility is that it is a combination of the Phoenician *Am*, which means "mother" and *Azon* or *Adon* for "lord" (Sobol, 1972).

13. Atalanta survived her father's (Zeus) attempt to kill her when he abandoned her as a baby on a mountain. He wanted a son! But Artemis interceded and sent a she-bear to nurse her. Atalanta was raised by hunters and became a legendary wrestler and runner, refusing to marry any man who could not outrun her in a footrace (Salmonson, 1991, p. 23).

14. Cavin (1985) suggests that the Amazons of northwestern Africa are thought to be the original Amazons (p. 63). Some archaeological evidence exists to show that Amazons existed around the Nile, the Sahara and in central and west Africa (see Loth, 1987, pp. 59-64). A book written by Garcirodriquez Montalvo in 1510 about the Spanish explorations, cited in Cavin, describes black women living without men on an island. The "island," named by these explorers after Califia, an Amazon queen, is supposedly California (Cavin, 1985, p. 69, 250). The reference by Montalvo to black women may refer to Native Americans or Pacific Islanders.

15. Kleinbaum (1983) cautions that Bachofen's comment should not be construed as an endorsement of powerful women. She explains: "Bachofen's Amazon is universal and hence natural. The glory of human civilization has been in overcoming and conquering nature" (p. 180).

16. A couple of contemporary incarnations come to mind. The Guerilla Girls, "an anonymous group of women seeking to transform anger into fun," have taken on the white male art establishment (Gillespie, 1993, p. 69). The second is the film *Thelma and Louise*, which despite its patriarchal overtones and phallic imagery shows female violence in such a context.

17. We could include swimmer Diana Nyad, softball player Joan Joyce, golfer JoAnne Carner, race car driver Janet Guthrie and on and on. However, not all athletes would be included. For example, I would disagree with Bolen's (1984) suggestion that Chris Evert is an Artemis archetype, and I would hesitate to include her on the list. Thousands of physically strong and athletic women throughout American history should be included in the volume. The first women cadets at West Point, for example, had to prove that they had the "upper body strength" to make the team (Friedan, 1981). Women pioneers, women in the Klondike, on the farm, in the wars, have also exhibited physicality that rivals that of males. They may differ, however, from the

examples of the athletic archetype to the extent that they have not developed their strength in a conscious or self-possessed manner.

18. Steinem's characterization of Wonder Woman has been criticized for its portrayal of her as peaceful and nonviolent; she often used her physicality to over-power oppressors and aggressors, much like another incarnation, the muscular Linda Conners in the 1991 movie *Terminator II* (see Chapter 12 by Molly Merryman).

19. Another novel, Cleo Birdwell's (1980) *Amazons*, is billed as an intimate memoir of the first woman ever to play in the National Hockey League. Unfortu-nately, I read the entire book before I realized that it was fiction. It focuses on the sex life of the 23-year-old main character Cleo. The only item of note in the book is the recognition of the marketing potential of her image as an Amazon; she is offered the job of spokesperson for new crackle-snackers from Kelloid's—Amazon Ringos, Ama-zon Discos, Amazon Nuggets and Amazon Noshes (p. 315). Manon Rheaume was the first woman to play in the NHL for the Tampa Bay Lightning in 1992 (Kaufmann, 1993).

20. Former heavyweight boxing champion Mike Tyson presents a larger-than-life example of the athlete who lives by his own rules and dominates his environment and his women. Tyson's recorded acts of violence against women include wife beating, sexual assault and harassment. In March 1992, the 25-year-old boxer was sentenced to six years in prison on a conviction for raping an 18-year-old Black Miss America contestant. At the sentencing, Tyson maintained his innocence saying, "I didn't hurt anyone—no black eyes, no broken ribs. When I'm in the ring, I break ribs; I break their jaws. To me, that's hurting someone" (Thigpen, 1992, p. 60). As we learn through the media of the other excesses by male athletes like Tyson, we may think that we have at last reached a re-visioning point—a rupture point—with our sport/gender metaphor. Yet Tyson's sentencing may not signal a change. Tyson can easily be con-structed as different, as another cultural archetype—the "black beast," by the race- and class-based hierarchy in sport (Hoch, 1979).

21. King, Lieberman and Navratilova have written autobiographies in which each describes both heterosexual and homosexual experiences.

22. The issue of physiological differences between male and female athletes is not addressed in any depth in this book. A number of excellent resources on the subject are currently available. Jarratt (1990), however, supplies some insight that is relevant to the focus of this book: "Women have performed as well as, and occasionally better than men in many sporting events; the best female performances in swimming and running are approaching the best male performances in these sports; and highly trained female athletes are very similar to highly trained male athletes in the physiological capacity for sport and exercise. They may even have some advantages over men in some areas such as body heat regulation and buoyancy" (p. 494).

23. Women's interest and participation in heavy contact sport has a long history. According to Euripides and Plutarch, "young Spartan women were not to be found at home but in the gymnasia where they tossed off their restrictive clothing and wrestled naked with their male contemporaries" (Stone, 1976, p. 53).

References

Adler, Margot. (1986). *Drawing down the moon*. Boston: Beacon Press.

Bachofen, J. J. (1967/1861). *Myth, religion and mother right*. Princeton, NJ: Bollingen.

Bem, Sandra L. (1974). The measurement of psychological androgyny. *Journal of Counseling and Clinical Psychology, 42,* 155-162.

Birdwell, Cleo. (1980). *Amazons.* New York: Holt, Rinehart & Winston.

Blue, Adrianne. (1987). *Grace under pressure.* London: Sidgwick & Jackson.

Bolen, Jean Shimoda. (1984). *Goddesses in everywoman.* New York: Harper & Row.

Bryant, Jennings & Zillmann, Dolf. (1983). Sports violence and the media. In Jeffrey H. Goldstein (Ed.), *Sports violence* (pp. 270-289). Newbury Park, CA: Sage.

Caprio, Betsy. (1982). *The woman sealed in the tower.* New York: The Paulist Press.

Carlson, Margaret. (1991, June 24). Is this what feminism is all about? *Time,* p. 57.

Cavin, Susan. (1985). *Lesbian origins.* San Francisco: ism press.

Chesler, Phyllis. (1982). The Amazon legacy. In Charlene Spretnak (Ed), *The politics of women's spirituality: Essays on the rise of spiritual power within the feminist movement* (pp. 97-113). New York: Anchor.

Colley, Ann, Nash, John, O'Donnell, Laurence & Restorick, Lesley. (1987). Attitudes to the female sex role and sex-typing of physical activities. *International Journal of Sport Psychology, 18,* 19-29.

Del Rey, Patricia. (1978). The apologetic and women in sport. In Carole A. Oglesby (Ed.), *Women and Sport: From Myth to Reality* (107-112). Philadelphia, PA: Lea & Febiger.

DiPerna, Paula. (1989). Lethal statistics. *Women's Review of Books, 7*(2), 1, 3-5.

Downing, Christine. (1988). *The goddess: Mythological images of the feminine.* New York: Crossroad.

duBois, Page. (1982). *Centaurs & Amazons: Women and the pre-history of the great chain of being.* Ann Arbor, MI: University of Michigan.

Eisler, Riane. (1987). *The chalice & the blade.* San Francisco: Harper & Row.

Ellenstein, Robert. (1991, March 29). Sugar & spice & takedowns are nice. *The Detroit Jewish News,* pp. 50-51.

Faulkner, Sandra (with Judy Nelson). (1993). *Love match: Nelson vs. Navratilova.* New York: Birch Lane Press.

Felshin, Jan. (1981). The triple option . . . for women in sport. In Marie Hart & Susan Birrell (Eds.), *Sport in the sociocultural process* (pp. 487-492). Dubuque IA: Brown.

Friedan, Betty. (1981). *The second stage.* New York: Summit Books.

Friedan, Betty. (1984). *The feminine mystique.* New York: Dell.

Gillespie, Margaret. (1993, March/April). Guerilla girls: From broadsides to broadsheets. *Ms.,* p. 69.

Hamlyn, Paul. (1967). *Greek mythology.* London: Paul Hamlyn.

Hancock, Emily. (1989). *The girl within: Recapture the childhood self, the key to female identity.* New York: E. P. Dutton.

Harding, M. Esther. (1935). *Woman's mysteries: Ancient and modern.* New York: Longmans, Green.

Hoch, Paul. (1979). *White hero, black beast: Racism, sexism and the mask of masculinity.* London: Pluto Press.

Janofsky, Michael. (1992, August 3). America's seventh wonder of the games. *New York Times,* pp. C1, C5.

Jarratt, Elizabeth H. (1990). Feminist issues in sport. *Women's Studies International Forum, 13*(5), 491-499.

Johnson, Buffie. (1988). *Lady of the beasts.* San Francisco: Harper & Row.

Jung, Carl G. & Kerenyi, Carl. (1969). *Essays on a science of mythology*. Princeton, NJ: Princeton/Bollingen.

Kane, Mary Jo. (1987). The "new" female athlete: Socially sanctioned image or modern role for women. In M. J. Adrian (Ed.), *Sports women* (pp. 101-111). New York: Karger.

Kaufmann, Elizabeth. (1993, January/February). The puck stops here. *Women's Sports & Fitness, 15*(1), 48-54.

King, Billie Jean (with Kim Chapin). (1974). *Billie Jean*. New York: Harper & Row.

King, Billie Jean (with Frank Deford). (1982). *Billie Jean*. New York: Viking.

Kleinbaum, Abby Wettan. (1983). *The war against the Amazons*. New York: McGraw Hill.

Lefkowitz, Mary R. (1986). *Women in Greek myth*. Baltimore, MD: Johns Hopkins.

Lenskyj, Helen. (1987). Female sexuality and women's sport. *Women's Studies International Forum, 10*(4), 381-386.

Leonard, Irving A. (1944). Conquerors and Amazons in Mexico. *The Hispanic American Historical Review, 24*(4), 561-579.

Lerner, Gerda. (1986). *The creation of patriarchy*. New York: Oxford University Press.

Lieberman-Cline, Nancy (with Debby Jennings). (1992). *Lady magic*. Champaign, IL: Sagamore.

Loth, Heinrich. (1987). *Women in ancient Africa*. (Shelia Marnie, Trans.). Westport, CT: Lawrence Hill.

Lumpkin, Angela. (1982). The contributions of women to the history of competitive tennis in the United States in the twentieth century. In Reet Howell (Ed.), *Her story in sport: A historical anthology of women in sport* (pp. 509-526). West Point, NY: Leisure Press.

MacKinnon, Catharine. (1987). *Feminism unmodified: Discourses on life and law*. Cambridge, MA: Harvard University Press.

Matteo, Sherri. (1988). The effect of gender-schematic processing on decisions about sex-appropriate sport behavior. *Sex Roles, 18*(1&2), 41-58.

McGough, Peter. (1993, August). The Bev Francis story: A career in focus. *Flex*, pp. 65-67, 150-156.

Messner, Michael A. & Sabo, Donald F. (1990). Introduction: Toward a feminist critical reappraisal of sport, men and the gender order. In Michael A. Messner & Donald F. Sabo (Eds.), *Sport, men and the gender order: Critical feminist perspectives* (pp. 1-15). Champaign, IL: Human Kinetics.

Metheny, E. (1967). *Connotations of movement in sport and dance*. Dubuque, IA: Brown.

Mitchell, Susan & Dyer, Ken. (1985). *Winning women: Challenging the norms in Australian sport*. Ringwood: Penguin.

Monaghan, Patricia. (1990). *The book of goddesses & heroines*. St. Paul, MN: Llewellyn Publications.

Mrozek, Donald J. (1987). The "Amazon" and the "American lady": Sexual fears of women as athletes. In J. A. Mangan & Robert J. Park (Eds.), *From "Fair Sex" to Feminism: Sport and the socialization of women in the industrial and post-industrial eras* (pp. 282-298). London: Frank Cass.

Myers, Linda J. (1988). *Understanding an Afrocentric world view: Introduction to optimal psychology*. Dubuque, IA: Kendall/Hunt.

Myers, Linda J., Speight, Suzette L., Highlen, Pamela S., Cox, Chikako I., Reynolds, Amy L., Adams, Eve M. & Hanley, Patricia C. (1991). Identity development and world view: Toward an optimal conceptualization. *Journal of Counseling and Development, 70*, 54-63.

Navratilova, Martina (with George Vecsey). (1985). *Martina*. New York: Alfred A. Knopf.

Nelson, Mariah Burton. (1991). *Are we winning yet?* New York: Random House.

Paris, Ginette. (1986). *Pagan meditations: Aphrodite, Hestia, Artemis*. Dallas, TX: Spring.

Preston, Mark. (1992, December). Farce & lobbing in Las Vegas. *Sports Illustrated*, p. 28.

Rich, Adrienne. (1979). When we dead awaken: Writing as re-vision. In Adrienne Rich (Ed.), *On lies, secrets, and silence*. New York: Norton.

Salmonson, Jessica Amanda. (1991). *The encyclopedia of Amazons*. New York: Anchor.

Schwab, Gustav. (1974). *Gods & heroes*. New York: Pantheon Books.

Smith, Barbara. (1992). Greece. In Carolyne Larrington (Ed.), *The feminist companion to mythology* (pp. 65-101). London: Pandora Press.

Sobol, Donald J. (1972). *The Amazons of Greek mythology*. New York: A. S. Barnes.

Sochen, June. (1987). *Enduring values: Women in popular culture*. New York: Praeger.

Sparhawk, Ruth M., Leslie, Mary E., Turbow, Phyllis Y., & Rose, Zina R. (1989). *American women in sport, 1887-1987*. Metuchen, NJ: Scarecrow Press.

Spretnak, Charlene. (1978). *Lost goddesses of early Greece*. Boston, MA: Beacon Press.

Steinem, Gloria. (1972). *Wonder woman*. New York: Holt, Rinehart & Winston.

Steinem, Gloria. (1982). Tales of a reincarnated Amazon: The invincible wonder woman! In Charlene Spretnak (Ed.), *The politics of women's spirituality: Essays on the rise of spiritual power within the feminist movement* (pp. 114-120). New York: Anchor.

Stone, Merlin. (1976). *When God was a woman*. New York: Harvest/Harcourt.

Thigpen, David E. (1992, April 6). The jock as a fallen idol. *Time*, p. 60.

Tyrrell, William Blake. (1984). *Amazons: A study in Athenian mythmaking*. Baltimore, MD: Johns Hopkins.

Walker, Barbara G. (1988). *The woman's dictionary of symbols and sacred objects*. San Francisco, CA: Harper & Row.

Walker, Barbara G. (1992). *Amazon*. New York: Harper Collins.

Wolf, Naomi. (1991). *The beauty myth*. New York: William Morrow.

Woolger, Jennifer Barker & Woolger, Roger J. (1989). *The goddess within: A guide to the eternal myths that shape women's lives*. New York: Fawcett Columbine.

12

Gazing at Artemis

The Active Female Archetype in Popular Film

Molly Merryman

Since the beginnings of human expression, myths have been key in defining who we are and where we are heading. Joseph Campbell (1988) stated that myth never decreases in importance and value because humans continually need scales through which they measure their actions. In today's electronic society, mythology has taken on a contemporary face—cinema and television are our culture's fireside storytellers. In place of Samson, Apollo and Beowulf, we have Batman, Captain Kirk and Indiana Jones. These modern mythological characters use their strength and power for justice or revenge, in quests and in escape.

The role of myth as a defining key has significantly less value for women, who have been systematically eliminated or reduced from original mythological constructs. However, some female mythological archetypes still exist. According to Gammon and Marshment (1989), movies and other stories of popular culture are the site of a struggle to shift the balance of power away from men.

From ancient Greek mythology arises an archetype of a true female, one who isn't defined by men as mother, lover or sister. Artemis, the huntress, is identified by her physical abilities and powers and is symbolized by her weapons. She is comfortable with violence, and she uses it in game and battle. As athlete, hunter and warrior, Artemis used the power of her body to further her goals. Artemis and her archetypes use the female body not only to give birth but to end life, so in effect, her body spills both blood and milk.

Within the myth of Artemis is a representation of women's physicality. Strong parallels exist between the athletic and battlefield achievements of Artemis and those of contemporary cinematic female athletes and heroes. Furthermore, the myth of Artemis has implications for a prototypical representation of contemporary female strength and power.

Ann Kaplan (1983, p. 200) writes that films for women speak of their experiences and show everyday images of their lives. Yet rarely is sport considered to be an experience of women, despite the thematic value of sport as a simplistic metaphor for struggle. The impact of Title IX caused a flurry of low-budget films in one of three categories —historical/political, instructional and motivational—to be produced in the mid-1970s (Moore, 1977). Esther Williams popularized water sports in several films in the late 1960s and 1970s, including *Bathing Beauty* and *Neptune's Daughter,* but only four major Hollywood releases (all of which will be discussed in this chapter) have invoked thematic constructs involving women athletes.[1] When women characters are placed in sport and action films, they go beyond the universe Kaplan defined for women's films, placing women in extraordinary places and intense experiences to demonstrate their abilities, talents and strengths.

According to Mayne (1990, p. 269), the images of women that "appear on screen may be largely the projections of patriarchal fantasies."[2] This projection leaves no space on the screen for expressions of realistic activities on the part of the characters. Women remain as objects in film, while men actively revolve around them.[3]

Furthermore, in the creation of movies, the concept of woman as spectator is lost. For example, de Lauretis (1984, p. 182) notes that the "idea that a film may address the spectator as female rather than portray women positively or negatively, seems very important to me in the critical endeavor to characterize women's cinema as a cinema for, not only by, women." In addition, Gentile (1985, p. 3) writes that films are "rarely read without reference to the dominant order of physical, sexual, political, spiritual, psychological, or cultural practice."

Films are representative of the cultural values of the presumed viewer. Within cinematic representations of women, the places that women occupy are few, and the representation of these women is as dream women, according to de Lauretis (1984, p. 21), "an imaginary fantasy, a fetish, a screen memory, a movie." These women do not do the things women in real life do. The women are not active; they are objects. Illustrating this are the remarkably few major release films that have examined the places of women in sporting events or action roles.

Only three major studios have released fictional accounts of women's athletics. The films are *Personal Best, Heart Like a Wheel* and *A League of Their Own*. Although these films portray women athletes, two do so by focusing on the cooperation between women athletes and do not develop an Artemis prototype. A widely distributed documentary, *Pumping Iron II*, addressed the sport of women's bodybuilding and revealed the Artemis prototype within. In addition, the films *Terminator* and *Terminator 2: Judgment Day* developed a proto-typical Artemis representation within the action and science fiction genres.

Personal Best (1982)

In *Personal Best*, the women athletes indeed perform their best, but they also work cooperatively, and they support each other in obtaining their best. The film traces the fictional track-and-field careers of two athletes: Chris Cahil (Mariel Hemingway) and Tory Skinner (Patrice Donnelly). It begins with the 1976 Olympic trial at Hayward Field in Eugene, Oregon, and ends with the 1980 U.S. Olympic Track and Field Trials, again at Hayward Field.

When *Personal Best* is compared with a similar film with male athletes, *Chariots of Fire*, an important distinction arises. Both films address the sport of track and field, including emphasis on technical details, by focusing on the friendships between two runners.

But in *Chariots of Fire*, the two male runners separate to train for the 1924 Paris Olympics. Clearly, the goal of both is to be the sole winner. Each focuses on his own training, and attention is placed on their individual achievements. In addition, the camera focuses on each athlete separately during races.

In *Personal Best*, races are shown in context of the entire field of runners, with neither Cahil or Skinner achieving autonomy. The two women runners are friends (and sometimes lovers). They train together and offer suggestions, despite being told not to do so by their male coach. The film concludes with Cahil running at a pace that could result in her losing the meet, in order to throw off the pacing of the other runners and allowing Skinner to place in the Olympics also.

Personal Best provides concentrated gazes on the sport of running and the beauty of strong, athletic females. As the film develops, the examinations of female bodies are almost distasteful in their objectifying gaze. The film's most disturbing flaw is its nearly pornographic focus on women athletes. Charlotte Brunsdon (1986, p. 205) writes that *Personal Best* is an objectifying movie in that it sexualizes the athlete, "rendering her powerless and again controlled by the male gaze."

There exists, though, an important difference between the camera's focus on bodies throughout *Personal Best*. For example, in one scene in which the runners are competing in the high jump, the camera focuses on their bodies, dissecting them, not showing any women in entirety. Instead, body parts and bodies with unseen heads are shown, sweaty and close to the camera. The difference is that the camera is stationary. What is moving are the women, their body parts propelled by their own physical strength. In effect, the camera is rendered inanimate by the actions of these athletic women.

Personal Best, despite its flaws, is valuable for its portrayal of women athletes as tough and competitive and as winners. In addition, it does not shy away from depicting the athletics, with detailed scenes of track-and-field events.

Heart Like a Wheel (1983)

In 1983, the second major film featuring female athletics was released, although this film did not get the distribution or have the box office success of *Personal Best*. *Heart Like a Wheel* is based on the life of three-time world top fuel racing champion Shirley Muldowney (Bonnie Bedelia).[4] This film differs from *Personal Best* because of its creation of the female athlete as autonomous warrior and hero.

Shirley Muldowney was the first woman to compete in professional automobile racing. She began running informal circuit races in 1956, progressing to the professional circuit in 1966 when she not only qualified for her license on her first attempt but broke the existing track record. She was constantly faced with discrimination and sexism, to the point that she could only get sponsored by a cologne company, and only with the name "Cha Cha" Muldowney, hot pink racing suits and an equally as hot pink top fuel dragster.

By 1976, Muldowney was the first racer to win two National Hot Rod Association national events. In 1977, she increased the number of national wins to three and became world champion. By this point, she had obtained more mainstream racing sponsorships and had regained her name, although sports commentators still referred to her as "Cha Cha." Significant to her success is that through all these victories, Muldowney was being discriminated against by many male racers, to the point of having her engines sabotaged.[5]

The records Muldowney established still hold, and she is the only racer to be a three-time world champion in top fuel. *Heart Like a Wheel* effectively documents the life of a successful athlete. Its portrayal is particularly valuable in that her achievements are as world-class athlete and not as "woman." In addition, the film is important because it does not shy away from the discrimination she faced because of her gender and reveals many of the impediments placed before her during her career.

Heart Like a Wheel focuses on the difficult struggle and independent battles Muldowney fought to get involved in and win at racing. On and off the track, the image of Muldowney in the film is as a crusader who fights alone against other racers, mechanics and sponsors to legitimize her participation in the sport and prove that she is a winner. In this context, Muldowney truly is an Artemis prototype, even to the point of naming her top fuel dragster "The Huntress."

A League of Their Own (1992)

In *A League of Their Own*, women obtaining legitimate status in team sports is a major aspect of this fictionalized account of the All-American Girls Professional Baseball League, which was founded during World War II. The film depicts the rise and dissolution of the league by focusing on one of the league's many teams, the Rockford Peaches. Unfortunately, the film loses a great deal of the exciting and important history of the league (which lasted from 1943 to 1954) through attempts at easy laughs and a focus on sibling (or female) rivalry.

In the movie's plot, a talent agent, whose job it is to find the athletes for the league, discovers two sisters on their farm. The two attend tryouts and make the league, becoming team stars. Dramatic conflict is supplied by the sisters, who struggle with one another for autonomy and support. Kit Keller (Lori Petty), the younger sister, has the greatest desire to be on the team but lacks the talent of her older sister Dottie Hinson (Geena Davis). This sibling tension provides a core to the larger tensions affecting the women. *A League of Their Own* reveals the dual roles women were expected to play as both athletes and beauty objects. Ball training is juxtaposed with etiquette and beauty training. Women who are too athletic or masculine are not invited to join the team.

A League of Their Own is commendable in that it focuses on the game of baseball and within that reveals the true athletic achievements of the players. It offers a forgotten piece of sports history to new generations and celebrates the genuine skills of its players. However, it does not offer an Artemis prototype but is a light relationship movie instead of detailing the personal and difficult struggles the individual athletes undoubtedly encountered.

Pumping Iron II (1984)

A muscular body is the supreme personal symbol of power, and as with other symbols of power, its possession has been forbidden to women. Within women's bodybuilding, a battle for the possession and display of developed female muscles is being fought publicly. The sport has yet to escape its beauty show beginnings, in which women who lifted weights were placed alongside exotic dancers and other female performers to provide entertaining breaks during male competitions.

In both male and female bodybuilding, a debate continues about whether bodybuilding is a sport, a performance art or both. Some regard the work in the gym to be the sport and the posing and choreographed competition to be art. The winner of the first World Women's Bodybuilding Championship, Lisa Lyon, stopped competing to appear at museums as a performance artist, a sculptor whose raw material was her own body (Mapplethorpe & Chatwin, 1983, p. 11).

Beauty versus strength is the dynamic focus of the 1984 documentary *Pumping Iron II*. In it, Texas beauty queen Rachel McLish is favored to win, despite the introduction of Australian powerlifter Bev Francis, who entered the contest expressly to challenge the beauty standards held in the contest.

Pumping Iron II was made when the sport of women's bodybuilding was only five years old. The first serious female bodybuilding contest took place in 1979, and women were required to wear high heels as part of their posing requirements.[6]

Bev Francis is a true Artemis prototype. She is revealed in the documentary as a warrior out to destroy the system that discriminates against female athletes in her sport. While other competitors socialize and see the sights, Francis trains, remaining hidden in her hotel room. Francis is in the game to win, and she intends to use her strength and the competitive skills she developed in power lifting to transform and win in this sport.

It is notable that Francis's posing routine invokes Artemis. She mimics the Greek goddess in her posing, even using a hunter's bow as prop. Fascinated with the connection between the sport of bodybuilding and power, Francis's goal to be powerful revolutionized bodybuilding and female muscularity (McGough, 1993).

The Cinematic Construct of Women's Weakness

Pam Creedon points out in Chapters 1 and 7 that there are close parallels between sports and violence. More than metaphorically, the playing field is an arena where players (who are more likely than not male) learn to express physical energy and anger within a set series of rules for positive gain. Catharine MacKinnon (1987) writes that women in our society are not allowed physical power, because the ideal woman is measured by the ease by which she can be raped.

To add to MacKinnon's conjecture, women are not allowed another manifestation of power—outwardly directed violence and action. Therefore, any power a woman has is diminished and poses no threat because she lacks the ability to direct violence outside herself. Women, untrained on the playing field, out of touch with their bodies and weighted down with messages from men and women that their violence is wrong, hold in that anger, energy and violence until they are manifested in self-damaging behaviors—insecurity, indecision and low self-esteem.

This is a reason why women's anger is frequently ignored or belittled—the anger has no external manifestation so it not seen as threatening. An angry woman only hurts herself. Physically and conditionally, she is unable to express in action her anger. Without power to manifest anger outside herself, the woman's well-stocked arsenal of anger turns inward, and the powerful source of energy serving progress and change is destroyed (Lorde, 1984, p. 127). A woman without the strength or physical ability to express rage in a crushing or violent fashion is left only with the option of cajoling her enemy, which further devalues her anger.

Women, who purportedly are more enabled to express a developed range of emotions, have been historically denied a significant expression: violence, or physically determined rage. Whatever anger women have is then self-sublimated or otherwise diminutively fostered. Because the full breadth of female anger is not allowed, the anger that is expressed is ineffectual and frequently humorous. Female anger is not a threat in a society stocked with male violence. Furthermore, women's anger is not well received, is ignored and is seen as irrational. Yet, as Marilyn Frye (1983) writes, anger simply implies a claim to domain.

Sports that involve self-defense or use of weapons get no audience attention. For example, in the XXVth Olympiad, a woman took the U.S. Shooting Team's only Gold medal, yet she received no network coverage for her achievements, despite the number of stations covering the Olympic events (Jones, 1992, p. 8).

Sport is defined as "an active pastime diversion, usually involving physical exercise and having a set form and body of rules"

(*American Heritage*, 1990). Action films have a role within this loose definition. Male actors in these films have muscular bodies, refined to fit the action-packed tasks and athletic stunts. In addition, action film stars such as Sylvester Stallone and Arnold Schwarzenegger are perceived by audiences as being athletes, their bodies sized to the near perfection of professional bodybuilders.

In cinema, women essentially are objects—love interests, damsels in distress, crime victims. According to Burchill (1986, p. 147), there exist two kinds of women—good and bad, and in cinema, the bad one is killed, raped or otherwise punished. In this cinematic universe, there are few active women, few female warriors.[7] This is part of Haskell's "big lie" (1973, p. 2), in which women are inferior to men and in which the movie industry is "dedicated for the most part to reinforcing the lie."

Despite this industry denial of strong women characters in film, the Artemis figure has made very brief appearances in cinema, as Joan of Arc or Queen Elizabeth. At the same time, the screen has been filled with women needing protection: Maid Marion and Princess Leia, wives and daughters in war films, victims in crime films. The female lead in cinema waits to be rescued, occasionally fighting a brief and usually comical battle, one from which she eventually needs to be rescued, rarely fighting alongside the male lead.

Even recent depictions of female violence are weak and fail as Artemis representations. *Bonnie and Clyde*'s Bonnie was defined by her relationship with Clyde (and, in fact, her violence was portrayed as a result of her sexual frustration). *Thelma and Louise*, touted by many as being the premier violent feminist film, still offers underdeveloped representations of violence as a direct and singular response to male violence. The characters are not perpetrators; they are victims followed closely by a cop / father figure who recognizes their innocence and works futilely to rescue them. Despite some affirming qualities of the film, including violent rejections of sexist attacks, there exist two major points that disqualify Thelma and Louise from being Artemis prototypes. First, all violence shown in the film is enacted singularly in response to male sexual perpetration —they kill and destroy, but only as victims fighting for survival— and furthermore, the two, like all good victims, do not survive, but neatly die at the end, in effect making the raping perpetrator successful in his crime of destruction. They are not heroes but victims reacting, albeit in a more active and positive manner than is usually shown in film.

There is a new model of female hero in action films, an Artemis prototype who strengthens her body visibly, who understands and uses violence and who expresses her anger in an active and external mode. She is Sarah Connor, who in *The Terminator* and *Terminator 2: Judgment Day* saves the world with her action and violence. Connor is played by Linda Hamilton, known mainly for her role in *Beauty and the Beast* (a role that followed *The Terminator*).

Hamilton worked out daily for nearly a year to obtain the body needed for this role. She also trained for several months with a former Israeli commando in weapons and combat techniques. In fact, Hamilton's physical training and new physique were the focuses of much of the publicity for *Terminator 2*.

Her body has not gone unnoticed in the realm of female bodybuilding. For example, in an article in a bodybuilding magazine that came out after the release of *Terminator 2*, former Ms. Olympia champion Corey Everson stated that "Hamilton has the type of body that gets women into bodybuilding" ("Terminator 2," 1991, p. 56). Everson went on to imply that cinematic showings of bodybuilding physiques do more for the popularity of bodybuilding than do the sport competitions themselves. This has certainly been true of male bodybuilding, where unprecedented numbers of men entered the gyms following the Hollywood popularity of Arnold Schwarzenegger and Lou Ferrigno, among others. With Hamilton being the first such image for women, it still has to be determined whether women will follow suit and build powerful, athletic bodies.

Sarah Connor: A Contemporary Artemis

Sarah Connor (Linda Hamilton) provides an autonomous and refreshingly powerful female archetype, a modern Artemis. Important to the value of this archetype is that the plots of these two films focus on the development of Sarah Connor from a timid but independent "every woman" to a world-saving Artemis warrior, who film critic David Ansen (1991, p. 57) described as a "fanatical matriarchal warrior" and critic David Denby (1991, p. 50) negatively described as a "She-Hulk."

In *The Terminator*, Sarah Connor is introduced as a common woman placed by science fiction fate in a situation in which she has tremendous purpose. In a future battle between humans and machines, her son (whom she trained and educated in weapons and strategies), leads a victorious battle. To prevent their destruction, the machines send through time an ultimate killing machine, one programmed to kill (or terminate) Sarah Connor. Also sent through time is Kyle, a friend of Connor's son in the future, as protector.

It is from Kyle that Connor learns about her situation and it is with him that she trains for battle. She does not rely on him as her protector; the two fight the terminator together, although it is Connor who destroys the terminator, killing a machine the video release display box states "no one can stop." Connor's killing of the machine does not involve so-called feminine wiles, but the crush of industrial machines.

Terminator 2: Judgment Day opens with Connor institutionalized for stating what no one believes and acting on what she knows to be true (a female condition portrayed notably in Charlotte Perkins Gilman's 1899 novel *The Yellow Wallpaper*). In the sequel, a more advanced terminator is sent through time to kill Connor's son John, who is now 10. Sarah Connor teams in battle with a second terminator sent through time to protect her son.

A central focus of the film is on actress Linda Hamilton's strong physique. In fact, the first image of Connor is of her developed biceps, the shot backing to show Connor working out. The context of the film is that Connor has spent the last decade procuring weapons[8] and military training and has attempted to alter the future (a nuclear war) by trying to destroy the company that makes the advanced computers that will in the future fight the humans and destroy the world.

The thematic construct of *Terminator 2* is that Sarah Connor confronts her destiny, thereby altering the destiny of the world. So by combating the traditional role of a peaceful and complacent woman, Connor saves the planet. Director James Cameron describes this construct: "The acceptance of destiny is an acceptance that life is dictated by fate and that there is nothing you can do about it, as opposed to believing you can control your life and rise above your circumstances" ("Terminator 2," 1991, p. 59).

What enables Sarah Connor to survive the film and save the world is her muscular physique, knowledge of violence and ability to express both physical power and violent power in an external fashion. She responds to situations with basic actions, clear missions and physical violence, but her violence differs from that in most action films in that it is driven by a greater good, the mission of saving the world. Joe Bob Briggs (1991, p. 10) writes: "No matter who or how many you kill, you can't be wrong, because if you don't do what you do, the world will end." Yet even within this faultless mission, Sarah Connor does not kill indiscriminately but when it is the only possible action and alternatives have failed. For example, in *Terminator 2*, Connor realizes the only way to prevent the machines from destroying the world is to stop their invention. She plans to assassinate Miles Dyson, the scientist responsible for their development. Yet she balks during her assassination attempt, instead enlisting Dyson's assistance in destroying all his records and research projects.

In her role as an Artemis archetype, Connor is important in the real-life debate over the viability of women in combat, because she is recognized as a woman warrior, albeit a fictional one. What is at issue with the United States military is that the image of a good soldier does not parallel the images of ideal femininity despite recruiting brochures that state: "Some of the best soldiers wear lipstick" (Isaacs, 1991, p. 24).

At the National Organization for Women National Convention on July 5, 1991, Gloria Steinem discussed the then-ongoing congressional trials to determine a woman's role in combat. From saying: "Can you imagine what would happen if every underpaid waitress, every sexually harassed secretary had two years military training," Steinem went on to speculate that violent actions may be the only change agent, when the achievement of more than 30 years' peaceful protest was being eliminated (Corbin & Kane, 1991, p. 1).

As an archetype for women, Hamilton's Sarah Connor displays important characteristics for women seeking equity in a violent society. She learns the rules of war and violence (much like the rules of sports games) and develops talents in these structures to function in her mission as peace emissary. Connor also reveals that these rules and lessons are only useful to someone who has the strength and power to carry them out; therefore, her body becomes her primary weapon. She displays the importance of obtaining an ownership of violence to move from being victim to aggressor without becoming a perpetrator. Connor demonstrates in film that women can master power and violence and that the manner of combatting violence is by using violence, that is, playing by the rules of the game. So Connor, rather than being a cheerleader on the sidelines, becomes a winning player.

Notes

1. Juvenile genre films such as *Bad News Bears* and *Lady Bugs* are not included in this analysis. However, the aspect of the juvenile Artemis as "tomboy" is certainly worth further research. Even Barbie dolls now come complete with a workout center, exercise cycle and dumbbells.

2. Leni Riefenstahl's *Olympia*, considered by some to be the greatest sports film ever made, is a documentary accounting of the 1936 Nazi Olympics that provides a rich mixture of mythology and patriarchy.

3. Rader (1991) suggests that the 1979 movie *10* glorified women who were "thin but physically fit, energetic, possessing some muscle definition" (p. 263). He adds that Bo Derek had done weight training and used a Nautilus machine for three months before the filming. The movie also tied beauty standards to the imprecise rating system use in gymnastics, diving and skating.

4. Shirley Muldowney served as the technical consultant to the film, as well as being the teller of her own story.

5. Sabotage resulted in serious injuries to Muldowney on more than one occasion.

6. During the 1979 Miss Body Beautiful Contest, competitor Georgia Miller-Fudge defiantly removed her shoes before posing, to the cheers of her competition (Weider & Kennedy, 1985, p. 16).

7. Female film detectives such as Kathleen Turner in *V. I. Warshawski* and television's Angie Dickinson in *Police Woman* were not included in the analysis.

8. An interesting aside is Connor's use of weapons in her first two fights in the film. Connor breaks off a mop handle to use as a riot baton, attacking first an orderly who attempted to molest her. The next weapon she uses is a hypodermic needle filled with pine-scented drain cleaner.

References

The American Heritage electronic dictionary. (1990). Cambridge, MA: Houghton Mifflin.

Ansen, David. (1991, July 8). Conan the humanitarian. *Newsweek*, p. 57.

Briggs, Joe Bob. (1991, August). In Terminator II, an ounce of prevention is worth a ton of death and destruction. *Hoot, 88*, 10.

Brunsdon, Charlotte (Ed.). (1986). *Films for women*. London: British Film Institute Publishing.

Burchill, Julie. (1986). *Girls on film*. New York: Pantheon.

Campbell, Joseph & Moyers, Bill. (1988). *The power of myth*. New York: Doubleday.

Corbin, Beth & Kane, Lisa. (1991). NOW national conference launches bold political agenda for the 90s. *National Times, 13*(5), 1-2.

de Lauretis, Teresa. (1984). *Alice doesn't: Feminism, semiotics, cinema*. Bloomington, IN: Indiana University Press.

Denby, David. (1991, July 15). The 90-million-dollar man: Terminator 2: Judgement Day directed by James Cameron. *New York, 24*(27), 50-51.

Frye, Marilyn. (1983). *The politics of reality: Essays in feminist theory*. Trumansburg, NY: The Crossing Press.

Gammon, Lorraine & Marshment, Margaret. (1989). *The female gaze: Women as viewers of popular culture*. Seattle, WA: The Real Comet Press.

Gentile, Mary C. (1985). *Film feminisms: Theory and practice*. Westport, CT: Greenwood Press.

Gilman, Charlotte Perkins. (1973/1899). *The yellow wallpaper*. New York: Feminist Press.

Haskell, Molly. (1973). *From reverence to rape: The treatment of women in the movies*. New York: Holt, Rinehart & Winston.

Isaacs, Rebecca. (1991). The implications of militarism: An interview with Cynthia Enloe. *OUT/LOOK, 4*(1), 22-24.

Jones, S. (1992). Meilie takes Olympic Gold in Barcelona. *Women & Guns, 10*(4), 8-10.

Kaplan, E. Ann. (1983). *Women and film: Both sides of the camera*. New York: Methuen.

Lorde, Audre. (1984). *Sister outsider*. Trumansburg, NY: The Crossing Press.

MacKinnon, Catharine. (1987). *Feminism unmodified*. Cambridge, MA: Harvard University Press.

Mapplethorpe, Robert & Chatwin, Bruce. (1983). *Lady Lisa Lyon*. New York: Viking.

Mayne, Judith. (1990). *The woman at the keyhole: Feminism and woman's cinema*. Bloomington, IN: Indiana University Press.

McGough, Peter. (1993, August). The Bev Francis story: A career in focus. *Flex*, pp. 64-67, 150-156.

Moore, Gaylen. (1977, October). Athletes foot. *womenSports, 4*(10), p. 18-19, 55.

Rader, Benjamin G. (1991). The quest for self-sufficiency and new strenuosity: Reflections on the strenuous life of the 1970s and 1980s. *Journal of Sport History, 18*(2), 255-266.

Terminator 2: Judgement (sic) day. (1991). *Muscle Training Illustrated, 2*(10), 56-59.

Weider, Ben & Kennedy, Robert. (1985). *Pumping up: Super shaping the feminine physique*. New York: Sterling Publishing.

13

Reawakening to the Co-Essence Model of Sport

Stanford's Tara VanDerveer Leads the Way

Pamela Sue Highlen

> To live in an evolutionary spirit means to engage with full ambition and without any reserve in the structure of the present, and yet to let go and flow into a new structure when the right time has come.
>
> Erich Jantsch (in Wheatley, 1992, p. 74)

The year is 2010. Commercialization, wealth, status and competitiveness no longer drive the sport world and the media that cover it. Sport is now recognized as a performing art, along with music, theater, art and dance. Athletes value cooperation, compromise, teamwork, synergism and something new called *co-essence*. Co-essence, the athlete's co-creation with self and with competitors, allows sport to be a total experience, "a way in" to heightened awareness. Force, conflict, aggression and a win-lose mentality in sport have given way to creativity, effortless movement, beauty and grace. Competitors

AUTHOR'S NOTE: This chapter is based on transcribed interviews with Tara Van-Derveer and members of the Stanford University women's basketball organization in 1990. My thanks to Marla Oberhausen and Pam Creedon for reading the manuscript numerous times. Their suggestions greatly improved the final version of this chapter.

strive together in synergistic union to fully express their creative energies.

The media have also been affected by this transformation. More women and people of color report sporting events. Sporting events are reported in commentators' "own voices." As a result, written and verbal sport commentary is more creative and artful. On television, sportscasters emphasize skill, courage, dedication, brilliance, satisfactory effort, improvement, cooperation, unselfish play and honorable performance in their reporting. Newspapers have dropped the sport section and have expanded the entertainment and arts section to include sports.

Innovations in media coverage have enhanced the vicarious experience of sport. Gone is the slick production packaging of sporting events. Instead, the media focus on the essence of what sport truly is: an art form. In television, more cameras are used to capture sport from diverse perspectives. Viewers have five perspectives from which to watch the televised event. In basketball, for example, one camera perspective follows the "action" of the game in the traditional way. Another focuses on specific athletes, so that a viewer can watch the game entirely from one player's perspective. Another option captures the artistic essence of performance. The camera follows a player through the entire shooting sequence of a three-point shot, thus minimizing whether or not the shot was made. The inherent art and skill of the movement is captured. The other two options focus on the offensive and the defensive play of the game. Viewers may watch all five "boxes" simultaneously, shift to full screen coverage of one or have full screen coverage of one with smaller "boxed" versions of any of the other perspectives.

Events such as the World Figure Skating Championships are commonly shown on two channels: one with commentary, the other without. Camera coverage of the wordless presentation emphasizes the event as an art form. Audiences appreciate the elegance of athletic performance without the interference of words. In fact, many wordless telecasts, such as figure skating and the Olympics, are used as meditation tools for centering the mind, body and spirit.

Another shift in media coverage has occurred. No longer do the media predominantly cover professional and elite athletes to the exclusion of amateurs. Amateur athletes and teams tell their own stories.

Audiences support recreational and local sport telecasts within their communities, because sport is recognized as a vehicle for self-expression and for understanding others. This programming brings diversity of cultural and ethnic perspectives to the viewing audiences. Coverage of pickup basketball games in the barrios of Los Angeles, for example, often features participants telling their own stories.

Advances in technology have revolutionized the sport experience. Holography makes it possible to learn from and play with "master" athletes. This experience is much like the holodeck portrayed in *Star Trek: The Next Generation*, a television series popular in the 1990s. Through sophisticated programming and three-dimensional holographic projection, master athletes can be called forth in any sport of interest. For example, if participants want to improve their vertical leap, they can call forth Michael Jordan as master teacher. In addition to skill mastery, interaction with masters is possible. In ice dancing, for example, Torvel and Dean, the legendary ice dance team from England, can be called forth to do routines with participants. Groups, as well as individuals, can participate in the holographic experience. A basketball team and its coaching staff can play games with holographic master teams. Degree of difficulty ranges from novice to master levels, so that the sport holographic experience can support participants at all levels of skill and experience. Holographic projections begin with meditative activities that bring participants into their own state of co-essence. This heightened sense of self allows the holographic experience to be the best for all, regardless of skill level.

Audiences see sport as athletes striving together to bring out the best in themselves and in their competitors. Since spectators no longer focus on the importance of outcome, they express less violence and aggression at sporting events. Gone are the frenzied death scenes of riots after soccer matches, so common in the last century. Betting on favorite teams is also a relic of the past. Instead, individuals contribute money to help athletes create, as is done with the other performing arts. In the Olympics, athletes and teams compete without national identification, thus enhancing true appreciation of sport as a performing art.

Overall, positive, creative sport participation has dramatically increased people's self-esteem. This greater sense of well-being has also increased people's appreciation of others. It has helped people turn their attention to issues that really matter, the well-being of the earth, including ecology, conservation of natural resources and the feeding and clothing of the world's people.

The Sport World: 1993

The year is 1993. What could possibly happen in less than two decades to create this transformation in sport and society? What would need to occur to cause such a dramatic shift in worldview? In order to transform the world of sport, we must first transform the worldview from which sport professionals operate and then, second, use this transformed worldview to change the infrasystem of sport. In order to assess the need for a new model of sport, we must first explore the infrasystem of the dominant worldview governing society and sport. Second, we must examine the historical roots of the female model of sport, as well as alternate models of sport that have been proposed. The Co-Essence Model of Sport (CEMS) is proposed as a new paradigm for sport professionals. Using the CEMS, individuals can transform the infrasystem of the sport world in the 21st century.

Infrasystem Underlying the Dominant Sport Model

Pam Creedon (1993) defined *infrasystem* as the foundation of institutional values and norms that determine an organization's response to its environment. In other words, the worldview, values and ways of thinking and making decisions held by the members of the institution determine behavior. Gloria Steinem (1992) asserted that the dominant worldview in the United States of America is shaped by patriarchy and racial divisions. She identified this dominant worldview as being characterized by three parts: (a) *either/or thinking*, which sees two parts to almost everything: good or bad, win or lose, masculine or feminine; (b) *linear thinking*, in which, among other things, people are graded and defeating others is the goal of accomplishment; and (c) *hierarchy*, in which all authority flows from the top. African-American scholar Linda James Myers (1988) has described this dominant worldview as the "suboptimal conceptual system." While agreeing with Steinem's characterization, Myers further depicts this suboptimal system as primarily oriented to (a) materialism, (b) the acquisition of objects, (c) individualism, (d) a segmented or fragmented perspective and (e) conditional acceptance of others.

This dominant worldview within society and within sport reflects a transactional model. This transactional perspective views relationships from a "quid pro quo" perspective, that is, the exchange involves "something for something." An example of this quid pro quo mentality is: "You are a good athlete and can help us win. We will give you an athletic grant-in-aid."[1] This transactional worldview is also characterized by an emphasis on outcome, where there is only one winner, where competition means to beat your opponent and, in many cases, to beat them at any cost. The coach is viewed as an entrepreneur, and the system is driven by an "either/or" mentality. The prevailing value system within the sport infrasystem is also nonsupportive of differences. Conscious or unconscious sexism, racism, classism and heterosexism are practiced. Nonsupport is often reflected in overt homophobic behavior. Often lesbian coaches do not feel free to openly discuss their lifestyles. For example, where heterosexual coaches could openly discuss job possibilities for a spouse prior to a move, lesbian coaches traditionally feel more constrained in discussing these concerns with prospective employers.

Although this infrasystem dominates the sports world today, other models based on different values have operated.

Overview of the Female Sport Model

From a historical perspective, women's sport in the U.S.A. developed in an educational context (Highlen & Fassinger, 1984; Oglesby, 1978). By 1875, physical education for women was incorporated into the curriculum at Vassar and Wellesley (Oglesby, 1978). The credo for women in intercollegiate sport was the "greatest good for the greatest number." In the 1950s women administrators in physical education, perhaps anticipating the problems with contemporary sports, opposed female participation in intercollegiate sports, as well as in the Olympics, because they feared such participation would lead to commercialization and professionalism (Oglesby, 1978, p. 11). This female model of sport was inclusionary, as opposed to exclusionary, focused on cooperation, not on hierarchy, stressed intrinsic satisfaction and enjoyment, regardless of winning or losing, and magnified personal performance as opposed to beating the opponent (Moseley, 1979, cited in Boutilier & SanGiovanni, 1983). In the 1960s, some female physical education leaders supported intercollegiate competition for women, which led in 1971 to the establishment of the Association of Intercollegiate Athletics for Women (AIAW). Consistent with its heritage, the AIAW grounded female sports participation within an educational model. In contrast, men's sports evolved from club sports apart from educational involvement.

With the passage of Title IX of the Higher Education Amendments Act in 1972, greater funding of women's sports occurred. As one result, coaching female athletes became more attractive to male coaches because of the increase in the number of sports offered for women, as well as the increase in salary and prestige for coaching female sports. Athletic administrators, mostly European American males, looked for the "best qualified" people to coach these sports. Since people tend to hire people with similar values, the "best qualified" were often seen to be similar to the individual doing the hiring; that is, males tended to hire males with similar functional philosophies. Often women were deemed dissimilar in philosophy, since their orientation was viewed as "glorified" recreation.

At the institutional level, the National Collegiate Athletic Association (NCAA) initiated a takeover of women's intercollegiate athletics, and in 1982 after the AIAW lost an antitrust lawsuit against the NCAA, it ceased to exist. The NCAA victory ensured that the dominant model of sport would prevail for women. Title IX and the NCAA takeover of women's sports had a profound impact on hiring practices. More men were hired to coach women's sports for at least two reasons: they had been in coaching longer than females, and they embraced the dominant sport model. In 1977, before Title IX, 90% of women's intercollegiate sports were coached by women. In 1990, only 47.3% of women's sports were coached by women (Acosta & Carpenter, 1990).

Alternate Sport Paradigms

Perhaps in response to these changes, several authors proposed an androgynous model that combined the female and the dominant sport paradigms. The androgynous model advocated the use of expressive (feminine) and instrumental (masculine) characteristics (Duquin, 1978; Highlen & Fassinger, 1984; Oglesby, 1978). Conceptually, a balance between process and outcome seemed to be a logical compromise to integrate the best of both models, while minimizing each model's shortcomings.

In the mid 1980s, several egalitarian models were suggested. Denis Waitley (1985) proposed a "win-win" philosophy. "When you win (whether you are my teammate or my opponent), then I win, too." This cooperative approach encouraged all participants to be the best they could be. Waitley identified enjoyment, having purpose beyond self, earning respect of others, practicing synergism and win-win communication, never trumpeting status, never defining a loss as losing (i.e., always learning regardless of outcome), using the spiritual dimension and developing self-esteem as elements of this philosophy. By following these tenets, Waitley suggested that all participants could "win" by realizing their potential.

In *The Chalice and the Blade*, Riane Eisler (1987) documented past cultures that flourished using what she termed a *partnership model*. In this model, cooperation, based on trust and reciprocity with others, occurred; interdependency was stressed, and power was viewed as "power to" or "power with" (versus "power over"). In *Are We Winning Yet?* Mariah Burton Nelson (1991) endorsed Eisler's model as fitting women's experiences in sport. Nelson noted that the word *competition* comes from the Latin *competere*, which means "to seek together." These egalitarian models directly spoke to the heritage of females in sport.

Critique of Existing Models of Sport

Problems exist with each of the depicted models. First, the "either/or" mentality implicit in the dominant and early female models is limiting. The dominant model exclusively emphasizes outcome:

"It's whether you win or lose." The early female model exclusively emphasized process: "It's how you play the game." Second, although the androgynous model utilizes "both/and" thinking by integrating outcome with process perspectives, it does not identify "core" elements that could make the model viable within the existing sport environment. Third, under pressure to compete and win, coaches and athletes using androgynous or egalitarian models may succumb to the outcome-oriented mentality needed to survive. When all is well with the outer world (e.g., the team is winning), coaches can maintain this androgynous or egalitarian stance. However, adhering to either model proves difficult under adverse circumstances. As the competitive challenges intensify—for example, when key players are injured; top recruits are lost; losses increase; fans and administrators become disgruntled—many coaches abandon the androgynous or egalitarian models and revert to tactics associated with the dominant model. Fourth and primarily, all of these models focus on the external world (i.e., how we are in relation to others) and either omit or minimize the importance of the inner world (i.e., how we are in relation to self, notably how we love and respect the self). As a group, women tend to value being in relation *to others* (Gilligan, 1982). Unfortunately, as a group, women do not honor themselves as readily as they honor others. A key to transformation is to identify core inner elements that will help women, as well as men, honor themselves.

Co-Essence Model of Sport (CEMS)

The Co-Essence Model of Sport (CEMS) paradigm is grounded in a worldview that existed before patriarchy and continues to be practiced by Fourth World indigenous peoples.[2] Indigenous peoples have honored both their inner and outer worlds throughout time. Their respect for nature, their methods of resource management, social organization, values and culture speak to us today. Therefore, the Co-Essence Model of Sport worldview is not new. The values and tenets on which it is based have been ignored by the dominant culture in the First World (highly industrialized societies) for several hundred years.

The tenets of the Co-Essence Model of Sport are presented here, followed by an elaboration of the model's components. Tara Van-Derveer, head coach of the Stanford University women's basketball program, is used to illustrate an operational CEMS philosophy and its effect on her basketball organization.[3] Interviews with Coach Van-Derveer and members of the Stanford basketball organization were conducted in September 1990, after Stanford won its first Division I NCAA championship.[4] Components of the Co-Essence Model of Sport are presented in Table 13.1.

Tenets of CEMS

At the core of the Co-Essence Model of Sport is the belief that spirit and matter are unified; that "life and intelligence are present not only in all of matter, but in energy, space, time, the fabric of the entire universe" (Bohm, cited in Talbot, 1991, p. 50). Quantum physics and holographic theory support this construction of reality (Capra, 1975, 1982; Talbot, 1991). Four tenets of the CEMS follow from this belief.

1. All forms of life are unique manifestations of spirit.
2. All of life is connected and hence is interdependent.
3. The highest value is in positive interpersonal relationships among people.
4. The world is experienced from a "both/and" rather than an "either/or" perspective.

Tenet 1. When all life is seen as unique manifestation of spirit, then self-worth is inherent in each person and, thus, is independent of external realities (Myers,1988; Myers et al., 1991). When reflecting on winning her first NCAA Division I Women's Basketball Championship in 1990, Stanford University Coach Tara VanDerveer conveyed this principle in the following way: "Leland [her cat] doesn't know whether we won or lost. After the Final Four he treated me the same way he always does." In other words, Coach VanDerveer recognized that she is the same person regardless of her external accomplishments.

TABLE 13.1 The Co-Essence Model of Sport (CEMS)

Tenets
1. All forms of life are unique forms of spirit.
2. All of life is interconnected.
3. The highest value is in interpersonal relationships.
4. The world is experienced from a "both/and" rather than an "either/or" perspective.

Components

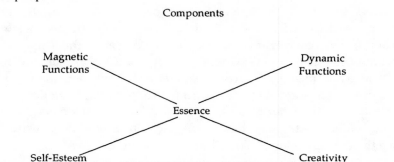

Magnetic Functions — Dynamic Functions — Essence — Self-Esteem — Creativity

Tenet 2. What does it mean to say all of life is interconnected? Imagine a spider web with a filament coming to your center and filaments extending to every person on the earth. When one moves mentally, emotionally, physically or spiritually this movement affects the whole web. As a coach, if I want the players to perform to their best potential under pressure, I will realize that my behavior has an impact on them. I can choose to be anxious and yell at them, or I can choose to remain calm and talk about what the team needs to do. When Stanford played Auburn for the 1990 NCAA Division I Women's Basketball Championship, Stanford lost an 11-point lead at one point in the first half, which resulted in a 41-41 tie at intermission. At halftime, Coach VanDerveer said to her players: "The score is 0-0. We've got to come out and play the better second half. Once we get the lead, we can't let them come back." She then praised the team for coming back to tie the game.

Tenet 3. The highest value is in relationships, not in material things or accomplishments (Meyers, 1988; Meyers et al., 1991). According to

Coach VanDerveer, "Winning the national championship doesn't matter unless it makes us happy. What matters is the closeness with a set of people who experience the same thing. That is what matters. Records are irrelevant. If we have touched peoples' lives in a positive way with our team that's great."

Tenet 4. The "both/and" perspective allows for everything that is true to stand, even if it appears on the surface to be contradictory. For example, as a coach I may care deeply for a player on the team and feel upset with her unwillingness to follow coaching instruction. In an "either/or" mentality the coach would identify only with the anger and frustration and not the deep caring. In a "both/and" mode both feelings would be valued and expressed. Coach VanDerveer's patience with athletes who have struggled illustrates this principle (see the example under "The Ultimate Challenge").

Core of the Co-Essence Model of Sport

The new sport model is called the Co-Essence Model of Sport because one's core or essence is the key. The word *essence* comes from the Latin *essentia* meaning "to be." Essence means the most important quality involving the inward nature of anything. In the CEMS this essence is the soul, the spiritual portion of our existence. It is at the soul/essence level that our life's purpose is known; it is where we accept ourselves unconditionally; it is where we connect with the Source; it is where creativity is born. Co-essence at the deepest level is where our soul is one with the Source and co-creates with it.[5]

The ego or personality is needed to manifest the soul's mission. Typically, however, the ego wants to control this unfolding process, rather than to surrender this role to the soul. The ego is prone to compare self to others, to judge self and others and to act out of fear instead of love. To operate from our deepest level of being, we must let go of the need to control. Ego, by cooperating with our essence, co-creates with our soul. The key to co-essence or co-creation is to accept self fully, believing in our inherent worth and oneness with the Source.

Self-Esteem

The word *esteem* comes from the Latin *aestimare*, meaning "to value." Therefore, for our essence to fully complete its purposes of loving and acquiring knowledge we must value self unconditionally. Valuing self unconditionally is perhaps the hardest task each of us faces.

Arrien (1989) identified love, respect and trust as the three universal ingredients of self-esteem across cultures. Movement into fear, fixation and control occurs as we move away from our true self (Arrien, 1989; 1993). Whenever we experience fear, we move away from love; whenever we become fixated, we move away from respect; and whenever we experience a need to control, we move away from trust.[6]

Love. The first aspect of self-esteem is love, which is viewed as an expanding and deepening experience (Arrien, 1989). In areas where we love ourselves, we feel open and expanded. Where we move out of self-love, we move into fear, or the constriction of energy. As we practice self-love, it extends to others. Coach VanDerveer said that the most important thing about Stanford's first Final Four appearance in 1990 was that people couldn't stop hugging each other. Assistant Coach Renee Brown described the Stanford basketball organization as: "People who care about themselves and want to succeed. They're confident about the people they're around. I wonder how many people could really stand up and say, 'I love' and really mean it. . . . that I love our Manager Marla, and I love the eleventh person on our bench and really want them to do well."

Respect. Respect, the second aspect of self-esteem, comes from the Latin *respicere*, which means "the willingness to look again" (Arrien, 1989, 1993). The opposite of respect is fixation or being stuck. Being fixated keeps us from looking at solutions to our problems. Fixation is a common problem in our culture. Communication with self is often grounded in negativism and criticism. We get fixated on and overidentify with the parts of ourselves that engage in behaviors that we don't like. When we look again at other parts of who we or others are, we extend respect to self and others. After Stanford's only loss of the 1989-1990 season to Washington, Assistant Coach Brown recalled that Coach VanDerveer told the team that "we lost because we didn't do this and this, and this. These are the things we are going to work on. She didn't belittle anyone on the team."

Trust. The third part of self-esteem is trust, which means "covenant" in German. Where we have covenant or agreement with ourselves, we have the capacity to have it with others. When we move out of trust, we feel the need to control a relationship, to control a task or to control the environment. Each person on Coach VanDerveer's staff has a lot of responsibility and a lot of input. She asks people for their ideas, because she trusts her staff. She knows that the Stanford program is better because of their input.

Creativity

One definition of *create* is "to bring into existence." When our soul is connected to the Source, we are fully able to bring into existence the unique talents and abilities we possess. The "flow" or "being in the zone" are ways athletes describe the height of their performance that comes when they are in this deepest of creative spaces. "Effortless," "rhythmic" and "at one with" are other descriptors often used. As the Chinese would say, the athlete is in the Tao of the moment. When an athlete enters a state of total awareness, the right movement happens by itself, effortlessly, without any interference from the conscious will. Stephen Mitchell (1988) described this effortless athletic movement as *wei wu wei*, or "doing not-doing." As Mitchell (1988) says, "Nothing is done because the doer has wholeheartedly vanished into the deed; the fuel has been completely transformed into flame. This 'nothing' is, in fact, everything. It happens when we trust the intelligence of the universe" (p. ix).

According to Coach VanDerveer, the three-point line revolutionized basketball. In their 1988 tour of China, Coach VanDerveer saw a Chinese guard score ten three-pointers against her team. Given Coach VanDerveer's assessment of Stanford's inability to go one-on-one with top collegiate teams, she incorporated the three-point shot into Stanford's game plan. In their 1990 championship game against Auburn, Stanford set a record for the number of three-point shots attempted (26) and made (11).

Dynamic and Magnetic Forces

Arrien (1989) identified eight universal qualities, which she has labeled *dynamic* and *magnetic*. In prepatriarchal Eastern philosophy, their counterparts are *yang* for dynamic and *yin* for magnetic energies.[7] The more we operate from our essence, the more fully we can access these magnetic and dynamic energies to bring forth our creativity.

Dynamism is defined as energy moving outward. Dynamism involves beginning or initiating. In contrast, *magnetism* is opening and deepening energy. Therefore, magnetism is the capacity to draw or to pull opportunities, people and situations to us.

Language. The first dynamic force involves our relationship with words and language. Do we enjoy using words? Are we effective in communicating our ideas to others? If so, then this dynamic function is well developed. To be a good coach is to be a good teacher. Coaches must have command of their sport and the ability to effectively communicate this expertise to the players and staff. The first time Assistant Coach Brown watched a game film with Coach Van-Derveer she was told: "Renee, I want you to think of this tape as a brain. We're going to pick it apart, and you're going to train your eye to see the game strategically."

Productivity. The second dynamic energy is productivity. If we enjoy bringing things into form, then this function is well developed. Coach VanDerveer wanted to win the National Championship in the 1989-1990 season for three seniors who came to a program with a 5-23 record. "To win for them is what got me out of bed in the morning," she said. "Doing things for other people is a big motivator for me and makes it so much more worthwhile. I can get what I want eventually, but it's more fun when it is for other people and doing it with other people."

Power. Power is the third dynamic function. The ability to empower myself and others is a dynamic force. If we assume our own leadership capabilities and inspire others to do the same, then we honor this dynamic force. Authentic power comes from inside; it does not mean power over others. Some coaches have asked Coach VanDerveer why she is so calm on the bench. She believes that her work is often done when she gets to the game. "There's no sense for me to stand up and scream. I don't like the 'grab the athlete' approach. And if it's not fun for the players, then why should they do it? Or why should I do it if it's not fun for me? There's an extra little spark or a spirit. If you don't have it, you're never going to be really, really good. If someone kills that in you or if you let it die, you're never going to be the best you can be. Coaches can do this to players. Enjoyment is the reason we do it. Otherwise we'd do something else."

Meaning. The last dynamic force is the curiosity to explore the meaning and the significance of life. If we want to understand what is significant, then this dynamic force is well developed. Coach Van-Derveer constantly searches for ways to make herself and her team better. "We're never satisfied with what we know," she said. Coach VanDerveer invites basketball experts to critique the team. Practices are videotaped and later assessed with the players.

Intuition. Intuition and vision comprise the first magnetic force. If we trust our intuition, then we have developed this magnetic force. After Coach VanDerveer's Ohio State team lost in the 1985 East Regionals to eventual champion Old Dominion, one of her assistants told her that the Stanford job was open. "The first thing out of my mouth was 'I'm going to take that job.' I had not interviewed. I had not talked to anybody. I got on the airplane and Linda Daniel, our head trainer, said, 'You're leaving, aren't you?' Also, when I was a graduate assistant coach at Ohio State before I left for the head coaching job at Idaho, I told Phyllis Bailey, Associate Athletic Director, that 'I will be a head coach in the Big 10 some day, and I will win the Big 10, and it will be a round-robin.' I don't know where I got that. It was just something I felt. I've always felt I could see things out there before they happened."

Nurturance. The ability to beautify and nurture is the second magnetic energy. We cannot heal or nurture unless we open to the depths of who we are. If we only nurture others, then we are not nurturing ourselves. Or if we care for others only in terms of what they can do for us, then we have inhibited this magnetic force. Trisha Stevens, player on the 1989-1990 Stanford Championship team, said that "Tara really cares a lot about all the players on the team as people first. She's always telling us first that she expects each of us to be a great person and to have a great attitude and to work hard. As long as you have a great attitude and you're working hard, she's going to be happy with your performance. She doesn't treat one person on our team who will play 40 minutes any better than someone who doesn't play at all. I think that's rare among big-time coaches. It's more that they just care about you as a player, and they want results."

Ritual. Ritual and ceremony comprise the third magnetic force. By bringing a sense of tradition through ritual and ceremony, we honor this magnetic force within ourselves and others. Coach VanDerveer talked about daily rituals they did during the 1989-1990 season to get comfortable with winning the national championship. "Every day something would come up in practice about how we needed to rebound better to win a national championship. When we were stretching someone would say, 'Picture stretching in Knoxville' [site of the 1990 Final Four], or 'Put another weight on. This one's for the Final Four.' When we huddled up at the end of the year as we got closer and closer to Knoxville, we moved more and more toward the center circle. We would give our cheer at the end of practice with everybody saying 'Number one.' As we did it more and more and more, people believed it more and more and more."

Organization. Organizing and systematizing comprise the fourth magnetic energy. For a deed to be completed, organizing and systematizing are necessary. In other words, organization and paying attention to details is essential for efficient productivity. After losing to Tennessee by 23 points in 1988, Coach VanDerveer watched tapes of Tennessee weekly. She learned how to prepare for the Lady Vols and how to improve her own team (Ryan, 1989, p. C2). Stanford won their rematch with Tennessee in 1989. Tennessee Coach Pat Summitt said, "After we played them last year, Tara VanDerveer said that Tennessee had taught Stanford a great lesson. Well, I hope we learned the same lesson tonight. The stat sheet said we have three more rebounds than Stanford, but I wouldn't have believed it. Their post game just ate our lunch. We just got whipped" (Ryan, 1989, p. C2).

The example of Coach VanDerveer suggests that the Co-Essence Model of Sport is achievable even in today's outcome-oriented environment. When individuals follow the CEMS, they are in a position to effect changes within the infrasystem of sport organizations.

Creating a Transcendent Infrasystem

Administrators and coaches, operating with a CEMS philosophy, create transcendent, as opposed to transactional, infrasystems. In the transactional system, athletes are viewed as commodities; the unitary goal is to win; conscious or unconscious sexism, racism, heterosexism and classism are practiced; the coach is an entrepreneur; and the system is driven by an "either/or" mentality.

In contrast, in the transcendent system, athletes are valued as human beings rather than as "objects" who perform; goals are multidimensional; diversity is valued; the coach is an educator and facilitator of growth; and the system is led by "both/and" thinking. Furthermore, criteria for evaluating coaches and all staff are multidimensional and reflect values inherent in the CEMS perspective. Performance criteria for coaches are based on helping athletes achieve their full potential individually and as a team. Academic progress of athletes is valued, as is the human development of the student-athletes. Salary is based on comparable worth, meaning that staff members doing any job within athletics requiring substantially equal skill, effort, responsibility and working conditions receive equal pay. Lifestyle diversity is welcome, and affirmative action is a part of the fabric of the institution. All job applicants, for example, are asked if their partners would like assistance in relocating. Order is created through discovery, not through imposition of authority. A sense of camaraderie and cooperation permeates this environment.

With the transcendent approach, self and others are valued for who they are, not for what they can do. As a result, all people working within the system are appreciated and acknowledged for the unique contributions they make to the organization. The atmosphere is positive. People feel free to risk becoming the very best they can be. Suggestions for improvement are actively solicited from everyone. In September 1990, I attended a viewing of the new Stanford recruiting video, which was being revised. Coach VanDerveer conducted the meeting in a collegial and egalitarian fashion, soliciting opinions from everyone, including me. She valued my input as an impartial observer with a different perspective.

With the transcendent approach, change is valued as positive and as a constant, so members are readily able to adapt to unexpected conditions. During the 1991 West Regionals, Stanford lost Tricia Stevens, their star post player, to a knee injury. Despite this adversity, Stanford won the West Regional and went to the Final Four in New Orleans as the defending champion. During the warm-up before their semifinal game with Tennessee, Julie Zeilstra, another starter, suffered an injury and was out for the game. With two starters on the bench, other players came forward; at the half, Stanford led. Although Stanford lost the game to eventual champion Tennessee, their play illustrates an important point. Players rise to the occasion when each is valued for her role on the team.

"Sunshine." Within the transcendent infrasystem all contributions are acknowledged, which helps bring out the best in all, given the attributes each possesses. The story of Angela Taylor, a nonrecruited "walk-on" who made the Stanford team, illustrates this point. In the middle of the 1989-1990 season, Coach VanDerveer asked each player to write down what she thought her role was on the team. Angela wrote, "Spread sunshine." Angela fulfilled her role so well that by December Coach VanDerveer gave Angela a grant-in-aid. "She's such a good person," Coach VanDerveer said. "Her talent has a long way to go, but I thought that type of behavior should be rewarded." Coach VanDerveer recalled, "Angela would be the last one to go into games. I'd say to her, 'Do you want me to put you in the game with one minute left?' She'd say, 'Yeah. I want to play.' At the end of the championship game with Auburn, there's a picture of Angela coming off the bench with her hands in the air, a big smile on her face. She hadn't played one minute in that game. Later I joked with her and said, 'You didn't play a minute. Does that ring mean anything to you?' And Angela replied, 'Just try to take it off my finger.' " Later when I talked with Angela about her role for the upcoming 1990-1991 season, she told me that she wanted to contribute physically on the court to help the team go back to the Final Four. She said she had studied videotapes of Sonja Henning and Jennifer Azzi (two

starting guards), concentrating on how they read the defenses and
made passes. Angela told me that the team goals were her first
priority. Her individual goals were second and twofold: to perform
at her best and to reach her potential. In the 1991 Final Four semifinal against Tennessee, "Sunshine" Angela Taylor started the game
for Stanford.

Tara VanDerveer: Visionary for the Future

Without doubt, Coach VanDerveer is an exceptional basketball
coach: She is both an excellent teacher of fundamentals and a superb
strategist. What sets her apart from most coaches is that she fully
embraces the CEMS tenets and philosophy. Coach VanDerveer co-
creates with herself and with others. Her belief in herself and in
others remains constant. In her first year at Stanford her team had
a 13-15 record. In her fifth year, Stanford won the Division I NCAA
championship. (See Table 13.2 for a listing of some of her accomplishments.) Although many examples could be given to illustrate
Coach VanDerveer's creativity, use of dynamic and magnetic functions and knowledge of the game, the ones that follow best capture
the essence of how she lives the CEMS philosophy.

After winning her first national championship in 1990, Coach
VanDerveer said that the Stanford players operate in a spiritual
way; that they have a sense of oneness where everyone is important; that beyond the game all people are connected. "The players
won't remember the scores of any games," Coach VanDerveer stated,
"but they'll remember how they felt a certain camaraderie, a sense
of togetherness."

Renee Brown, then an assistant coach at Stanford, captured Coach
VanDerveer's essence when I talked with her in 1990.[8] "I think the
most important thing about Tara is that she approaches life with a
big heart. She's willing to share and, in turn, not only do you want
to give and share back, you feel like, 'I'm going to work hard no
matter what.' I worked hard before I met Tara, but there's a special
part of Tara that makes me work even harder. It rubs off on the team;
it rubs off on our secretary; it rubs off on everybody. Tara doesn't
yell. Tara doesn't do any of that kind of stuff. She's taught me so

TABLE 13.2 Tara VanDerveer Career Coaching Record

Year	School	Record	Pct.	Post-Season
1978-1979	Idaho	17-8	.680	—
1979-1980	Idaho	25-6	.806	AIAW
1980-1981	Ohio State	17-15	.531	—
1981-1982	Ohio State	20-7	.741	—
1982-1983	Ohio State	23-5	.821	NCAA
1983-1984	Ohio State	22-7	.759	NCAA
1984-1985	Ohio State	28-3	.903	NCAA
1985-1986	Stanford	13-15	.464	—
1986-1987	Stanford	14-14	.500	—
1987-1988	Stanford	27-5	.844	NCAA
1988-1989	Stanford	28-3	.903	NCAA
1989-1990	Stanford	32-1	.970	NCAA Champions
1990-1991	Stanford	26-6	.813	NCAA Final Four
1991-1992	Stanford	30-3	.909	NCAA Champions
1992-1993	Stanford	26-6	.813	NCAA
Idaho	2 years	42-14	.750	1 appearance
Ohio State	5 years	110-37	.748	2 appearances
Stanford	8 years	170-47	.783	5 appearances

National Coach of the Year
Converse, 1988-1989   Naismith, 1989-1990

SOURCE: Information from S. Raczynski (1992), *1992-93 Stanford women's basketball media guide.* Stanford, CA: Stanford University.

many lessons, but the most important lesson she's taught me is to believe in me. If I believe in me, I can handle whatever is out there. She totally believes in Tara, and I think that rubs off on a lot of people." Assistant Coach Brown continued, "Just because Jennifer Azzi [two-time All-American and Naismith Award winner] is getting all the media attention, is Jennifer Azzi treated any differently than Angela Taylor who doesn't get any? No way. Just because my title is Part-Time Assistant, I'm not treated any differently than Amy Tucker, who is Tara's number one assistant. I know that the role I have within our organization is just as important. Whereas I think that Angela Taylor (the eleventh player of eleven) knows the role that she has is just as important as the role that Jennifer has. I think that Tara has made that significantly clear to everyone, and it starts with her and begins to filter. Like a flower, I think it blooms. Tara had to plant the seed and water it."

Assistant Coach Julie Plank described the essence of Coach Van-Derveer: "I think a lot of people wonder about her, what type of person she is because she's not really the dynamic outgoing person to people on the outside, because she just does her own thing. She goes about her business, and she's not cocky in the least bit. Awards, she deserves them all, but it doesn't go to her head. And she's willing to listen to other ideas and to listen to her players."

Assistant Coach Renee Brown concurred: "Tara never puts anyone down to make herself look better. She's very humble in her approach to a lot of different things. You know how a lot of head coaches don't give their assistants credit. Assistants work hard. Tara was once an assistant, and she knows that. Tara was speaking at the MacGregor Club with 400 men and 25 women in the room. One coach said to Tara, 'Your post people, Coach VanDerveer, they look great. They're posting up strong.' And Tara says, 'Well, hey, you know, Renee Brown works with our post players.' And another coach said, 'The recruits that you're bringing in, they're great players. They look really good. Jennifer Azzi is a great player.' And Tara says, 'Amy Tucker identi-fied Jennifer Azzi, and Julie Plank recruited her.' Another said, 'Your players are in good condition. Boy, they look strong.' And Tara says, 'Julie Plank is our conditioning coach.' She will give it back. But you know if she gave it back that you deserved it. At the end of the Stanford-Auburn championship game on CBS, it thrilled so many people that on national television Tara could acknowledge her assistants."

All-American Jennifer Azzi remembered how Coach VanDerveer systematically rebuilt the Stanford program: "My freshman year was really tough, because Tara and I are both really a lot alike in certain ways. We really want to win, and we're willing to work hard for the things that we really want. It was hard because I wanted it right away. As a player I only have four years, and I envisioned us [making the] Final Four three out of the four years. Using the first year to build was fine. After that we'd be right in there. She was looking to develop the long-term program. We would lose a game, and she'd say something like, 'Jennifer, you need to work on your pull up shot, that's really going to help your game a lot. It's going to help the team. You need to be able to pass the ball into the post better.' The little things that really can't be changed overnight. I would get mad, because I kept saying, 'I don't care. I want to win the next game. I'm not looking at the future right now. I'm looking at right now.' I think the thing that makes Tara really successful is this: She starts at the lowest level and builds from there. She doesn't really overlook much. Sometimes as a player it can be tough, because I just wanted to forget about the little things. But it's the little things that win games and win championships. She's gotten our team to screen and do things that not a lot of teams with our talent do, because we could win 25 games just on talent, but winning those extra seven games is due to just doing the little things right."

The Ultimate Challenge

It is easy to work with mature athletes who want to be the best they can be. The ultimate challenge a coach faces is bringing out the best in each player. Many coaches, when faced with a "problem" athlete, move into a space of control and authority. This dynamic creates a "win-lose" scenario in which the coach always wins, since she or he has more power. Ultimately the coach, the player and the team lose, because energy is taken away from the common goal of excellence for everyone.

One Stanford player, who was struggling, sat next to Coach VanDerveer on a plane trip. Coach VanDerveer confronted the athlete with the problems she saw. The athlete proceeded to tell Coach VanDerveer what she didn't like about playing for her. For an hour they "had it out" on the plane. This challenge continued into the player's junior year. Finally, Coach VanDerveer showed this athlete letters she had received from former players and told her that she was missing the best part of playing on a team. On their last road trip together, Coach VanDerveer received a card from this outstanding athlete thanking her for all she had done to support her growth both on and off the court. Through Coach VanDerveer's patience, this athlete realized that the best part of playing on a team involves relationships that endure long after the basketball career has ended. In an atmosphere of love and support people come into their own. In this noncombative state, the "problem athlete" encounters only resistance from herself and realizes that it is her choice what to make of her life.

Conclusion

What Coach VanDerveer remembers most about her career in basketball are the relationships—the connections that are maintained across time, never to be broken. To paraphrase Ghandi's words, Tara VanDerveer's life is her message. Through the Co-Essence Model of Sport, Coach VanDerveer has made a positive difference in the lives of those around her and in the infrasystem of her basketball organization. The future of sport and this society will be influenced by the worldview each of us embraces. As we examine our own worldview, we can ask the following questions: What message do I want my life to convey? How will my message impact the lives of those around me? What is my vision of the 21st century? The Co-Essence Model of Sport offers one option for us to consider.

Notes

1. Phyllis Bailey, Associate Athletic Director at The Ohio State University, provided the following information about grants-in-aid (personal communication, March 11, 1993). A grant-in-aid is aid given to university athletes. The maximum amount for a grant-in-aid can be tuition and fees, room and board and a loan of books. The NCAA determines the number of grants-in-aid that may be offered for each sport. This number varies for men's and women's teams. Some sports are designated as "head count" sports, which means that if an athlete receives any portion of the grant-in-aid package, it counts as one grant-in-aid. In women's intercollegiate athletics, basketball, volleyball, gymnastics and tennis are designated as "head count" sports. In NCAA Division I women's basketball, a maximum of 15 grants-in-aid can be given to players at any time.

2. George Manuel, World Council of Indigenous Peoples, says that "the Fourth World is the name given to indigenous peoples descended from a country's aboriginal population and who today are completely or partly deprived of the right to their own territory and its riches. The peoples of the Fourth World have only limited influence or none at all in the national state to which they belong" (Burger, 1990, p. 19). Indigenous peoples are often referred to as *first peoples* because their ancestors were the original inhabitants of their lands, which were subsequently colonized by foreigners. The term *indigenous* is widely accepted by these peoples themselves and is now adopted by the United Nations.

3. Coach VanDerveer was chosen to illustrate the CEMS approach because she fully lives this model. There are other outstanding coaches who embody many of the CEMS principles, such as self-esteem, and the dynamic and magnetic functions. Coach VanDerveer is exceptional because she acts out of her co-essence, and this is the core of the CEMS approach.

4. I conducted interviews with Coach VanDerveer and members of the Stanford University basketball and athletic organizations during one week in September 1990, after Stanford had won the Division I NCAA basketball championship. These interviews were tape-recorded and subsequently transcribed. These transcriptions served as the basis for the quotes contained in this chapter.

5. I am grateful to my teacher, Conrad Satala, Fort Wayne, Indiana, for introducing me to the concept of *co-essence*, which originated from Mesoamerican (Middle or Central American) cultures. Co-essence means "companion spirit," a supernatural being with whom a person shared her or his consciousness. Conrad Satala (1991) characterizes co-essence as being in the deep feminine energy within us that is linked with the Source. This feminine energy is characterized as an inner space that is expanded, that has a profound level of inner silence and deep compassion. From this inner feeling a larger sense of self begins to emerge—one's co-essence. One's known inner boundaries are no longer present. Co-essence or co-creation begins with the self and can then extend to co-creation with others.

6. Angeles Arrien, raised biculturally in the Basque and United States cultures, has had a profound impact on me. I honor her for her ideas on self-esteem and dynamic and magnetic functions, which she derived from cross-cultural study. Her formulations were chosen because of the "truth" they spoke to me and for their universal applicability across cultures.

7. According to Vicki Noble (in Stein, 1987), in predynastic China, women were the healers or shamans and were called *Wu* (meaning "to heal"). The *I Ching* (the ancient Chinese *Book of Changes*) had its origins in the prepatriarchal times in ancient China and the Wu. The *I Ching* was only put into written form during the patriarchal dynasties in China and has gone through major modifications since then, including a distortion of the meaning given to yin and yang. Diane Stein's The *Kwan Yin Book of Changes* (1987) reclaimed the content of the ancient *I Ching*. The original concept of yin and yang form an integration of magnetic and dynamic functions available to all. In other words, yin is not female and yang is not male, but they reflect the magnetic and dynamic forces that unite the universe and all of life. Yin and yang, therefore, are not dualistic opposites. In this chapter, the magnetic and dynamic functions are defined in this original, ancient, prepatriarchal way.

8. Renee Brown is now an assistant basketball coach at the University of Kansas.

References

Acosta, R. Vivian & Carpenter, Linda J. (1990). *A longitudinal study—thirteen year update*. Unpublished manuscript. Brooklyn College, New York.

Arrien, Angeles (Speaker). (1989). *Healing all our relationships*. [2-tape-set cassette recording]. Angeles Arrien, P.O. Box 2077, Sausalito, CA 94966 ([415] 331-5050).

Arrien, Angeles. (1993). *The four-fold way: Walking the paths of the warrior, teacher, healer, and visionary*. San Francisco: Harper San Francisco.

Boutilier, Mary A. & SanGiovanni, Lucinda. (1983). *The sporting woman*. Champaign, IL: Human Kinetics.

Burger, Julian. (1990). *The Gaia atlas of first peoples: A future for the indigenous world*. New York: Anchor Doubleday.

Capra, Fritjof. (1975). *The tao of physics*. New York: Bantam.

Capra, Fritjof. (1982). *The turning point: Science, society and the rising culture.* New York: Simon & Schuster.

Creedon, Pamela J. (1993). Acknowledging the infrasystem: Toward a critical feminist analysis of systems theory. *Public Relations Review, 19*(2), 157-166.

Duquin, Mary E. (1978). The androgynous advantage. In C. A. Oglesby (Ed.), *Women and sport: From myth to reality.* Philadelphia, PA: Lea & Febiger.

Eisler, Riane. (1987). *The chalice and the blade.* San Francisco, CA: Harper & Row.

Gilligan, Carol. (1982). *In a different voice: Psychological theory and women's development.* Cambridge, MA: Harvard University Press.

Highlen, Pamela S. & Fassinger, Ruth. (1984). *An androgynous model of sport.* Women's Services Presentation, The Ohio State University, Columbus, Ohio.

Mitchell, Stephen (Trans). (1988). *Tao te ching.* New York: Harper Perennial.

Myers, Linda J. (1988). *Understanding an Afrocentric world view: Introduction to optimal psychology.* Dubuque, IA: Kendall/Hunt.

Myers, Linda J., Speight, Suzette L., Highlen, Pamela S., Cox, Chikako I., Reynolds, Amy L., Adams, Eve M. & Hanley, Patricia C. (1991). Identity development and world view: Toward an optimal conceptualization. *Journal of Counseling and Development, 70,* 54-63.

Nelson, Mariah B. (1991). *Are we winning yet? How women are changing sports and sports are changing women.* New York: Random House.

Oglesby, Carole A. (1978). *Women and sport: From myth to reality.* Philadelphia, PA: Lea & Febiger.

Raczynski, S. (1992). *1992-93 Stanford women's basketball media guide.* Stanford, CA: Stanford University.

Ryan, Joan. (1989, December 14). Stanford topples Tennessee. *San Francisco Examiner,* p. C2.

Satala, Conrad. (1991). *Passion—an inner focus.* Unpublished manuscript.

Stein, Diane. (1987). *The kwan yin book of changes.* St Paul, MN: Llewellyn Publications.

Steinem, Gloria. (1992). *Revolution from within.* New York: Harper-Collins.

Talbot, Michael. (1991). *The holographic universe.* New York: Harper-Collins.

Waitley, Denis. (1985). *The double win.* New York: Berkeley Books.

Wheatley, Margaret J. (1992). *Leadership and the new science.* San Francisco, CA: Berett-Kochler.

Author Index

Subject Index

About the Contributors

Susan Birrell is Chair of the Women's Studies Program and Professor in the Department of Sport, Health, Leisure and Physical Studies at the University of Iowa. She earned her M.A. and Ph.D. in Sports Studies from the University of Massachusetts and her B.A. from St. Lawrence University. Her work focuses on cultural criticism of sport from a feminist cultural studies perspective. Her forthcoming work includes an edited book with Cheryl Cole, *Women, Sport, and Culture* and four chapters on "The Cultural Context of Women's Sport," coauthored with Nancy Theberge for the book *Womensport: A Multidisciplinary Approach.* She is currently studying the connections between sport and tourism.

Cheryl L. Cole holds an Ad Hoc Interdisciplinary Ph.D. in the Sociology of Culture and Women's Studies from the University of Iowa and a Ph.D. in Sport Studies from the University of Southern California. She is currently Assistant Professor in the Department of Kinesiology at the University of Illinois at Urbana-Champaign where she teaches courses on the cultural politics of the body. Her current research focuses on the technologies of sport and the production of deviant bodies; she is co-editing two forthcoming anthologies: *Women, Sport & Culture* (with Susan Birrell) and *Exercising Power: The Making and Remaking of the Body* (with John Loy and Michael Messner).

Anne Cooper-Chen is Associate Professor and Director of the Center for International Journalism at the E. W. Scripps School of Journalism at Ohio University. During 1992-1993 she was a Fulbright Scholar at the Center for International Programs, Chubu University, Kasugai, Aichi, Japan. She has recently completed a book called *Games in the Global Village: A 50-Nation Study of Entertainment Television*. She earned her Ph.D. from the University of North Carolina, her M.A. from the University of Michigan, and her AB from Vassar College.

Judith A. Cramer is Assistant Professor of Communication Arts at Long Island University, Southampton. She earned her M.A. in Communication Arts from the University of Hartford in Connecticut. Her master's thesis was titled, "Athletic Heroes and Heroines: The Role of the Press in Their Creation." She earned her B.S. in Sports Information/Journalism from Keene State College in New Hampshire. She has worked as a news and sports reporter, news director and talk show host and producer in commercial and public radio in Ohio.

Pamela J. Creedon is Associate Professor of Journalism at The Ohio State University where she is also an associated member of the graduate faculty of the Center for Women's Studies. She organized an interdisciplinary Big Ten Women in Sport conference at Ohio State in 1991 and was a member of the steering committee that organized and ran the second conference in 1992. She joined the Ohio State faculty after a 14-year career in public relations, both in the corporate and nonprofit sectors. As Director of Public Information at Mount Union College in Alliance, Ohio, she managed its sports information program. She earned her M.A . degree in journalism from the University of Oregon and her B.A. in English from Mount Union College. She is the editor of *Women in Mass Communication*, also published by Sage.

Karlene Ferrante, a native of Wisconsin, is Assistant Professor of Communication at the University of Wisconsin-Stevens Point. She teaches courses in popular culture criticism, social change, cultural diversity and research methods. She holds a Ph.D. from the University of Texas at Austin, where she wrote her dissertation titled "Moving into the Circle of Politics: The Process of Personal Enfranchisement." Her research interests include enfranchising social movements, the social construction of gender and feminist pedagogy.

Elizabeth H. Granitz is Assistant Professor of Economics at Long Island University, Southampton. She served as director of the School of Business at the university for four years. She earned her A.B. from Cornell University and her M.A. and Ph.D. from the University of California at Los Angeles.

Susan L. Greendorfer is Professor in the Department of Kinesiology at the University of Illinois, Urbana-Champaign. Her A.B. and M.A. degrees are from the University of California, Berkeley, and her Ph.D. is from the University of Wisconsin, Madison. A sociologist of sport, she is recognized as a pioneer researcher on the topic of women in sport and has published several articles related to gender and race differences in the sport socialization process. Her recent research encompasses a more comprehensive perspective that focuses on gender ideology and women's physicality, and her latest project represents an analysis of culturally constructed media images of women in sport. She is cofounder of the North American Society for the Sociology of Sport and a member of the Advisory Board of the Women's Sport Foundation, and she has been inducted into the American Academy of Physical Education.

Pamela Sue Highlen is Associate Professor in the Psychology Department at The Ohio State University. She is a licensed psychologist in private practice specializing in growth, development and personal empowerment issues. She has been a sport psychologist for the Ohio State Women's Basketball Team, Tennis Team, Field Hockey Team and a Columbus-based age-group gymnastics team. She served on the Ohio State President's Committee on Salary Equity for the Department of Athletics during 1991-1992 and was a member of the steering committee that organized and ran the Women in Sport Conference at Ohio State in 1992. Currently she is writing two books: one relates her Co-Essence Model of Sport to the coaching philosophy of Stanford University's Women's Basketball Coach Tara VanDerveer; the other focuses on the model as it relates to business management.

Mary Jo Kane is Associate Professor in the School of Kinesiology at the University of Minnesota in Minneapolis. She also has a joint appointment with the Department of Women's Studies and the Center for Advanced Feminist Studies. She received her Ph.D. from the University of Illinois, Urbana-Champaign. She has taught courses in sport sociology and sport and gender at both the graduate and undergraduate levels. Her primary research area of interest involves media portrayals of women in sport and physical activity. More recently, she has begun to focus on the role of sexual violence against women in men's athletics. She has written numerous research articles on women and sport and also serves on editorial review boards of a number of scholarly journals, most notably *Signs: Journal of Women in Culture and Society.*

Molly Merryman earned her MA in Journalism from the School of Journalism at The Ohio State University and her B.A. from Ashland University. A published poet, she worked in government and non-profit public relations before starting her doctoral program in American Cultural Studies at Bowling Green State University, where she is currently a teaching associate in women's studies.

Linda D. Williams, a native of Chadbourn, North Carolina, is on the faculty at North Carolina A&T State University. She completed her undergraduate and master's degree work at the University of North Carolina-Chapel Hill and earned her Ph.D. at The Ohio State University. She has served as a co-investigator for two major media studies sponsored by The Amateur Athletic Foundation of Los Angeles. The first, *Gender Stereotyping in Televised Sports,* was released in 1990, and the second, *Coverage of Women's Sports in Four Daily Newspapers,* was released in January 1991.

Printed in the United States
120403LV00001B/165/A